When Empathy Fails

How to stop those hell-bent on destroying you

By Kathy Marshack, Ph.D.

Are You a Victim of:
False Arrest?
Wrongful Prosecution?
Assault?
Frivolous Lawsuits?
Stalking?
Cybercrime?
Fake News?
Parental Alienation?
Dangerous Lies?

**Life Lessons on
Empathy Dysfunction (EmD)**

© 2018 Kathy J. Marshack, Ph.D.
700 N. Hayden Island Drive, Suite 274,
Portland, Oregon 97217-8172
info@kmarshack.com
www.kmarshack.com / 503-222-6678

All rights reserved. No part of the material protected by this copyright notice may be reproduced or used in any form or by any means, electronic, or mechanical, including photocopying, recording, or by any information storage and retrieval system, without prior written permission of the copyright owner.

Edited By: Janet Herring-Sherman
Map Illustrations By: Eric Savage
Cover Illustration: Kathy Marshack and Ron Lee

Font: Century Schoolbook, Arial Black, & Arial
ISBN: 1979969000
ISBN: 9781979969000
Library of Congress Control Number: 2018936786
US~Observer – 2051 West Jones Creek Road, Grants Pass, Oregon 97526 / 541-474-7885 / www.usobserver.com

Publisher's Cataloging-in-Publication

Marshack, Kathy, 1949-

When Empathy Fails: How to stop those hell-bent on destroying you—life lessons on Empathy Dysfunction (EmD) by Kathy J. Marshack.--1st ed.-- US~Observer – 2051 West Jones Creek Road, Grants Pass, Oregon 97526 / 541-474-7885 / www.usobserver.com

1. When Empathy Fails: How to Stop Those Hell-bent on Destroying You—Life lessons on Empathy Dysfunction (EmD) — Empathy Dysfunction Scale — Empathy — Empathy disorder —Narcissism — Sociopath — Bullying — Traumatic Brain Injury (TBI) — Athlete concussions — Sports medicine — Asperger's syndrome — Autism — High-functioning autism — Concussion — Brain scans — Mild traumatic brain injury — TBI — Chronic traumatic encephalopathy — CTE — Addiction —Alcoholism — Brainwashing — Domestic violence — Coercive Control — Mental disabilities — Aaron Hernandez — NFL — Liars — Radiant empathy — Codependency — Perseverance —Psychology — Counseling — Soccer mom — Personality change — Evil. 2. Vancouver, Washington, history — Local government — Toxic neighbors — Law-breaking city officials — False arrest — Attorneys — Lawyers — Predatory Prosecution — Wrongful Prosecution — Police — Neighbors — Bad neighbors — Rights of Way — Easement rights — Property rights — Civil rights — Trespassing — Mob mentality — Prosecutor — Ombudsmen — Citizen Advocate — Lawsuits — Harassment — Code enforcement — Rogue government employees — Politicians — Political — Immoral politicians — Unethical politicians — Abusive politicians — Small town politics — City councils — City attorneys — Judges — Hiding evidence — Suppressing facts — Home-based business — Law enforcement — Conspiracy — Mental disabilities — Injustice — Moralities — Public Access — Public Affairs — Train Horn Noise Quiet Zone — Train track safety — Railroad crossing safety. 3. Cyberstalking — Cybercrime — Fake news — Facebook — Social media — Stalking — Private investigator — Hacking Amazon — Personal threats — Exploitation — Women 4. Parental alienation — Interpersonal communication — Marriage — Parenting — Divorce — Family relationships — Divorce attorney — Child safety. 5. Jungle — Rainforest — Panama — Mike Dooley — Tutters — Travel — Travelogue — Blue Morpho butterfly — Hero — Heroine — Brave mom — Warrior Mom — Matriarch — Maternal love — Healing — Dreams — Investigative journalism — What dreams mean — Animal companions — Pets — Pacific Northwest train history — Pacific Northwest steamboat history — Columbia River history — Road history, Vancouver, Washington — Reality-based. I. Title When Empathy Fails. II. Title.

HAVE YOU EVER

Felt victimized, been swindled or lied to by your best friend;

•

Loaned money to loved ones who squandered the gift and never paid you back;

•

Had to fight unscrupulous prosecutors for your freedom;

•

Been forced to defend yourself from your vengeful ex or your ungrateful children;

•

Bumped into a beguiling, but shifty, stranger?

If so, you've crossed paths with someone operating with Empathy Dysfunction (EmD).

•

It's time to out these EmD people.

•

Keeping silent about them is what harms—even kills—their victims.

•

In the following pages, you'll see how to identify and beat people bent on hurting you.

•

You will find encouragement to fully express your loving and lovable authentic self: to be—and to live—unafraid.

Also by the Author

"Entrepreneurial Couples: Making It Work at Work and at Home" — *1998*

"Sixty Things to Do When You Turn Sixty" — contributor, *2006*

"Going over the Edge: Life with a Partner or Spouse with Asperger Syndrome" — *2009*

"Out of Mind–Out of Sight: Parenting with a Partner with Asperger Syndrome (ASD)" — *2013*

> "God, grant me
> the serenity to accept the things I cannot change,
> the courage to change the things I can,
> and the wisdom to know the difference."
>
> Author Unknown

TABLE OF CONTENTS

TABLE OF CONTENTS vii
DEDICATION xvi
FOREWORD xvii
PREFACE xxii
ACKNOWLEDGMENTS xxvi
INTRODUCTION 1
- Cap'n Jack is, well, cursed with Empathy Dysfunction 1
- Meet my tour guide to the Multiverse 5
- The Multiverse explained 9
- Yet another sociopath 12
- Marianne hooks me 13
- The anger trap 18
- Dingbat or sociopath? I wonder. 20
- Don't judge the spider or the sociopath 22
- Chapter by chapter 24

PROLOGUE: "THE RIVER, THE ROAD AND THE TRAIN" ---
A CONSPIRACY THEORY TRIED AND FOUND TRUE 33
- Behind—and before—the creation of the Empathy Dysfunction Scale 33

PROLOGUE IN BRIEF (ABRIDGED): FROM TRASHED TO TRIUMPHANT 38
- You need to know only two things 38

PROLOGUE (UNABRIDGED): A TRUE CRIME STORY 44
- A True Crime Story 44

- The Main Players 45
- Two land deeds to the rescue 48
- Railroaded, literally 50
- A conspiracy theory—really, truly! 58
- P.S. Phoebe used to call me her hero 71

CHAPTER BY CHAPTER OVERVIEW
CHAPTER ONE: NO ONE CALLS ME MOM ANYMORE 75
- They might be out to get you 75
- September 11, 2001 76
- A life hijacked 79
- "Mom is my hero" 81
- Like it's a bad thing 84
- Stalked, sued, slandered 92
- Lies, damned lies—and still more 97
- For this mom, it's personal 99
- Chapter One Highlights 102

CHAPTER TWO: EMPATHY DYSFUNCTION (EMD) IN-DEPTH 104
- From zero to radiant 104
- Empathy is an experience 105
- We long to belong 108
- Empathy Dysfunction (EmD)—what it is and isn't 110
- EmD-0—having zero degrees of empathy but not intending harm 111
- EmD-1—narcissists, sociopaths, and others out to harm 113
- EmD-2 – mental illness or brain damage 117
- EmD-3—addiction, ADHD, Bipolar Disorder 118
- EmD-4—the good at heart 121
- EmD-5—epitomizing empathy 123

TABLE OF CONTENTS

- Heroin addict with a smile 124
- Jailer with a sense of humor 126
- The redhead, the jailer, and the girl who screamed in her sleep 127
- Empathy Dysfunction (EmD) in a nutshell 129
- EmD Assessment Tool 130
- Chapter Two Highlights 131

CHAPTER THREE: BRAINWASHING MOM 133
- Veiled in brainwash 133
- Coercive control 136
- Abuse the child to control the mom 139
- How coercive control begins 146
- Blame the victim 151
- Resilience ignited by guilt and Parental Alienation Syndrome (PAS) 154
- Chapter Three Highlights 160

CHAPTER FOUR: MY DAUGHTER IS AUTISTIC 162
- Empathy Dysfunction score? Zero. (EmD-Zero) 162
- Frightening and frightened 164
- Rage, bluster, and tears 165
- She's hunting me, her own mom 168
- Life-and-death struggle with herself 168
- Relief is at hand 169
- She inflicts pain on herself 170
- Finally, she looks at me 170
- At last, her spirit is soothed 171
- What's empathy got to do with it? 172
- The argument for self-knowledge 175
- Meltdown or temper tantrum? 175

- Utterly rejected 180
- Politically incorrect 182
- Loving Bianca through my writing 184
- Chapter Four Highlights 187

CHAPTER FIVE: IMPACTED BY MILD TRAUMATIC BRAIN INJURY 190
- Empathy as it comes and goes—EmD-2 190
- Getting your "bells rung" 191
- My daughter has brain trauma 199
- "You need to protect yourself" 203
- The night it finally happened 205
- Like a light switch 209
- Fighting back and fighting mad 212
- Another night in Clark County Jail 213
- Mom always said to "sore [sic] with the eagles" 216
- Chapter Five Highlights 221

CHAPTER SIX: ON BECOMING A WARRIOR MATRIARCH .. 222
- How it begins—EmD-3 222
- "Po' white trash" 223
- Genealogy—a back-to-the-future affair 227
- Shamed by the shameless 230
- "I'm an addict" 232
- Sinking to a new low 239
- The love of a Matriarch Warrior 242
- Chapter Six Highlights 243

CHAPTER SEVEN: HOW MOB MENTALITY MATERIALIZES ... 245
When a neighborly chat won't work 245
- Believe in nice 245

TABLE OF CONTENTS

- "Call Richard Landis" 256
- "All the best" 264
- Police: political pawns or peacekeepers? 270
- The terror of being cyberstalked 277
- The lie that just won't die 280
- Chapter Seven Highlights 283

CHAPTER EIGHT: JUST PLAIN MEAN 285
- Why me? 282
- "The" memo 289
- Increasing lies and run-up pressure 296
- Vigilante justice 304
- Flat out obstruction of justice 310
- The truth or the "take?" 318
- Chairman of the Board 319
- Postscript 326
- Chapter Eight Highlights 329

CHAPTER NINE: IN THE CROSS-HAIRS OF CYBERATTACKERS 330
- On being cyberattacked 330
- A reputation under fire 333
- Disinformation defined 338
- Cybercrime at City Hall 349
- Cyberstalkers believe their victims are in the wrong 345
- More cyberstalking—yes, more of the same madness 349
- Faked news 352
- Be outrageous and power down cyberbullies 356
- Chapter Nine Highlights 362

CHAPTER TEN: RADIANT WARRIOR, RESILIENCE EPITOMIZED 364

- The bright side of Empathy Dysfunction 365
- The liftoff dream 366
- A brand new theorem: Dr. Kathy's Theory of Relativity ... 370
- Ride the wave 372
- Warrior in training 376
- Training in the trenches 379
- Responding to the pairing of gossip and shame with robust resilience 384
- Shedding the shame 388
- Becoming a Radiant Warrior (EmD-5) 392
- Chapter Ten Highlights 395

CHAPTER ELEVEN: CONCLUSION - HOW I SURVIVED THE DECADE-LONG PERFECT STORM AND LEARNED TO DANCE AS IT RAGED 397

- The witch-hunt that led to something good: creation of the Empathy Dysfunction Scale 397
- Tip One: Keep your channel clear 400
- Tip Two: Just keep going 405
- Tip Three: Stop! Do anything else! 408
- Tip Four: Embrace your worst fear 416
- Tip Five: Forgive yourself 416
- Tip Six: Do a little bit more 419
- Tip Seven: You are enough 422
- Postscript: Another letter from God 425

EPILOGUE: BRAVEHEART 428

- How many attorneys did it take? 427
- The overpowering loneliness 434

TABLE OF CONTENTS

- Who am I if no longer Mom?... 436
- An epilogue is another beginning................................... 437

AFTERWORD 441

APPENDIX 450

- Documents, reports, correspondence

    Fig. A.1 Prologue, in brief..452
    Chapter Two Empathy Dysfunction Scale

    Fig. A.2, Prologue, unabridged..453
    1908 Railway Right-of-way Deed

    Fig. A.3, Prologue, unabridged..455
    The land at the center of the author's battle with neighbors has a long and complex history. Here an 1847-1922 map of Lower Clark County (the location of the author's land) compares to a 1922-2014 map of the same area. They show the development of the modern road system.

    Fig. A.4, *Prologue, unabridged*..456
    Here a before-and-after set of maps pinpoints the pivotal Steamboat Landing, which grew up as an important port for farmers and lumbermen to ship their products via steamboats on the Columbia River. Over time, Steamboat Landing has given way to mostly recreational sailboats, motor boats, kayaks, and canoes—prompting the land grab efforts of the author's neighbors and developers.

    Fig. A.5, *Prologue, unabridged*..457

Phoebe's loving letter to her mom in 2005

Fig. A.6, Chapter Seven 458
Fire Marshal's report about how unsafe the Old Camas Highway stretch in front of the author's home had become

Fig. A.7, *Chapter Eight*..450
Text from author's 2004 letter to Jim Jacks, asking for help

Fig. A.8, *Chapter Eight*..464
Fateful and libelous—and false—memo written by Jim Jacks, Vancouver Citizen Advocate, about the author in 2004

Fig. A.9, *Chapter Seven* 46t
List of Alternative Facts involving Richard Landis in the River, Road, Train saga

Fig. A.10, *Chapter Seven* 483
2004 emails between Richard Landis and Shana Druffner of BNSF

Fig. A. 11, Chapter Seven 486
Samples of 2004 Pat Owens' correspondence with Richard Landis about the author's road research and Landis' interest in the same old roads

Fig. A.12, Chapter Seven 506

TABLE OF CONTENTS

    2008 Dan Lorenz letter to Judge John Nichols requesting help in getting records from the City Prosecutor and police

Fig. A.13, Chapter Eight 513
    2005 Dan Lorenz letter to BAR regarding Josephine Townsend's handling of the author's Diversion agreement

Fig. A.14, Chapter Eight 517
    2006 Subpoena for Raylene McJilton, Vancouver's Records Clerk, to appear in person in Clark County Court with any and all documents making allegations against the author or her property

Fig. A.15, Epilogue 520
    By-the-numbers list of the author's costs and losses during the perfect-storm years

Fig. A.16, *Epilogue* 522
    Letter to Kathy Marshack from Uber driver, who relays how enormously helpful the Empathy Dysfunction Scale has become in her work

Dedication

"Dogs are not our whole life, but they make our lives whole."
— ***Roger Caras***

*Simon Templar, the epitome of loyalty—
and gifted at providing comic relief when needed most.*

To my best friend, Simon Templar,

Simon did not inspire this book. He didn't offer clever or insightful feedback on my writing. He wasn't critical either.

He gave me nothing except unconditional love, adoration, and undying loyalty. Most of all, he made me smile every day—exactly what I needed during those long, lonely writing days when the work was emotional and cathartic.

No matter how painful the memories, or how much I struggled to get the manuscript just right, Simon was always there to bring me back to the present moment, which is all any of us have. So it is with immense gratitude that I dedicate this book to Simon Templar, my black Labrador retriever, this woman's best friend.

Thank you and woof

Foreword

Empathy Dysfunction (EmD)—not yet a household term—explains so much about the state we're in these days. Have you ever had your wallet stolen by someone who looked you right in the eye? Or had a good friend lie to you, repeatedly? Or been blamed for interfering when you tried to rescue a loved one from their bad choices? Or known the heartache of having your children turn against you?

These are examples of Empathy Dysfunction (EmD) as described by Kathy Marshack, Ph.D., in her book "When Empathy Fails."

Dr. Marshack has spent 40 years observing and treating those with empathy problems, such as sociopaths, autistics, alcoholics, and the brain-injured. Along the way, she made a surprising discovery.

Regardless of their medical or psychological diagnosis, these patients had one major thing in common: Empathy Dysfunction. Dr. Marshack realized that this problem with empathy was what was causing the greatest damage to their relationships.

With this insight, Dr. Marshack developed the Empathy Dysfunction Scale (EmD Scale) to help the rest of us more clearly understand our loved ones' challenges with empathy. She has given us a way to assess the level of Empathy Dysfunction in others.

In a fearless manner, Dr. Marshack uses her personal story to show us how to counteract the effects of those who scramble relationships with predatory, irrational, convoluted, and non-empathic logic. Dr. Marshack is more than a psychologist: She is someone who has had her heart broken and her confidence stolen by people with Empathy Dysfunction. Who better to guide you in learning how to protect yourself from those with EmD?

Hapless victims who have suffered (or are suffering) at the hands of those with EmD will benefit most from this book. It's time for you to take back your life from people so self-absorbed that they frequently leave you holding the bag. This revealing book should also be on the bookshelves of attorneys, physicians, psychologists, clergy, and others who deal with people problems. Instead of helping the dysfunctional, how about finally helping their victims?

"When Empathy Fails" is one of the first books of its kind for the *US~Observer,* an on-line and print investigative news source. We are devoted to helping innocent victims mitigate false charges and prosecution; however, we don't often get the chance to hear from those we've helped.

Once justice has been served and the smoke has cleared, people tend to put all of the terror and heartache behind them: They don't want to rehash it. With Dr. Marshack's latest book, we get an in-depth look at her life before, during and after the painful episodes with EmD relatives, neighbors, and representatives of local legal and criminal justice systems. When the *US~Observer,* through its investigative

When the *US~Observer,* through its investigative reporting, spotlighted the injustices she had endured, this brilliant woman was totally exonerated.

FOREWORD

reporting, spotlighted the injustices she had endured, this brilliant woman was totally exonerated.

We hope Dr. Marshack's is the start of a line of *US~Observer*-published books focused on the aftermath of institutional abuse. It is imperative to learn more about the extensive damage to victims of false charges and prosecution—the kind of harm that legal exoneration alone cannot heal.

We are journalists, so we report the facts and expose the injustices in our efforts to vindicate the innocent. As a psychologist, and the victim of false allegations, government harassment, assault, and defamation, Dr. Marshack is in a unique position to take the story a step further.

We are very proud of our part in the development of this book. The *US~Observer* carefully investigates each and every allegation. We use original sources and verify testimony with multiple witnesses. We print the facts. We are not biased. If a claim is vague, exaggerated, or just not supported by the facts, we don't print it. We wouldn't be serving our readers if we made cavalier accusations or endorsements.

When the *US~Observer* discovered Dr. Marshack's story back in 2011, she was still singlehandedly trying to settle her lawsuits with her neighbors and the City of Vancouver, Wash. Because of her amazing courage, we researched her efforts and in 2011 and 2012 published several news stories that summarized the preceding nine years of her struggle.

That exposure served as a catalyst for additional people in similar situations to contact us with allegations about the corruption in Vancouver. It seemed like a natural fit to offer this psychologist a position as an investigative reporter for the *US~Observer*. Since then, Dr. Marshack has used her professional skills and personal experience to bring injustice to light, thus benefitting the mission of the *US~Observer*.

As the title of chapter one implies, Dr. Marshack lost her children through this ordeal. She fought the injustice on many fronts. She won most of the time, but she didn't escape unscathed. The legal bills were horrendous. More than once, she nearly lost her business and psychologist licenses to practice.

The most unbearable loss has been the estrangement from her children. One highly-effective method that narcissists, sociopaths, and the like use to undermine the confidence of their falsely accused victims is to alienate the ones the victims love. That's exactly how it played out with Dr. Marshack. Sadly, she lost this most critical battle.

It is a heartbreaking story; but if this book were just a rehash from *US~Observer* archives or an emotional re-telling of Dr. Marshack's personal story, it would not be enough. By combining her expertise as a psychologist with her experiences, Dr. Marshack takes us into the world of abnormal psychology to help us better understand the workings of sociopaths, narcissists and other toxic people. She introduces the reader to the Empathy Dysfunction Scale (EmD Scale), an innovative tool she developed to help quickly identify people who may be out to hurt you.

"When Empathy Fails," is not another dry and academic psychological treatise. In addition to the EmD Scale, Dr. Marshack gives you tips on how to: identify those with Empathy Dysfunction; protect yourself; survive unscrupulous attacks, and retake your life. Not everyone we help through our investigations gets beyond exoneration to psychological wellness. We are pleased that Dr. Marshack is one of the ultimate survivors and now wants to help you be one, too.

FOREWORD

During the past quarter century, the *US~Observer* has investigated more than 4,000 cases involving innocent victims. We have been to every state in the Union to interview prosecutors, judges, trial attorneys, politicians, criminals, and victims. Our goal is to expose corruption in our government, especially in the judicial system that falsely arrests, prosecutes, and imprisons innocent people.

Often this is because the accused are unsophisticated and up against rogue prosecutors, such as Josephine Townsend of Vancouver. While "When Empathy Fails" exposes one corrupt city attorney, there are many more still creating chaos and sorrow in the lives of far too many innocent people.

We wish the best for Dr. Marshack and cheer for the success of this first-ever, one-of-a-kind book. It shows the other side of wrongful prosecution—the damage that was done to one woman and her family. Her book is a triumph. With courage and caring, Dr. Marshack takes us behind the scenes to show us how to take on the system and prevail.

Sometimes people are truly out to get you. Without having experienced the abuse of corrupt public servants, neighbors, and even family, Dr. Marshack may never have discovered EmD or developed the EmD Scale. Now you, too, have this tool and will know what to do when trashed by narcissists, sociopaths, and other toxic people who assume carte blanche to ruin you.

This book is an imperative read for victims as well as for law enforcement personnel; all those working in the legal system; and anyone living or working in the shadow of Empathy Dysfunction.

Edward Snook
Publisher, US~Observer
Grants Pass, Oregon
September 25, 2017

Preface

Empathy: Everyone has at least a little, right? It seems a lifetime ago (starting on Sept. 11, 2001) when I began the journey that would prove otherwise. What I discovered led me to create a scale that measures the amount of empathy or lack thereof. I call it the Empathy Dysfunction Scale (EmD Scale). It's a tool that teaches about the range of empathy—from none to a lot.

This unique Scale demonstrates how to protect yourself from those without empathy—people who seem out to get you. These were the kind of toxic people who catapulted me into years of horrible pain and loss.

My setbacks, mistakes and successes are captured and documented in "When Empathy Fails." No person should have to endure the trauma and agony I did at the hands of people mired in Empathy Dysfunction! If reading my story of mistakes and triumphs helps you to navigate around the empathy-lacking people in your life, then I consider the outcome of my perilous journey to be a win.

I hope you can appreciate your life's journey, too. It is a miracle; because you have free will, you have the opportunity to choose right from wrong. And because God loves you, you keep getting more chances to get it right, even if you miss it the first or the fiftieth time. No matter, it is striving to do the right thing that is important. Free will and the chance to make conscious choices are powerful tools along the path to enlightenment. Individuals without empathy are some of our best teachers.

Forgiving myself for all of my mistakes is an ongoing process since, like all humans, I keep making poor choices; however, each time I forgive myself, I see other options.

PREFACE

Self-forgiveness is essential to rebooting your life especially when others may not forgive you. As you read this book and discover how I negotiated a perfect storm of ruthless people—people who shamed and abused me—you will see that forgiving yourself is essential to your survival.

> **Self-forgiveness is essential to rebooting your life especially when others may not forgive you.**

In the throes of coming to self-forgiveness, a dream held a powerful message for me: That I am always forgiven and have countless chances to do my life correctly.

I dreamt that I was swimming in the ocean on a beautiful sunny day. Others were swimming and surfing also. I could see them in the sea just a few hundred yards from the wide sandy beach on the Oregon shore of the Pacific Ocean. It was bordered by boulders and forest.

Suddenly, a massive tidal wave was heading our way. The pleasant summer swim turned into panic. We swam madly for the shore but couldn't escape. I watched in horror as the wave caught the swimmers, then me, tossing us violently onto the rocks and into the trees. Everyone was killed.

In the next dream scene, the group of swimmers was sitting in a classroom discussing the event. Our teacher was asking how we might have prevented this disaster. It was peaceful in the classroom—as if our deaths were not the issue. I don't recall what the group discussed.

It appeared, though, that I'd learned nothing because the dream repeated itself that same night.

Again, I found myself swimming in the ocean and thoroughly enjoying myself—until a tidal wave swept me up and killed me on the rocks. Then there I was, back in the classroom with a new bunch of people, still trying to reason out the lesson in the deadly waves.

The dream sequence happened a few more times before my "dreaming self" took a different tack.

This time, as I watched the panic set in, I decided to fly up out of the ocean like an eagle and soar over the rocks and trees to safety. As I soared, I looked down at the terrified swimmers and wondered why they hadn't realized how easy it is to escape certain death. On returning to the classroom, I found no one there, not even the teacher.

I awoke from the dream to the realization that life is a perpetual discovery of who we are. More importantly, we are being called to be our true, authentic self.

"When Empathy Fails," is a book title with a caveat: My daughters still won't forgive me the years of toxic battles and the accompanying trauma and drama that stole their childhood. They refuse me any contact, meaning I'm estranged from my young grandson as well.

Dozens of people call me "Mom," including young friends and clients. A 9-year-old client of mine asked his mother if he could claim me as his grandmother since his own had passed on. In a heartbeat, I accepted! I am blessed and proud to be Mom and Grandma to those who need me and genuinely love me. It is an honor.

My fervent hope is that you will read this book and learn that you are blessed even if you are enduring the pressure of defending yourself from: hostile neighbors; a vindictive ex-spouse; wrongful prosecution; or hurtful actions by ungrateful children.

I hope you will find help, even solace, in these practical tips for protecting yourself and surviving the attacks of those who have Empathy Dysfunction. Even more, I hope you will find and believe in your God-given ability to rise to the level of abundant Radiant Empathy; then you will be able to soar with the eagles—no matter the toxic chaos around you.

Kathy J. Marshack, Ph.D.
Portland, Oregon

Acknowledgments

My deepest gratitude and heartfelt love go to my former executive assistant, Michelle Lathim. For more than nine years, Michelle was my trusted sidekick. I could never have kept up my warrior strength during this span of ordeals if it hadn't been for this amazing, loving and devoted employee and friend.

Michelle came to work for me after two former assistants had been overwhelmed by the job. The strain of managing the office for my psychology practice and handling the relentless harassment proved to be too much for them. Imagine coming to work one morning to find that your boss had been arrested the night before.

In my office, Michelle never really experienced the "ordinary" office job. She, too, was impacted by all that threatened me: lawsuits; code enforcement investigations; police intimidation: and harassment by my neighbors and ex-husband. In organizing hundreds of pages of evidence for my attorneys, Michelle became an unofficial but masterful paralegal.

Since she worked out of my home office, Michelle endured my daughter Bianca's intense emotional meltdowns. Sometimes Bianca stood in Michelle's office screaming at the top of her lungs. When my younger daughter Phoebe started stealing from us, Michelle had to lock up her purse. Once, Michelle had gotten up in the middle of the night to try to rescue me from jail (in 2013 following my false arrest after an altercation with Phoebe). That kind of dedication was above and beyond anything I'd expected or had ever experienced.

ACKNOWLEDGMENTS

Michelle was also there to share in the triumphs. Each time I won in court, we celebrated. When my books on Asperger Syndrome were published, she'd proudly bragged to others about my accomplishments. When I sold my house to Kent Kresa, my neighbor's developer, she helped me pack up 30 years of my life and career for our move to my new home and office in Portland, Ore.

Michelle is like a sister to me. When I was overwhelmed—especially when my daughters turned on me—she was always there offering her support. Frequently, she would forward an email from a satisfied client or reader to remind me that I was appreciated. She never forgot my birthday or holiday—or Mother's Day.

One of my favorite Michelle memories is a wry comment she made. I was living in a perfect storm of calamities that no one believed was real. She'd said, "The reason they don't believe you, Kathy, is that it's just so unbelievable!" I still laugh when I think of Michelle's face as she delivered that line. Yes, our life together during those uncommonly harsh years was unbelievable.

Three years ago we were at last done with courts and lawsuits, and the final legal entanglement wrapped up. I was able to move to a lovely home in a peaceful setting on the Columbia River. Settlement money had paid the mountain of bills. Freedom! Michelle and I were finally going to have time to breathe and laugh and indulge in creative projects (like this book).

Then, with hardly a word, she was gone. I suppose she'd needed a break from all that had happened. Michelle remains an angel with Radiant Empathy, the highest and best kind. (I call this EmD-5 on the Empathy Dysfunction Scale.) I have no doubt that she is having the time of her life with her family and friends. She deserves it.

My psychotherapist, Frank Colistro, Ed.D., offered a counterbalance to Michelle's unequivocal encouragement. He was kind, of course, and respectful, but it was his objectivity I valued most. He challenged me to think things through. Psychotherapy is not always helpful if you have no clarity about your problems. When I felt all alone and terrified, Frank reminded me of my strengths and helped me fashion a strategic plan. I am forever in his debt for helping me see that to take on the hero's journey, I had to suit up.

Two other health care practitioners, the epitome of empathy, deserve my deepest gratitude: Dr. Robert Allen, my chiropractor; and good friend and naturopath, Dr. Julie Glass. Both have stood by me for years.

Drs. Allen and Glass took care of me even when I could not pay for their services. Without the benefit of their incredible skills, my aches and pains would have grown into full-blown chronic illness. Thank you for your healing touch and loving hearts.

My dear friend and minister, the Rev. Lawrence King, deserves my thanks as well. Larry was not there for the entire decade-plus journey, but he showed up when I needed him the most.

I had just sold my Vancouver home and moved back to Portland. I felt alone and adrift until I found the Portland Center for Spiritual Living (PCSL). I'd long known that I needed to find a new spiritual home. Larry welcomed me into the PCSL community, which has become my new family. Together we founded the PCSL Writer's Group. Without Larry's loving guidance, this book would have languished unfinished. Thank you for being a spiritual guide and kindred spirit. There is no better example of Radiant Empathy than Rev. King.

ACKNOWLEDGMENTS

It has been a joy to reconnect with my editor, Janet Herring-Sherman, who helped me edit the book, "Out of Mind – Out of Sight." Janet has survived her own hero's journey, so she was absolutely the perfect person to help me smooth out the wrinkles in the manuscript of "When Empathy Fails."

Janet has an uncanny ability to understand me and what on earth I am trying to say. With deft comments, she gets me thinking about a better way to express myself. How could I have finished off this book without Janet to fine-tune the text? She fixes things like pronouns and punctuation and suggests global shifts to make complicated themes and terms easier for the reader to follow. Thank you, Janet, for being a beautiful and talented soul.

Of course, I wouldn't have written this book at all if it weren't for the *US~Observer's* publisher, Ed Snook, and his staff. It was the amazing work of these investigative journalists that finally convinced people to believe my story. Without their research and factual revelations, I might be sitting in prison.

Ed and his reporters poured over the facts, making sure of accuracy at every turn. Their fearless determination to expose government corruption enabled me to reclaim my life. When Ed asked me to work alongside his reporters as an investigative journalist, I was both honored and thrilled. Thank you, Ed, for believing in me: I am forever in your debt.

Many others were there for a part of my journey. Radio personality Lars Larson donated his considerable talent to help expose Vancouver's corrupt City Hall. David Madore donated his studio and the production talent of Naylene Frunk to make a marvelous video to help me reveal the corruption surrounding the Train Horn Noise Quiet Zone issue near my home.

I hope I haven't overlooked others who helped along the way. Please know that I appreciate each and every one of you. Whether you were there for a moment, a day, a year, or longer, know that I couldn't have written this book without you. Thank you for your kindness, love, support, and inspiration. Honestly, none of us can get through this life on Earth without each other.

INTRODUCTION
What I Learned in the Jungle

(or, This Trip Was No Disney Cruise)

"I always wondered why somebody doesn't do something about that. Then I realized I was somebody."

— Lily Tomlin

Cap'n Jack is, well, cursed with Empathy Dysfunction

PANAMA—September 14, 2014. Wild tropical birds fly through the windowless lobby bar of Panama's Gamboa Rainforest Hotel where I am seated. Below are the Chagres River and the cloud-covered, rain-soaked jungle. The enlivening sounds there rise and reach me over the hotel music and gentle Spanish-speaking voices. I am reminded that this rainforest world belongs to the animals and birds living there: I am only a visitor.

This is the day I decide to start writing a story about another jungle—civilization— where people who are sociopaths, narcissists or have Empathy Dysfunction can be as deadly as any predator in the Panamanian jungle.

Just as my Arnold Palmer drink is delivered and I type the first sentence on my iPad, Cap'n Jack Sparrow appears. Local actor Jorge portrays the loveable character from the Disney

The author during her 2014 trip to Panama's Gamboa Rainforest. This stand-in for the Disney character Cap'n Jack Sparrow appeared at her side just as she began to draft the manuscript for this book.

movie series, "Pirates of the Caribbean." He is quite happy to pose for photos with the tourists, so I ham it up.

Too often, filmmakers present the Sociopath as a lovable con artist who has a heart of gold and does the right thing in the end. Hollywood capitalizes on our need to believe this.

There is nothing redeemable about a Sociopath who steals your heart, your money, and your confidence. How ironic that Cap'n Jack showed up right then—a messenger from the Universe,[1] reminding me to take my work seriously. Sociopaths, even those like Cap'n Jack, who seems less sinister, are no laughing matter.

I am writing this book to help you recognize, understand and defend yourself against those who have pernicious Empathy Dysfunction.

---

[1] Occasionally, I may use metaphysical terms such as "the Universe" or "Karma," or even a very loose definition of "angel." I may also interchange the word "God" with "the Universe." Although I was raised a Christian by my Lutheran mother and my Baptist father, I am equally at home in a Catholic cathedral, Buddhist temple, or non-denominational New Thought church. According to the Bible, God created us, and God is omnipresent, omniscient, and omnipotent, which makes all of us God-infused incredible Souls. In other words, wherever the Spirit within is acknowledged and expressed, regardless of religion, that is where I believe we are at our best.

INTRODUCTION

Accept it or not, sociopaths, narcissists and other toxic people walk squarely among us. They wreak emotional, psychological, and spiritual damage—and havoc when they lift your wallet or hack your bank account. Others with Empathy Dysfunction can be good souls whose empathy brain circuits have been damaged by alcohol and drug abuse or by traumatic brain injury.

Even well-meaning people with healthy, well-functioning empathy circuits can detour into Empathy Dysfunction when their moral code is suspended because they are scared, hurt or angry. You may be adept at spotting sociopaths and protecting yourself from their cons. But have you considered that you also need to protect yourself from people who don't mean to harm you?

I developed the Empathy Dysfunction Scale (EmD Scale) to help you identify the kind of people you're dealing with in your life. Plus I have tips for how to handle each type of Empathy Dysfunction from zero degrees of empathy (EmD-0) to Radiant Empathy (EmD-5). You needn't worry about EmD-5 folks: These are the angels who arrive in the nick of time to guide, support, and love us. They steer us away from disaster and help us untangle from it afterward.

Recognizing these EmD-5s, then following them into the light is a fantastic experience: It's the perfect antidote to those with Empathy Dysfunction. My trip into the jungle would provide me the opportunity to be tested by an EmD-1 (sociopath) and touched by an EmD-5 (Radiant Angel).

I left the past behind on Aug. 7, 2014, when I sold my house and finally moved away from the place so filled with trauma the previous 12 years. With the sale proceeds, I paid off the rest of my legal debts, bought a lovely new home in another state, and scheduled a sixty-fifth birthday trip to Panama. Just when I'd thought I had a handle on my life, the Universe saw fit to send me a reminder—named Marianne—that I was not entirely in control.

I met Marianne[2] on the first leg of my journey to Panama when we both got bumped from our flight to Houston, Texas. Ah yes, syrupy-sweet Marianne, the sociopath who could have ruined everything, had I let her. Marianne is a marvelous example of those everyday sociopaths who slyly slip into our lives, leaving a trail of destruction so convoluted they get away with their plots and schemes. Not this time. I am calling her out.

> **[There are] two unquestionable merits of being a genuine truth seeker: Your view of others (inside and out) takes on the clarity of high-powered binoculars. This enhanced, X-ray-like vision and acute awareness serve as your shield against the sociopaths that would pillage your life.**

First, I want to tell you about Iker, who turned out to be a philosopher and a Radiant Angel (EmD-5). Iker helped me recognize that life is about seeking truth, love, joy, and renewing yourself each day. To be prepared to meet an evil person, like Marianne, you must first turn your attention inward. That's where you must dwell—in a state of truth, love, and joy.

Unknowingly, Iker showed me two unquestionable merits of being a genuine truth seeker: Your view of others (inside and out) takes on the clarity of high-powered binoculars. This enhanced, X-ray-like vision and acute awareness serve as your shield against the sociopaths that would pillage your life.

---

[2] Marianne is not her real name. However, the details of my encounter with her are very real.

INTRODUCTION

Meet my tour guide to the Multiverse

The day the official Panama group tour ended, the other Tutters[3] boarded the busses that would take them to their flights home. I stayed, and scheduled myself for a guided tour through the jungle. Alone for the first time in eight days, I was already missing my mellow roommate, Elizabeth. I was looking forward to meeting new travelers and swapping adventure stories. When I'd reported to the tour desk, I was surprised to find I'd be traveling alone with the tour guide, Iker Lorente.

Iker was dressed in safari khakis with the Gamboa Rainforest Resort name on his shirt pocket.

> ...those binoculars would become a metaphor for seeing deeper into myself.

To enhance looking deep into the jungle, he had binoculars for each of us. Before the day was done, those binoculars would become a metaphor for seeing deeper into myself. For that, I would use mental field glasses. The vision of taking a selfie with these telescopic lenses was close at hand.

He'd handed me a bottle of water, then politely asked me to climb into the bed of the truck that would take us to the trailhead. It was a short, bumpy ride as Iker and I sat on an unforgiving wooden seat. The driver tried heroically to avoid potholes in the road; however, in this tropical environment any pavement or gravel turns to muck in short order. Plants and trees, growing at

---

[3] Mike Dooley, the author of many books, including the best seller, *Infinite Possibilities*, offers tours to destinations around the world for members of his organization, TUT. He refers to his co-travelers affectionately as "Tutters."

a ferocious rate, quickly reclaim the places where humans have made pitiful attempts to tame Mother Nature.

Not long after we'd ventured onto the Pipeline Trail, I realized that Iker was not very well-versed in the names of the surrounding flora and fauna. He referred to his guide book often. (Or could it have been that recognizing the thousands of species in the rainforest is an impossibility?) Iker did have a solid working knowledge of the jungle itself. A college history major, he was a critical thinker who could look at the big picture and see the repeating nature of human interaction with the dense jungle.

He made sure I didn't slip off the muddy, rotting, wooden foot bridge. He found me fairly stable ground to circumvent the huge mud puddles—and reassured me that the pack of wild dogs I thought I'd heard was a troop of noisy Howler monkeys. I was particularly proud of spotting a flock of parakeets, and Iker shared my joy. Showy displays of jungle life were few, and I was about ready to head back. My bucket list was waiting at the hotel, and I was anxious to cross out the line about traversing a bewildering rain forest trail.

Things got a bit more exotic when the rare and elusive Blue Morpho butterfly showed up. Excited, I unwrapped my waterproof camera to take a photo. Gently, Iker warned, "It's not easy to get a picture of the Morpho."

The minute the Blue Morpho lands on a leaf, it closes its fluorescent

The minute the rare Blue Morpho butterfly in [Panama rainforest] lands on a leaf, it closes its fluorescent blue wings, showing only the brown underside. To our surprise, the Blue Morpho landed and kept its beautiful wings open. Mesmerized, I managed to take a photo, ecstatic over my good fortune. In the next instant, I was horrified at what I saw through my camera lens.

INTRODUCTION

Blue Morpho Butterfly

via katelynoDESMA9

Rare and elusive, this beautiful butterfly was caught in a photo the author took during a vacation in the Panamanian rainforest. She felt a significant change come over her as she observed the blue morpho. Later, she would discover that the color blue in a butterfly is often thought to symbolize joy, color, or a change in luck. Sometimes, a blue butterfly is viewed as a wish granter, or a symbol of Spirit speaking through transformation and change—a divine and unexpected gift: exactly what it turned out to be for the author.

blue wings, showing only the brown underside. To our surprise, the Blue Morpho landed and kept its beautiful wings open. Mesmerized, I managed to take a photo, ecstatic over my good fortune. In the next instant, I was horrified at what I saw through my camera lens.

The butterfly was caught in a spider web. In seconds, the spider devoured the body of the struggling butterfly, leaving the delicate blue wings stuck in the invisible web. Iker and I watched in amazement, me with horror, and he with reverence. He told me, "It is a rare honor to see a predator capture its prey. We are very lucky today."

Iker's comment clung to me: As only an EmD-5 angel can do, he'd reframed a painful moment and spun it into a beautiful life lesson. In a flash of insight, I knew I must let go of expectations about the tour and give myself over to a different kind of journey.

I felt a strong urge to know more about Iker, another Earth traveler (a Radiant Angel in a human body), who seemed to be operating on a deep spiritual plain. He was about to teach me things that would change my life. I put my camera away and cracked my water bottle open for a big swig.

Then, I turned to Iker and re-introduced myself, the genuine, curious me—the "me" I protect and rarely show to anyone. I'd shed my self-absorbed expectations of the jungle. Quite mysteriously, I'd become open to seeing the truth there—and in my world back home.

I asked Iker about his life and what was important to him. I've come to call him my tour guide to the Multiverse[4] (more about the Multiverse later). In three short hours, Iker had opened my eyes—and my soul—to more, and different, levels of being.

Iker came into my life at the perfect time. Unwittingly, he helped me understand how I was moving from my former universe (way of being and thinking), filled with upheaval and heartbreak,

---

[4] "Multiverse," sometimes referred to as a parallel universe, is the hypothetical set of possible universes, including the universe in which we live. Together, these universes comprise everything that exists: the entirety of space, time, matter, energy, and the physical laws and constants that describe them. Don't get lost in the complexities of this term. Instead, ride along with me. I think my story will help define the Multiverse for you. It's a sometimes confusing futuristic term that has made its way into popular parlance though the concept has shown up in literature since somewhere around 1666 when Duchess Margaret Cavendish wrote "The Blazing World." Think also of modern works by Stephen King, Isaac Asimov, and Michael Crichton plus films, such as "Minority Report," and "The Butterfly Effect," and TV shows, such as "Twilight Zone," "Stargate," X-Files," and "Dr. Who." Then there are all of the Multiverse-style superheros in Marvel and DC comics.

into my new universe—the one where I went on tour in Panama and began writing a book.

Iker's presence and philosophy helped me to refocus and keep myself from backsliding into my two-dimensional world. His spontaneous, innocent appreciation for the cycle of life opened me to a new way of seeing things. I felt like I was traveling on a new plain, which I decided to call my Multiverse.

The Multiverse explained

This is not a metaphysical (a reality beyond what is perceptible to the senses) book, even though, between the lines, I reveal my spiritual philosophy: namely, that we are not alone in the Universe, and we are all connected spiritually.

My "contemporary" spiritual belief structure is built upon the teachers of New Thought, Religious Science, and Science of Mind (developed by such early 20th century teachers as Emmet Fox, Thomas Troward, Emma Curtis Hopkins, and Ernest Holmes). Fox, for example, explains that the Bible is a textbook of metaphysics that shows how Jesus teaches us to develop our soul and shape our life into what we wish ("Sermon on the Mount," 1934).

According to Fox, universal power "is the real source of all things that exist. It needs only to flow into your being and transform itself into health, into true prosperity, into inspiration, or into anything else you may be needing. This Power is there. It is present everywhere. It belongs to nobody in particular because it belongs to all. It is waiting at all times for men and women to call it into use—not merely in crisis, but in every problem however small every day of your life."

To my mind, Fox's philosophy is not unlike the view of the many scientists who teach us that the Universe is composed of billions of interacting systems of stars. "Interacting" is the key word here. These galactic systems affect each other and every living thing in the Universe.

Furthermore, our Universe is expanding, a factoid that just blows my mind, because it not only explains the Multiverse, but my life.

As many as 700,000 universes are thought to exist. Within each of these are at least 100 constellations, and within each constellation, 100 local solar systems. That makes 7 billion solar systems with 7 trillion habitable planets—Earth being only one of them; hence the Multiverse.

I'm not making up this stuff. Check for yourself. Stephen Hawking and other well- respected physicists postulate this theory. NASA scientists recently discovered—just forty light years away—a new-to-us solar system with seven Earth-size planets, three potentially habitable. Don't you wonder just a teensy bit about the possibility of intelligent life elsewhere? And if our Universe is expanding, how many more habitable planets and sentient beings are out there waiting to emerge?

I am neither a scientist, nor a spiritual teacher. I am a person trying to make sense of her life. To me, a person's "internal" multiverse is comprised of a trio of individual universes: emotions, spirituality and mindfulness.

The concept of multiverses resonates with me since it is the only thing so far that explains the wild, crazy, convoluted, miraculous—and interacting—connections in my life. This ever-expanding Multiverse, filled with millions of stars, solar systems, and life-supporting planets, is a metaphor for the quirky (and sometimes painful) happenstances that lead to marvelous moments of insight and personal growth.

INTRODUCTION

How else do you explain my meeting Iker (the Basque tour guide in the Panamanian jungle), who, in an intimate moment with a rare butterfly, shared how he sees the meaning of life; hence inexplicably pointing me to a new manner of thinking about my life and death.

I'd been considering writing the story of my entanglement with hostile neighbors, corrupt city government, and the oppressive jurisprudence system for several years. Initially, I'd planned to begin with the early-American history of the land where I lived. I'd wanted to emphasize the similarities between my neighbors and the ruthless Indian-hating EmD-1 frontiersmen[5] who had "settled" the land.[6] I'd wanted to weave in how battles like these, old and new, impacted my children, friends, and clients.

These subplots had rolled around in my thoughts for years, but I'd never found the right way into my story. That barrier collapsed when I finally sold my "troubled" house, moved away, and took an adventurous tour. How fitting to celebrate my freedom from EmDs by swinging through the jungle on my sixty-fifth birthday!

---

[5] It would turn out that Silas Maxon, the original settler of my property, was party to the U.S. Cavalry's massacre of entire Pacific Northwest villages of Native Americans in the 1840s. He was reported to have been present at the first hanging in the Oregon Territory when five Cayuse men were hung for war crimes in order to save their people from further persecution. At his execution, one of the five, Tiloukait, said, 'Did not your missionaries teach us that Christ died to save his people? So we die to save our people."

[6] In another interesting twist, my genealogical studies revealed that the land adjacent to mine, occupied by Scott and Jody Campbell, had originally been homesteaded by B.T. Olney, a descendant of Thomas Olney, a colleague of my colonial ancestors Obadiah Holmes and Chad Brown.

The Universe, though, had other plans for me. If I was going to write a meaningful book on how to survive encounters with relentless EmDs, I apparently needed one more experience to bring it all home.

The first leg of my Panama trip was from Portland to San Francisco, which is where I met Marianne: She would turn out to be an EmD-1 sociopath. At our initial meeting, I'd begun to feel like Alice in Wonderland—as if I'd fallen into a rabbit hole and was trapped in an alternate reality. I'd easily slipped into Marianne's custom Universe, a reality polluted with lies, schemes, and ridiculous rationalizations.

Yet another sociopath

It was a simpler, quicker lesson this time. Even after the years of suffering at the hands of sociopaths (EmD-1) in my hometown, the Universe had decided I needed an indelible reminder that I would never be free of such people. Sociopaths make up about 4 percent of the general population in the world and around 25 percent of the American prison population; hence you and I are bound to bump into one now and then.[7]

> Sociopaths seek us out. That's right. They thrive on causing pain, actively hunting for victims. I would wager that each of us is the target of a sociopath at least once a year.

Sociopaths seek us out. That's right. They thrive on causing pain, actively hunting for victims. I would wager that each of us is the target of a sociopath at least once a year.

---

[7] According to Martha Stout in the 2005 book, "The Sociopath Next Door." New York: Broadway Books.

INTRODUCTION

The lesson: It is best to be prepared to detour around the rabbit hole when a sociopath sneaks up, intending to push you down that portal. You can't avoid sociopaths; however, you can mitigate their damage by employing the tools I will teach you about in "When Empathy Fails."

The reason this Marianne character got as far as she did with me: I was traveling on the notion that I was leaving the bad guys behind. Not true. This irrational belief gave me a blind spot that rendered me vulnerable. It only takes one bad guy or gal to spoil your day—or your life.

Enjoy the loving people you meet. Invite them into your life with positive thoughts and prayers. Give your love and joy to others without hesitation. Doing so generates a powerful anti-sociopath defense system in you. Be ready for sociopath attacks of every kind. "Arm yourself" is my motto.

Marianne hooks me

I met Marianne when our flight from San Francisco to Houston was canceled. All passengers had boarded the plane before the announcement came: The first officer was too ill to fly; there was no replacement for him. The inconvenienced passengers began leveling complaints. I too, was concerned, worried that I would miss my two remaining connections to Panama.

United Airlines' employees assured us they would find alternative flights—tomorrow. I sucked it up and got in line with everyone else who was waiting to get a hotel room, blanket, toothbrush, and new flight schedule.

In the line to my left, a blonde, middle-aged woman was fretting and crying noisily about missing out on her Panama plans. "I've been waiting all year for this trip," she said. "I wasn't sure if I should go or not," she added, still carrying on. "It cost a lot of money. Now I think I should cancel and go home. But if I cancel, the airline should pay for it. That's the least they can do."

She was turning and talking to everyone. Most, busy with their own troubles, ignored her. Not me. Nope. I have broad shoulders, right? I decided to help, so I turned to Marianne and said, "Are you part of the TUT tour?"

She stopped her screaming and turned a smile in my direction. "Yes," she said, her eyes wide with glee as she hooked me. In a delighted, but childish, voice, she responded, "I recognize you from your beautiful picture on the website. You're Kathy aren't you?" She reached out both arms and hugged me. What's worse is that I'd let her hug me.

I'd wondered how she recognized me from the tiny little picture on the TUT Panama tour Facebook page since I rarely posted anything there. Only later did it dawn on me that Marianne had investigated all the tour's participants as potential victims for her shameful shenanigans. She was on the hunt.

Her loud, dramatic scene prompted an airline employee to open another computer terminal. He motioned Marianne over. Others who were waiting patiently and quietly didn't receive this kind of personalized service. Nope. Only the sociopath did; because the airline staff wanted to shut her up.

Marianne milked it even more. "I'm so afraid I'll miss the most important part of the tour. I'll be too late for the trip to the native village," she moaned.

Again I stepped into appease, saying, "Oh I don't think we'll miss the trip to the Embera village. That's on Monday. Today is only Saturday. Even with this delay, we'll still get there on Sunday night."

With crocodile tears she said, "That's right. The natives are called Embera. Are you sure? I don't want to miss this. It's the highlight of the trip for me." When I nodded to her reassuringly, she tried to hug me again, but this time I stepped aside. She looked into my eyes, those big tears dripping down her cheeks, and said effusively, "Thank you, thank you for saving this trip for me. If it weren't for you, I would have just given it up and missed the trip of a lifetime!"

A bit over the top you say? I was uncomfortable with her unrestrained gratitude, but I chalked it up to the midnight hour and the confusion caused by the flight cancellation. Experienced in handling a crisis, I don't get as ruffled as others might. I thought Marianne might be more reasonable after rested. She'd said as much, explaining that she was getting over a stress illness brought on by the recent Alzheimer's-related death of her dear mother. How could I not feel sympathetic?

"Could you help Kathy, too?" she asked the United employee. Marianne turned and motioned me over to the computer terminal. Speaking to the United employee while keeping her eye on me, Marianne continued, "We're on the same tour, so we have to get the same connecting flights to Panama. We could even go to the same hotel. Wanna' share a room, Kathy?"

I was stunned by the heft of her spontaneous manipulation. I hesitated, "Well. . . I . . . um." The United rep looked at me, waiting for an answer. Noting my hesitancy, Marianne offered, "Well, if you are uncomfortable with that, it's okay. You may want a separate room." Both of them looked in my direction, waiting for my response. Behind her tall counter, the airline staffer looked back at her computer and said, "Act fast, rooms are filling up."

Feeling pressured, I said, "Well, sure. That would be okay," even though I wasn't sure about it at all. I longed to get out of the airport and into a bed. We would have long hours of travel the next day since they'd re-routed us from San Francisco east to Newark, N.J., then on to Panama.

I was tired. My thoughts and feelings were jumbled. Marianne was acting like a dingbat. Her tears and manipulations were coloring and controlling everything, including our revised flight and overnight accommodations. She even got extra stuff out of the United employee by complaining long and loud. My mistake was allowing myself to make decisions that didn't feel right. Marianne was grooming me, sucking reason out of me and setting me up to accept her lead unconditionally.

As we were leaving the airport, I saw other passengers cozying up with their United-issued blanket. They'd found napping spots on airport chairs and benches. I wondered why I hadn't made that choice. By the time we got to the hotel, we would only get three hours of sleep anyway. Marianne was chipper now, stopping to grab free cookies and juice from the United staff. Acting as if she didn't have a care in the world, Marianne chatted up passersby, too. The word "dingbat" came to mind again.

On the 1 a.m. ride to the hotel, Marianne opened her tattered backpack and pulled out a used cottage cheese carton full of tuna salad. She munched happily even though the rest of us choked on the tuna smell. She turned around from her front passenger seat and sweetly asked if the tuna smell bothered anyone. No one answered her, including me.

We were all allowing her to inconvenience us because, well, it's not polite to refuse someone. Having no consideration for the van's passengers, she dug herself in deeper when she said, "Gosh, I know it smells, but I am so hungry I just have to eat. My roommate back home insisted on packing food for my trip."

Beyond annoying, Marianne talked nonstop en route to the hotel; the rest of us sat stone silent. She told the driver all about her college years and favorite professors and the films she'd watched in her classes. By the time we got to the hotel, I wanted to strangle this selfish woman. Then, she handed me her airline vouchers and asked that I handle the process of checking in for both of us! She was so overwhelmed by the ordeal, you know.

Really? I obliged; after all, we were sharing a room, and I'd get through the process faster. At last, I got the room number and the key then headed for the elevator. Marianne hung back to score more cookies from the desk clerk.

No surprises by now, right? Wrong. The room had one bed! The desk clerk confirmed that there were indeed no other rooms to be had—even in the massive DoubleTree San Francisco Airport Hotel. Why hadn't I slept in the airport?

"I hope you don't mind that I snore," Marianne said as she tossed me foam earplugs. How had she known that she needed to carry spare earplugs? "I have lots of these," she said cheerfully.

I thought, "Of course you carry ear plugs for your victims," but I said nothing. This kook had me spellbound.

"I'm glad I planned ahead for this eventuality," Marianne pattered on. "I have a nightgown and a change of clothes in my carry-on."

Hmmm, I thought suspiciously. I had nothing except my jungle backpack. I had Band-Aids, aspirin and motion sickness pills, but no clothes except what I was wearing.

Everything else was in my suitcase, probably stuck on the wrong airplane and headed for Houston, Texas. Marianne turned her back to me as she slipped into her nightie. I crawled into bed fully clothed to nap before the shuttle returned to take us back to the airport.

"Hope you don't mind," Marianne said ever so sweetly, "but I am a heavy sleeper. Would you mind waking me when it's time?"

> Marianne fell asleep instantly, then set to snoring—all night. I must have dozed off, because the alarm woke me. I turned on the light to rouse Marianne, and there she was next to me—buck naked!

"Sure," I responded, secretly wishing she would sleep through the alarm and miss the flight. Marianne fell asleep instantly, then set to snoring—all night. I must have dozed off, because the alarm woke me. I turned on the light to rouse Marianne, and there she was next to me—buck naked!

The anger trap

I wish the Marianne saga had ended there, but it didn't. I got fed up with her, but because I was angry, she still had a hold on me. My anger blinded me to her machinations. Think about it: As a sociopath, Marianne had no feelings one way or the other about me. Concern for inconveniencing me didn't even come into play. She was only interested in having me in the palm of her hand. Far worse than being a dingbat, this dangerous woman was a cold, calculating predator, who was reveling in toying with me.

As we boarded the hotel van to go back to the airport, I looked at her tattered backpack and frayed, cloth rolling carryon for the first time. I wondered if she had any money at all. How had she paid for her trip? I started to suspect that she may have wheedled a freebie out of the TUT organization or some unsuspecting person.

By now, I had a niggling feeling that she was lying to me about most everything, even though I couldn't prove it. What to do about it was the question. I hoped that once we got to Panama, I could rid myself of her and enjoy my vacation.

INTRODUCTION

I didn't see Marianne for the rest of the flight to Panama City. When we landed, and I'd passed through Customs, there she was, waiting outside with our hotel van driver. Wearing a cheesy, condescending smile on her face, she said, "I thought you were already out here since you left the plane before me."

"Well," I said, "It took me awhile because my luggage didn't make the flight. I had to file a report with United. They said my bag should be delivered to the hotel tomorrow by 1 p.m."

Marianne gave me a startled look, and those crocodile tears reappeared. "Luggage?" she questioned. "Oh no! I forgot my bag. I have to go back inside," and she abruptly turned to re-enter the building.

"You've got to be kidding," I exclaimed. (I couldn't help myself.) "Why didn't you get your bag at the luggage carousel? I mean, if it wasn't there, you would have known to file a claim like I did. What were you thinking going through Customs without your bag?"

Marianne whined, "I don't know. I am so tired and stressed. Why didn't you tell me to get my bag? Did you see my orange duffel bag on the carousel? I have to go back in right now."

It was stunning. Marianne was blaming me for her failure to claim her luggage! This melodrama was all for show. As I later learned, there was no bag, no orange duffel to be claimed. It was never delivered to our hotel. It was never loaded onto the bus for transfer to our next hotel. Not her travel roommate or anyone else on the tour ever saw an orange duffel.

Over the next day and a half, I had to schlepp around in rapidly deteriorating clothing. Marianne, on the other hand, wore a variety of outfits. She had a swimsuit for a dip in the pool plus colorful capris and a change of shoes for our trip to the Embera

Village. It was pretty clear that she carried everything in her worn out carry-on and backpack, which sufficed as her luggage.

Dingbat or sociopath? I wonder. . . .

Do you still think I am overreacting? Most of what I have told you about Marianne could also describe a disorganized person—except that she'd lied outright: She'd had no checked luggage. Blaming me for failing to remind her to retrieve her non-existent luggage was purely a setup. Being naked in the bed had been beyond rude. Sociopaths are like that. They drag us into situations so outlandish and embarrassing that we keep quiet about them.

The next afternoon, when we returned from the tour to the Embera village visit, I asked the desk clerk if my bag had arrived. It had not. Marianne sidled up to me at the hotel's front desk and announced to all within range, "I called the airline for you and told them we didn't need our bags until this evening because we would be on tour all day. In fact, I told them to hold your bag until they could find mine, so they wouldn't have to make more than one trip." She smiled at the desk clerk, dragging her into the scheme.

"You did what?!" I exclaimed, furious. I turned my back on her and walked over to the concierge. I asked him to please call United and request that my bag be delivered immediately. Really? I'm supposed to wait for my bag until Marianne's non-existent missing bag is located?

Marianne looked at me with mock hurt in her eyes. "I was only trying to help," she said tearfully, scurrying off to the free dinner with the rest of the tour group.

That was the last straw. I was so angry that during the remainder of the trip I called her out whenever she caused me trouble. It wasn't easy: Every time I turned around, she was standing next to me, listening to my conversations and insinuating herself into the groups where I mingled. I felt like I was being stalked.

When she tried to sit next to me on the bus, I announced loudly enough for all to hear, "Marianne, I don't want you near me. You are a stalker and a sociopath. I don't care if you have to stand up the entire trip. You will not sit in that seat." The whole bus was silent. The tour guide's smile vanished. Marianne went into her act. She burst into fake tears, begging someone at the back of the bus to help her out. And a man did by trading seats with her. A win for me.

By the trip's end, there were still some who remained unconvinced Marianne was a liar and master of manipulation. She had lost a few more "believers" with the story that her only child had died of typhoid fever. The rest of the tour members tumbled when they observed Marianne stealing food from the trip farewell banquet. When she thought no one was looking, she'd pulled Ziploc bags from her pocket, surreptitiously shoveled buffet food into them, then hidden them in her backpack.

I was finally able to let go of my anger when Dooley, our host, gave a farewell speech, thanking all who'd made the tour a success. When he handed out awards, Dooley honored Marianne for making the trip to the Embera village so memorable—because she'd spoken to the people there in fluent Spanish. Or so he'd thought, since he is not a Spanish-language speaker.

I wasn't shocked, but I was amused. The coup de grace came in seeing that this toxic sociopath had successfully conned even a celebrity like Dooley. That realization helped me to forgive—and stop judging—myself for falling prey to her sociopathic wiles. Marianne may have even deserved an award—for helping me kick-start writing, "When Empathy Fails."

Don't judge the spider or the sociopath

A big difference exists between the jungle spider and Marianne. As Iker observed, the spider killed the butterfly for food in the natural cycle of life. Marianne targets her victims solely for the pleasure of shutting down their sense of safety: No honor in that. How fitting to observe this cycle in the tropical rainforest.

Most of us living in the jungle we call civilization have lost our fight-or-flight edge to survive to a sense of complacency. Well-fed and well-educated, we are, mostly, unprepared to survive when, suddenly falling into a rabbit hole, we drop into place where a more primitive mental level of life reigns—the kind of place where the likes of Marianne thrive. This guide to Empathy Dysfunction will help to change that.

> **When you judge others according to your personal and narrow world view, you become a perfect candidate for victimization.**

Iker taught me another valuable lesson: to be non-judgmental about life. He wasn't horrified when he saw the lovely butterfly twitching as it was eaten alive. Iker was instead honored to share a brief moment in the butterfly's cycle of life.

When you judge others according to your personal and narrow world view, you become a perfect candidate for victimization. Think about all of the judgments I made about Marianne, and even Iker[8], before I saw that I could no more blame the spider for its actions than I could blame Marianne for hers.

---

[8] I'd been puzzled why Iker hadn't known more about the Panamanian jungle, especially the Spanish names for the flora and fauna. I chuckle even now at my foolish assumption. My tour guide to the Multiverse is not a native Panamanian. He's not even a native Spanish

INTRODUCTION

Had I been able to remain neutral and observant, I could have avoided—or much sooner shaken off—this woman's destructive grip on me. My cost for judging her: several days lost to irritation and inconvenience when I wanted to be relaxing and enjoying my dream vacation. "Don't judge. Stay neutral. Observe." This is another of my mantras.

Consider how differently things might have turned out had I ignored Marianne that fateful day in the San Francisco airport. The other passengers did.

Or, what if I'd abruptly changed my mind and decided to sleep in the airport? I could have ignored her when she pretended to lose her luggage; then hailed a cab to take me to the hotel. To make those healthier decisions, I would have had to suspend my notions of propriety and goodwill. Therein was the catch.

This exemplifies precisely what I want to teach you in this book: Don't assume you must go with the flow for someone else's sake. Vow to be flexible enough to care for yourself when you are targeted by EmDs.

The real heroes in life are flexible. They can be charitable to others yet still have the common sense to take care of themselves. Travel through life as an observer, so you can fly away from, instead of fluttering into, an EmD's spider web. When a Marianne drops into your life

The real heroes in life are flexible. They can be charitable to others yet still have the common sense to take care of themselves. Travel through life as an observer, so you can fly away from, instead of fluttering into, an EmD's spider web.

---

speaker. He's Basque (that little region between France and Spain). No wonder he had to keep consulting the guide book.

like a spider on a mission as it descends from the ceiling, take heed and quickly get away.

If it's a small spider that doesn't bother or threaten you much, perhaps you'll let it go. On the other hand, a brown recluse is a spider to be reckoned with: Kill it on the spot. Likewise, if a major sociopath drops into your life, trust your gut: You can feel the presence of a predator who is stalking you. Don't, for an instant, question your intuition. Take swift action to protect yourself.

Chapter by chapter

Sociopaths, like Marianne, inspired me to create this book. I had an inkling that I needed to learn far more about empathy and Empathy Dysfunction if I were to write anything meaningful or helpful. I began charting the course of my life—spotlighting the toxic period when I'd been trashed at every turn: I realized that non-sociopaths could have dysfunctional empathy circuits, too.

I will introduce you to the spectrum of Empathy Dysfunction, which I now define as the EmD Scale. This Scale can help identify the level of empathy in someone who has autism, or is brain injured, developmentally disordered, chemically dependent, or sociopathic. It also applies to typically empathic people who occasionally dip into thoughtless and unkind behavior.

For perspective, I give you examples of highly empathic angels with Radiant Empathy who showed up unexpectedly during my years-long perfect storm of multiple EmD encounters. One of the most critical angels was Ed Snook, the publisher of the *US~Observer,* a newspaper with a mission of exposing injustice. When he and his staff of investigative journalists took up my cause, I began to feel vindicated.

INTRODUCTION

Finally having the ear of someone who valued truth and integrity had filled me with renewed hope. After covering my ongoing story for about a year, Ed acknowledged my research prowess and invited me to work as an investigative reporter for the *US~Observer*. Again, the sense of being hammered by the world abated a little with his offer.

In surviving the storm and its aftermath, I've become smarter about how to be a human being. I learned how to take my life back from the users and abusers. I hope you will benefit from my misfortunes and my musings.

A synopsis of each chapter, beginning with the Prologue, follows....

Prologue: "The River, The Road and The Train" --- A CONSPIRACY THEORY TRIED AND FOUND TRUE

The examples I use to illustrate the different types of Empathy Dysfunction (EmD-0 on the low end through EmD-5 on the high end) are taken from a far-reaching back story. Yet, the scenarios are meaningful as they are—without explanation of when or where they occurred. You can actually read chapters out of order and still benefit from the education about Empathy Dysfunction.

If you are a reader who wants to know the underlying story because: you're curious; need to confirm all that happened to me really did; or truly want to know the person who lived through all of this—read the entire *Prologue* that follows. You'll read about the exhaustive illegal, unethical, immoral, hateful—unimaginable— actions my neighbors engaged in to force me to give up my property rights. It will help you grasp how they lost, and I won—in the end.

History buffs, you may want to go directly to *figs. A.2, A.3, and A.4*, deeds and maps that tell the story of my property and the environs back to pioneer times.

For clarity, you may find yourself using it throughout as a reference. My life from 2002 to 2014 was so convoluted and filled with chaos that even I had difficulty keeping it all straight. I am still coming to terms with the trauma of those years. In some instances, I am just now connecting the dots.

If you choose to skip the in depth *Prologue* for now and hurry on to the main part of the book, there's a two-page synopsis of it.

In essence, you have three options: skip the *Prologue* altogether; read the synopsis of it; or read the whole darned thing. It's up to you.

Chapter One—No One Calls Me Mom Anymore

Outlined here are the first bewildering years when those with Empathy Dysfunction besieged me. Beginning in 2002, I was harassed, assaulted, stalked, sued, and falsely arrested—all because of others' greed over real estate development. It took me awhile to catch on to the destruction EmDs could cause. Their irrational attacks were so frightening that my children became casualties, too.

A year after the first lawsuit was filed against me in 2005, my eldest daughter, Bianca, turned on me and has not spoken to me since. Taking you off guard is how EmDs start their decimation. Before I got back on my feet, I made several serious mistakes—which I now offer as warnings for you.

INTRODUCTION

Chapter Two—Empathy Dysfunction (EmD) In-depth

After introducing you to Empathy Dysfunction "in the raw" in *Chapter One,* I walk you through the definition of empathy and Empathy Dysfunction, then explain the six levels of EmD from zero to five. Autistics are basically EmD-0 because of their inability to connect. Sociopaths are EmD-1. Those with traumatic brain injury are EmD-2. Alcoholics and addicts fall into EmD-3.

Those who function normally, except when victimized by sociopaths and other EmDs, are considered EmD-4. Finally, there are rare EmD-5s who, like angels, provide the most incredible, caring support. I've included EmD-5s in the mix: It's important to recognize them as blessings. If it weren't for the EmD-5s in my life, I might very well have succumbed.

Included is the Empathy Dysfunction Scale I developed for you to gain the kind of insight that can help to keep you safe around people with low levels of empathy.

Chapter Three—Brainwashing Mom

Prior experience has groomed many EmD victims. Here I describe brainwashing and the kind of coercive control, imperceptible to outsiders, that turns us into EmD targets. Again, I use myself as an example. Leaving an abusive marriage, along with the strain of caring for two disabled children, rendered me psychologically unable to handle the onslaught of harassment.

When I awoke to the bludgeoning abuses, I faced a desperate scramble to regain ground—and my sense of self-worth. I will teach you how to stop insidious abuse in its tracks.

Chapter Four—My Daughter Is Autistic

Autistics are EmD-0 not because they are worse than sociopaths, but because they have no degree of empathy. Sociopaths, EmD-1s, have just enough insight to assess a person's weaknesses, then take advantage of them. They could care less if you suffer.

On the other hand, autistics can't fathom how you think, but they do have a moral code, and their intention is seldom to harm you. In this chapter, I tell you the story of my daughter Bianca, who has Asperger Syndrome, also referred to as high-functioning autism. I struggled to relate to this child I so loved. For that, she has forsaken me. I ask that you take heart; there is hope for good relationships with autistics.

Chapter Five—Impacted by Mild Traumatic Brain Injury

Study after study has verified that repeated head injury from concussions has caused brain damage to players in the National Football League (NFL). The League denied the obvious for far too long, allowing more and more professional athletes to succumb to the illness known as Chronic Traumatic Encephalopathy (CTE).

I came face-to-face with CTE when my younger daughter, Phoebe, was evaluated for brain damage from repeated concussions during her soccer years. In this chapter, I describe her descent into Empathy Dysfunction.

I watched my bright, shining, compassionate daughter become increasingly deceitful, belligerent, and combative during her middle- and high-school, years. Then, when she was 23, Phoebe assaulted me so fiercely that I feared for my life.

INTRODUCTION

I learned how to protect myself from Phoebe, but that caused her, and my infant grandson, to fall away from me as her older sister had. Fortunately, there are things you can do to help your EmD-2 loved ones—if they'll let you. I am especially encouraged by California psychiatrist Daniel Amen's protocol for healing a battered brain.[9]

Chapter Six—On Becoming a Warrior Matriarch

Taking on a career drug addict is not easy, especially when he is a member of your family and someone you love dearly. I have many family members who are alcoholics/addicts, some in recovery, and some not. I watched my father lose one battle after another with some of these addict family members (cousins, aunts, uncles, and extended kin). Although Dad lost most battles with his troubled (EmD-3) family members, I learned many things from his mistakes, including: send love and prayers for their recovery.

Here I show you how an EmD-3 can grow to have more empathy once in recovery for addiction. When they are actively using, EmD-3s can descend to the level of EmD-1. With abstinence, exercise, proper nutrition, and competent psychotherapy, these folks can rise to the level of EmD-4. Recovery is so remarkable for some that they want to give back to society just as EmD-5s often do.

Chapter Seven—How Mob Mentality Materializes

EmD-4 describes the majority of people, those who live a good life, raise healthy children, pay their bills, and contribute to

---

[9] Daniel Amen, M.D. is a well-known psychiatrist and pioneering clinician who uses brain scans to better diagnose mental disorders.

society. In this chapter, you'll have the realization that EmD-4s think more about fitting in than about how to live a meaningful life.

Narcissists and sociopaths aim to use these EmD-4 innocents for harm. For example, my ordinary EmD-4 neighbors became submerged in mob mentality because a couple of sociopaths manipulated them. Wanting to fit in, my once-nice neighbors ran full-out with gossip, doing their level best to bring harm to my children and me. It's important that EmD-4s learn to do what's right and be responsible for their actions even—or perhaps especially—when that means standing apart from the persuasive crowd.

Chapter Eight—Just Plain Mean

This is the meat of the book. It's where I describe how three EmD-1s created a host of problems for me when they set out to destroy my family, my career, my finances, and my freedom. The most accurate way to describe EmD-1s is "just plain mean."

It is critical to understand that EmD-1s are truly out to get you. I want you to comprehend how these conscienceless people operate. The sooner you spot them, the better. What you are about to learn will enable you to stop them cold.

Chapter Nine—In the Cross-hairs of Cyberattackers

The U.S. Presidential election of 2016 brought to public awareness how EmDs use cyberattacks to destroy opponents. These political criminals didn't just hack into private email accounts or use ordinary propaganda; they also used the Internet to spread gossip, in the form of "fake news" and "alternative facts."

INTRODUCTION

  The EmDs in my life were no less destructive. My neighbors and others engaged in hacking, cyberstalking, fake news, and lying by way of using alternative facts. Their evil intent was to destroy my finances, my professional reputation, and my family.

  The Internet makes it phenomenally easy and efficient to launch a campaign of cyberattacks at lightning speed. Don't assume that because you aren't rich, famous, or in the public eye, you're safe from EmD (1,2,3, or 4) mayhem. In our brave new world where the unthinkable can happen—it takes only one EmD to press the send button and wreak havoc.

Chapter Ten—Radiant Warrior, Resilience Epitomized

  Diverging from the dark side of Empathy Dysfunction, in this chapter I show you what is possible when you function as an EmD-5, or Radiant Angel. These people live at a level where it is as important to stand up for others as it is to protect themselves.

  They have resilience, which I suspect comes from a lifetime of surviving hardship. Most probably, EmD-5s have worked through life lessons and emerged more enlightened and loving. I haven't always functioned at EmD-5 level, but I have been there a time or two: It has made all of the difference in living a meaningful life.

Chapter Eleven—Conclusion – How I Survived the decade-long Perfect Storm and Learned to Dance As It Raged

  Just as I was wrapping up the manuscript of this book, I got a letter from the Archdiocese of Portland asking for my help in processing an annulment request for my ex-husband. It was a surprising request since he's Jewish, and I'm not Catholic. After thinking it through, I realized it was a very fitting (albeit ironic) conclusion to the book.

It confirmed two of the lessons I set out to teach you. First, never be surprised by the things people with Empathy Dysfunction do. Second, when EmDs cross you, let them go completely and utterly: Never look back.

Follow the seven basic tips outlined in this chapter, and you will be able to take back your life. Never again will you be waylaid by those with severe Empathy Dysfunction.

Epilogue—BraveHeart

I spent $564,744 on legal fees from 2002 to 2014. This amount doesn't even include the half a million dollars (or more) my title insurance company paid my attorneys.

I hired 16 attorneys to handle more than 20 legal matters (divorce, lawsuits, harassment and contempt orders, false arrests, stalking protection, city code violations, and licensing board complaints).

I collected $125,951 in settlement damages from those EmD neighbors and the city of Vancouver. Let that sink in. This is the price of justice in America. The lawyers get their exorbitant cut, and clients---already victims---like me get to make payments on horrendous legal debt. And that leaves a good many of us struggling to clean up our credit score—if we can.

On the other hand, in the Epilogue I can proudly call myself BraveHeart. I weathered this perfect storm and came out on the other side, transformed. I live in a beautiful river setting with my dog Simon Templar and my three cats (Neo, Trinity and Seven of Nine).

**Thank you for picking up this book
and taking the time to peruse the *Introduction*.**

PROLOGUE

"The River, the Road, and the Train," a Conspiracy Theory Tried and Found True

"But you have to see how all the pieces fit together before you can draw final conclusions."

Cliff Sloan, associate independent counsel during the Iran-contra investigation

Behind—and before—the creation of the Empathy Dysfunction Scale

This is the back story for "When Empathy Fails" where I detail the events behind the development of the Empathy Dysfunction Scale.[10] Believe it or not, the saga that led to the birth of the Empathy Dysfunction Scale started centuries ago. I have included maps *(See below or figs. A.3 and A.4)*[11] to show where these events took place in a contemporary suburban neighborhood along a lovely stretch of Columbia River waterfront.

---

[10] To view the Empathy Dysfunction Scale *(See below, Chapter Two. or fig. A.1)*.

[11] As my story begins, I encourage you to review these maps, old and new. Refer to them for clarity as you read through the related sections of "When Empathy Fails."

WHEN EMPATHY FAILS

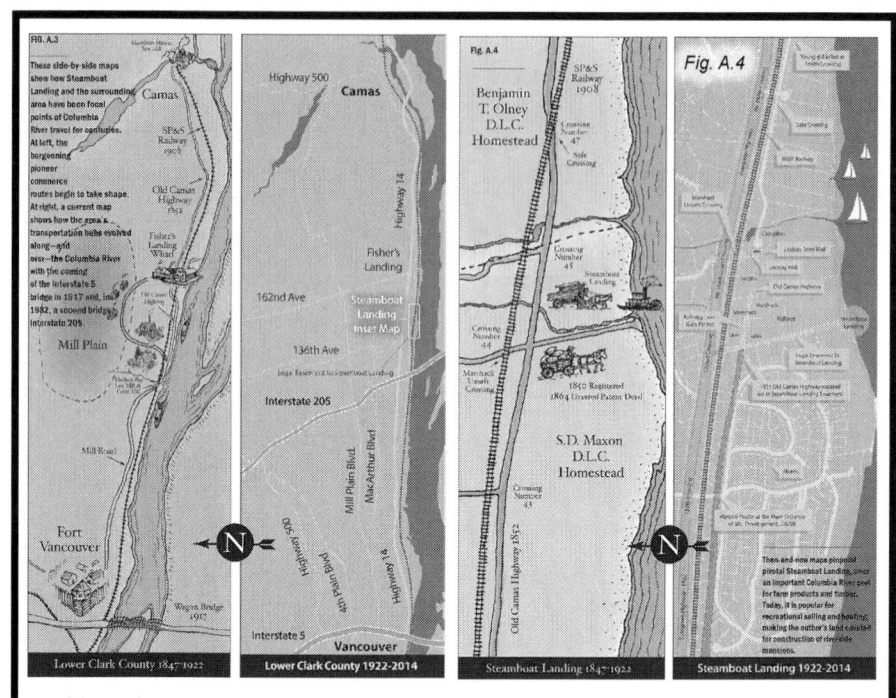

Maps that help explain the history of the author's land and the surroundings as time marched into the 21st century. Highlighted is Steamboat Landing, the area where the author's story took place. Once an important Columbia River port for produce and timber, SBL is now popular for recreational boating, one of the reasons her neighbors coveted the author's land. The places—and people—called out on these maps were integral to the creation of Dr. Marshack's Empathy Dysfunction Scale. (See Figs. A3 and A.4 for a larger view.)

    For historical perspective, I've also included maps from as far back as 1852 when the land still belonged to the First People of the Pacific Northwest (i.e. the Chinook and Cayuse tribes). Later came British fur trappers, and still later, land-hungry American settlers—both involved in the massacre of thousands of First People.

PROLOGUE --- THE RIVER, THE ROAD, AND THE TRAIN

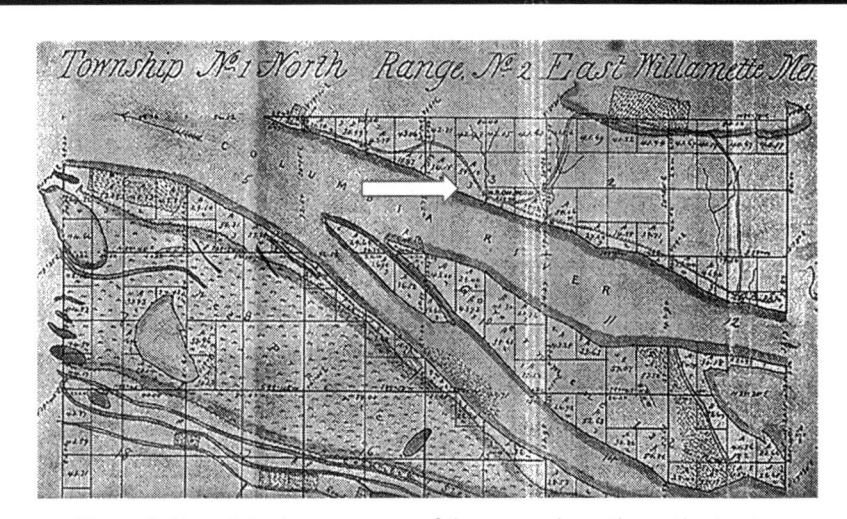

Above *is the original survey map of the area where the author's story took place. It was created by Americans in 1852 and shows the Columbia River and the parallel Old Camas Highway north of the river (see arrow).*

Below *are Surveyor notes that accompanied the Township map. They read: "The above map of Township No. 1 North of Range No.2 East of the Willamette Meridian, Territory of Oregon is strictly conformable to the field notes of the survey thereof on file in this office which have been examined and approved. – Surveyor General's Office, Oregon City December 17th 1852." The signature appears to be that of B. Grestun, Surv. Genl.*

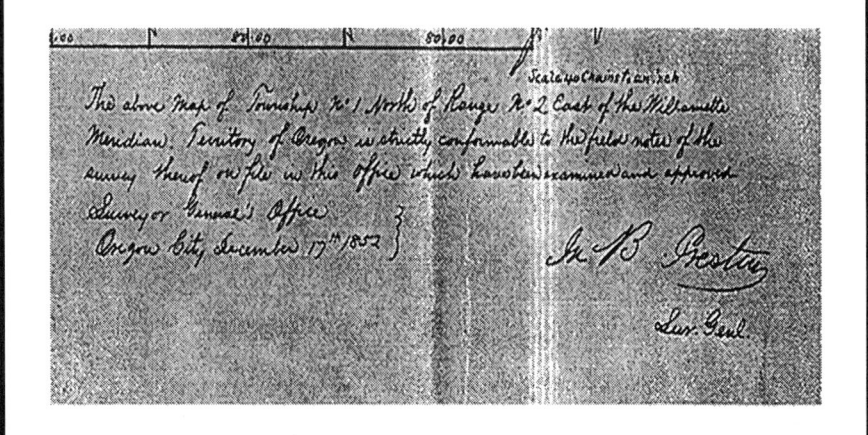

> • This 1852 survey map of Joseph Hunt's shows the *"Columbia City to Cascade City Road"* leading through the S.D. Maxon DLC. H.J.G.' survey of Township 2 was recorded in 1860, probably completing the road survey to

An example of the historic documents that the author uncovered in her quest to prove the solid history and legality of the in-perpetuity easement rights attached to her property in Vancouver. The language here connects to the Surveyor's map and notes above.

I think it will be helpful for readers to know this underlying story, but it is not necessary to understanding the concepts introduced in "When Empathy Fails."

The examples I use to illustrate different types of Empathy Dysfunction (EmD-0 on the low end through EmD-5 on the high end) are taken from this back story. Yet, the scenarios are as meaningful as is without explanation of where they came from. You can read chapters out of order and still benefit from the education about Empathy Dysfunction.

If you are a reader who wants to know the back story because: you're curious; need to confirm all that happened to me really did; or truly want to know the person who lived through all of this—read the entire *Prologue*.

For those of you who want to skip the in depth prologue for now and hurry on to the main part of the book, there's a shortened version of the "story."

In essence, you have three options: skip the Prologue altogether; read only the synopsis of it; or read the whole darned thing. It's up to you.

I suggest that the *Prologue* (even the nutshell version) will come in especially handy when reading *Chapters Seven* and *Eight*. My head still spins with disbelief when I think of those days when the Train Horn Noise Quiet Zone (THNQZ) mob came after me, all the while encouraged by people who were just plain mean.

PROLOGUE IN BRIEF

From Trashed to Triumphant

"There are 869 different forms of lying, but only one of them has been squarely forbidden. Thou shalt not bear false witness against thy neighbor."

— Mark Twain in "Following the Equator" from the chapter "Pudd'nhead Wilson's New Calendar" (1897)

You need to know only two things

You have no reason to believe that I know anything about how to stop unscrupulous people in their tracks, but for this: For more than a decade, I was trashed repeatedly, then, eventually, came out on the other side of it all triumphant and at peace.

This book would be nothing more than another titillating memoir if it was only about my personal and tragic experiences, such as my encounters with corrupt government officials, unethical civic leaders, false arrests, assaults, cyberstalking, lawsuits, and betrayal by my children.

My attorney Mick Seidel told me, "A jury will never believe that you went through all of this. It's just too outrageous to be real." If I had a dollar for every time I've heard a similar comment, I'd be wealthy.

> **My attorney Mick Seidel told me, "A jury will never believe that you went through all of this. It's just too outrageous to be real."**

PROLOGUE IN BRIEF

Sometimes, truth is stranger than fiction—and in my case, it was. The truth doesn't always show its face unbidden. Nope. I'd needed to take step after step to set the record straight and reclaim my life.

When I'd considered writing about the perfect-storm decade I'd lived through, I'd known that I wanted to offer readers more than a story of my triumph over bad people. But what?

For years, I'd puzzled over what toxic people had in common. In time, I'd made two important discoveries, one for you and one for me. The discovery for you is the purpose of this book. It had finally occurred to me that my enemies all had one thing in common: deficiency in empathy to some degree or another. I was excited then. It explained everything.

I'd felt a sense of relief as I'd gained this clarity about why I'd been so rigorously victimized. As I'd poured over evidence (depositions, emails, and other incriminating evidence) and researched the psychological theories of empathy, I'd realized it had been a variety of bullies who'd attempted to have their way with me.

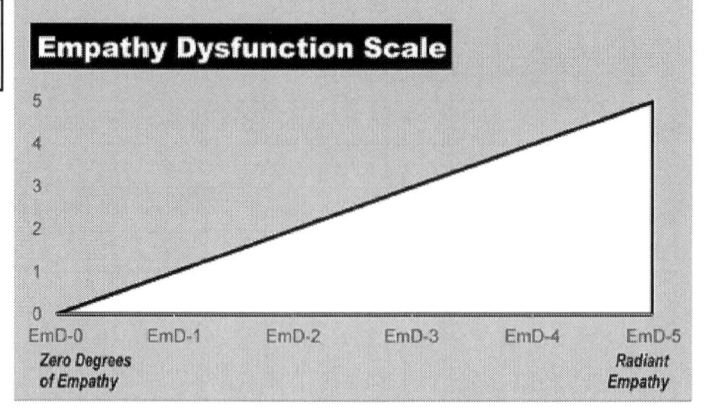

Fig. A.1 — Empathy Dysfunction Scale

(Scale from 0 to 5, with categories EmD-0 "Zero Degrees of Empathy" through EmD-5 "Radiant Empathy")

Understanding the Varying Degrees of Empathy in Humans

EmD-0 *Zero Degrees of Empathy*—struggle to understand the empathic reciprocity of normal communication, but they are not out to get you. Deep down, they have a moral code; or they can be taught about morality. **Examples:** *autistics and young children.*

EmD-1 *Self-Absorbed individuals*—only interested in their own agenda; hence usually cause serious harm. It only takes a single EmD-1 to destroy everything their victim has worked for. **Examples:** *narcissists and psychopaths/sociopaths.*

EmD-2 *Organic Brain Injury/Illness*—unpredictable mental functioning that creates chaos in their lives and the lives of their caregivers and loved ones. **Examples:** *the mentally ill and traumatic brain injured (TBI).*

EmD-3 *Controllable Mental Illness*—can function at much higher levels of empathy if their disorders are treated with medicine, psychotherapy, and psychosocial education. Otherwise, their empathy is intermittent, depending on their stage of illness. **Examples:** *alcoholics, addicts, and those with bipolar disorder.*

EmD-4 *Basic Good-enough Empathy*—psychologically unaware yet good citizens and neighbors most of the time; however, they are prone to gossip and codependency. **Examples:** *unless asked to do more than they desire, most are trustworthy.*

EmD-5 *Radiant Empathy*—fearless individuals with empathy fully functioning nearly all of the time. They have clear boundaries for themselves and others. **Examples:** *the devoted friend who accepts all of your flaws; the 88-year-old man who plants saplings for future generations; the Medal of Honor winner; the woman who fights for those who are disenfranchised; and the mother who always forgives.*

(fig. A.1)

Copyright Kathy J. Marshack, Ph.D. 2017

Next, I'd had the revelation that I could categorize these bullies according to their level of empathy (or non-empathy). My hunches and hard work had begun to take shape and evolved into the Empathy Dysfunction Scale (EmD).

The most important thing I want you to take away from reading "When Empathy Fails," is how to spot people with Empathy Dysfunction, then stop them dead in their tracks, using the tools that worked for me—before they damage you or your loved ones.

Some of you may also be interested in the underlying story that weaves in and out. It holds the key to the chaos and confusion that generated the Empathy Dysfunction Scale in the first place.

As you read this book, you may struggle to keep track of all of the players, the lawsuits, the attorneys, and the tragedies. I know I did even as I lived it! The chronology of my life during these trying times did not play out in a straight line and is definitely complex.

Your best bet is to refer to the *Appendix*. There I have: included maps of my neighborhood showing the disputed spots; displayed images of historic deeds and incriminating correspondence from this bully to that; and presented a detailed account of the big-picture story behind the "River, the Road, and the Train" chapter of my life.

The book, itself, takes you step by step through my encounters with the Empathy Dysfunctional people who goose-stepped into my world (City officials Richard Landis, Josephine Townsend, and Jim Jacks as well as neighbors Scott Campbell, Don Morris, and several others.

While jaw-dropping, not all of these details necessarily further my goal to help you understand Empathy Dysfunction, or what I refer to as EmD. My personal story may fascinate a handful of readers, or even become the plot line for a Hollywood movie, but it is not the purpose of this book.

WHEN EMPATHY FAILS

> **It made no sense that they'd all gotten together clandestinely to generate a huge plot—that covered multiple private and civic issues—laser-focused on taking me out, distressing my children, and continued this despicable ploy for years.**

First, I'd "gotten it" that these bullies had one thing in common: defective empathy brain circuits. Why the lot of them was working in some sort of dramatic conspiracy against me was extremely confusing.

It made no sense that they'd gotten together clandestinely to generate a huge plot—that covered multiple private and civic issues—laser-focused on taking me out, distressing my children, and continued this despicable ploy for years.

Sometimes, things are simpler than they appear—just like the straightforward Empathy Dysfunction Scale had turned out to be. The sole reason they'd come after me? Greed. A brand of greed that escalated to extreme and abusive proportions. This is the most essential thing you need to know to put the whole story in context.

In 2001 (when the housing market was about to skyrocket), a handful of my wealthy neighbors had begun investigating the possibility of implementing a Train Horn Noise Quiet Zone (THNQZ) to silence the train horns that blasted as they passed our homes dozens of times each day. How better to further enhance their property values in one fell swoop?

> **The sole reason they'd come after me? Greed. A brand of greed that escalated to extreme and abusive proportions. This is the most essential thing you need to know to put the whole story in context.**

In order to create this political designation, the THNQZ proponents had needed the help of local, state, and federal agencies, plus the backing of the private owner of the train tracks. The only obstacle standing in their way was me.

I had a variety of rights that confounded them, primarily my property rights, my home occupation permit, and my right to a safe train crossing. And, oh yes, my civil rights! As nutty as it seems, the neighbors' selfish agenda sucked me into more than a decade of legal action and harassment. It cost hundreds of thousands of dollars to defend myself against all of it only to lose my family.

The second—and far worse—realization I'd had while researching this book was that "no one calls me Mom anymore" (hence the title of Chapter One). This upper class mob's barrage of unsettling disparagement hadn't been limited to me.

Neighbors and police had hurled accusations and employed downright hateful actions against my two daughters. Essentially, the three of us were living in a mental and emotional (and sometime physical) war zone, land mines all around. One by one, the girls left, presumably to live where they'd feel safe. They cut off contact with me as well.

I lost far, far more than time and money to these louts. The bullies' flat-out greed cost me the ultimate—my family. I pray always that my daughters, grandson, and I will be reunited—and even live in harmony.

Triumphant, still? Yes. I cleared up the mystery of why those with Empathy Dysfunction banded together to destroy me, and I stopped them. Identifying and defining the EmD Scale was a bonus. I consider it a success that I made these two discoveries.

Next time I won't waste so much time letting my suffering interfere with silencing unscrupulous attackers. Now that I have the Empathy Dysfunction Scale, I can quickly size up these creeps, and make plans to dispatch them.

Read further for the rest of the story behind "When Empathy Fails."

UNABRIDGED PROLOGUE
A True Crime Story

"Each of us is a book waiting to be written, and that book, if written, results in a person explained."
— Thomas M. Cirignano, The Constant Outsider

I filed for divorce in early spring 2002, having finally given up on a 23-year marriage to a divorce attorney who leveled daily verbal abuse at our two adopted daughters and me. I knew it wouldn't be easy to get a divorce in our smallish town, Vancouver, Wash., where my husband held sway with the entire legal community (judges, attorneys, police, and even City Hall officials). You can just imagine the set up I walked into.

Very quickly, my life had turned into an unparalleled nightmare of intrigue not unlike a Hollywood crime mystery script. I felt like Julia Roberts in the movie "The Pelican Brief," wondering how she'd gotten herself into such a mess, then being forced to learn on the fly how to protect herself from a group of unscrupulous conspirators.

Very quickly, my life had turned into an unparalleled nightmare of intrigue not unlike a Hollywood crime mystery script. I felt like Julia Roberts in the movie the "Pelican Brief," wondering how she'd gotten herself into such a mess; then being forced to learn on the fly how to protect herself from a group of unscrupulous conspirators.

In my case, it wasn't a fictional plot. It is a true crime story about a suburban mom in the eye of a perfect storm of greedy neighborhood bullies wrongfully enlisting the aid of pawns—several of them elected—in judicial, legal, and law enforcement systems.

As this storm of modern witch hunting grew stronger, it swept up more and more players; so many it became increasingly harder to keep track of them.

My decade from hell had begun with a sad, but not uncommon, divorce story: My scorned husband used parental alienation to harm me. His efforts were effective: Neither of my daughters has spoken to me for years.

Following the divorce, I was besieged by a host of unethical and absolutely selfish power brokers, who stirred up a hateful and destructive mob. This partial list of characters reads like an Agatha Christie whodunit:

THE MAIN PLAYERS
- Rogue Prosecutor
- Auto Tycoon
- Newspaper Publisher
- Train Corporation Executive
- Scorned Husband
- Sneaky Civil Servant
- Real Estate Heir
- Professor
- Podiatrist and His Wife
- Fiercely Loyal Dog
    and
- Me, the Suburban Soccer Mom

The list of minor players is even longer, though their actions were no less deadly. Here are just a few of them: the multimillionaire who drilled a well into a wetland near the Columbia River; the nephew who sent threatening emails; the HOA President who mocked up and publicly displayed a Kathy Marshack "Wanted Poster."

Believe it or not, Presidents Lincoln and Clinton show up in this true-life melodrama. Sadly, my daughters are also among those who were victimized by the perfect storm of dangerous players in our lives: In turn, my two girls victimized me.

> **Each and every case involved my treatment by people who were lacking or deficient in basic empathy. It was so prevalent that I began to call the phenomenon Empathy Dysfunction.**

Except for a few, the players in my drama wanted to harm me. They believed I stood in the way of their goals to acquire even more power and money. Once they'd sustained several legal losses on my account, what they wanted most was revenge.

By the time this perfect storm was spent, I had hired 16 attorneys—costing me more than half a million dollars[12]—to represent me in 20-plus legal matters that were presided over by eight judges. Each and every case involved my treatment by people

---

[12] Another approximate half a million dollars was paid out to attorneys by my title insurance company because they had insured my deeded property rights when I'd purchased the land. A title company makes sure that the title to a piece of real estate is legitimate, then issues title insurance for that property. Title insurance protects the lender and/or owner against lawsuits or claims against the property that result from disputes over the title.

who were lacking or deficient in basic empathy. It was so prevalent that I began to call the phenomenon Empathy Dysfunction.

Although I survived, I lost my children to the oppressive year-in-and-year-out psychological warfare I'd been up against. The tragedy, and travesty, of losing my beloved daughters has been intensely painful, as you can imagine. My grief and longing to see them recur daily. No mother should have to go through this.

Aside from my daily prayers, one thing kept me going: the research for this book. For some reason, I have been gifted with a talent for research and writing. During the course of those lonely, stormy years, I wrote two books on Asperger Syndrome (or Autism Spectrum Disorder (ASD), my eldest daughter's disability) and a chapter in the book, "Sixty Things to Do When You Turn Sixty."

I was also busy preparing PowerPoint presentations for my attorneys, not just to underpin my defense against menacing neighbors, but to clarify the history of the real estate and deeds they were disputing.

The history of the land along the Columbia River where I lived at that time goes back to the founding of the Oregon Territory and the commerce that followed: which was why I titled one of my presentations "The River, The Road and The Train." While preparing these PowerPoints, I found I had another talent—investigative reporting.

A shattered mom who knew she might never see her children again, I'd continued to work as a practicing psychologist and healer. I had to do more than survive (although survival was utmost on my mind every day).

Even as the merciless hounding and battering had continued, I'd known I needed to find meaning in my life again. While trying to see connections and extract reasons for being bullied, I began to integrate the people involved, their obvious pathologies, and their apparent ravaged empathic abilities. (Plus, I had nothing left to lose, right?[13])

My deductions inspired me to develop the Empathy Dysfunction (EmD) Scale *(see fig. A.1)*. It's a tool to help us gauge how much empathy (from a lot to none) is at work in the people who frequent our lives; hence, better know how to interact with them. I didn't set out with a psychological scale in mind, it just kind of happened. I believe it is my mission to bring you this new way of perceiving how feelings are, or aren't, shared.

Two land deeds to the rescue

At stake were (1) my legal right to gain access to the Columbia River via a couple of roads, and (2) my legal right to safe passage across a busy transcontinental train track.

Two deeds—two old and brittle pieces of paper—foiled the outcome of the foolish and mean players in this true crime story. The deeds are associated with a piece of real estate where I lived for 30 years (14237 S.E. Evergreen Highway, Vancouver, Wash.). At stake were (1) my legal right to gain access to the Columbia River via a couple of roads, and (2) my legal right to safe passage across a busy transcontinental train track.

Once my legal land rights had been made clear, my opponents were stymied in their goal to legitimately claim my

---

[13] This is a philosophy that originated with General Sun Tzu, the Chinese military strategist and philosopher, who lived from 533 to 496. B.C. He is credited as being the author of the influential book "The Art of War."

deeded easements for themselves. At that point, this growing mob had chosen to subvert my rights in any other way they could. I'll explain more about why these deeds were so disconcerting to my neighbors; for now, I want to familiarize you with the content. It will prove extremely important in tying together the seemingly far-flung pieces of the conspiracy theory.

First came this small addendum to the property description for my two parcels of land[14] (which my now ex-husband, Howard Marshack, and I purchased in 1984 while married):

*"**TOGETHER WITH** an easement: For ingress and egress over and across a strip of land 30 feet in width, as said roadway now exists, leading from subject property to the "Steamboat Landing" as well as leading over and across that tract of land described as the "Old Camas Highway."*

Second was the train crossing deed given to my predecessor by the Spokane, Portland and Seattle Railway (SP&S) in 1908. Back then, the train company was buying land along the Columbia River in order to lay the first train track in Washington State. As SP&S had bought up land, they'd agreed to grant a perpetual (north-to-south) right of way across the tracks to local landowners.

In addition, my deed states that the train company had agreed to build a "crossing" and a road to that crossing for ease of access. *(See an excerpt of the deed below or see fig. A.2).*

---

[14] The easement rights discussed throughout the book applied to both parcels, the one where my home stood and the adjoining vacant lot.

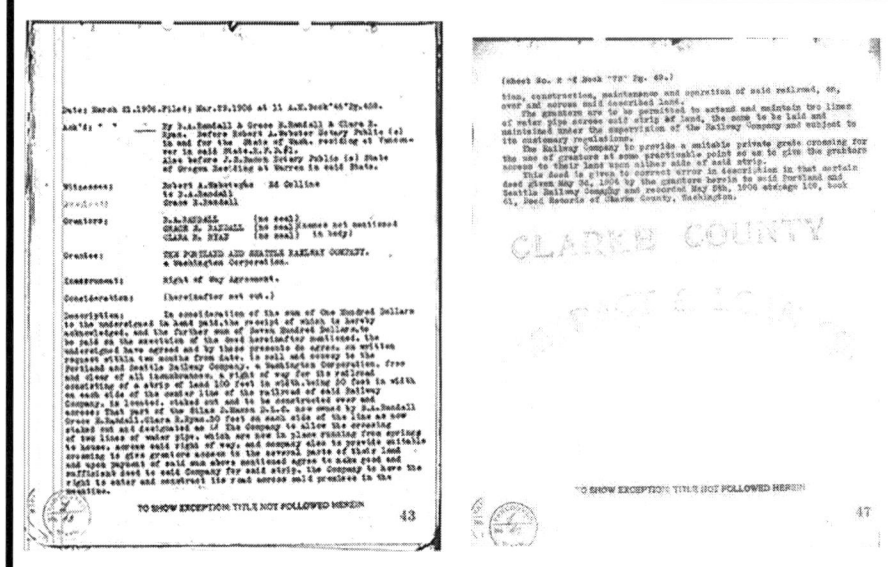

In the 1908 "Right of Way Agreement," (and Warranty Deed) the SP&S Railway Co. had agreed "to provide a suitable private grade crossing for the use of the grantors at some practicable point so as to give the grantors access to their land upon either side of said strip." The "strip" refers to the 100-foot-wide right of way for the west-to-east train track that runs parallel to the Columbia River and Old Camas Highway. (See fig. A.2)

Railroaded, literally

You've now seen how these two deeds were critical to the reasons I was sued, harassed, assaulted, arrested, and shunned. It may, however, still be unclear how, or why, I got ensnared betwixt and between dozens of people with Empathy Dysfunction.

Why did this blustery wind of EmD destruction swirl around me for 12 years? It can't be as simple as a run of bad luck with unconscionable people. Nor am I a masochist who thrives on victimization. Neither am I like the fictional character Jessica Fletcher of "Murder She Wrote," who just happens into a new crime scene, TV episode after TV episode.

UNABRIDGED PROLOGUE

Nope. There was a plot behind this action. It hadn't been obvious until many years later when I put together the long-lost puzzle pieces. It is a story of incredible criminal activity that grew and grew until it involved an entire town and launched me on a trajectory of loss and lifetime sorrow.

This vicious plot required a cohesive bevy of bullies. In *Chapter Seven,* I will take you on a deep dive into the mob mentality that was stirred up against me and why.

There was a plot behind this action. It hadn't been obvious until many years later when I put together long-lost puzzle pieces. It is a story of incredible criminal activity that grew and grew until it involved an entire town and launched me on a trajectory of loss and lifetime sorrow.

If this were a gripping Christie murder mystery, there would be six or seven main characters, and only one would be guilty. In Christie novels, the protagonist, Miss Marple, voluntarily braves danger to ferret out culprits. It always ends well for Miss Marple (obviously not for the murder victim, or the mob victim in my case).

In my story, I am the lone protagonist fighting off multiple attackers not just one. My attorney Dan Lorenz told me that my attackers were like sharks: They may not have planned the perfect storm, but they were opportunistic and used the storms created by others to wreak more damage.

My weaknesses (fear over losing my licenses; financial distress from the divorce and multiple legal issues; trying to protect my client's rights to privacy when their license plates were being photographed) provided them several opportunities to come after me as well as my children. Thank God, no one was murdered, but it was no less frightening for me—or my girls in some instances.

Imagine this scene is from a film about the story of how I was railroaded.

In 2009, the protagonist, Dr. Kathy Marshack, is pouring over pages of documents sent over by City of Vancouver Attorney Allison Chinn as a result of a long-stalled public records request that had been made by Marshack's attorney. (Legally, these records should have come to light during the multiple requests for public records made from 2006 to 2008, and during the discovery process in the 2008 lawsuit Marshack had filed against Vancouver.)

It's late. Her daughter Phoebe is in bed. Exhausted from the ordeal of years of harassment (divorce, arrests, court hearings, and the loss of her older daughter Bianca to their father's vile manipulations), Marshack works into pre-dawn night after night to protect herself from the next attack. Hunched over her computer, Marshack scrolls through hundreds of pages of Vancouver government documents that have been scanned to CDs.

Glare from the computer screen lights up her haggard face, then reveals a look of shock. Marshack is seeing, for the first time, a libelous memo—that erroneously refers to her as a functional sociopath—written by Vancouver Citizen Advocate Jim Jacks in 2004 with the help of City Prosecutor Josephine Townsend and Code Enforcement Officer Richard Landis.

Wide awake now, Marshack is overcome with tense excitement as she continues her scroll through hundreds of emails corroborating her suspicion. What suspicion? That she had been purposely victimized by her ex-husband, her neighbors, the Vancouver Police, the Mayor's Office, the City Attorney's Office, Code Enforcement, The Columbian newspaper, and the Burlington Northern Santa Fe Railway (BNSF) train company (formerly the SP&S).

The scene fades to black while the audience ponders the mystery and anxiously awaits the next scenes. As the story unfolds, the players in this mob are implicated in multiple illegal plots and are supported by corrupt government officials.

Unceremoniously, most of these true criminal activities ended in legal settlements rather than jury verdicts.

Unceremoniously, most of these true criminal activities ended in legal settlements rather than jury verdicts. In truth, Vancouver had engaged in criminal activity against me in many ways.

In truth, Vancouver had engaged in criminal activity against me in many ways.

Three rose to the surface, because they were the most obvious:
1. Hiding the falsified Jacks' memo from me for five years—even in discovery for the court cases *(See fig. A.8);*

2. Shredding my Diversion file AFTER I had sued the City instead of preserving those records as required by law;

3. Concealing covertly-taken videotapes furnished to the City by my neighbor Don Morris.

Here are the "excuses" Vancouver's City Attorneys provided for these crimes against me:
1. Jacks' libelous memo had been believed to be factual and true;

2. My Diversion files had been shredded because it is routine to destroy them when they are "expired;"

3. The City's declaration that the Morris videos were non-existent; followed by the excuse that the tapes had been "lost" on the messy desk of City Planner Chad Eiken.

Why had I been so vehemently picked on en masse? Because a handful of wealthy neighbors wanted to increase the value of their posh properties, situated between the Columbia River and the railroad tracks, by eliminating the safety horn blasts made by passing trains as they approached my deeded track crossing.

Why had I been so vehemently picked on en masse? Because a handful of wealthy neighbors wanted to increase the value of their posh properties, situated between the Columbia River and the railroad tracks, . . .

UNABRIDGED PROLOGUE

The idea, quite possibly tossed around since 2001-2003 (if the City's email stash is any indication), had been named the Train Horn Noise Quiet Zone for East Clark County (THNQZ). For a look at the list of 87 actions regarding the Zone from 1992 to 2012 *(see A.9)*.

It involved a complex process of:
- Getting community support;
- Conducting engineering feasibility studies;
- Drafting and passing Washington State legislation to allow for a taxing authority (Local Improvement District or LID) that would fund the Quiet Zone;
- Coordinating with railroad owner Burlington Northern and Santa Fe Railway (BNSF) to design enhanced safety equipment at the train crossings;
- Applying for a THNQZ permit from the Federal Railway Administration (FRA);
- Holding public meetings;
- Voting by homeowners who would be impacted by the prospective THNQZ tax.

Coincidentally, about the same time I received this first batch of delayed "discovery" documents from Chinn in August 2009, I received an invitation to attend a meeting at the Vancouver Water Resources building to celebrate the success of the THNQZ process. The THNQZ state legislation had passed; my neighbors had overwhelmingly voted for the designation; the FRA permit was in hand; and BNSF had plans to soon begin improvement of the safety features at the three public train crossings in the area.

Everybody who was anybody in Vancouver was in attendance at the lavishly- appointed party: Mayor Royce Pollard (who preceded

Mayor Tim Leavitt), BNSF and FRA representatives, members of City Council, several City Attorneys, City Manager Pat McDonnell, a throng of my neighbors, wealthy civic leaders who lived along the Columbia River, and members of the press.

I was there as was the FRA Representative Christine Adams. I'd filled a plate with food, grabbed a glass of wine, and sat down next to Adams and BNSF Safety Manager David Agee, whom I'd met before.

**"I [FRA rep Christine Adams] wasn't aware of any other train crossing in the area. There was nothing about it in all of the reports I received from the City.
I'd like to see this crossing."
.... The next day, Adams and Agee [from BNSF] visited the antiquated crossing near my house. They were appalled at the poor visibility and unsafe conditions.
In fact, Adams learned from Agee that, according to the engineers who steered trains past it each day,
my tiny train crossing had been deemed the most dangerous in Clark County.**

After some introductions, I questioned Adams, "I'm curious why the plan for the THNQZ doesn't include safety equipment at my crossing? I see from the plan that there is safety equipment at S.E. 164th, S.E. 147th and at S.E. 139th but not my crossing at S.E. 144th Court. Is there some reason for this?"

Adams looked puzzled. Agee already knew the answer since he was the one who had discovered the malfeasance by the THNQZ committee and pointed it out to me. She said, "I wasn't aware of any other train crossing in the area. There was nothing about it in all of the reports I received from the City. I'd like to see this crossing."

UNABRIDGED PROLOGUE

Continuing our discussion, I learned that during the multi-year process to acquire a THNQZ permit, my neighbors and their City co-conspirators had failed to advise the FRA of the existence of my "private" train crossing. Incredible! Instead, they'd engaged in the most nefarious harassment in order to destroy my family and shut down my psychology practice to make me—and my safe-crossing issues—go away.

The mob's goal had been to destroy my credibility, handicap me financially, and demoralize me by harming my children. All because they'd wanted to save the cost of $20,000 to upgrade my dilapidated train crossing—when they were spending an average of $72,000 on each of the other three.[15]

The next day, Adams and Agee visited the antiquated crossing near my house. They were appalled at the poor visibility and unsafe conditions. In fact, Adams learned from Agee that, according to the engineers who steered trains past it each day, my tiny train crossing had been deemed the most dangerous in Clark County.

Adams and Agee agreed that the THNQZ would have to wait until there was a better safety plan in place. It wasn't sufficient to allow 40 to 50 trains a day to rush past this crossing at 60 miles per hour without one bit of safety equipment (and potentially no train horn sounded) to warn motorists and pedestrians.

Brent Boger, an Assistant City Attorney, threatened to sue the FRA for the delay of the Quiet Zone permit, complaining that

---

[15] Because of the years of work on the THNQZ, there were many other costs in addition to that of construction work at the crossings. These included: engineering analyses; petitioning the State Legislature for a new law allowing the formation of a Local Improvement District; and paying City and County officials to negotiate with the train company, the Federal Railway Administration, and the community.

it would cost the City lots of money. Subsequently, commercial pilot Roger Parsons, also the Citizen Chair of the Quiet Zone Committee, sent out an email to all residents in the proposed THNQZ (except for me of course), stating that the approval process had hit a snag because of a phony problem at the 144th Court private train crossing.

It took four more years before the THNQZ was approved in 2013, and it still only included minimal safety equipment at my crossing.

A conspiracy theory—really, truly!

Still not convinced that there was a huge conspiracy going on? Let me explain. I had not opposed the THNQZ. I would have benefitted, too, by no longer hearing the horn blasts day and night. Undoubtedly, the Zone would also have improved the value of my property.

Plus, with train crossing improvements (such as new crossing guard barriers, bells, and flashing lights), my worries would have been resolved for family, friends, and clients who used the 144th Court crossing to get to my house (which also served as my home office for my psychology practice).

It hadn't been my opposition that stirred up the conspiracy. It was that dispensing with my private crossing entirely—by simply revoking my home occupation permit—would have been a lot easier.

Home occupation permit? Perhaps I should mention a third piece of paper that confounded the mob. I'd acquired a Home Occupation Permit in 1997 when the City of Vancouver annexed my area of Clark County. Since I'd had an existing home office at the time (since 1986), I was supposedly "grandfathered" in without having to meet any special requirements. Standby. Just as with my deeds, this legal document would prove vital to defending my rights.

UNABRIDGED PROLOGUE

The sneaky civil servant involved was Landis.[16] He was front and center in almost every action to thwart my rights and grease the wheels for the THNQZ. He thought it would be easy. Landis knew that a private train crossing becomes a public train crossing if used by the public to reach a business location.

Landis had been in regular contact with BNSF officials on this point. Since I had a home occupation permit to meet with my psychology clients at my house, the crossing was technically public; hence, requiring safety equipment under the THNQZ rules.

On the other hand, if I had no home occupation permit, the City and my neighbors could totally ignore the safety conditions at my crossing and save money on safety upgrades (which would be paid for by the one-time LID tax. Upkeep of and future improvements to the improved safety equipment would have fallen on BNSF.)

Landis' first plan of attack was to find a way to revoke my home occupation permit. His first opportunity came in January 2004 when my neighbor Jody Campbell, wife of *The Columbian* newspaper publisher, Scott Campbell, filed a bogus complaint that my clients were endangering her.

The maps of my neighborhood *(see figs. A.3 and A.4)* may also help you understand why the Campbell's did not want safety equipment at the private crossing, located right next to their home.

---

[16] Since Vancouver Code Enforcement Officer Richard Landis shows up again and again in "When Empathy Fails," I've included a chronological list of his transgressions—titled "Alternative Facts,"—regarding the THNQZ (*See fig. A.9*). Landis had started investigating me in 2003. However, back in 1992, City Attorney Ted Gathe had written City Council a memo regarding how to vacate a territorial road (such as the Old Camas Highway that fronted my property). The City had covered up this document: City staff hadn't wanted me to know that legal steps were required to vacate the road—steps the City of Vancouver had ignored.

Remember, those new clanging bells and flashing lights that would have to be installed if this crossing were to be improved? The Campbell's clearly didn't want that disturbance.

Besides, they had another public crossing available to the east of their house at S.E. 147th (a crossing that I occasionally used when my private crossing was too unsafe for passage, as in winter when it was iced up). Landis was ever so helpful to the Campbells, providing them with inside information that he was moving to revoke my home occupation permit.

Meanwhile, my divorce had become a long-suffering battle: In 2003, I was falsely arrested for assaulting Howard's secretary. It had actually been her who'd assaulted me. City Prosecutor Josephine Townsend, a colleague of my ex-husband as well as Landis, had taken on my case with relish.

To get Townsend off my back and keep her from putting me in jail, my attorney at the time, Bob Yoseph, had encouraged me to sign a Diversion agreement. Foolishly, I took his advice and agreed to the Diversion terms in June 2004. By September, Townsend would try to revoke it and put me away.

Also in September of 2004, about the time the THNQZ research was getting started in earnest—by the City, BNSF, and Landis (of course)—my longtime neighbors Mary Kellogg, and Dr. Joseph Leas and his wife, Julianne Leas, decided to sue me over the river easement road that I shared with them and other neighbors.

Kellogg's son Don Morris—who stood to inherit a tidy sum from his mother's real estate—and his wife Melanie Mooney (a professor at Clark College in Vancouver, Wash.) began a campaign of harassment against me. They'd wrongly assumed they could wear me down and force me to relinquish my rights to the easement roads, making way for them to develop the adjacent stretch of riverfront.

UNABRIDGED PROLOGUE

The two couples must have known they stood little chance of quieting (i.e. dismantling), my title to the easement since it had been deeded to me with ironclad terms. Guess who leapt to help their cause? Landis, of course.

With his counsel, the City Planning Office authorized a permit for the Leas to build a gate that blocked my access. This, even though the City was well aware of my river easement rights. Landis also encouraged Kellogg, Morris, Mooney, and the Leas to send in a barrage of complaints regarding my home business, my use of the easement to access the river, and the way I parked on my property.

While I was successful at fighting off these numerous assaults on my rights, Landis finally struck pay dirt with the citation he issued for parking my 1987 motorhome on my old gravel driveway next to my garage. As evidence of this "terrible" infraction, Landis used photos that had been covertly taken by the Leas. An Administrative Judge, hired by the City of Vancouver, upheld the Landis citation.

While I was successful at fighting off these numerous assaults on my rights, Landis finally struck pay dirt with the citation he issued for parking my 1987 motorhome on my old gravel driveway next to my garage. . . .

Landis contacted Townsend, who promptly moved to revoke my Diversion agreement (because committing a crime—even a code infraction— was grounds for terminating it).

With my conviction in hand, Landis contacted Townsend, who promptly moved to revoke my Diversion agreement (because committing a crime—even a code infraction—was grounds for terminating it). For good measure, and to make sure I never surfaced again, Townsend and Landis had helped Citizen Advocate Jim Jacks draft the libelous memo that claimed I was a "diagnosed functional sociopath."

Are you seeing the growth of the mob at Landis' hands here? He'd reasoned that if I was worried about being thrown in jail for five years—because the way I'd parked on my property had been questioned, therein putting my Diversion agreement in jeopardy—I would certainly stop spending time complaining about the lack of safety at my train crossing. Not so much.

When Kellogg and company (Morris, Mooney, and the Leas) had continued to lose to me in court over easement rights, they'd complained about me to another group that used the easement to access the river: neighbors living to the west of the easement road in the private, gated community known as Steamboat Landing (SBL).

The mob of five warned the SBL residents that I was dangerous and crazy and should be stopped from using the river easement road—which all SBL parties also had legal access to utilize. The other mobster, Landis, offered support here, too.

Meanwhile, according to SBL Homeowners Association (HOA) meeting minutes, the Vancouver Police Department had encouraged the SBL residents to prevent me from "trespassing" by: harassing me, building a fence to block my legal access, and—emboldened by Code Enforcement's help—installing a Wanted Poster with my photo at SBL's front gate. I sued SBL in 2008, and Steamboat Landing had to pay the price for that bit of 2006 stupid, jump-on-the-bandwagon folly.

That's not all. Landis outright lied to the police about my rights. This was probably the most frightening of all the mob's out-to-get-me actions—because local law enforcement had been given the power to arrest me at will, over nothing. Sadly, the police believed Landis and not the easement-related court documents I showed them.

Lt. Dave King was in frequent communication with Landis and with Toni Montgomery, President of the HOA Board at Steamboat Landing. He'd assured Montgomery that I had no deeded rights and that she should call him whenever she saw me trespassing on the easement.

I was under investigation for trespassing for many years and, indeed, I was arrested because Landis misled police. Ultimately, I was vindicated in court.

Landis even interfered in the lawsuits my neighbors brought against me over the river easement road and the Old Camas Highway. He reported to the Assistant City Attorney Charles Isely that the roads in question in my deed had never existed.[17]

Subsequent surveys showed that the Old Camas Highway dated back to 1852, and the right to use the adjoining road to the river was documented back to the mid-1800s and the land's original homesteader Silas Maxon.

Isely and Vancouver Assistant City Attorney Brent Boger had questioned the legitimacy of my deed, claiming records that far back in time had been lost in a courthouse fire, or were, inexplicably, so old they didn't count anymore.

---

[17] Over the years, Landis asserted several qualifiers about the river easement road and the Old Camas Highway. He said that: my deed was "vague;" the Old Camas Highway (OCH) had never been built; the Old Camas Highway was my neighbor's "private driveway;" there was an underlying easement on my property for a county road but it was not the Old Camas Highway; there was no survey to show whether the OCH was north or south of the train tracks; the OCH was "never a public road." In other words, Landis kept coming up with ways to interfere with my rights by making contradictory statements about the old roads.

The author spent many hours in this Clark County building, which houses archival material as well as today's records. In the County Surveyor's Office, the author discovered several old maps and the pioneer petition for the road past her house. What she found here helped the author win her rights back.

However, I had copies of all the deeds to my land and the easements dating back to 1864. It hadn't taken much investigation to locate historical documents for the land and the roads from the 1850s forward. I'd easily found stuff in the County Surveyor's Office and at the Clark County Historical Society: So much for the lame courthouse fire excuse. All that I unearthed was legitimate in spite of the bureaucrats' bullshit rationale.

When I'd started to question the wisdom of the THNQZ, Landis made contact with Shana Druffner, (a BNSF executive and attorney). In several emails, they discussed how to solve the problem of my supposed intransigence. While Landis came after my home occupation permit, Druffner focused on how to discredit the legitimacy of my train crossing deed, which granted me the right to use the crossing for any reason in perpetuity.

In several emails, they discussed how to solve the problem of my supposed intransigence. While Landis came after my home occupation permit, Druffner focused on how to discredit the legitimacy of my train crossing deed, which granted me the right to use the crossing for any reason in perpetuity.

Druffner figured if she could abolish my right to perpetual access to the crossing and to the adjacent roads, she could help all of the parties get their THNQZ that much faster. No matter that my deeded train crossing rights were as secure and unbreakable as those in my deed to use the river easement road.

Her approach to bullying me came as a threat to bill me for any accidents at the crossing and for its regular maintenance. In fact, Druffner offered to sell me insurance to cover these costs through BNSF's authorized broker—with a $50,000-a-year premium: My homeowners insurance company had refused to add BNSF to my policy.[18]

Would you believe—even for an instant—that you are responsible for train company property because you live next to its train tracks and drive to and from across a private train crossing installed by that company? Incredible!

There's more. Others involved were emboldened by Landis. The mob grew exponentially when the real estate market busted in 2008. My neighbors' dreams of making millions on waterfront development, enhanced by a THNQZ, came crashing down. That left these players, used to getting their way, plenty mad.

In their twisted thinking, their properties' devaluation wasn't being caused by the weak economy. No, it was my fault. Unilaterally, the mob members decided to punish me because of my determination to maintain my deeded rights on two fronts, river access and train crossing safety.

Campbell stepped in and had his faithful reporter Stephanie Rice write stories that demeaned me, which were

---

[18] An insurance company, authorized by BNSF, usually grants policies to construction companies using BNSF property on a temporary basis; however, this arrangement did not extend to me, a private citizen who uses the train crossing to get to and from her home.

published in *The Columbian*. For example, when I was once again falsely arrested and had to stand trial after Mooney assaulted me on the river easement July 4, 2006, Rice wrote a story comparing my plight to that of the women in the popular television series "Desperate Housewives," which aired from 2004 to 2012.

Rice attempted to draw parallels between the series' fictional cul-de-sac setting, Wisteria Lane, and the circle drive in front of the Leas' house and the river easement road bordering Steamboat Landing. Her writing inferred that my struggles and claims of conspiracy were no more than drama playing out within a group of indulged and gossipy women.

Further, when, in desperation, I'd tried to sell my home to escape the growing mob, Rice found reason to treat it as a "news" story. She found an expert to testify that my property was not as valuable as my asking price. Really, that's worth a reporter's time and considerable space in a community newspaper?

Campbell's money problems were twofold. The dot.com era swing to online news coupled with the Great Recession had brought his newspaper business to its knees. He was forced into bankruptcy, which required the sale of his brand new downtown Vancouver building, designed to house *The Columbian,* and his beautiful Columbia River home next to mine. He'd turned to Landis, Leavitt, and the City Attorney's Office for help. They'd obliged.

Campbell sold his office building to the City and his home to David and Martha Lindsay. The Lindsays bought the home with the proviso that they would be allowed to claim as private the portion of the still-public Old Camas Highway in front of their house (and mine). Campbell had signed a document stating that he would be responsible to the Lindsays if it happened that they could not claim the road as private after all.

UNABRIDGED PROLOGUE

The author's neighbor Scott Campbell sold his home (in the background) to David and Martha Lindsay. They wasted no time in blocking her passage on the stretch of the still-public but seldom-used Old Camas Highway that passed by their home. Next, the couple tore up the road to make way for a multicar garage. Then came the drilling of a well adjacent to a federally protected wetland pond feeding into the Columbia River.

This photo is witness to environmental damage the digging of the well caused. The surface of the once-clear pond turned into algae scum, which was consequently treated with herbicide—killing fish in the process. The Lindsays were granted city permits for this construction—despite the host of wetland-related federal and state regulations. Some, when ignored, are considered criminal offenses.

WHEN EMPATHY FAILS

> As I would learn years later, many of my mob-member neighbors had been meeting with City officials secretly (not publicly as required by law) at the home of auto tycoon Dick Hannah just down the street to the east of millionaire David Lindsay's...home.

The couple had barely moved in when they tore up the old road and built a $300,000 garage on the spot. In the process, they'd drilled a well into the wetland surrounding a trout pond that fed into the Columbia River. And, the Lindsays built a steel wall blocking my access, and that of all those living to my west, to "their" Old Camas Highway stretch; therein cutting off our ability to use the safe public train crossing at S.E. 147th. The clincher: This environmental abuse and caviler approach to people's welfare was all done with approval by the City of Vancouver.[19]

Wouldn't you think that cutting off access to a safe public train crossing would have encouraged BNSF, the FRA, the City of Vancouver, and the neighbors impacted to consent to reasonable safety upgrades to the little old train crossing near my house? But

---

[19] Interestingly, when Campbell first built his luxury mansion (2002-2004), he was not allowed to build near the trout pond nor the stream that empties into the Columbia River. Environmental inspectors even filed complaints documenting dead fish and other environmental damage done during construction of his home. Nevertheless, the deal Campbell worked with the City apparently allowed even worse degradation of the environment as an incentive for the Lindsays to buy the Campbells' home, then make "improvements" no matter how that might impact the pond and surrounding wetland. Why not: Vancouver's mayor (at the time it was Leavitt) was getting a swanky new City Hall by buying Campbell's brand new downtown Vancouver newspaper building dirt cheap because Campbell was in bankruptcy. A clear case of "you scratch my back, and I'll scratch yours."

reason had not prevailed, because, by this time, the mob mentality had taken hold and the pack was gripped with anger.

As I would learn years later, many of my mob-member neighbors had been meeting with City officials secretly (not publicly as required by law) at the home of auto tycoon Dick Hannah just down the street to the east of millionaire David Lindsay's (formerly the Campbells') home. The agenda item: discuss how they could get Kathy Marshack out of their way.

No way was Lindsay going to acquiesce to flashing lights and clanging bells being installed at "the Marshack" train crossing right in front of his house (The train crossing was by then being referred to as the "Marshack" crossing in City and FRA documents.)

Brian Carlson, the City liaison for the THNQZ, would later report that tempers had been hot at these meetings; being reasonable had not been on the minds of attendees. Carlson also mentioned, in deposition, that when my name had been spoken, it garnered despicable epithets.

Under the pressure of this powerful and greedy group of people, the FRA granted the THNQZ permit with two conditions regarding the crossing that, because of the Lindsays' construction, had become the only ingress and egress left for me. With these minor modifications only, the THNQZ process had been allowed to proceed: (1) remove a stone monument that blocked visibility; and (2) install LED-lit stop signs.

Railroaded. True crime story. Yes, these are apt descriptions of the inexplicable conspiracy to deprive me of my livelihood, my property rights, my freedom, my safety, my family, and my peace of mind. At first blush, you may consider the conspiracy idea a product of paranoia; but in this book, I give you plenty of examples that fully document the conspiracy.

No one should be subjected to this kind of government corruption and vigilante justice. I made it out. I pray that you will, too, if ever you find yourself unable to fathom why you are being stalked, sued, falsely arrested, or wrongfully blamed when you've done nothing wrong. If you discover that an entire community is out to get you, please utilize the Empathy Dysfunction Scale *(See fig. A.1)* to help you strategize your survival maneuvers.

You might want to keep this overview and the area maps *(See figs. A.3 and A.4)* **readily available for handy reference as you read my story.**

I've done my best to explain the plot line that was unfolding beneath the surface as I developed the Empathy Dysfunction Scale (EmD Scale). However, with the many characters and the complex twists and turns in this story, it is easy to get lost. I hope you will stay the course as you read and face the detours and reverses of fortune.

Being without a compass in the chaos around me was how I came to be repeatedly victimized. Even I couldn't keep up with the unending machinations of all those who were set on my ruin at every turn.

It is only with time and healing from the perfect storm trauma that I have been able to re-look at and relive all this. That hindsight, admittedly both painful and cathartic, has enabled me to pull together my unbelievable true conspiracy theory episodes in the pages of "When Empathy Fails."

P.S. Phoebe used to call me her hero

I lost many friends over this true conspiracy. Mary told me that she was tired of hearing about the conspiracy theory. Chris told me that she couldn't be sure I didn't cause it all myself.

At my former church, the denomination's state president, Roland, told me that he didn't think I was stable enough to be a member.

Mick dissolved into a paranoid delusion and was afraid to testify on my behalf.

Pals Andy and Jody "forgot" to come to court to support me as I endured the absurdity playing out.

Phoebe, Dr. Marshack's younger daughter, poses with her message in the sand to her mom. Phoebe had been generous with her displays of love and respect for her mother until becoming mentally debilitated from the Traumatic Brain Injury concussions she'd suffered during the active soccer days of her youth.

Friends Dave and Jim, both married, offered sex instead of emotional support.

John, my chiropractor, said he would help my children, but not me.

Bianca, my autistic daughter, crashed and burned in 2005, then sent me a letter that said I was a "fuckwit" not worthy of remembering.

I held out hope that my daughter Phoebe would be able to survive the conspiratorial onslaught. We got away from it all as often as possible. I took her to Women's National Basketball Association (WNBA) games. We went on camping trips to the Oregon Coast and National Parks like Yellowstone. We took really cool vacations to Greece and Costa Rica and swam with dolphins at Disney World.

I was still holding forth as a soccer mom then, completely unaware of how her soccer-related concussions would drastically alter Phoebe's mental state and set her up for a dangerous and dysfunctional adult life.

More than once, I'd rescued Phoebe from parties where she'd drunk herself into a stupor. It was frightening to make midnight runs to the emergency room with my comatose daughter.

To shield Phoebe from the horrors I was going through, I'd tried to keep our family life as normal as possible. To this day, I doubt she knows it all.

Phoebe wrote a most loving email to me in 2005 when Bianca turned against both of us shortly after we'd returned from a trip to Kauai. We three had celebrated Bianca's graduation from high school there. Phoebe was 15 then. It is heartbreaking to read her email and be reminded of the degree she suffered when betrayed by her father and sister. I'd hoped that she knew I would love her and fight for her forever. Here's an excerpt.

(To read Phoebe's entire letter *(See fig. A.5)*

I'd clung to this loving message from Phoebe for many years after she left home. One night in 2013, she assaulted me, violently pushing me across the room into a plate glass door, then called the police. Phoebe told them I'd attacked her, and I was arrested. It was then that I'd had to let Phoebe go, too. And with her, my only grandchild.

So you see, I survived my personal perfect storm but not without casualties lost to Empathy Dysfunction. Not in spite of,

Mommy,

Fig. A.5
Loving note Phoebe sent to her mom in the summer of 2005 after her older sister left home to live with their father

i just wanted to tell you that i love you and i thank you in every single way for everything you've done for me.

you've been a strong person for who knows how long and i admire that. i admire you all together. i know when i was younger, i didnt understand things very well but having to grow up with a father and a sister with AS and then gettin myself into a relationship that turned out to be a mess just made me a more mature person. . . .

. . . knowing more about why i grew up the way i did and having a mom like you has made me more of a successful person in many different ways. no one but you understands what ive been and still am going through and at times as you can see i just hate it and cant take it anymore. i wish i had a father like a lot of my other friends have whos there for me and i know i can count on. . .

. . . but just know, even if i am only 15 years old, i will ALWAYS be here for you mommy. i love you to pieces and im a lucky girl to have such a great mother like you. we will both get through this. I PROMISE! just keep your head up and think all positive thoughts.

**Love always and forever,
Phoebe Irene Marshack #19**

I LOVE YOU MOMMY!

[2005]

but because of, all this, I've become a more self-aware warrior with an enhanced sense of doing things for the greater good. For this new meaning in my life, I'm grateful.

Coming out on the other side of the storm still standing has cemented my belief that all of the suffering on Earth is far from random. I hope you, too, will learn to use all of life's experiences—even those that seem wrong and insurmountable—to become a better human being. When I switched to this mindset, I moved from victim to victor.

. . . I hope you, too, will learn to use all of life's experiences—even those that seem wrong and insurmountable—to your benefit. When I switched to this mindset, I moved from victim to victor.

To my mind, it's like the concept of Karma, which is neither good nor bad; it just is. Karma encourages us to choose between good and evil. The choice can range from really bad Empathy Dysfunction to really good Radiant Empathy.

Pray that you make wise choices that will help you become a better, more empathic human being. That's something we all need to do each and every day.

Of that, I'm sure.

CHAPTER ONE

No One Calls Me Mom Anymore

> *"A successful woman is one who can build a firm foundation with the bricks others have thrown at her."*
> —gender-specific paraphrase of statement made by David Brinkley

They might be out to get you

Fifteen years is a very, very long time to endure hardship. My two daughters and I lived through some excruciating times while I was stalked, sued and slandered. I don't blame them for turning away from me. My daughters had to fend for themselves a lot while I was trying to protect our family. Becoming alienated from them has been the worst hardship of all: It shattered me.

Most days I would fall asleep at my computer after I worked a ten-hour day as a psychologist, followed by several more hours organizing evidence for my many legal matters. I don't think my daughters would have fared better if I had not defended myself. My caving would have led us down the path of homelessness and bankruptcy. Adults now, I hope Bianca and Phoebe will come to understand and forgive me for the upheaval in their young lives.

"When Empathy Fails" is more than a book about how I became estranged from my daughters. It's also about how people with Empathy Disorders create the kind of evil chaos that brings sorrow. In this chapter, you will learn how people with empathy disorders think and act. Since they know and consider only what is in their mind, they are self-absorbed and unable to relate to others.

Their decisions are selfish. Worse, when an empathy disorder—what I define as Empathy Dysfunction—is severe, you have a person who is unimaginably destructive to others.[20] We know them as narcissists and sociopaths.

The onslaught of attacks coming from all corners of my life bewildered me. I was a devoted suburban mom, working from my home office, so I could have a flexible schedule to accommodate my kids' needs. All this, and still I would never be respected as dictated in the *"Ten Commandments: Honor Thy Mother."*

A small group of greedy and power-hungry people was out to annihilate me and bring down my simple life. The outrageous lies of one woman set the stage for years of frightening abuse and the eventual alienation of my children.

My goal in writing this book is to leave you with tools to protect yourself from dangerous people. If you find yourself with: a rotten neighbor; friends who start believing the nasty gossip spread by your ex-partner; or a nagging feeling you're being watched—pay attention. It's not because you're paranoid (unreasonably suspicious). It's because "they" really might be out to get you.

September 11, 2001

I was getting ready for work early the morning of Sept. 11, 2001, when I got a call from my husband, Howard. He'd

---

[20] In Chapter Two, "Empathy Dysfunction (EmD) In-depth," I will define and explain the characteristics of empathy and its dysfunction.

left a few minutes before, headed for an appearance in court. "Turn on the TV. There's been a bombing in New York," he said urgently.

"What?" I asked lamely. I was confused and stunned by his urgent and unexpected call.

9/11

"Turn on the news," he repeated emphatically. "The Twin Towers have been hit and have collapsed." Howard—so inept at reading the nuances of human interactions that he freezes when invited to chit-chat at a party, Howard could be—was clear and decisive in an international catastrophe. I suppose this serves him well as an attorney. "Turn on the TV," he kept insisting. "This is important. I'll call you back later. I want to watch the news." Then he hung up.

I turned on the television in the family room and watched the scene in disbelief. Many of you have similar memories. I can't say that I consciously knew then how this cataclysmic event would change me. Even as it happened, we all knew the world had been irrevocably altered, particularly for Americans. We could no longer ignore the reality of terrorism. The amped up need for safety would soon engulf us 24/7.

By Dec.13, 2001, Osama Bin Laden and his organization, Al Qaeda, had claimed responsibility for murdering an estimated 2,700 people when two airliners, hijacked by Al Qaeda, had hit the

World Trade Center. Within minutes of the crash into New York City's Twin Towers, two additional hijacked jetliners had crashed, one at the Pentagon and one in a field in Pennsylvania.

The death toll rocketed. Americans reeled, especially on the East Coast. Those of us on the West Coast may have been the most confused. This disaster, of epic proportions, didn't affect many of us personally. The attacks on the East Coast felt as far away to us as Pearl Harbor had to mainland citizens during World War II.

Back then, we'd gone to war to retaliate for the attack on our shores. The War Effort had unified our nation: Young men had enlisted or drafted. Women, children, and older folks had kept home fires burning. How would America respond this time? How would our people unite around a terrorist attack of this magnitude?

I began to answer this question when a local radio station sought me out as a psychologist to interview about the emotional side of the 9/11 tragedy. The radio journalist asked me, "What can we, here in Portland, do to help those suffering in New York? People are scared. Children aren't sleeping. What can we do?"

I knew that question would be coming, and I'd prepared remarks. As I started to speak, I realized how inadequate my words were. "There are those who can fly to New York and help," I began. "They can use their skills in law enforcement, safety and medicine to care for the tired, sick and injured; and to help families of the deceased. The Red Cross needs volunteers. If you can't fly there, you can donate blood, supplies, or money."

The broadcaster prompted, "Besides helping out at Red Cross, what else can we do?" He obviously hadn't been satisfied with my canned response.

I stepped it up a notch then, saying, "Do what you can to help at home, right here. Help your elderly neighbor take her garbage to the curb. Volunteer for a worthy charity. Donate to a food bank. Hug your children more. Even if you can't be of direct help to those in New York, you can do things here at home to help make the world a bit better." Still, I felt that my response had been lackluster.

The journalist must have realized something more inside me was trying to surface. "Anything else?" he pressed me impatiently.

My response came out of nowhere; confident, I said with conviction, **"Yes! There is something else. Do everything you can; then do a little bit more!"**

The interview played and replayed on the radio at the top of every news hour for a week. Commentators referred to my words as powerful, hopeful and inspiring; that had revived my hope. I needed to hear those words as much as everyone else during the months following 9/11. I would come to need them many times during the next 15 years.

A life hijacked

By Patriot Day (the annual commemoration of the 9/11 Al Qaeda attack) on Sept. 11, 2006, my life had been hijacked. Here's what I'd survived in those five years. I'd:

1. Weathered a hostile divorce from a divorce attorney.

2. Had licensing board complaints filed against me by the Vancouver judge handling my divorce.

3. Spent three days in the county jail after being arrested on false charges.

4. Been sued by my next door neighbors over a property dispute.

5. Survived physical injuries at the hands of neighbors—broken foot, head and face bruises/contusions, and a human bite wound.

6. Been stalked by these same people, who'd sent in false complaints about me to Code Enforcement.

7. Had one particularly piqued neighbor take more than fifty secret video clips of me, then send them to Code Enforcement.

8. Been cited for innumerable bogus infractions by Vancouver, Washington's Code Enforcement Division.

9. Been dragged into court (civil, criminal and administrative) so many times that I had no less than three or four lawyers representing me, at any one time.

10. Been forsaken by Bianca, my eldest daughter, who'd gone to live with her father.

11. Received threatening emails from an anonymous cyberstalker for a year.

12. Endured having a wanted poster with my picture appear at the front gate of a neighboring private community, announcing to all that I was dangerous.

13. Had several false front-page stories maligning me appear in *The Columbian* newspaper, owned by one of my hostile neighbors.

This litany of abuses had begun when I'd filed for divorce shortly after 9/11. The following two years had been excruciatingly painful as I'd struggled to work as a psychologist and care for two disabled children while defending myself from Howard's mountain of costly court filings against me.

He'd refused to pay for his daughters' special health care and educational expenses, so I had. That had left me without money to pay my divorce attorney; so I'd borrowed against credit cards. He'd decided that since I wanted the divorce, I should pay for all of the children's special care and my attorney fees, too. Reasoning with Howard had, again, proven impossible.

"Mom is my hero"

I realize now that my greatest strength and my greatest vulnerability stem from motherhood. I am a mom—proud, loving and fearless in protecting my children. I'd thoroughly enjoyed the years of piano lessons, Girl Scouts, camping at the beach, and chasing bubbles and balloons in the backyard. Our summer road trips to national parks, such as Yosemite, Glacier, Yellowstone and Olympic, remain some of the fondest memories of my life.

Bianca's interest in paleontology had taken us to unexpected locations, including Canada's famous dinosaur pits in the badlands near Drumheller Alberta. Phoebe's prowess at sport had landed me at many a soccer tournament where I delighted her teammates by blowing the horn whenever they scored. I'd been head over heels for all of the girly stuff, too—shopping and makeup and slumber parties. It had been blissful falling asleep to the smell of popcorn and the sound of girls giggling in the family room.

Motherhood was what kept me going during the years-long barrage of attacks. It would turn out to be my Achilles' heel. I, like most mothers, knew the greatest threats to me were those leveled at my children. I would fight like a provoked mother grizzly to keep my "cubs" safe and sound. Still, I knew that using anger was not the best way to resolve problems. Mostly, my go-to approach was to use reason.

After Howard and I had separated, Phoebe came to me with a concern. She was about 12. "Mom," she said tentatively, "I want to tell you something about my dad, but I don't know if I should." (Phoebe had started referring to Howard as "my dad," instead of the usual "Dad." It was her clever child's way of distinguishing her two separate realities: Mom and Dad didn't belong to each other anymore, but she still belonged to both of us.)

Understanding Phoebe's dilemma, I said, "I know you don't want to betray your dad and tell me something that is private. Does it feel like you are stuck between a rock and a hard place? You know, like no matter what you do it will be wrong?" Phoebe nodded her head.

"Okay. Here's what we'll do," I continued. "Tell me what is bothering you. If it is something that you should handle with your dad, and I shouldn't be involved with, I'll tell you. On the other hand, if it is an adult thing that Mom and Dad should handle, I'll talk to Dad about it. Okay?" Again Phoebe nodded her assent.

"I just don't know what to do when my dad phones you," she said nervously, looking down at her feet and shifting her weight from one foot to the other. "Dad has your number on his cell phone with a code word. So you see, when he calls you, he picks up his phone and tells it to 'Call the Bitch.' I don't like it, but he laughs every time he calls you."

I found it amusing that Howard got some small delight from being disrespectful behind my back. Clearly, his empathy was so lacking that he had no idea how much his immaturity was harming his daughter.

I told Phoebe, "Of course I will talk to Dad for you. He shouldn't say this sort of thing. Don't worry. You're not in trouble. I will explain to Dad that you told me because you love us both and don't want to be caught in the middle." Seeming relieved, and satisfied that Mom would take care of the problem, Phoebe went off to play with the dog.

Howard was virtually assaulting Phoebe each time, in her presence, he phoned me, using his denigrating phone code. I called him and calmly pointed out that his behavior was out of line—reminding him that when

> **Howard was virtually assaulting Phoebe each time, in her presence, he phoned me, using his denigrating phone code ['Call the Bitch'] .... In the coming years, he would say and do worse things in front of his children. At least I knew that Phoebe knew I would stand up for her. I suppose that is why Phoebe used to post on Facebook, "Mom is my hero."**

you harm the mother of your children, you harm the children who love her.

I felt rather proud of the way I'd handled it. I think he listened, but I can't be sure: In the coming years, he would say and do worse things in front of his children. At least I knew that Phoebe knew I would stand up for her. I suppose that is why Phoebe used to post on Facebook, "Mom is my hero."

The divorce dragged on from early 2002 into the spring of 2004. The legal fees grew astronomically as Howard pressured me financially with repeated unnecessary court filings. I had spent more than $100,000 on legal fees by the time we were divorced—on what would have been our twenty-fifth wedding anniversary, April 28.

I was awarded custody of the girls and half of our community property, exactly what I'd asked for originally before all of my money was used up (Howard's legal fees were paid by his father, but I had no one to back my share). Meanwhile, being a mother had become increasingly difficult as I managed teenage rebellion at home and defended my freedom at the same time.

Like it's a bad thing

My divorce attorney, Bob Yoseph, was the last person I expected to hurl a false accusation at me. That's just what he'd done in 2003 when he'd said, "What did you do to make Josie Townsend [City Prosecutor for Vancouver] so mad at you? She's furious and wants to lock you up. If she has her way, you'll never work again. And you could lose custody of your children!"

Stunned, and instantly filled with fear, I asked incredulously, "Who is she? I've never met her before." (I'd still been in shock from being arrested and made to spend three days in county jail.) I wasn't sure if Bob was serious, or if he was using his attorney bluster to intimidate me. Attorneys can be like that, using intimidation on their clients to achieve abject compliance.

"Who is she?" he mocked, as if I'd been kidding. He went on, saying, "She's the head prosecutor for the City, that's who she is. She has taken a personal interest in your case. It had been assigned to a deputy prosecutor, then Josie took it on—because it's about you! What did you do to make her this angry?"

"I didn't do anything," I told Bob emphatically, getting an inkling of how things worked. I was divorcing a divorce attorney in a small town. On his turf, the world of courtrooms, judges, prosecutors and lawyers, I was playing way out of my league.

I continued my explanation though I could tell Bob was in no mood for it: "All I did was go to Howard's office last Friday, as you'd instructed, to pick up my belongings. I'd hired a moving company and asked a friend to help me. Phoebe and a girlfriend came along, too. Howard was supposed to have the furniture and Bankers Boxes ready for me. It turned out, he'd changed his mind.

"Arriving at Howard's old office, I'd found that he'd taken some of my stuff to his new office. I'd been confused because we'd arranged—in writing—exactly what I was to pick up that day. You even have a copy of that list in your files, Bob. I decided to drive to his new place to get my belongings. On the way, I tried calling him but got no answer. It seems he was in Seattle with his girlfriend.

"Finally, he answered his cell, just as I arrived in his office's reception area. I asked him about the missing items, and he told me, 'I need them. If you want them back, you'll have to get a court order.' Then things went bad. I was furious that Howard had lied to me once again. I spotted my stuff and told the movers to take it anyway. When Howard's then secretary, Esther, saw this, she tried to stop me, grabbing my left wrist. That's when it all escalated." Now at the end of my explanation to Bob, I was exhausted.

Apparently, Esther had felt the need to defend her absent boss. I tried to pull my arm away, but that only landed me up against a wall (with bruises to prove it). When Esther had grabbed me, I'd instantly flipped into "fight or flight" mode. With my daughter standing right behind me, I'd behaved like a protective momma grizzly might. As if hypnotized, I'd watched my right arm swing up involuntarily, my hand doubling into a fist.

I'd hit Esther in the face and watched my knuckles bend her nose as if in slow motion. Her head had bobbed back and forth like that of a bobblehead doll. At last, she'd let go of my arm and was screaming at me, "I'm going to sue you! I'm going to sue you!" I'd still been in shock when the building manager appeared and demanded that I leave." I did leave and thought it was over until the police came to my house hours later and arrested me for two misdemeanor crimes, Assault IV and Trespass. My daughters watched in tears as the Vancouver Police handcuffed me and stuffed me in the back of the cop car.

Arguing with me at that point, Bob stressed that I would never win this case as self-defense with Townsend on the warpath. He said, "She's a bulldog. And when she's this mad, she'll destroy you. You've already been in jail for three days over this.[21] You don't want to spend another six months locked up, do you? Or lose custody of your kids?"

He was very convincing. I felt terrified as I realized my life could go up in smoke over a couple of pieces of furniture. Not wanting my children to suffer anymore, I agreed to Bob's plan.

---

[21] I learned later that I was kept in jail for three days, even though I could have been released earlier, because the jail staff determined I was indigent. Even though the cops arrested me at my own house, with my name on my home office door, the Clark County officials wrote on the form that there was no way to verify that I had a home to go to.

He and Townsend negotiated the terms of a settlement for my assault charges for a few weeks. It came to this. All charges would be dismissed if I:

- Agreed to two years in a diversion program (meaning that I would stay out of trouble for two years);
- Signed an agreement that I was guilty of the two misdemeanors, but the charges would be dropped if I complied with all terms of the diversion agreement;
- Paid for Esther's medical care, about $50; the cleanup of Howard's office, about $50; and court fees;
- Engaged in 26 weeks of anger management treatment with forensic psychologist Frank Colistro;
- Reported to Townsend in person each month with a record of good behavior from my psychologist.

Bob had been mystified by this last demand, saying it was quite strange that two misdemeanors warranted the regular attention of the City's head prosecutor. He'd said, "I don't get it, but she's quirky."

The morning I was to appear in court to have the judge sign the Diversion agreement, I put on my best suit, a light blue silk. I thought I looked pretty even though the skirt and jacket hung loosely on my body, grown thin because of my stress diet. (I'd been eating next to nothing since my jail stay.)

I wanted to look and feel my best for the demoralizing day. Phoebe had already taken the bus to school, but Bianca was working herself into an autistic meltdown (something I will explain more in *Chapter Four*). She was 17 years old, 5-feet-3 inches tall, and weighed about 185 pounds. She was sobbing uncontrollably, pleading, "Don't leave. Don't leave me."

"I have to go, Bianca. I have very critical business to take care of," I calmly explained. I hadn't told the girls everything I was going through, doing my best to spare them the nasty details of the divorce and my wrongful arrest/prosecution. It probably wouldn't have mattered if Bianca had known. She is autistic, so her empathy skills are non-existent. When the stress chemicals rush through her brain and body at times like these, she is not reasonable. "I have to leave," I said again, trying to convince her, but Bianca was relentless.

"No!" she screamed and dropped to the kitchen floor, grabbing my legs. I was afraid to move (because in the past Bianca had become aggressive when I'd resisted her).

"Okay, Honey. I won't go," I lied. I saw no other choice.

"Really?" she said as she looked at me warily.

"Yes, I'll stay. Just let me go to my office upstairs. Why don't you go to your room and listen to some music to calm yourself down?" I was starting to panic. I had to get to court on time, or the diversion agreement would be toast. Imagine what Townsend would say if I used the excuse that my autistic teenager had been throwing a tantrum.

Bianca let go of my legs, and I walked upstairs, pretending to busy myself at my desk. I listened for sounds of Bianca returning to her bedroom. When I was sure she had, I crept back downstairs and out the back door to my car. I'd started the engine and barely backed down the driveway when Bianca ran outside looking wild with fear. She was barefoot and still in her pajamas. She flung her body on the hood of my car, pounding it with her fists while screaming, "Don't go! Don't Go! Don't go!"

I stopped the engine and got out, leaving the car parked in the middle of the street. "I am so sorry, Bianca. I shouldn't have lied to you. Please forgive me. I'll come back into the house with you right now."

Her body was limp, her face streaked with tears. She was distraught but couldn't explain her distress. As mothers of a disabled and/or dependent child generally are, Bianca and I were very close. Maybe she'd sensed that I was in danger. I hated that she was so frightened. A horrible guilt besieged me, because the last time I'd left her, I'd been handcuffed, then stuffed into a police car. I'd had no way to talk to her, console or explain things the three days I'd been in jail. Phoebe had stayed with a girlfriend. Bianca had been left alone in the house. Not even her father had come to comfort her.

I walked Bianca back into the house, and she calmed down somewhat. She agreed to go to bed as long as I sat with her. I made a cool, moist compress for her red and swollen eyes, then gave her a Klonopin to help her relax. (Bianca' psychiatrist had prescribed Klonopin to help when her anxieties were at a fever pitch). I held her hand and stroked her hair as she fell asleep. I softly said, "I love you, Bianca. I'm here for you. Don't be afraid my little one."

Bianca never knew that I left her again. She slept for several hours while I pulled my act together and drove to court just in time to sign the diversion document. I met Townsend for the first time. I felt incredibly alone and sorry for myself. Bob was there, but I had little faith in his ability to empathize with my misery.

Before I could catch my breath, Bob was reminding me that the judge signing my diversion agreement was a friend of Howard's secretary. It seemed Bob expected me to give permission for this ethics violation. Otherwise, my hearing would be rescheduled in another county. To avoid the delay and keep Townsend happy, Bob recommended I waive my right to have an impartial judge.

Why not? I already had been arraigned in front of Judge Jim Rulli, also my neighbor. My divorce proceedings were being presided over by Judge Diane Woolard, my attorney's ex-wife. Why not continue the pattern of legal abuse running rampant in a small town? I agreed to the terms, signed the papers and turned to leave. I felt completely drained and so badly wanted to get out of the courthouse and back to Bianca. Bob tried to say something, but I waved him off and turned to walk down the hallway.

I heard the click of Townsend's heels as she ran down the tiled floor after me. The sound made me think of a bulldog with too-long toenails crossing a hardwood floor.

"Oh, Miss Marshack? Miss Marshack?" she called out in a syrupy-sweet voice.

I shrugged, and with a heavy sigh, turned around. I said nothing as I looked down at Townsend.

"Miss Marshack, here's my card in case you need to get hold of me," she said, smiling with delight that she had me cornered.

My temper got the better of me. I couldn't stand this woman who seemed to enjoy tormenting innocent people. Even if Townsend had known about the traumatic hours right before I'd appeared in court—when I had lied to my distraught daughter and been forced to leave her alone—she wouldn't have cared that I now had to get home to Bianca.

I was thinking about that when I took the card from her outstretched hand. I looked at her condescendingly and said, "It's Dr. Marshack, thank you!" I turned my back and walked away. I thought it was over. I would find out differently.

I have never talked with Bianca about how she felt during this difficult time; because she could get so enraged or depressed that I learned to walk on eggshells to protect her from herself. A year later she moved in with her father and we have not spoken since.

On the other hand Phoebe has a way of letting you know where you stand through her actions. One day only a few months after I'd been in court with Townsend, Phoebe and I were shopping at Urban Outfitters, a funky little boutique in northwest Portland. She'd spotted a book that she thought was just what I needed. "Mom, Mom, you gotta take a look at this book! It's perfect for you," she'd said excitedly.

With a twinkle in her eye, Phoebe held up a small yellow book with the title, "You Say I'm a Bitch Like It's a Bad Thing." I laughed aloud, then pursed my lips in feigned disappointment, saying, "But I thought you said I am your hero?"

Phoebe laughed, too. Her eyes twinkled as she gave me a super hug. "You are my hero, Mom. And that's why you need this book." Quite a mature response from a 14-year-old young woman, wouldn't you say?

How had she known that I needed a reminder to forgive myself, especially since I never overtly explained to her the whole story behind my arrest? Because I'd been strong and protective, Howard and Townsend thought badly of me. I had started to fall into the trap of thinking that, too.

That was when my younger daughter's healing smile and sense of humor had made me feel loved and forgiven. I adore Phoebe for

> That was when my younger daughter's healing smile and sense of humor had made me feel loved and forgiven. I adore Phoebe for her insight—and for bringing me to my senses that day. I will hold that memory in my heart forever.

her insight—and for bringing me to my senses that day. I will hold that memory in my heart forever.

Stalked, sued, slandered

By Spring 2004, I was finally divorced and carrying out my Diversion requirements. The divorce was not big news in the little town of Vancouver, but my arrest for assault certainly had been. The local newspaper, *The Columbian*, ran the story on its front page (Oct. 5, 2003). The *Eugene Register-Guard* in Oregon, and the *Seattle Post Intelligencer* in Washington also carried the article.

A news editor at *The Columbian*, who is an acquaintance, told me about the news staff's discussion whether to run the story or not. He'd argued against the story, suggesting that an incident like mine was not that unusual during the stress of a divorce. My source told me later, "I can't figure out why they thought it was worth front page news, let alone news at all." He added that he didn't see why the newspaper had wanted to humiliate a good person.

As my story unfolds, you will understand why: the newspaper's owner and my neighbor Scott Campbell may have wanted to discredit me.[22]

Backing up a bit, on Jan. 29, 2004, before the Diversion or divorce papers were finalized, I'd found my secretary at the time, Marta, looking distraught as I'd walked over to her desk.

---

[22] Typically, and especially in America, the news department and the publisher of a newspaper have operated parallel with a sort of Mason-Dixon Line separating the publisher from influencing the who, how, what, when, and why of news coverage. However, today's tough climate for print media has seen some combination of the publisher and editor roles. This may have been the case with The Columbian publisher Scott Campbell.

She'd said, "I got this call from your neighbor Jody Campbell this morning. She was very angry. You were in session with a client, so I told her I would let you know and that you would call her back."

I'd asked, "Angry about what?" Marta had handed me the yellow phone message note. It read, "She has had several people knocking on her door looking for you, and she doesn't appreciate it." Campbell, who lived two houses from me, is the wife of Scott Campbell.

I worked out of my home office at the time, so I wondered if a new client had mistaken the Campbell's house for mine.

I'd asked Marta, "Do you suppose any of my clients went to the wrong house? Has any client mentioned getting lost? If so, we should make sure clients get better directions, so we aren't inconveniencing the neighbors."

Marta had responded, "I haven't heard from anyone that they got lost. We send out excellent directions. Plus there is a picture of your house attached. It seems highly unlikely that anyone would have gone to the wrong house. But Jody was extremely angry. She told me that she was going to report you to Code Enforcement for running an illegal business out of your house. Then she hung up on me," Marta had said, looking frightened.

I called Jody a few times but didn't hear back from her. I went over to her house and knocked, but she never answered. Two weeks later, Vancouver Code Enforcement Officer Dan Jones showed up to investigate a complaint by Jody Campbell. After assuring me that I did indeed have a legal permit for my home office, Jones told me Campbell was claiming that my business was disrupting her home life.

In Vancouver, home occupation permits are granted to businesses, such as my professional psychology practice, only if they are conducted quietly and do not disturb the ambiance of the residential neighborhood. Most communities have similar ordinances. I was surprised at Jody's alarm since I had operated my practice from home for twenty years with no complaints. Why now? My practice was still low-key and inoffensive.

Jones, trying to be helpful, said, "You are in compliance, and I don't think this is a problem that you can't take care of by talking with your very influential neighbor. As long as your clients don't bother Mrs. Campbell, I am sure it will be all right." He had given me a knowing wink as he'd said, "very influential neighbor."

I assumed this was his way of encouraging me to take her threat seriously. After all, her husband published the newspaper, and the Campbells were highly regarded. For the first time, I wondered if Jody's complaint was somehow related to why *The Columbian* had put the story of my arrest front and center.

By April 2004, my neighbors were stalking me in earnest. Joseph and Julianne Leas had moved in next door in March and had immediately begun filing dozens of complaints about me with Code Enforcement. This time, I received a written notice from Officer Richard Landis, demanding that I fire my secretary or close my business immediately. It was obviously time to hire an attorney.

The story of the next two years is pretty zany and hard to follow, so I'll give you the highlights. Hang tight: They're tough to fathom.

First, it took nearly two years to get the City to back off on its threats about losing my home occupation permit. In the end, I agreed to a special permit, written specifically for my situation. The agency had needed to save face for not honoring their City codes in my case; so they'd cobbled together a standard home occupation permit—with a few extra provisions. (I will explain these in an *upcoming chapter*.)

Second, my neighbors, along with Officer Landis, stepped up the code enforcement complaints, which had resulted in many site inspections. Supposedly, my clients continued going to wrong houses in the neighborhood while trying to find my office.

I was cited for: illegally parking in my old gravel driveway; having too many cars at my house; housing a barking dog; trespassing; and locating my fence in the wrong place. Each time my neighbors complained, Landis conducted an investigation and filed another citation against me.

Third, Townsend decided to revoke my Diversion Agreement, stating that I had broken the law by violating City codes. Receiving the "Notice to Revoke" had sent shivers racing through me. The ink was barely dry on the agreement, and now she was planning to withdraw it! The ramifications: I would be automatically found guilty of all charges; I could be sent to jail, potentially losing my license to practice; and, worst of all, lose custody of my children! I had to act swiftly.

I filed a Land Use Petition lawsuit against the City of Vancouver: Citizens have the constitutional right to reject the validity of City Codes. My lawsuit had stopped Townsend cold: It meant that I could not be considered guilty of breaking any law until I was convicted. Nor could I be sentenced until the codes had been ruled legal and constitutional or not, as determined by the Washington Superior Court. Townsend had no grounds to undo my Diversion Agreement!

Fourth, I realized how much of a menace Townsend was. It was hard to believe that I was the only Vancouver resident being legally stalked by her. (I would eventually hear from several of Townsend's victims.) I decided to go over her head to City leaders—the Mayor, City Manager, and City Council members. When I got little response from these, my elected officials, I wrote to Jim Jacks, Vancouver's Ombudsman, or Citizen Advocate.

He was the only person to write back to me. He apologized for being unable to help me, deeming that my cases were being handled appropriately through normal government channels. Meanwhile he'd thrown me under the bus at City Hall by writing a libelous memo calling me a functional sociopath. Yet another lie—but I wouldn't learn about all that until five years later during deposition after I sued the City of Vancouver for conspiracy—and won a settlement.

By Sept. 29, 2004, at the request of her boss, Chief City Attorney Ted Gathe, Townsend dismissed the revocation petition against me. It took longer to get the home occupation permit restored. The neighbors continued to harass me for nearly another decade. More lawsuits were to come.

The most shocking discovery came five years after I'd contacted Jacks for help with the unreasonable conduct of City employees Landis and Townsend. In August 2009, I read, for the first time, Jacks' secret and libelous memo about me. It was what had kicked off the years-long campaign to stalk, sue and slander me.

According to the 2013 depositions of Jacks and Townsend, the two had met in early September of 2004 to investigate my complaints of being unfairly treated by Townsend and Landis. Gathe had told Townsend to show my Diversion file to Jacks, which she had never done. Instead, Townsend had verbally shared with Jacks an entirely concocted story about me.

On Sept. 7, 2004, based on Townsend's word, Jacks had written a memo to his boss, City Manager Pat McDonnell. In turn, McDonnell had passed Jacks' memo along to the Mayor and City Council. In it, Jacks had claimed his findings about me were factual. In truth, it contained outrageous accusations and falsehoods. The statement that jumped off the page at me: "Ms. Marshack is a functional sociopath."

> Mark Twain once said, "A lie can travel halfway around the world while the truth is putting on its shoes."

Lies, damned lies—and still more

Mark Twain once said, "A lie can travel halfway around the world while the truth is putting on its shoes." Being honest is a virtue but not much help when you are a victim of secret and damaging gossip spread by people in power.

Jacks had said I was a sociopath and written that I was likely to lose my license to practice, because of the code violations. Worse still, Jacks had claimed that my trusted psychotherapist, Dr. Frank Colistro, had testified in court against me. According to Jacks, Dr. Colistro had diagnosed me as a "functional sociopath," who "should NOT be a practicing psychologist." (Dr. Colistro never testified in court, for or against me, and he has vehemently denied ever saying these things about me).

Jacks had sent his memo to Townsend and Landis for their endorsements before forwarding it to the City officials. Townsend had known it all to be false, but had said nothing.[23]

From there, the gossip spread like wildfire. How was I supposed to get any support from my elected officials when they

---

[23] The terms narcissist and sociopath are actually traits of diagnosable personality disorders. They are not diagnoses per se. Neither is the term "functional sociopath" actually a diagnosis. It is a term entirely invented and perpetuated by Jim Jacks. I use the terms narcissist and sociopath primarily to describe characteristics among those who are EmD-1. However, other EmDs can demonstrate narcissism and sociopathy from time to time.

believed Jacks' observations that I had no regard for other people and felt no remorse? Why would the police believe anything I said when Jacks had written that I have explosive anger management problems? Even Clark County judges had looked at me askance because they'd believed Jacks when he'd written, "She is resentful of authority and thinks that society's laws do not apply to her." It took years for me to unravel this mess.

These lies had circulated for five years before I discovered the Jacks' memo. I found it as a result of the public records request I'd made after suing the City of Vancouver and my neighbors for all of the harassment.

> **... I was shocked to discover that the City had dozens of boxes of documents about me—going back as far as 2003!**

When the request came through, I was shocked to discover that the City had dozens of boxes of documents about me—going back as far as 2003! As I sorted through the reams of emails and letters, the Jacks' memo popped up. It had, no doubt, been purged from the files of the City manager, mayor, City council members, Landis and Townsend. Someone had botched the cover-up, neglecting to remove Jacks' records.

Despite the memo and its damned lies, it took me five more years to settle my lawsuit against the City of Vancouver for Townsend's treachery and the collateral damage. Another surprising coup came two years later. On Aug. 15, 2015, the Disciplinary Board of the Washington State Bar Association filed a petition against Townsend for professional misconduct. After years of numerous complaints about her—mine and those of many others—Townsend was finally called out for her lies, manipulations and deplorable lack of integrity.

Still, no criminal action was taken against her. Like so many with Empathy Dysfunction and the absence of a conscience, Townsend will more than likely move to another arena and continue to tell lies and cause untold suffering.

The years lost in this battle cannot be restored, my girls' childhood never salvaged. Writing this first chapter, though, has helped to further my healing. It is very satisfying to be introducing you, dear reader, to ways that will help you avoid, or better manage, the chaos and destruction caused when Empathy Dysfunction slips into your world.

Whether Empathy Dysfunction is the result of narcissism or autism, mental illness or brain injury, sociopathy or greed, you need to remember that, without empathy, people can cause incredible pain and suffering. They have a fervent determination to meet their needs—and their needs only.

On the darkest side of empathy disorders are those who do know how you feel but don't care: They want you to feel worse. Simon Baron-Cohen, author and professor of developmental psychopathology at the University of Cambridge in England, describes sociopaths as having "zero degrees of empathy" in his book, "The Science of Evil."[24] He calls sociopaths "zero negative," because as horrifying as it sounds, these individuals revel in your distress.

For this mom, it's personal

The events of Sept. 11, 2001 woke me up to the fact that I needed to take my life more personally (I'll explain in a moment). At first the awakening was just emotional, not personal. I knew

---

[24] Baron, Cohen, Simon. (2011). "The Science of Evil: On Empathy and the Origins of Cruelty." New York: Basic Books.

that something wasn't right in my world, but I didn't fully understand what it was I needed to change.

The catastrophe in New York frightened me and propelled me to take action, but it was action without a plan. Filing for divorce was my first action step. I finally had the courage to break out of a destructive marriage. But this still wasn't personal; it was an action to move away from someone, a way of life that was not safe for me. There still was no proactive plan for my life.

I got an inkling of an idea about my life of the personal when I spent three days in the county jail, following my first false arrest. The obvious is that I recognized it was not going to be so easy to divorce a divorce attorney in a legal system where he held all of the cards. I needed to learn how to stand up for myself and quickly before I lost everything. Not so obvious was the lesson I learned from a tiny pamphlet left in my jail cell by volunteers from Catholic Charities.

Desperate for something to distract me from my plight (and my migraine headache) I read the story of the suffering of Mother Mary as she watched her son Jesus carry his cross to Calvary where he would be crucified. I literally wept with Mary as she described her feelings of anguish, fear and anger. . .but held strong her resolve that the son she bore would die for something far greater for all of us.

As the years rolled by and I was sued and stalked and defamed and arrested again. . . as first one daughter left me, then the second, I learned more about the life of the personal. It is actually a source of strength.

What does Mary's story have to do with the personal? At that first "visit" to jail, I could definitely relate to a mother's suffering, but it would only occur to me later how much a mother may be called upon to sacrifice. As the years rolled by and I was sued and stalked and defamed and arrested again... as first one daughter left me, then the second, I learned more about the life of the personal. It is actually a source of strength.

Taking one's life personally means to realize how incredibly important you are. You were born to be You in every way possible. You are an amazing, one of a kind Soul and with every step you take you walk on hallowed ground. There is no way any of us can truly understand the enormity of God's plan, but to know you are loved is enough. Mother Mary knew this, which is why she could be strong for her son and all of the rest of us who weep at her feet.

In other words, the action plan for taking your life personally is to relax and know that you are an instrument of God's love for you. Throughout this book you will see me ignore this knowledge, struggle to control the outcome... and fail repeatedly, even though I had this lesson early on in my fight against injustice.

I am still learning to take my life personally, to enjoy the beauty of life and to count even adversity as a blessing. (After all, adversities drove me to write this book).

Regardless of what I said on the radio following 9/11—and with Mother Mary's help—I think I finally understand the lesson of living the life of the personal. Because only YOU can do it. Living personally is to do everything you can as the God creation that you are... and then do a lot more.

That realization led me to discover the connection between empathy and Empathy Dysfunction. That's what I'm excited to share with you.

"No One Calls Me Mom Anymore" Highlights

1. Wake up. No matter how nice you are, there truly are people out to get you. Stay neutral and be prepared.

2. Do all that you can to defend yourself; then do a little (or a lot) more.

3. Where's your Achilles' heel? Don't abandon your standards of morality. Be prepared to take a few hits where you are most vulnerable.

4. Stay out of court if at all possible. Once you've been identified in "the system," you will remain a target.

5. Kids are kids. They are not your allies. They may love you, but they can't fight for you.

6. Don't lose your temper or dissolve into tears. That's how those with empathy disorders snag you.

7. Lots of people use others' misfortune to better their position and power. Don't take this personally. Instead, do what you can to shut them down.

8. Government employees are not friends. Nor are they here to serve you. Do not volunteer information about yourself to them.

9. Never open the door to the police, code enforcement officers or any other law-enforcement agency. Do not step out of your home if they

come to your house. They cannot enter your home without a warrant or your permission.

10. If you find yourself in a legal predicament, hire competent private help. Do not trust your public servants to help you.

11. Never cross a psychopath. They are vindictive. Fight as if your life depended on it.

12. Trust in God and the Universe to guide you.

CHAPTER TWO

Empathy Dysfunction (EmD) In-depth

"Such is the human race. Often it does seem such a pity that Noah and his party did not miss the boat."

— **Mark Twain**

From zero to radiant

High IQ, artistically gifted, natural athletic ability, or psychological diagnosis as healthy—none of these characteristics exempt people from having Empathy Dysfunction (EmD). It is my belief that once you understand how empathy works and how it can become dysfunctional, you will have a better handle on navigating life.

Empathy is what binds all humans. It is in the act of relating and connecting to others that we become more human and develop our identity within the human family. EmD can divide us from that human family. Attempting to engage with someone who has Empathy Dysfunction leaves us feeling unheard and unimportant. This disconnect brings us down emotionally and creates chaos in our lives in no time flat!

In *Chapter One* you were introduced to Empathy Dysfunction in the raw as I walked you through a few of my close calls. In this chapter, I discuss the Empathy Dysfunction Scale.[25] *(See Prologue or fig. A.1)*

I could regale you with more personal stories; then the point of the book would be missed. I want to empower you with tools to handle EmD people, so they will never again derail you from the incredible life you are meant to live.

Protecting yourself from EmDs requires two vital skills. First, as soon as you suspect or identify EmD in a person, disengage as soon as you can. Second, cultivate your own empathy, so that you operate at the highest level, EmD-5. As long as you keep your empathy hovering at EmD-5, your loving intent and firm personal boundaries will win the day. I'll show you how. I will explain empathy and Empathy Dysfunction; then introduce you to the unofficial Empathy Dysfunction Scale, which I created as a guide to understanding the spectrum of empathy.

People on the lower end of the Scale, from Zero (EmD-0) to Three (EmD-3), operate with serious Empathy Dysfunction. Type Four, average empathy, is where most people land. While learning about type Five, you will recognize the Angels in your life, those who make you feel loved even when you have made the worst of blunders.

Empathy is an experience

Empathy is multidimensional (having many different features or types). Believe me when I tell you that empathy is far

---

[25] Please understand that this Scale is not based in scientific research, nor is it considered a professional diagnostic tool. Rather, it is based on anecdotal evidence and my personal experience. I designed it to give readers perspective on empathy and Empathy Dysfunction. It is by no means official or definitive; however I hope it is groundwork for future research.

more than sensitivity, or caring, or reading social cues, or even being compassionate.

It is more holographic than two dimensional or the sum of its parts, meaning that the act of empathizing can begin at any point in the empathy system (kind of like the Multiverse). Empathy is the capacity to recognize, honor and acknowledge the intentions and emotions of others while knowing your personal intentions and emotions.

Empathy is a dynamic, evolving process—not a human trait. From empathy comes the ability to hold dear the feelings and thoughts of others.

Those with highly-evolved empathy skills do not confuse the psychological boundaries between themselves and others. They can care, feel compassion and sympathize without taking on the responsibility for another person's intentions or feelings. This distinction is critical. Empathy is respectfully allowing the other person to take responsibility for their life. (In AA and other 12-step programs, the ability to do this is called detachment.)

A symphony may best represent the dynamics of humans empathizing. A great composer creates a musical score that allows for the best use and sound of each instrument while staying faithful to the melody and the meaning of the piece. Sometimes we hear a solo. Other times we embrace the resonance of the horn section or the rumble of the tympani. Often the room is filled with what sounds like a thousand string instruments. We may feel thrilled, calmed, or seduced by the music.

A symphony is not complete without the audience, which provides energy to the musicians. Have you noticed how much more alive a performance is when the audience emotionally joins with the orchestra? Empathy is like this, too. It is far more than the sum of its parts. It is the sense that everyone in the room is breathing the music. So, too, empathy creates a powerful oneness that lets us know we are not alone.

The inability to fully integrate the multidimensional elements of empathy equates to "Zero Degrees of Empathy" (Simon Baron-Cohen, a British psychologist).[26] One person can have cognitive empathy with a high level of concern for justice—a trait of many on the Autism Spectrum; another may possess emotional empathy with a sensitivity to the feelings of others. This is true of many who are codependent, doing for others what they should do for themselves.

Unless the two are integrated, it is the same as having no empathy. For what is justice without mercy? Or compassion without the courage to value yourself? Genuine empathy is more than combining the two parts. When engaging in an empathic moment with someone, another reality emerges. The Sanskrit word, "Namaste," best captures sharing empathy with another. It means, "I bow to the divine in you," and is spoken as a greeting to another person.

> **For what is justice without mercy? Or compassion without the courage to value yourself?**

Traditionally the greeting is offered with the hands pressed together in prayer fashion, fingers pointing toward Heaven, thumbs touching your heart center while gently bowing the head, hands

---

[26] Baron-Cohen, Simon. (2011). "The Science of Evil: On Empathy and the Origins of Cruelty." New York: Basic Books.

pointed toward the other person. It matters not whether you share age, gender, culture, interests, beliefs or habits with that person.

What matters is beyond the trappings of Earth. It comes in greeting an individual in as worthy a manner as you would a divine being. The concept that we are all divine beings (or Souls), greeting each other with the gesture of Namaste, honors the Soul within us as well as the Soul of the other person. It highlights the complementary nature of empathy.

We long to belong

I believe that empathy underlies everything we are as human beings. The theory of Dialectical Psychology (as developed by Klaus Riegel, a developmental psychologist), presupposes that we come to know who we are by relating to others.[27] Humans are highly social beings. We long to belong so to speak. This need to connect and belong leads us to compare ourselves to others and, reciprocally, others compare themselves to us.

From the social dialectic of humans connecting, we develop introspection that leads to empathy. Phoebe was about 8 or 9 years old when she'd asked, "Mommy, if I'm adopted, what do you call the other kids?" Although I hadn't had a good answer for her, I'd smiled, proud of her thoughtful question. Phoebe had been observing others and comparing herself to her friends. Recognizing she was different because she was adopted, Phoebe was looking for a way to position herself as a child in a family. At that time, Phoebe had normally developing empathy with budding introspection.

Phoebe's sister Bianca (also adopted) is different. Even as a child, because of her Autism, she'd struggled with empathy. When

---

[27] Riegel, Klaus. (1979). "Foundations of Dialectical Psychology. United Kingdom: Academic Press.

EMPATHY DYSFUNCTION (EMD) IN-DEPTH

Bianca was about 12, she'd asked me if I would order a couple of magazines for her, "Teen" and "Cosmo Girl." I'd been delighted to help her since I was already well aware of how socially isolated Bianca had become. This pre-teen interest had come as a welcome relief to me after years of Bianca being friendless and burying herself in science and fantasy fiction.

After reading the magazines for two or three months, Bianca had told me to cancel her subscriptions. She'd said, "They are no help. The girls at my school don't wear these clothes or use this makeup." With zero degrees of empathy, Bianca had been trying to fit in by reading magazines instead of by making friends. While she'd had the same human need to belong, she had not been equipped to reach out to the other girls to learn about being a pre-teen.

She'd tried comparing herself to the girls in "Teen" and "Cosmo Girl;" however, relating to her actual classmates had not occurred to her. She'd been unable to recognize their unique qualities or to invite them into her world of pre-teen fashion curiosity.

From childhood through adolescence and into young adult-hood empathy is taking shape neurologically, cultivated by a loving family and healthy social interactions. It is further refined in adulthood by meditation, prayer and commitment to living a passionate life. To love and to heal from life's tribulations requires being highly aware of empathy's importance. I suppose that's why wisdom (held by those who have Radiant Empathy, EmD-5), grows stronger with age and surviving tragedy.

If your empathy is repressed or non-existent, life will be rocky. Sociopaths and narcissists will zero in

> **To love and to heal from life's tribulations requires being highly aware of empathy's importance.**

> **Head injuries, dementia, drug abuse, and social pressure that cause fear, anger, or greed can thwart natural empathy.**

on these weaknesses to manipulate you. Others without strong empathy skills, such as autistics, do care and are deeply troubled by their lack of social connection.

Head injuries, dementia, drug abuse and social pressure that cause fear, anger or greed can thwart natural empathy. The bulk of people have healthy empathy (EmD-4) and can dial it up to the higher EmD-5 level with conscious effort. Choosing to recognize the divine in each person is what opens hearts and advances empathy.

Empathy Dysfunction (EmD)—what it is and isn't

It is sometimes easier to understand empathy by defining what it is not. Most of us intuitively recognize when another person is lacking empathy. We certainly know when we have been "burned" by a disrespectful or abusive person.

We feel it in our gut. I want you to have the cognitive tools to recognize these people and to define their level of EmD from zero to five. With this knowledge, you will be in much better shape to protect yourself from those who would use your empathy against you.

I might add that choosing to dial up your empathy is the best defense against those with any degree of EmD. By knowing yourself well—and knowing what another person is capable of—you can more easily connect with love or remove yourself from an unworkable relationship.

As you become more familiar with Empathy Dysfunction, you will see how it is a dynamic process along a spectrum. Empathy shifts on the Spectrum as it ebbs and flows, expands and contracts, declines or refines. A (+) or a (-) can be used along the spectrum to fine-tune the nature of a person's Empathy Dysfunction.

In the *Introduction* and *Chapter One*, you saw several examples of people with EmD-0 to EmD-5. In succeeding chapters I delve more deeply into each type of EmD, giving you a better picture of how people with Empathy Dysfunction can weave webs of chaos, create damage and inflict heartbreak. However, not everyone with EmD is trying to harm you.

> **Autistics have no idea what another person is thinking or feeling... Because they are "mind blind." Autistics make decisions solely on their analysis of a situation.**
>
> **EmD-0 autistics exist in a silent, sad world where they develop rigid rules of conduct. They are capable of lying and manipulation just like any other human being, but they do not usually intend to harm anyone. They are trying to achieve a solitary—and very literal—goal.**

EmD-0—having zero degrees of empathy but not intending harm

Autistics best represent the EmD-0 type: They have zero degrees of empathy because they cannot integrate its dimensions. Significantly different than narcissists, autistics do not intend to harm you. They do, however, suffer from their lack of empathy.

As Bianca did, they struggle to relate to others. They often remove themselves from society as a way to cope with the pain of being unable to connect. Alternatively, autistics may set up a life where they can be in complete control of outcomes, such as self-employment.

Autistics do not have a "theory of mind," which is another way of saying they have no idea what another person is thinking or feeling; hence do not react to it. Because they are "mind blind," autistics make decisions solely on their analysis of a situation; as when Bianca had researched pre-teen behavior without connecting with the girls in her class.

With EmD-0, autistics exist in a silent, sad world where they develop rigid rules of conduct. They are capable of lying and manipulation just like any other human being, but they do not usually intend to harm anyone. They are trying to achieve a solitary—and very literal—goal.

An autistic college professor once told me that members of his department frequently ask him to have coffee; however, he rarely accepts the invitation. When I'd asked why, he'd said, "Well, they usually ask me after I have already had my coffee, so there is no need to go along."

When an autistic behaves badly, it may not be the result of a malicious intent. A young autistic grad student at Stanford was arrested, tried and convicted after joining what he'd thought was a "Green" group on campus. The group's focus had been purported to protest the sale of gas-guzzling SUVs.

One night, the student joined the group for a rally—only to watch in horror as the students firebombed the SUV/car sales lot. He hadn't expected the students to set fire to vehicles, and he was shocked by their actions. Since he'd participated in the protest, he was arrested, found guilty, and is serving several years in a California state penitentiary.

On the other hand, an EmD-0+ woman has dedicated her life to helping those with autism. I diagnosed her as autistic for the first time in her life when she was age 42. She was stunned into silence when I suggested Asperger Syndrome. As she mentally digested the diagnosis, she slowly raised her left leg to set her ankle on her right knee, revealing her panties underneath her skirt. To my surprise, she'd exclaimed, "Fuckin' A!" She'd continued unabashed, "Do you suppose that explains every fuckin' problem I've ever had in my fuckin' life?[28]"

After considerable medical and psychological intervention, this woman has gone on to dedicate her life to helping others with Asperger Syndrome. She has: volunteered for private organizations that assist disabled adults; written extensively on the subject of women with autism; and been a national speaker. Kudos for this Zero (+) woman!

EmD-1—narcissists, sociopaths, and others out to harm

Narcissists and sociopaths best represent this type (EmD-1).[29] While narcissists may not intend to harm you, they do so anyway, because they feel entitled to do as they please. They fully believe that their wish is your command. Sociopaths, on the other hand, actually do want to harm you, getting a thrill from your suffering. They have learned that the rest of us are saps and will allow them free reign with our minds and hearts. Why are we saps? Because we hold the false belief that all people have a full range of empathy skills when this is just not true.

> ... While narcissists may not intend to harm you, they do so anyway, because they feel entitled to do as they please. They fully believe that their wish is your command.

---

[28] Coming from an intelligent, college-educated woman, this obvious lack of social skills (i.e. saying "Fuckin'A" and sitting in an indiscrete and inappropriate manner) is one symptom of Asperger Syndrome.

[29] The terms narcissist and sociopath are actually traits of diagnosable personality disorders. They are not diagnoses per se. I use the terms primarily to describe qualities among those with EmD-1. Other EmDs can demonstrate narcissism and sociopathy from time to time.

Narcissists and sociopaths have enough perception to know how to manipulate us but feel no obligation to treat us fairly. Unlike autistics with zero degrees of empathy, an EmD-1 without a conscience employs empathic tricks; such as pretending to sound sincere. This type of EmD will not change. No amount of rehabilitation will work, which is why many state prison systems do not allow early release for inmates diagnosed as psychopaths (another term for sociopath).

Not all EmD-1s are criminals or in prison. Many are in our workplaces, neighborhoods, and families. A classic EmD-1 is a former neighbor of mine, Don Morris, who had nothing but venom in his heart for me. He engaged in extreme measures that were clearly illegal, yet he was never held fully accountable. The disdain this man held for me only increased with each event that I foiled. Such is the nature of a stalker. Here is a partial list of his attacks on me from 2004-2014.

This neighbor:

1. Threatened to kill my mostly Hispanic yard crew, whom he called "Wetbacks."

2. Promised to dig up the cable the Comcast guys were installing at my house if they dared to step onto his property.

3. Along with his wife, drove their recycling bins to my driveway, then placed them under my car. This outlandish behavior went on for months until a judge ordered them in contempt of court.

4. Turned his yard sprinklers on precisely as my children and I walked by, leaving us soaked.

5. Drove across my lawn repeatedly with his car.

6. Dug holes along our shared dirt/gravel road to the river, disguising them with yard debris. I fell into one of these holes and broke my foot.

7. Planted rebar stakes on the river bank and in the Columbia River, putting anyone who dared walk, swim or boat by in danger.

8. Took fifty secret videos of me, my daughter, my dog, and my guests; then turned the videos over to Vancouver Code Enforcement as evidence that my psychology practice endangered the community.

9. Placed a toilet by my fence and in full view of my dining room.

10. Hired a crew to cut down at least ten of the 50-year-old rhododendrons on my property, costing me thousands of dollars to replace.

11. Assaulted me from behind, knocking me to the ground.

12. Aimed a rifle at me as I walked by; then shot overhead to scare me.

No other description fits this man except EmD-1 (-). EmD-1s are very effective at convincing others to gang up on their victim.

This man convinced the entire next door neighborhood (Steamboat Landing in Vancouver, Washington) I was so dangerous that my photograph and a warning should be posted at their entrance gate. It read that, should I pass through the gate, a call to the police should be made.

This bit of libel was actionable and cost their Homeowners' Association about $100,000 in legal fees and damages when I sued. The foolish neighbors at Steamboat Landing were just as much victimized by this man as I was. This type of chaos and harm caused by an EmD-1, who feels entitled to have what he wants, no matter how many people get hurt. I am without even one example of an EmD-1(+); this cannot exist where there is no conscience and the intent to harm.

The author's EmD-1(-) neighbor, with severe Empathy Dysfunction, convinced an entire neighborhood (SBL) that the author was profoundly dangerous. To warn her off, SBL's HOA foolishly put up this sign at their compound gate:

"SBL Homeowners – Kathy Marshack, who lives east of this community, is not permitted on SBL property at any time. A restraining order has been filed on 7/6/06. If you see Ms. Marshack in SBL, do not approach her! Immediately call the Police."

This bit of folly cost SBL about $100,000 in legal fees and damages when the author sued.

EmD-2 – mental illness or brain damage

Brain damage is the simplest way to explain why the EmD-2 level exists. EmD-2 individuals may have a severe mental illness, such as Schizophrenia or Alzheimer's. Or their good brains may have been damaged by drug/alcohol abuse, a car accident, or high impact sports. Because the brains of these individuals are deteriorating, they frequently have limited empathy as well as other damaged cognitive functions. EmD-2s may occasionally have an empathic moment, like a little window opening to the person they used to be. Still, it is vital to protect yourself from their potentially dangerous, and unpredictable, choices.

EmD-2 has come into the spotlight as we've learned more about the tragic circumstances of NFL football players who have experienced concussions. These athletes were once the cream of the crop. They had fame, money, power, and careers as coaches and sportscasters following their playing days—for awhile. Then, their too-many football collisions caught up with them, leading to Traumatic Brain Injury or TBI. Now we know that TBI can lead to Chronic Traumatic Encephalopathy (CTE), a progressive and debilitating disease that leads to death.

Sufferers of CTE create havoc for themselves and their families. Struggling to understand their minds and the minds of their loved ones, these men can become confused, paranoid, and violent. Just because they used to have empathy, doesn't mean you can count on it after the disease takes hold. The heartbreak is that sufferers often know something is wrong but can't explain it.[30]

---

[30] Utecht, Ben. (2016). "Counting the Days While My Mind Slips Away." New York: Howard Books. This is just one of many stories about the suffering of retired football players.

Furthermore, their loved ones cannot connect with a person who no longer resembles the person they'd loved.

Much more than Empathy Dysfunction complicates these conditions. For those of us who live with and love these people, it is the disrupted empathy that we need to understand and address—for our emotional well-being. Often there are subtle symptoms of brain injury that show long before the disease is apparent. Family members see these things and wonder why the empathic connection is crumbling. Knowing that you are doing all you can, as well as grieving the loss of empathic connection, may bring you some peace, even if you can't change the outcome.

My niece is a sad example of an EmD-2 who was at one time an EmD-3. She is at the stage of deterioration where she is unreasonable and unreliable, but not yet psychotic or violent. Empathy is seldom present. She is late for everything—as much as four hours late, because of her obsessive/compulsive need to clean and organize.

She chooses not to take showers and instead cleans her body with wet-wipes. She has severe tooth decay and is constantly daubing her inflamed gums with pain reliever. She is terrified of meeting new people. Her chronic body inflammation and irrational anxieties constrict her life immeasurably. Our relationship ended when I refused to loan her more money after she'd repeatedly lied about repaying her debt. Feeling angry and misunderstood, she cut me off. I worry about her, but I cannot reach her. I take comfort in knowing I did my best.

EmD-3—addiction, ADHD, Bipolar Disorder

In Greek mythology, Sisyphus, a self-aggrandizing, deceitful king, was condemned to live in Eternity rolling a boulder uphill again and again: Similarly, EmD-3s have a lot of work to do to maintain their empathy and avoid backsliding. Typically these individuals have ADHD, Bipolar Disorder or Alcoholism: When they adhere to a recommended course of treatment, their developmental disorders or diseases either stop progressing or progress slowly.

The backbone philosophy of Alcoholics Anonymous is that alcoholics are never fully recovered even when they are abstinent. Rather, they are "recovering," because staying sober/clean requires the daily rededication to looking after their physical, mental, emotional, family, and spiritual health.

It's a lot of work to keep rolling that boulder uphill. Many EmD-3s fail time and again, bringing additional harm to themselves and others. It's as if they have temporary insanity, or temporary Empathy Dysfunction.

One alcoholic got so drunk he decided to outrun a police car as the officer was trying to slow him down. Soon three cop cars were after him, each from a different direction. One officer put down tack strips to puncture his tires, but this guy drove over the strips and continued, driving on his rims. When he ran into the police vehicle ahead of him, another one T-boned him. A third police car smashed into the rear end of his car. Amazingly, no one was severely injured.

When the driver later visited my practice to get help, I was able to refer him to chemical dependency treatment. He is back on track, but may still be facing some jail time. His family is frightened for his future.

EmD-3s are capable of slipping into EmD-2 status if they abuse drugs for too long, get into one too many accidents, or alienate the wrong people. For many years, Marlena had been a wonderful and supportive executive assistant. On looking back, her boss realized Marlena had been slowly deteriorating over a couple of years (because of a yet-to-be-diagnosed health problem impacting her brain). When he'd finally noticed her increased incompetence, he'd perceived it as a sudden change.

Over a two-year period, she'd stopped operating as an EmD-4 and an occasional EmD-5, and had slipped to a level where she'd caused such chaos that her boss was relieved when Marlena quit. She'd: mangled her boss's calendar by double- and triple-booking appointments; shredded important documents, such as bank records, continuing education files, and passport records; and failed to complete billing paperwork, which resulted in $40,000 of receivables so old they had to be written off.

It took a full year with a new executive assistant to clean up the mess that Marlena had created when her mind was temporarily insane.

Worse was the heartache for her employer, who had trusted and loved her. Marlena had quit her job in a huff, never fully understanding that she was suffering from Empathy Dysfunction and never taking responsibility for the damage she'd caused. Instead, she'd blamed her boss for creating too much work for her.

With proper diagnosis and treatment, EmD-3s can operate as EmD-4s and EmD-5s. I have had many clients with ADHD, Bipolar Disorder, and addiction who are well aware that they occasionally have moments when they are not empathic: They grieve the harm this causes others.

Some of these dedicated individuals find their disorder

to be a catalyst for helping others. Knowing firsthand how hard it is to avoid slipping backward, they: become AA sponsors in service to others seeking sobriety; volunteer for charitable organizations; or work as ministers and chemical dependency counselors.

EmD-4—the good at heart

In some ways, it is easier to be an EmD-4 than any of the other types. EmD-4s have good brains and were raised by parents with good brains. They are mostly free from the health problems, poverty, and life traumas that sabotage the development of empathy in those with autism, TBI, and addiction issues. Without the wisdom that comes from soul-searching, an EmD-4 will not be able to advance to the status of EmD-5.

A simple example is the woman who takes yoga classes for fitness but does not embrace the holistic spiritual discipline of Yoga. Or perhaps you have a friend who contributes generously to his church, but fails to see that his elderly neighbor needs help getting her garbage can to the curb.

My friend Frank is like this. He is retired and visits his neighbors each day as he walks his dog. He invites his friends to dinner, and often they reciprocate. If he goes fishing, he shares his catch. He even keeps a garbage can at the end of his long driveway, so neighbors walking their dogs have a convenient place to toss their dog's waste. Frank's not one to be ostentatious, preferring to live simply since his wife passed away. He spends his money for his basic needs, using the rest for his surfing hobby, or to buy a bouquet for his girlfriend.

The problem is that Frank doesn't think outside his white-privileged world. At a restaurant one evening, he made a comment that alerted me to his unwitting thoughtlessness. When our waiter spoke, it was obvious that English was his second language. I

> ... the bulk of the population is EmD-4, having what I call "good enough" empathy. ...
>
> EmD-4s are good-hearted people who: don't take the last piece of chicken on the platter; do clean up after their dogs; read some of the voters' pamphlet; volunteer in their community; bring a thoughtful gift for the birthday boy; and genuinely enjoy making others happy. They tend to accept the status quo.

couldn't quite place the accent, so I asked. When he told me that he and his parents were Syrian refugees, I was amazed.

Before I could learn more about his journey from Syria to Portland, Ore., Frank blurted out, "Better here than there!" Then he laughed and dug into his burrito. The young man was quiet. He smiled politely, asked us if we wanted anything else, then left.

The positive side to this horrible breach of empathy is that Frank responded graciously to my criticism. "Frank, I can't believe you said that!" I scolded. "Do you understand how much this young man has endured? He had to leave his country and seek asylum in the United States. He has his parents thank goodness, but who knows what horrors he has seen and who he had to leave for dead."

A little sheepishly, Frank said, "I didn't mean any harm by it, but I get it." When the waiter walked by again, Frank motioned to him to stop at our table. He apologized to the young man for his rash comment. Afterward, he left a large tip and smiled at me, recognizing the need to repair our relationship, too. I wouldn't call Frank's revised behavior EmD-5, but as an EmD-4, he was able to see the other side of things. Like Frank, EmD-4s usually accept criticism graciously and make amends where they can.

In my experience, the bulk of the population is EmD-4, having what I call "good enough" empathy. Frank's comment demonstrates EmD-4 (-), but his apology was EmD-4 (+).

EmD-4s are good-hearted people who: don't take the last piece of chicken on the platter; do clean up after their dogs; read some of the voters' pamphlet; volunteer in their community; bring a thoughtful gift for the birthday boy; and genuinely enjoy making others happy. They tend to accept the status quo.

If an EmD-4 is to grow to the level of an EmD-5 (Radiant Empathy), life must be embraced at a deeper level: This is where EmD-4s learn to recognize that it requires more than being nice to do life. It takes courage and resilience... and love.

EmD-5—epitomizing empathy

You'd think the least likely place to experience empathy would be in jail. However, human beings are who they are wherever they are—on a college campus, in a corporate boardroom, behind bars, or at the grocery store. When I'd been in Clark County Jail—for running afoul of those with the predatory kind of EmD—I'd discovered that even inmates run the gamut of human empathy.

By now you have an idea that EmD-5 is the epitome of empathy and not

> **You'd think the least likely place to experience empathy would be in jail. However, human beings are who they are wherever they are—on a college campus, in a corporate boardroom, behind bars, or at the grocery store.**
>
> **When I'd been in Clark County Jail—for running afoul of those with the predatory kind of EmD—I'd discovered that even inmates run the gamut of human empathy.**

an Empathy Dysfunction. It serves as an anchor for the spectrum. I think of EmD-5s as having Radiant Empathy, because they seem to radiate an angelic glow when I am around them. EmD-3s and EmD-4s are capable of reaching EmD-5 level. You don't have to be Mother Teresa or Nelson Mandela or Malala Yousafzai to achieve this state, although these saintly people are incredible role models.

EmD-5s are not without flaws. They may eat too much, or get divorced, or sow too many wild oats when young. What they have in common is a mission to make better the lives of others.

Ralph Waldo Emerson has been credited for one of my favorite quotes regarding Radiant Empathy; no one is sure who the original author was. It reflects EmD-5 perfectly.

> *"To laugh often and love much; to win the respect of intelligent persons and the affection of children; to earn the appreciation of honest critics and endure the betrayal of false friends; to appreciate beauty; to find the best in others; to give of one's self; to leave the world a bit better, whether by a healthy child, a garden patch or a redeemed social condition; to have played and laughed with enthusiasm and sung with exultation; to know even one life has breathed easier because you have lived—this is to have succeeded."*

The following three examples, taken from my jail experiences, are very typical of EmD-5s, who we usually encounter for only brief moments.

Heroin addict with a smile

On my first trip to jail (at age 54), I sat in the holding tank with Laura for hours. She was a beautiful young woman, with long, thick, curly dark hair that fell in waves around her face.

Laura was softly crying when I entered the cell. I learned that she was a heroin addict, living with her boyfriend in a van. Both had been arrested for some minor infraction. She was worried that all of her worldly possessions would be confiscated, leaving her with nothing. Curious about her lifestyle, I asked how she managed on the street with no shower or toilet. "You would never guess that you live in a van," I blurted out. "Your hair is beautiful."

Laura stopped crying when we began to chat and even smiled when I showed some interest in her. "Oh," she said, warming to the conversation. "There are lots of places to clean up and get food and even wash clothes. You get to know the city when you live on the street. My boyfriend is good to me. It's his van, you know."

She had offered me her sack lunch, which had been provided by the jail staff. I'd been in no mood to eat; in hindsight, I should have reconsidered. I was kept me in the tank for seven hours before being booked. Besides Laura, no one had offered me anything to eat.

Three days later, when I was being released, I saw Laura again. She had spent her first three days in solitary confinement, detoxing. I'm not sure if she had medical help to do so, but she looked radiant when she came up to congratulate me for getting out. She stretched out her arms to me for a big hug. As we embraced, she whispered in my ear, "Good luck to you Kathy. When I get out, I'm going to stay clean this time. I mean it!" I hugged her again and whispered back, "I know you will."

Mostly an EmD-3, Laura clearly had the ability to dial it up to a higher level of empathy, such as EmD-4 or even EmD-5. If she is unable to avoid heroin, the addiction will cause enough brain damage to push Laura down to EmD-2.

She'd gained nothing by promising to stay clean. She'd been sincere (not attempting to butter me up before asking for money—which she never did). Her promise to stay clean had come from her heart—a gift to say she appreciated me for having comforted her. She'd been thanking me by offering something she thought I would like—her sobriety. In that moment, she had been EmD-5.

Jailer with a sense of humor

The sergeant who'd booked me, had asked, "What are you doing here?" He already knew why I'd been arrested because he had the police report. His question had surprised me. I guess he'd been incredulous to see a 54-year-old, well-dressed white woman standing at his window in handcuffs.

"I'm divorcing a local divorce attorney, Howard Marshack," I'd said weakly. It was the first thought that had popped into my head. I'd been in shock over the ordeal that my ex-husband had just put me through. It was quite the trap I'd walked into at Howard's office. I should have known better.

The sergeant had laughed but seemed oddly sympathetic. "Wow!" he'd said. "I'm sorry. What bad luck." In that brief moment, he'd made me feel like I was going to make it through this ordeal. Just as quickly, he'd been back to business. In exchange for three dollars, he'd given me a pocket comb, a plastic cup, a toothbrush, and a pencil. He'd put the rest of my stuff in a plastic bag for safekeeping; then another jailer had led me off to my cell.

I didn't know much about the sergeant, but for an instant, he'd given an EmD-5 empathic response. It had been short, but thoughtful. He'd recognized me. He'd seemed to understand my predicament. He hadn't judged me, acknowledging that bad stuff happens sometimes.

The redhead, the jailer, and the girl who screamed in her sleep

You can find plenty of EmD-1s in jail, like the male jailer who'd repeatedly ordered the gorgeous young redhead to shower, so that he could watch her strip. (Yes, male wardens guard female inmates!) Or the prisoners who'd hovered over me to see if I would finish my meal, eager to claim the leftovers.

Then there was the young woman no one had wanted to share a cell with: She had scabies (a contagious disease) and screamed in her sleep.

A game jailers play is to move inmates around every few hours.

A game jailers play is to move inmates around every few hours. Each time my cellmate was released, I moved to the lower bunk, so I didn't have to sleep under the flickering fluorescent light. Almost immediately, I'd be ordered to move to a new cell. The newbie always gets the top bunk. You have to crawl up with no ladder and jump down onto the cold, concrete floor, which was pretty painful on my feet and legs. I'm sure the jailers thought it was amusing to watch the frightened and confused old lady try to find her bearings.

I'd been pretty much in shock the entire weekend I was in jail this first time. I'd had a migraine headache and been shivering. Whenever I'd made it to the front of the line to make a collect call to my children, no one answered the home phone.

My daughter Bianca, I'd later learned, had been home alone, but she is afraid of answering the phone. Phoebe had found refuge with a friend. Their father, Howard, had stayed in Seattle with his girlfriend rather than come home to comfort his children.

When I'd been allowed out of my cell into the common room, I'd sat huddled in my one thin blanket, trying to calm myself while the TV blared and the voices bounced off the cinder block walls. Once in a while, a young woman would approach me and ask incredulously, "What's a mom like you doing in this place?" Mostly there had been little interaction among the inmates.

On the first of the jail cell swaps, I'd faintly heard my name called with instructions to report to a new cell. Not entirely sure what to do, I'd looked around perplexed. A young woman had noticed my confusion and told me to get my stuff and move upstairs.

Obediently, I'd gone to my old cell on the lower level to pick up my few possessions (pillow, bunk mat, plastic cup, comb, and pencil). I'd shuffled along slowly as if my body were heavily weighed down. The blanket was slipping from my shoulders, but I'd tried to hold it close as I'd clumsily dragged my mat from the bunk.

Just as I'd reached the stairs, the same young woman who had spoken to me earlier, the woman who had scabies and screamed, had moved up close beside me and whispered in my ear, "You need to act quickly, or the guards will punish you!" Then she'd grabbed my mat and pushed me upstairs.

I never got her name, but I'd thanked her before curling up into a ball on my bed. I hadn't seen her after that, probably because I hadn't been able to remember much about her appearance. I'd been so overwhelmed with the fatiguing migraine that I'd paid little attention to anything or anyone. Someone told me that she screams in her sleep because she'd been gang raped.

In spite of the torment she must have experienced each day, this young lady had enough kindness and courage to help me, risking punishment for doing so. I'd later learned that the guards viewed any kindness shown to another inmate as dangerous fraternization. She hadn't asked for anything in return. She hadn't even given me her name. I consider this EmD-5 conduct, and I am thankful that God sent me an Angel when I most needed one.

Empathy Dysfunction (EmD) in a nutshell

Seldom will you meet a solid EmD-5, but when you do, you will feel bathed in radiant love. It is remarkable. When you meet an EmD-0, I hope you will have compassion for their empathy missteps and see them with an awareness of their good intentions.

Be wary of EmD2s and EmD3s. You can certainly send compassion to these souls from a safe distance: Remember, their motivations are unpredictable.

Living with EmD-4s is relatively easy since they are amiable, and make good neighbors and friends.

I must insist that—for your own good—you disengage from an EmD-1 the moment you recognize signs of their total self-absorption. You are no match for a narcissist or a sociopath. They have the ability to harm you—probably for the rest of your life.

EmD Assessment Tool

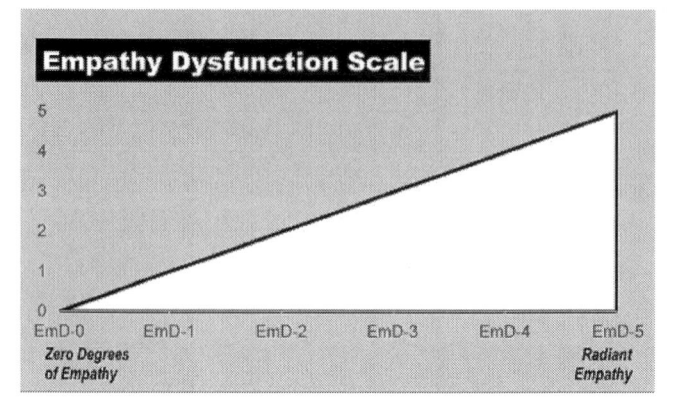

Fig. A.1

Empathy Dysfunction Scale

(Graph showing values 0 through 5 on y-axis, with EmD-0 through EmD-5 on x-axis. EmD-0 labeled "Zero Degrees of Empathy"; EmD-5 labeled "Radiant Empathy". A diagonal line rises from 0 at EmD-0 to 5 at EmD-5.)

Understanding the Varying Degrees of Empathy in Humans

EmD-0 *Zero Degrees of Empathy*—struggle to understand the empathic reciprocity of normal communication, but they are not out to get you. Deep down, they have a moral code; or they can be taught about morality. **Examples:** *autistics and young children.*

EmD-1 *Self-Absorbed Individuals*—only interested in their own agenda; hence usually cause serious harm. It only takes a single EmD-1 to destroy everything their victim has worked for. **Examples:** *narcissists and psychopaths/sociopaths.*

EmD-2 *Organic Brain Injury/illness*—unpredictable mental functioning that creates chaos in their lives and the lives of their caregivers and loved ones. **Examples:** *the mentally ill and traumatic brain injured (TBI).*

EmD-3 *Controllable Mental Illness*—can function at much higher levels of empathy if their disorders are treated with medicine, psychotherapy, and psychosocial education. Otherwise, their empathy is intermittent, depending on their stage of illness. **Examples:** *alcoholics, addicts, and those with bipolar disorder.*

EmD-4 *Basic Good-enough Empathy*—psychologically unaware yet good citizens and neighbors most of the time; however, they are prone to gossip and codependency. **Examples:** *unless asked to do more than they desire, most are trustworthy.*

EmD-5 *Radiant Empathy*—fearless individuals with empathy fully functioning nearly all of the time. They have clear boundaries for themselves and others. **Examples:** *the devoted friend who accepts all of your flaws; the 88-year-old man who plants saplings for future generations; the Medal of Honor winner; the woman who fights for those who are disenfranchised; and the mother who always forgives.*

(fig. A.1)

Copyright Kathy J. Marshack, Ph.D. 2017

Following the epiphany moment when the idea to rate levels of Empathy Dysfunction came to me, I developed the EmD Scale. It provides a simple and straightforward way for you to get a general idea of the depth and constancy of a person's empathy—or lack thereof. When you've pinpointed a level, refer to the chapter that focuses on that type of empathy to learn more.

"Empathy Dysfunction (EmD)" Highlights

1. Empathy exists on an ascending continuum from EmD-0 to EmD-5. It helps to know what level of Empathy Dysfunction you are facing.

2. Empathy is at the core of all relationships. Don't take it for granted. Be observant, so you will notice if someone is short on empathy. A relationship with an empathy-lacking person can cost you dearly.

3. The best way to protect yourself from low-level EmDs is to cultivate your empathy, so it grows to Level 5.

4. Empathy is the ability to hold dear the feelings of others. A symphony, where the composer, director, musicians, and audience mutually respect and appreciate each other, is a metaphor for the empathic process.

5. "Namaste" is the Sanskrit word that describes empathy as honoring the Soul within us as well as in another person. It is the belief that we are all divine beings.

6. People who have autism, traumatic brain injury, narcissism or addiction issues, do not have the full range of empathy. Don't assume they do. Stay safe by staying aware.

7. EmD-0 folks don't always mean to harm you, but they can. As long as they stay true to their moral code, you should be okay.

8. EmD-1 folks mean to harm you and they will in a flash.

9. EmD-2 folks will hurt you because their head injuries and brain damage make their behavior erratic.

10. EmD-3 folks can rise to a higher level of empathy when they stick with their professional medical treatment and recovery program. They have a tough row to hoe, so often fail to remain at EmD-3 level.

11. EmD-4 folks are usually good friends and neighbors. They are susceptible to the influence of EmD-1s through EmD-3s since they are not always conscious of how much they feel obligated to others. Be wary of an unaware EmD-4.

12. EmD-5 folks are the Angels who walk among us. They remain empathy-neutral, which gives them the awareness to navigate all levels of the Empathy Scale.

13. Utilize the EmD Scale to gain insight about the level of empathy you or people in your life possess—or don't possess.

CHAPTER THREE
Brainwashing Mom

"No person is your friend who demands your silence, or denies your right to grow."

— Alice Walker

Veiled in brainwash

A fog settles in the minds of brainwashing victims and consumes them. When your reality is repeatedly denied, your life becomes a series of mildly-depressing days with nothing to look forward to. You just exist. The following example is typical of the brain fog I suffered because of the brainwashing at the hands of my husband during our marriage.

It had never occurred to me to ask my husband to take me to the hospital for my surgery. This was early in our marriage, but I had already come to expect nothing from him. Howard never inquired about me or showed emotional support. Unless I could manage life on my own, I was an inconvenience to him. So when I had a breast cancer scare, and the surgeon recommended a lumpectomy, I'd automatically made plans for the operation without consulting him.

> Howard [the author's ex-husband] never inquired about me or showed emotional support. Unless I could manage life on my own, I was an inconvenience to him.

I'd arranged my work schedule so I could have the surgery on a Thursday, take Friday off work, and recuperate over the weekend. I'd packed a little overnight bag just in case there were surgical complications that would keep me in the hospital overnight. On the day of the surgery, I'd sent my children off to school after Howard left for work. All alone, I'd driven myself to the hospital.

After being admitted, I'd been escorted to my room and instructed to take off all of my clothes and wrap up in a hospital gown and a blanket. After that, I'd sat quietly on the bed waiting for the nurse to take me through all of the legal stuff that is required before surgery. The nurse had been puzzled when I'd explained that no one had accompanied me. She'd said, "I thought you understood that you will be given a general anesthetic, which requires you to have someone to drive you home after the procedure."

I'd felt foolish. Of course, the medical staff would expect me to have a helper, most likely a loving husband concerned that his wife is about to have a lumpectomy, a biopsy for cancer. I'd said, "Well since it's just a day surgery, I thought I could drive myself home." In my brainwashed, delusional world, I suppose I'd thought this made sense.

The nurse had looked at me with an odd expression of patience, but she was all business. "We will have to cancel your procedure unless you arrange to have someone who will take you home," she'd said. For good measure she'd added, "And they need to be here now before you go into surgery so that they can sign the forms that they will be responsible for you."

I had been thoroughly humiliated. I blamed myself for not insisting that Howard take the day off, so he could drive me to the hospital. It never occurred to me that the situation was not my fault; that I had been the victim of such intense coercive control, I now believed I was not worth being cared for or about. Why hadn't Howard insisted that he would be there to comfort me and hold my hand when I was afraid?

I'd called Howard and, as it turned out, he'd been able to come to the hospital after all. He'd been annoyed that he'd had to leave work; but when I'd explained that the hospital staff insisted, he'd relented. The procedure went well. Howard waited there until I recovered from the surgery.

The nurse explained to him how to take care of me over the next couple of days, but I am not sure he really listened. When we got home, I crawled into bed exhausted. Howard didn't hang around to help. Instead, he left me alone and went out for the evening.

Brain fog. That's the best way to describe it. Others have a reality in which they are important enough to be respected, considered and loved. In fact this enables them to do the same for their friends and loved ones. That's the nature of empathy; its' reciprocal. On the other hand, my reality had crumbled so extremely that it no longer included me.

It still stuns me that I endured this type of abuse for 25 long years. Like the proverbial frog in the pot of water that is slowly heated, I hadn't realized that I should jump out until I was already boiling. I did eventually figure out how to take back my life. It has been a long hard slog, but this book is evidence that I have been at least partially successful.

In this chapter, I focus on the narcissistic dimension of EmD-1 that revels in brainwashing. It matters not that EmD-1s, such as narcissists, do not **mean** to cause harm to others. With zero degrees of empathy, their actions inevitably damage others.

One narcissist boldly told her sister that "empathy is a marvelous weapon." If causing you harm is not the narcissist's ultimate goal—and getting their way generally is their goal—you may be able to stop him or her at their game.

Why engage with someone who never considers how you feel, is unwilling to accommodate you, and considers your empathy a tool to use against you?[31]

Coercive control

Long before Vancouver City Prosecutor Josephine Townsend and crony Jim Jacks, Vancouver's Ombudsman, concocted the story that I was a "functional sociopath," I had spent years defending myself and my children from the type of domestic violence known as "coercive control," (which includes brainwashing). That made me a sitting duck for the abuse that Townsend and Vancouver Code Officer Richard Landis dished out.

I was desperately trying to break out of a destructive marriage; however, my self-esteem was still pretty low. I hated dragging my children through a divorce, but I also knew that we could not live under the oppression being dished out daily by my husband. Naively, I'd thought that I could get away from the abuse by filing for divorce: Instead, I learned that abusers, like Howard, never relinquish control over their victims.

---

[31] The terms narcissist and sociopath are actually traits of diagnosable personality disorders. They are not diagnoses per se. Neither is the term "functional sociopath" actually a diagnosis. It is a term entirely invented in a memo written by Jim Jacks, Citizen Advocate in the Vancouver City Manager's office (and later a Washington State House Representative). I use the terms narcissist and sociopath to describe qualities among those with EmD-1 primarily. However, other EmDs can demonstrate narcissism and sociopathy from time to time.

Most of you have no trouble seeing the lack of empathy in those who use domestic violence and coercive control. Author Simon Baron-Cohen refers to these predators as having zero-negative degrees of empathy in his book, "The Science of Evil."

What he means is that when a lack of empathy is unchecked by morality, you have a very dangerous person. Some EmD people (such as autistics) have a moral code and would never intentionally harm their friends and loved ones. However, people who engage in coercive control are devoid of a moral code. They want power over their victims and will stop at nothing to get it.

> ... when a lack of empathy is unchecked by morality, you have a very dangerous person.

Psychologists and the courts used to believe that domestic violence was limited to physical and/or sexual battery. Now we realize that long before these problems erupt, the victim has endured years of insidious verbal abuse and social isolation.

Not infrequently the coercive control or domestic violence comes to the fore when the victim finally strikes back. One woman was horrified to find that her boyfriend was watching pornographic videos with her 12-year-old son. She walked into the living room one day and exploded when she saw what was on the television. She tore the tape out of the tape deck and mangled it. Then she threw the video player on the floor cracking it beyond repair.

> Psychologists and the courts used to believe that domestic violence was limited to physical and/or sexual battery. Now we realize that long before these problems erupt, the victim has endured years of insidious verbal abuse and social isolation.

When her boyfriend tried to stop her by pinning her to the wall, she struggled to get free. As she broke loose, she scratched him with her fingernails.

Trying to protect his mother, the son called 911. The police arrested the mom for assault and destruction of her boyfriend's property (i.e. the pornographic tape), then tossed her in the Clark County Jail. The boyfriend went free. It was a horrifying miscarriage of justice.

This is similar to what happened to me. After years of coercive control, where my reality had been denied and criticized; my children kicked and yelled at by their father, and the entire family danced around Howard's needs, I was plain worn out.

I crashed, landing in jail myself. That was where I'd met the mother who'd destroyed the pornographic tape. We'd swapped stories, wondering how we could have been foolish enough to put up with the abuse for so long. That's how coercive control rolls: It sneaks up on you.

It is important to understand that brainwashing is a propaganda tactic where information is twisted or spun, selectively omitted to favor the abuser, or presented falsely with the intent of making victims doubt their memory, perception, and sanity.[32]

---

[32] Propaganda is the term used to describe dissemination of false information to the public. Similarly, brainwashing includes using lies and confusion techniques to undermine the victim's sense of reality.

Certainly, this is what had been in Townsend's mind when she'd lied about me to Jacks. She'd put me on the defensive for years; because the police, newspaper owner and other influential people in my small town believed her lies.

Quite effectively, they had all continuously treated me as if I was crazy and dangerous. My ex-husband was only too happy to help stir up animosity against me. The lies were devastating. Even more, crazy-making things were happening behind my back.

Turns out, it's easy to brainwash a mom. Even with my level of education and professional credentials, I'd been fooled. I'd loved my husband and wanted to make the marriage work. I'd wanted to protect my girls from the anguish of their parents divorcing. I'd stayed and put up with one mind-numbing brainwashing experience after another. So had my children—until my resilient nature took over.

Abuse the child to control the mom

I'd like to tell you that things got better in 2004 and 2005, but the persecution escalated. In:

- **April 2004**   I was divorced;

- **June 2004**   I had signed my Diversion agreement for assault and trespass against my ex-husband and his secretary.

- **Sept. 9, 2004**   I was sued for the first time by my neighbors Mary Kellogg, and Joseph and Julianne Leas to quiet title to my right to use the Old Camas Highway and the river easements granted to me in my deed.

- **Sept. 29, 2004**   I had fought Townsend's Diversion revocation petition successfully;

- **March 2005**   I'd won the Kellogg and Leas lawsuit in summary judgement (i.e. the judge determined that legal documents upheld my deeded rights) without need of a trial.

But oh no, this was not to be the end. The summary judgment order had further angered my neighbors. They'd escalated their harassment of me and refiled their lawsuit with new grounds. In an attempt to force me to comply with their wishes, my neighbors began targeting my children.

So did Howard. He'd remarried shortly after our divorce was granted. That did not deter him from stepping up his control over me by way of the children. He chose Phoebe's fifteenth birthday in April 2005 to make his stand.

"Mom, I want a boy/girl party for my birthday. Is that okay?" my younger daughter, Phoebe, had asked.

"No problem for me, honey, but it's on your dad's weekend; so you'll have to ask him," I'd answered.

"Ummm," she'd whispered as if once again pausing to find the right words to help explain a conundrum. "Well I already did ask my dad, and he said I couldn't have any friends for my birthday."

"Why's that?" I'd asked casually, foolishly thinking that Howard might have a good reason.

Phoebe had looked uncomfortable, the same way she had when revealing that Howard used the code word, "Bitch," to call up my number on his cell phone.

She'd explained, "Ummm, well, ummm. My dad said that he doesn't want a mess at his house. So I am not allowed to invite friends to my birthday."

"Well, you could wait two weeks until you are back home with me," I'd offered. I know how important it is for children to celebrate their birthdays on or near their birthdate, but I was once again accommodating Howard's coercive control.

"Mommy," she'd wailed. "That won't work. I want a slumber party with the girls. The boys are coming over for pizza and cake and hanging out. Then they have to go home, so the girls can sleep over and watch movies and stuff. You know I want a party with all of my friends. But my dad won't let me." She looked angry and hurt.

"Okay. Okay. Let me see what I can do," I'd answered, relenting. "Maybe Dad will swap weekends with me. Would that be okay with you? You can stay with me and have your birthday party. Then you can go with your dad next weekend. He shouldn't mind. Maybe you and Dad could celebrate privately sometime the week before or after the party. What do you think?"

Phoebe liked the idea. So I set about to make it happen. I called Howard with the suggestion. He flatly refused. He told me it was "his" weekend, and that he didn't want a bunch of noisy kids at his house. He said that he and Susan (his new wife) would take Phoebe to dinner, but no guests were allowed whatsoever.

I suggested that if we swapped weekends, it was a win-win. He could still have dinner with Phoebe, and she could have a boy/girl party at my house. Plus he would have no mess to clean up since I was willing to take on the teenagers at my house. Nope. He remained adamant.

Next, he threatened: If she failed to be at his house this weekend, Phoebe would not be allowed to come to his house again. Neither Phoebe nor I believed that Howard would go that far, so we'd planned her party.

I said, "Give Dad time to settle down. He can't mean he won't ever allow you to visit him again. That's ridiculous. On the other hand, I can't tell you to disobey your dad and swap weekends. Talk with him, and let him know you love him. I'm sure he will get over it and enjoy your visit next week."

Howard didn't get over it. He stuck to his word: Phoebe was never again allowed to go to Howard's house. He stopped contacting her entirely. He even blocked her phone calls and emails.

For years, she was not permitted to attend any holiday function with his extended family. Howard rarely sent a birthday card or holiday gift. I was surprised that his wife would allow this abuse. After all, she was a mother and a grandmother. But there was no appealing to her either. I guess she also believes that I am a dangerous and crazy bitch, raising a teenage version of myself.

For several years, I'd tried to reconcile Phoebe and her father. I offered to pay for reconciliation therapy for them. Howard never responded to my emails; he blocked my phone number from his home, cell and work numbers, just as he'd done with Phoebe. I called and emailed his brother, his cousins, and even his last living aunt.

The single response I received was from his Aunt Gloria Londer. She told me during a brief phone call that she had asked Howard about his estrangement from Phoebe. He'd told her that he wasn't ready yet. Wasn't he ready to see his own daughter? Are you kidding me? All because she'd wanted a birthday party with her friends? No one seemed to comprehend that this was coercive controlling BS (pardon me).

Phoebe tried another time to get through to her dad on her birthday. We were driving home from the restaurant where we had just celebrated her seventeenth birthday. Two of her girlfriends were in the car with us. She told her friends how Howard had cut her off. The friends hadn't believed her because it was such an outrageous notion.

"No, really," said Phoebe. "I'll prove it to you."

She put her phone on speaker and dialed Howard, getting the automated message that her number had been blocked. Then she asked one friend to borrow the girl's phone to make a call to Howard. He answered that call right away.

"Hi Dad this is Phoebe," she said to her father nonchalantly.

"Who?" he asked, not recognizing the phone number.

"You know, Dad. This is your daughter Phoebe," she responded. Phoebe turned to her friends with a look of smug satisfaction that she had proven her point. Both friends' jaws had dropped in surprise.

"Oh yes. Hello, Phoebe. How are you?" Howard sounded as though he was talking to a business associate.

"Well it's my birthday today, Dad, and I haven't heard from you." Phoebe pushed to see what he would do.

"Oh it is?" he said. "Happy Birthday Phoebe. I've sent something in the mail for you. I've got to go now." Howard's tone was smooth with no trace of distress. Then he hung up.

Phoebe's friends were stunned. One of the girls offered that Howard had at least said a gift was on its way.

Phoebe laughed and said, "I doubt it. He lies about stuff like that. If you don't believe me, let me show you." She asked for the phone of her girlfriend again and redialed her dad. The response that came over the speaker was, "This Verizon customer is no longer accepting calls from this number." Within minutes of Phoebe's second call, Howard had blocked her friend's number, too.

Phoebe was also right about her father's promised birthday present. Nothing came in the mail for Phoebe from Howard. Nothing. As Phoebe had grown older, she'd begun to confront her father about his coercive control.

She sent the explosive and heartbreaking email (on the next page) to Howard after years of being shunned by him and her older sister Bianca. It was the result of a lifetime of confusion from the mental abuse of brainwashing, then three years of active parental alienation[33] efforts by Howard.

It was a painful irony that once, after a fight with Bianca, Howard had filed a motion to split the custody of our children: He'd wanted Phoebe, and I could have Bianca.

When Phoebe had finally had enough and sought retribution, her anger spewed forth with the force of a geyser—like the subterranean water slowly heating and brewing until it can't take any more pressure and erupts with great momentum.

---

[33] Parental alienation refers to the destructive tactic one parent (in this case the father) uses against the other parent and/or their children to emotionally and physically undermine the relationship the offspring have with the other parent (in this case me). Parental alienation is not limited to young children. Older teens and young adults are also vulnerable. Generally, a mother has far less legal ability to protect her vulnerable children from this kind of abuse.

I cried for Phoebe when I'd read her email to her father. Just a teen then, Phoebe had not been equipped to be strong like I'd been. She'd tried mightily—though she finally succumbed to the abuse her father continued to inflict through his neglect.

As you can see manifested in Phoebe's pain at the loss of her sister and her childhood, the domestic violence wrought by coercive control can destroy an entire family.

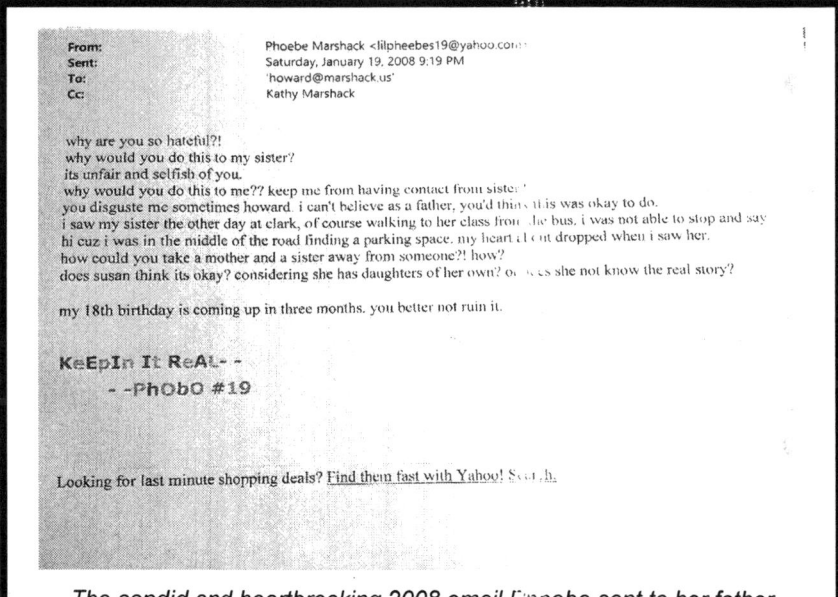

> **From:** Phoebe Marshack <lilpheebes19@yahoo.com>
> **Sent:** Saturday, January 19, 2008 9:19 PM
> **To:** 'howard@marshack.us'
> **Cc:** Kathy Marshack
>
> why are you so hateful?!
> why would you do this to my sister?
> its unfair and selfish of you.
> why would you do this to me?? keep me from having contact from sister?
> you disguste me sometimes howard. i can't believe as a father, you'd think this was okay to do.
> i saw my sister the other day at clark, of course walking to her class from the bus. i was not able to stop and say hi cuz i was in the middle of the road finding a parking space. my heart i c nt dropped when i saw her.
> how could you take a mother and a sister away from someone?! how?
> does susan think its okay? considering she has daughters of her own? or does she not know the real story?
>
> my 18th birthday is coming up in three months. you better not ruin it.
>
> KeEpIn It ReAL- -
>   - -PhObO #19
>
> Looking for last minute shopping deals? Find them fast with Yahoo! Search.

The candid and heartbreaking 2008 email Phoebe sent to her father reads: "why are you so hateful?! Why would you do this to my sister? its unfair and selfish of you. why would you do this to me?? keep me from having contact from my sister? you disguste me sometimes howard. I can't believe as a father, you'd think this was okay to do. I saw my sister the other day at clark, of course walking to her class from the bus. I was not able to stop and say hi cuz I was in the middle of the road finding a parking space. my heart dropped when I saw her. how could you take a mother and a sister away from someone?! how? does susan think its okay? considering she has daughters of her own? or does she not know the real story? my 18th birthday is coming up in three months, you better not ruin it. keEpIn It ReAL – PhObO #19"

How coercive control begins

The set up for more serious abuse, like my arrest in 2003, came from the years of being treated with high disregard and being terrorized by Howard's abuse of our children. My ex-husband had been so self-absorbed that nothing was on his radar except what suited him. It still stuns me that I'd tolerated it, losing a little more of me each time. Here's how it started.

At first, I'd thought Howard was just a quirky bachelor. When we'd first met, he'd owned three televisions (in the days before personal computers and flat screens), yet only one of them worked. Still, he'd kept them sitting out as if ready to use. His house was always in disarray, never vacuumed, never dusted, and never organized. He never made repairs either. It was so bad that when guests had stopped by, they'd asked if he had just bought the house as a fixer-upper.

Nor had Howard ever bathed his dog, even when she'd suffered from annoying and uncomfortable hot spots. I hadn't been sure if he even cared for the dog because he never walked her; he just opened the door and let her run the neighborhood. Hamburger Helper had been his menu for most every meal; no fruit or vegetables were included in his diet, not even a salad.

Plus, he'd had lots of odd habits, like cleaning his kitchen counters with a whisk broom, brushing crumbs to the floor for the dog to lick up. He would cover left-overs with a paper towel and place them in the refrigerator. Instead of blowing his nose, Howard would stuff huge bandanas into each nostril.

He would tear off the waistband elastic from his worn out underwear, then use it to tie up things most people would bind with Zip Ties, rubber bands or Velcro. Rarely had Howard combed his hair in the morning unless I reminded him. On weekends he'd never shower since he didn't have to go to work (never mind that he slept with me). When I'd mused aloud about some of his quirkiness, Howard ignored me. It was like it had never occurred to him that he had a girlfriend who he might want to accommodate just a little. And I'd put up with it.

When we got married, Howard started imposing some of his rigid ways on me. He insisted that I shouldn't carry cash, only a credit card or a check. I pointed out that I liked to have some cash because it helped me budget. Howard insisted that was unreasonable. When I wanted to toss out his grandmother's ancient and smelly hand-me-down couch, he resisted, saying it was an heirloom (broken springs, torn fabric, foam padding so old it was crust).

I couldn't get him to mow the lawn or do a load of laundry without a fight. He'd become very upset when I'd wanted to buy a can of paint to spruce up a room. Worse yet, he thought vacations were "boondoggles." If I wanted to spend a little money on gas and a hotel for a weekend at the beach or up in Seattle, he'd be furious. It was all he could do to manage his life let alone share one with me.

> **Worse yet, he thought vacations were "boondoggles."**

By the time we adopted our children, it was painfully obvious to me that I could not count on Howard to parent, or help with any of the household maintenance. We both had developing careers by then. Howard was an attorney, and I was in graduate school as well as working full time as a psychotherapist.

To make it all work, I'd run myself ragged. I hadn't even gotten a break on Sunday nights because that's when I cooked and prepared an array of frozen meals for the week ahead. Howard even complained about that. He argued that I was always telling him what to do, even when all I asked was for him to bring in a pound of hamburger from the freezer in the garage.

I finally hired helpers, lots of helpers, then worked more hours to pay for them. We had nannies and gardeners and house cleaners because Howard would help with nothing. Lest you think Howard was making significant money in those days, he'd started at Weber & Gunn Law Firm in Vancouver in 1985 and made $15,500 annually.

Even in those days, that salary was dramatically low, about a third of what most new attorneys received. I've always suspected the law firm had offered him a paltry salary because they'd wanted him to go away. I didn't like his work situation and had asked him to look for other jobs. Howard insisted that it was a good deal. So I endured.

I found ways to juggle the myriad of responsibilities he refused to share. I worked more and more hours to pay for expenses that he couldn't or wouldn't cover. But when it came to protecting our children, I couldn't trust him. Here's one example.

At the Clark County Fair one summer, Bianca was about age 6 and Phoebe was just 3 years old. I'd needed to go to the ladies room, which was a hike across the fairgrounds toward the horse barn.

"Howard, do you need to go to the bathroom? I do," I'd said.

"No," he'd answered flatly.

"Well okay then!" I'd expressed annoyance in my tone of voice because he'd never acknowledged me.

"Girls, do either of you need to go? I'd asked more cheerily. Neither one of them did. Like most children, they didn't think about going to the bathroom until they were nearly peeing their pants; then we'd have to rush.

"Are you sure?" I'd repeated. "You can go with Mommy now or wait with Daddy." I wanted them to come with me, so there would be no accidents later; but I also allowed them to make their decisions. They both shook their heads. "No? Okay then. Mommy's going to be right over there." I pointed in the direction of the restrooms. "You stay with Daddy by the fountain. I'll be right back."

Assuming that Howard was listening to all of this (as any responsible co-parent would), I turned my back to them to walk toward the restrooms. Still, I had my doubts about Howard. I turned around to caution him to watch the girls carefully while I was gone. Already, Bianca was walking up the path to the llama pen, and Phoebe was wandering into the food court. It had taken only a few seconds for the girls to get away. Howard was sitting on a bench playing with his new iPAQ (personal data assistant, a predecessor to the smartphone). He was totally oblivious to his girls.

"Howard!" I screamed as I ran back. "Stop Phoebe. She's headed toward the food court." He looked up, startled but made no move. I ran and scooped up Phoebe. As I passed Howard, still sitting on the bench, I handed him the baby and said, "Stay here! Hold Phoebe. I'll be back." I dashed after Bianca. She wasn't moving too quickly, which made it easy for me to reach her.

When Bianca and I got back to where Howard was sitting with Phoebe, I scolded him. "Howard, why weren't you watching the girls? They could have gotten lost, or hurt, or kidnapped. You can't just look away and expect them to be okay. We're at the county fair for God's sake with thousands of people. What were you thinking?"

"I was watching them," he said glaring at me. "They were right here. They weren't far. What's your problem?"

That's the kind of response I got all the time with Howard. He never apologized. He never took responsibility. He always blamed me. It was beyond infuriating. As the years rolled by and the responsibilities grew, I assumed all of the mounting work. After the girls' disabilities had become apparent (i.e. autism, ADHD, and sensory processing deficits), I became hypervigilant.

> This is how coercive control works: The victim keeps thinking that she just has to work harder and faster to make things right.... She gives him [her abuser] more credit than he is due. She covers it up so well that no one else has a clue what she's experiencing.

I got more and more headaches. My back ached, so I started to get weekly massages, which made Howard complain. My shoulder "froze" so I went to the chiropractor. My digestion gave me fits, so I went to the naturopath. I needed a couple of glasses of wine to make it through the evening, or I couldn't sleep. While Howard watched TV non-stop, then later immersed himself in his computer, I managed the evening chores: homework, bathing, folding clothes, and cleaning up the kitchen. A sustainable life this was not. Clearly, I was losing it.

This is how coercive control works: The victim keeps thinking that she just has to work harder and faster to make things right. She believes that she and her spouse only do things differently, not that he is unreasonable. She gives him more credit than he is due. She covers it up so well that no one else has a clue what she's experiencing.

The controlling partner is very effective at isolating his victim from social contact. Since Howard never wanted to socialize with anyone, if it hadn't been for my work, no one would have known I existed. By the time I'd had the courage to file for divorce, I'd felt like I'd been imprisoned in a Texas bunker with no idea what was happening in the outside world. No wonder I'd blown my cork and slugged Howard's secretary.

Blame the victim

For decades, I'd been blamed for: things I did not do; upsetting Howard; having a different opinion; wrongly wanting respect, and conjuring up dangerous and willful acts of independence. It has taken me many years to mostly recover from the brainwashing, although I still get triggered from time to time.

I may muse over a past event with a nagging feeling that it was no small thing, but I can't put my finger on it. I know that it happened. I remember it. But to survive the brainwashing, I dissociated from the feelings I'd had at the time. I still suffer distress and terror, primary symptoms of Post-Traumatic Stress Disorder (PTSD).

When a victim has given up her confidence to an abuser, she is no longer able to judge for herself; hence the victim quietly puts the memory away for self-preservation. As she recovers, little by little, she starts to realize that her memories are real and that she was terrorized. Recovering the memories and accepting the truth is part of the recovery process for victims of brainwashing.

Memories from back then keep surfacing as I explore the layers of my guilt. As a psychologist, I know the guilt is an artifact of my empathic need to resolve the problems with my loved ones (more about the concept of guilt in the next section). When I'd finally realized that I had been conned, trashed, and abused, I saw that real resolution with an abuser is impossible.

Ironically, those memories now give me hope; because, rather than continuing to let them trigger guilt, they help me to accept that I was a good wife and mother, who did her best against high odds. I can even honor myself for going way above and beyond the call of duty. Here's an example of how I freed myself from blame and guilt.

Only recently did I remember, and piece together, what had happened during the early spring of 1997. I'd decided to clear out the overgrown and seldom-used side yard next to the garage on the far side of our house. As I turned the corner, I was curious about a black plastic tarp that was loosely thrown over a pile of something.

Since we'd had a large 1-acre lot covered with evergreen trees and rhododendrons, there was always a lot of post-winter cleaning up and hacking back the spring onslaught of blackberry and English ivy vines. I didn't remember putting a black tarp out there and figured it must have been put there by Howard. I decided to explore.

When I'd pulled the tarp back, I'd lost my breath. Next, I'd burst into tears. There in the side yard, where the rain had drenched them through fall and winter and into spring, were my parents' antique furniture and several cardboard boxes containing my childhood mementos; right where Howard had piled them up with great abandon. Under the black tarp, blown loose by rain and wind, things precious to me had been destroyed—deliberately.

"Howard!" I screamed as I went into the house to find him. He was sitting in front of his computer. With tears blurring my vision, I asked, "Howard, why did you put my parents' stuff and my childhood mementos out in the side yard?"

"What are you talking about?" Howard responded, taking a moment to turn away from his computer. He watched me blankly. I could tell he was not paying attention.

Distressed as I was at his lack of interest, I'd been forced to explain. "Howard, I found my stuff and Mom's furniture under a plastic tarp near the garage. Why would you have put this stuff out in the weather all winter?" I was incredulous and suffering. I still couldn't believe he'd done such a horrible thing.

"Oh that. You told me to," Howard said without a shred of empathy for my distress.

"What? Are you kidding me? I never told you to put my stuff out in the rain," I exclaimed, confronting the absurdity of his answer.

"Well you didn't tell me not to," he said coolly. I listened with disbelief. "Last summer you told me to move the stuff out of the garage to make space so that the remodeling contractors could work out there. I distinctly remember asking you what to do with that stuff. You told me it didn't matter, just that it needed to be out of the way. So I put it outside under a plastic tarp. It should all be okay." With a straight face, this grown man was telling me this ridiculous excuse.

I was angry now. "Howard," I continued, "Never in a million years did I dream that when I told you to move my stuff out of the way, you'd think it made a wit of sense to put it outside in the elements for six months. You put it on dirt, under an unsecured plastic tarp where the weather destroyed everything. My childhood scrapbooks. My dolls. The stuffed dog my mother gave to me when I was three. Mom's few cherished family heirlooms. All destroyed. I don't know what to do." I was heartbroken.

Howard stayed calm and cool; no remorse on his face and no hint of concern for me. He spoke in the same tone he would use with Phoebe on her birthday a decade later. He said, "Well then, you shouldn't have asked me to take care of it," then turned back to his computer.

> Nearly everything Howard focused on in those days demonstrated crazy-making, heartbreaking disregard for me. For years, I'd been hoodwinked into excusing his behavior as merely thoughtless or careless.

Thoroughly demoralized, I'd gone back outside and tried to save what I could of the mess. Nearly everything Howard focused on in those days demonstrated crazy-making, heartbreaking disregard for me. For years, I'd been hoodwinked into excusing his behavior as merely thoughtless or careless. Cruel domestic violence is what it really was; designed to destroy my confidence.

If I had called it what it is back then, I would have had to face that I was in a terrible bind. In truth, I wasn't that brave. Instead of acknowledging that I was living with a man who was destroying our children, and me, I'd put up with many more years of his cruelty.

Resilience ignited by guilt and Parental Alienation Syndrome (PAS)

I'm no longer embarrassed that it took me decades to wise up. Neither should any of you feel that way if you are a victim of coercion? It's not easy to trust yourself when your significant other is determined to undermine your sanity.

> I'm no longer embarrassed that it took me decades to wise up. Neither should any of you feel that way if you are a victim of coercion.

If you are up against a wily spouse, who knows how to use the legal system against you, it's significantly harder to break free. I have had women tell me there is no way they would file for divorce from their attorney spouse. One woman, an attorney herself, knows better than to challenge her husband, so she chooses to stay and suffer coercion. The kicker: Her husband is a judge!

> Guilt is an interesting phenomenon: It is a catalyst for resilience. If you can experience guilt, unlike those with EmD-1, you are capable of recognizing your part in a situation gone wrong.... It's guilt that signals our resilience and accountability to step up.

Howard and Townsend used their legal skills against me more than once. I was horrified to learn that the two of them had helped each other out by jointly victimizing me. In 2010 I'd filed a complaint with the Washington State Bar against Townsend for the libelous memo she'd helped Jacks write. That was when she'd appealed to Howard to provide evidence against me. In an email to Townsend, dated June 11, 2010, Howard agreed to help her out, writing, "I am sorry my ex is causing you more troubles."

Guilt is an interesting phenomenon: It is a catalyst for resilience. If you can experience guilt, unlike those with EmD-1, you are capable of recognizing your part in a situation gone wrong. That's how guilt teaches us to respond differently when something similar occurs. It's that guilt that signals our resilience and accountability to step up.

The desire to find a solution that's agreeable to the person harmed is also a byproduct of guilt. However, folks like Townsend and my ex-husband aren't interested in a win-win solution: It's a win-lose world for them. The more you compromise, the more they will take advantage of you.

In the email mentioned above, Howard had admitted that the Divorce Court eventually awarded me the things I'd tried to take from his office. Even more telling is how he'd relished the fact that I'd broken some of that stuff in "my rage." He'd taken no responsibility for lying to me and setting me up.

The year 2005 held a major lesson for me regarding the resilience necessary to combat EmD-1 people. Still, it ended sadly. I took both girls to Kauai to celebrate Bianca's high school graduation.

The trip had proved too much for Bianca, my autistic child. The heat, the bugs, the people all terrified her. I tried in vain to find something she would enjoy in that tropical paradise: a visit to the arboretum or a catamaran cruise to see ocean wildlife. Even when dolphins were jumping and spinning off the bow of our boat, Bianca chose to remain below deck safely reading a book.

Hardly a day went by when Bianca didn't devolve into an autistic meltdown, throwing herself to the floor crying, sobbing, and screaming. One time, hotel security came to our room to investigate because neighboring hotel guests had called with concern. Later, we nearly missed our plane at the Kauai airport: Bianca had a meltdown when I temporarily misplaced her passport.

When we got home from what should have been the trip of a lifetime, I called Howard and asked him to take Bianca for a couple of weeks. Phoebe and I both needed a break from Bianca's rage-infused abuse. I love Bianca, and I understand that her autistic nervous system gets overwhelmed. Enduring her spells was none the less harmful to my own nervous system.

Howard had agreed to my request, a little too readily in hindsight. The next week, I got a FAX from Howard saying that he was out of the country and had left Bianca with a house sitter. He specified: (1) I would be unable to reach him; hence ruin his vacation; and (2) that his housesitter had been instructed to call the police if I attempted to go to his house and bring Bianca home. His cruelty left me traumatized. Thinking of my autistic daughter being left alone with a stranger was terrifying.

Bianca never returned home. Howard has been quite effective at alienating her from me. I've made several attempts to reconcile with Bianca and have now waited more than 11 years to hear from her. My heart continues to feel broken, but my deep love for my oldest child remains unchanged. The difference now is that I no longer feel guilty about what happened to separate us.

I wish I could say that the guilt vanished easily, but it has been a slow process. It has taken many years to move on in my life—without Bianca. Without a way to speak with her or to get past Howard's grip on her mind, I finally had to accept that I did all I could and a lot more than "a little bit more." I was valiant. Even then, this mother couldn't win all of the battles.

This points to another phenomenon that was playing out then. It's called Parental Alienation Syndrome (PAS), and it is the result of long-term brainwashing. Howard was a PAS black belt.

Parental Alienation Syndrome (PAS) Primer

PAS is a type of domestic violence where one parent uses the children as a weapon to destroy the other parent. Sadly, it is often very effective, sometimes causing lifetime estrangement. Both the children and the targeted **parent are vulnerable because of the fear and chaos aroused by the EmD-1 parent (like my ex, Howard)**

He did everything in his power to keep me from my daughters. He refused to allow me contact with Bianca. He rejected Phoebe for years, which broke her heart and made her vulnerable to alienation, too. Howard supported my neighbors and the City officials who maligned me, especially regarding my parenting skills.

He withdrew financial support for our children, forcing me to work excessive hours to make ends meet. He was so effective at convincing others I was a terrible parent that his own divorce attorney, Danielle Liebman scolded my attorney, Bob Yoseph, for daring to represent me, "Why would you represent that bitch?" This lack of objectivity didn't seem a problem for Liebman, who went on to become a local judge

In spite of his callous abuse of his family, and even in our darkest moments with their father, I encouraged our daughters to stay connected with Howard. I'd wanted to make sure the girls knew they didn't have to choose between their parents. One example: shortly after we'd separated, the girls were visiting their father at his apartment when Howard had angrily kicked Bianca and knocked her to her knees (I'd filed a child abuse report, but since Howard knew the child abuse investigating team, it went nowhere).

Plus, Howard testified to the divorce judge that I was so difficult and he was so stressed by the divorce that he hadn't been able to help himself from accosting his daughter! The judge accepted this excuse. I, on the other hand, was not allowed to make these kinds of "mistakes." Nope, I'd been hauled off to jail.)

After a few days of cooling off, I arranged a meeting for the two of them at a safe and public place. At first, Bianca had refused. I knew that avoiding her father would never help her to resolve the abuse he'd inflicted on her; so, I insisted she meet Howard at an IHOP® restaurant in Vancouver. I'd done all of this in spite of Howard filing a complaint against me for interfering in his parenting rights. Completely unable to accept responsibility for assaulting Bianca, Howard had even asked the court to split up our daughters, preferring to take Phoebe and leave Bianca with me. This was an obvious ploy to eliminate his child support payment.

Later, on another visit, when he'd refused to send Bianca home, he'd promptly cut off all child support payments. He'd assumed that if Phoebe lived with me and Bianca with him, it would split the difference financially; hence he wouldn't have to pay me a dime more for their care. (I never told the girls about their father's narcissism.)

When Howard and Bianca had ignored Phoebe for years, I still drove Phoebe to Howard's house, so she could leave gifts for their birthdays and holidays. Yes, we had to package the gifts in black garbage bags and throw them over a locked gate, but we made an effort anyway. (Neither Howard nor his wife, Susan, would open the door for Phoebe.) I wanted Phoebe to know that I supported the love she had for her father and her sister.

It hadn't occurred to me that Howard would not honor his duty as a father. It took many years for me to give up trying to overcome his mulishness about Bianca after she'd gone to live with him. When I'd asked Howard for time with Bianca to celebrate her twenty-first birthday, he'd sent a curt email, "Bianca doesn't want to see you." He'd made no effort to help our autistic daughter resolve problems with her estranged mother.

Even worse was his behavior when Phoebe was delivering her first baby, our first grandchild. Phoebe had needed an emergency caesarian delivery, requiring several units of blood. Baby Jameson was in the neonatal intensive care unit for a couple of days.

Despite these harrowing circumstances, Howard refused to visit his daughter in the hospital—unless I guaranteed that I would not be there lest we see each other. Even at this special (and critical) time in his daughter's life, Howard had insisted on using the fictional excuse that I was too dangerous for him to be around. These tactics are very common among abusers who employ PAS. It is nearly impossible to fight back if you are up against a powerful ex-spouse, with political, legal and financial resources.

While writing this book, I heard from a former babysitter who had lived with us for a year.[34] Somehow she'd learned that I was estranged from both of my daughters and could hardly believe it. She wrote:

> *"When I lived with your family 25 years ago, I sincerely thought that your girls would have a brilliant future. They were beautiful and clever, and they had a great strong mother who worked hard to reach freedom as a woman. But I should admit that I always thought Howard was a strange, crazy guy. [However] I couldn't have imagined this sad outcome. Let's keep faith that one day things will change and time will bring Phoebe and Bianca a better life."*

This message brought me much comfort! She was only 22 when she'd lived with us; however, she'd known what hell my life had been then. It also confirms what psychotherapist Sarah Swenson meant when she wrote that women who leave these EmD-1 relationships lose twice.[35]

To escape a spouse's coercive control and reclaim her spirit, a woman divorces. Then, most of the time, she also loses her children. After growing up in an environment where their mother endured chronic disrespect, children can come to believe that Mom deserved it.

---

[34] She was a young woman from Portugal who had lived with us for a year to practice her English and learn about American culture.

[35] Swenson, Sarah. (April 20, 2016). "Married with Undiagnosed ASD: Why Women Who Leave Lose Twice" in www.goodtherapy.org

The babysitter echoed my belief in resilience and affirmed that I'd done the right thing to leave. I hope that by remaining tough—and refusing to cave to brainwashing and coercive control—I've helped my daughters to achieve a better life.

"Brainwashing Mom" Highlights

1. Brainwashing, brain fog, and gaslighting are all tools of coercive control. They can be used by any dysfunctional EmD. The most coercive control is employed by EmD-1s to inflict mental abuse. Living with this is a mind-numbing experience.

2. The terms narcissist and sociopath (or even malignant narcissist) are not mental diagnoses. Rather they are symptoms of those with EmD-0 through EmD-4.

3. Coercive control is almost invisible to others and often surfaces when the victim strikes back.

4. The target of coercive control is usually a woman with children, who is kind, nurturing, hardworking, and prone to seek win-win solutions.

5. Coercive control starts imperceptibly as the victim accepts one demeaning experience after another. She becomes willing to accept almost any abuse because she has been primed for it.

6. Coercive control is complete when the victim no longer trusts her perception of reality.

7. Those victimized by coercive control are more susceptible to other dysfunctional EmDs. Thus the abuse cycle repeats.

8. Guilt is a tool of competency. We tend to feel guilty for the bad that happens to us and our loved ones. Oddly, the guilt gives us hope that we can correct the problem.

9. Most victims of coercive control have incredible resilience. The ticket is to use it to break away from the abuser and start life anew.

CHAPTER FOUR
My Daughter Is Autistic

"Are you proud of yourself tonight that you have insulted a total stranger whose circumstances you know nothing about?"

— **Harper Lee's** *character Atticus Finch in her novel " To Kill a Mockingbird"*

Empathy Dysfunction score? Zero. (EmD-Zero)

Bianca, the author's oldest, and estranged, daughter has the challenge of living with Autism Spectrum Disorder. When Bianca and other autistics miss intuitive and nonverbal communication cues, they are left stranded and unable to navigate social interaction. Often, these misfires send autistics into dramatic emotional meltdowns like the one Bianca is experiencing in this photo.

Polar opposites in many ways, narcissists and autistics do share one thing: severe Empathy Dysfunction. The critical difference is that autistics have zero degrees of empathy. Narcissists can understand another's point of view even when it's not relevant to their goals. Sociopaths, on the other h and, also understand a lot about you; but they absorb and use this information to make you the target for their charm and harm.

The last thing autistics want is to cause harm. They really do want to connect and belong to a family. With zero degrees of empathy, this is a painful struggle.

Another key difference is that autistics can develop a moral code and often have a strong sense of justice while EmD-1s consider this a tedious goal. This moral code is what guides the autistic's actions when they struggle to understand another's feelings or point of view.

As long as those with autism clearly see that they are doing the right thing—and they get feedback that they are not harming others—they can navigate the social world.

> **This moral code is what guides the autistic's actions when they struggle to understand another's feelings or point of view.**
>
> **As long as those with autism clearly see that they are doing the right thing—and they get feedback that they are not harming others—they can navigate the social world.**

The problem is that the rest of us interact with others using a variety of intuitive, non-verbal communications bathed in reciprocal empathy.

When autistics miss these cues, they can become emotionally overwhelmed. Often, the sad result is that they shut down, or are marginalized by others, because of their inability to track social interaction.

In this chapter, I guide you through a tiny slice of the world of my autistic daughter, Bianca. She is typical of those brilliant, sweet, creative autistic people struggling to find their footing in the world. Even though Bianca has forsaken me, I will welcome her back when she is ready to let her mom love her again.

Frightening and frightened

One of the great tragedies of my life is the loss of my daughter Bianca. When she was 18, under pressure from her father, she chose to abandon me. Howard took her to live with him and refused to allow me contact—yet another demonstration of the coercive control he exerted over me.

I have made many efforts to reconcile with Bianca over the years to no avail: She and her father hold firm in the position that I am dangerous. I don't know if Bianca realizes her father is telling her lies about her mother; however, I fear after all of these years, the parental alienation is complete, leaving little hope for she and I to reconcile.

Bianca is my oldest daughter, about age 17 in the photo above. She suffers from Asperger Syndrome, or high-functioning autism, as it's now classified under the umbrella of Autism Spectrum Disorder (ASD). Bianca is brilliant, having taught herself to read before kindergarten!

Still, I think it is a misnomer to classify individuals with Asperger's as "high-functioning" when these sufferers experience extreme emotional outbursts known as "meltdowns." Bianca is anything but high-functioning when she loses emotional self-control, then collapses into fear and rage. Autism may be the only empathy disorder that is as terrifying for the family as it is for the autistic.

Let me take you through one of my daughter's meltdowns. The purpose isn't to shock you or to gain your sympathy. It is to help you know the mind of an autistic, who lacks the empathy to understand herself, let alone her mother. With EmD-Zero, the autistic is trapped in a confusing and chaotic world of unnamed, and sometimes unchecked, emotions.

Even with the ability to feel empathy, I'd felt trapped: I didn't know how to enter the world of my enraged and frightened daughter to help her out of her misery. In this chapter, you will observe that even when empathy is offered, it does nothing to sooth the broken heart of an autistic child—especially one who has lost faith in her mother's love.

Bianca and I were very close. She'd come to depend on me to protect her from the world and guide her through difficult social situations. When I couldn't protect her from her father and later from the frightening neighborhood battles, Bianca's faith in me was snuffed out.

Rage, bluster, and tears

One time, when Bianca came into my home office in the throes of a meltdown I'd felt terrified—like I was being hunted by those smart, birdlike velociraptor dinosaurs seen hunting in packs in the movie "Jurassic Park." She'd looked crazed as she'd lunged at me.

For some reason, she had disintegrated into an emotional storm earlier in the afternoon. It might have been triggered by her younger sister's taunting. Or because she was hungry. Or as a result of a simple misunderstanding with me. In any case, Bianca had been furious, first dissolving into tears, then escalating into a rage.

I'd tried comforting her, but nothing I said had helped. My attempts to soothe her had only enraged her more. She'd screamed louder and cried harder. When I'd walked away to give her space, Bianca had followed me around the house, accusing me of being a terrible mother. At one point, she'd repeated an oft-used phrase, "If you loved me, you would kill me!"[36]

---

[36] Sadly, Bianca would manipulate me with this threat. It was a double bind: If I protested that I didn't want her to talk like that, she would twist that into a lack of understanding on my part.

I'd ignored her crazy tirade while attempting to stay neutral. Calmly, I'd asked, "Would you like something to eat?" I'd hoped that a snack would distract her from her rage.

Continuing, I'd offered another suggestion, "Would you like some Klonopin? (This is a type of tranquilizer prescribed by her psychiatrist for times like these to help her relax.) I can bring you a cold washcloth for your face. How about if you go to your room and get some rest? We can talk later."

I knew better than to offer Bianca physical comfort during these times. She did not like to be touched. In the past, she had clawed at me and put her hands around my neck as if to strangle me. So I'd stayed clear, near enough to talk to her, but far enough away to avoid injury.

> **I knew better than to offer Bianca physical comfort during these [meltdown] times. She did not like to be touched. In the past, she had clawed at me and put her hands around my neck as if to strangle me.**

With scary, mind-blowing Aspie logic, she'd retorted, "Just like you to try to get rid of me. You don't care about me. All you care about is what the neighbors will think!" (By the way, "Aspie" is a term invented by those with Asperger Syndrome, so it is not a sign of disrespect).

After another hour or so of this impenetrable illogic and emotional abuse, I'd caved to her bullying and tried to make my escape. I'd gone to my office at the top of the stairs, closed my door and locked it. I'd thought, or rather hoped, that Bianca would take my cue to go to her room. Instead, Bianca had followed me up the stairs while issuing loud, blood curdling screams. When I'd shut the door, she'd pounded it with her bare fists. She'd demanded that I let her in and "Stop being a coward." I'd felt bewildered, frightened, and hunted.

Sitting in my desk chair at my computer, I'd listened to the frightening screams and the pounding thuds on the door. My door is very robust; if Bianca kept beating it, her hands would be bloodied and bruised. If I'd let her in, I—or both of us—could have been injured.

It was at times like these when I'd wished for a supportive spouse to help me. Even before we'd divorced, Howard had ignored Bianca's meltdowns unless she attacked him. Then he'd screamed as loudly as his daughter, often hitting or kicking her. Too often, I'd literally been trapped between these two as their empathy disorders festered and burst.

With trepidation, I'd decided to unlock the door to Bianca. Before I did, I'd looked helplessly around my office for anything that might protect me. I'd gravitated toward the new camera I had been testing out. (It's one of those waterproof cameras that I'd dreamt of using when taking my children on river rafting trips—like that happy delusion would ever happen.)

I'd picked up the camera, placed it in the "point-and-shoot" position in my hand, and slowly walked toward the door. I'd even glanced over my shoulder to count the steps necessary to make

During one of her daughter's autistic meltdowns, the author, desperate to shield herself from a possible physical assault, grabbed her camera and instinctively raised it to the point-and-shoot position in front of her face.
As Bianca had advanced, and her high-pitched velociraptor-like screams escalated, the author snapped a series of photos. This picture and those that follow depict the extremity of Bianca's rage.

a quick retreat to my chair. I can't figure out why I thought my chair would be a safe place. I guess it was the only thing in the room that represented comfort to me.

She's hunting me, her own mom

Bracing myself for Bianca's explosion, I unlocked the door. The first photo I snapped appears earlier in this chapter. It is a bit blurry; I'd been scared and trying to maneuver backward to my chair. As predicted, Bianca looked like she was on the hunt.

Oddly, her passion was dinosaurs, and the velociraptor topped her list. (This kind of fixation is also known as a "special interest" in the autism literature.) She'd even pretended to scream like a velociraptor. It is the most frightening thing to hear your daughter's screams, then to realize that she is yelling at and hunting you!

Bianca seemed startled when I'd snapped that first picture. "What are you doing?" she snarled. I'd felt a sense of relief since that was a sign Bianca was again coherent. She stopped her attack behavior enough to ask a question. Photographing Bianca seemed to be working, so I took another picture. Even though she'd burst into yet another blood curdling velociraptor scream, I'd kept taking pictures. And with each photo snapped, she stopped moving toward me for a moment. I managed to get the upper hand—barely.

Life-and-death struggle with herself

"What are you doing?" Bianca had asked again, still hostile.

"I'm taking your picture," I'd replied without further explanation. Neutral, stay neutral. I'd been trying to follow the advice I give my clients.

"Go ahead and take my picture!" she'd shrieked. "Take all the pictures you want. I don't care." She'd now been ranting and struggling for hours. She'd tossed her head backward, her long beautiful hair sweaty and tousled, a mirror of her tangled emotions. I could see she was still tormented. But there was more. The grimace on her face was proof that she'd been trying to choke back her emotions. She'd stopped her attack on me and entered into a life-and-death struggle with herself.

The grimace on Bianca's face showed that she'd been trying to choke back her emotions during the autistic meltdown she was experiencing.

Relief is at hand

Bianca had then stood in front of me as if posing for another photo. I'd taken it. I had successfully protected myself from my daughter with my camera.

I fear for Bianca when she is in the throes of palpable agony, but my fear of my daughter had been greater. I'd been willing to hold my ground because I'd hoped she would find her way out of her Hell and back to me.

Thinking back on this episode with her autistic daughter, the author candidly revealed, "'I fear for Bianca when she is in the throes of palpable agony, but my fear of my daughter had been greater."

She inflicts pain on herself

Swiftly, Bianca had reached under her damp hair, grabbed a chunk and pulled it out by the roots. Like a hunter or warrior, she'd displayed the stands of hair as symbolic of a coup.

But hers had been a crazy, self-inflicted coup. Bianca had turned on herself in a hateful display. The pain of torn hair had been preferable to the pain in her mind. I'd felt safe then, but at a horrible price: watching my daughter in such torment and being unable to do anything to help but take pictures. It feels that way all over again as I write about the event.

Swiftly, Bianca reached under her damp hair, grabbed a chunk and pulled it out by the roots. Like a hunter or warrior, she'd displayed the stands of hair as symbolic of a coup. The pain of torn hair had been preferable to the pain in her mind.

Finally, she looks at me

For the first time in hours, Bianca looked at me. Her tear-streaked face was puffy and red, but she'd finally looked at me,

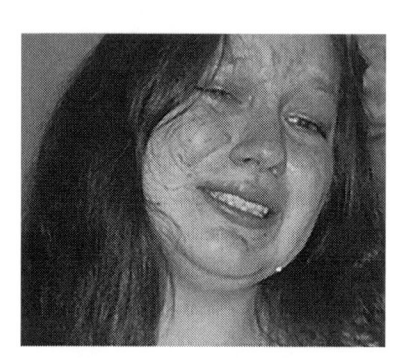

After hours of autistic raging, Bianca finally makes eye contact with her mother.

actually looked at me. The rage was gone, and I could see some light in her eyes again.

I'd known then that she was back in her body instead of possessed by her unmanageable primitive emotions. Together we'd fought the demons in her mind. It had been a victory of sorts.

At last, her spirit is soothed

As Bianca let the tears flow, she'd self-soothed by stroking her beautiful chestnut hair. I'd risen from my chair, the camera still in my hand in case I should need it for protection again. I'd held back my tears as I'd asked her, "Would you like to sit down? Why don't you sit on Mom's couch?"

Bianca had obliged but said nothing. She'd kept sobbing.

Gently, I'd put the camera back on my desk and picked up a box of tissues. "Would you like a tissue?" I'd asked, slowly moving the box out in front of Bianca as a gesture of peace.

Bianca had taken the box and put it in her lap.

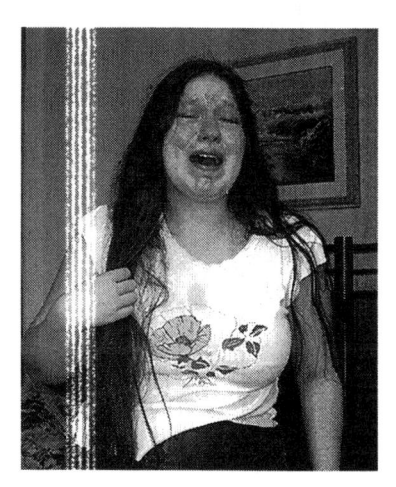

As Bianca let the tears flow, she'd self-soothed by stroking her beautiful chestnut hair. . . . My arm around her as she'd rested her head on my shoulder, I'd cried softly. . . . My little girl had at last been able to allow herself to feel comforted. She'd needed my strength, and I'd provided it. Seldom are autistics aware that accepting another's love can be an antidote for their agony.

I moved over to the couch and, ever so gently, lowered myself down to the cushion. Even a subtle movement could reignite a meltdown. This time Bianca had allowed me to sit next to her. I'd pulled a tissue from the box and handed it to Bianca. She'd accepted it.

"Why don't you blow your nose, honey?" 'I'd asked. Then, I'd taken a handful of tissues and wiped the tears and snot from her face.

My arm around her as she'd rested her head on my shoulder, I'd cried softly. My love for her had washed over me. My little girl had at last been able to allow herself to feel comforted. She'd needed my strength, and I'd provided it. Seldom are autistics aware that accepting another's love can be an antidote for their agony.

I'd let my tears fall then. We'd sat there for a while, feeling the aftermath and allowing the love to seep in. Eventually, I'd asked her to go back downstairs with me to her bedroom where she could rest. I'd brought her a damp washcloth to soothe her burning eyes. She'd agreed to take a Klonopin, then crawled into bed. With her spirit soothed, she'd soon been asleep.

What's empathy got to do with it?

The underlying reason for an autistic's meltdown is an overly sensitive nervous system that is a set up for sensory overload. Years of feeling misunderstood and alone contribute to an Aspie's defensiveness.

The underlying reason for an autistic's meltdown is an overly sensitive nervous system that is a set up for sensory overload. Years of feeling misunderstood and alone contribute to an Aspie's defensiveness. In Bianca's case, there is also a high IQ, which leaves her with a Mr. Spock[37] command of logic yet no skills to reason herself out of agony.

I believe that EmD-Zero explains it all. Meltdowns are the product of the unbearable emotional load that the autistic carries each and every day. Trying to navigate the emotional meanings that dominate our social world is horrendous for Aspies.

They don't read between the lines. They rarely catch the non-verbal cues that signify a potent moment between people. When Aspies do try to engage, often they are rebuffed because their comments are a little off or because, well, they have an odor.

Many Aspies are unable to remember why it is important to shower or change clothes. (Notice in the photos, the yellow splotch on Bianca's T-shirt, acquired from a long-ago spill and her subsequent—and common—failure to put on clean clothes for days.) She'd seldom showered unless I insisted.

After all, social skills and etiquette serve no purpose for the autistic.

After all, social skills and etiquette serve no purpose for the autistic.

Ill-equipped to comprehend how the rest of us relate many Aspies prefer to be alone. Bianca wanted to eat in her room instead of with the family. She preferred the comfort of her obsessively cluttered bedroom, surrounded by things she loved, such as her computer, her tunes, and her stacks of magazines.

---

[37] *Mr. Spock* is the resolutely logical human-Vulcan first officer of the U.S.S. Enterprise starship in the science fiction television series and movie "Star Trek."

The first step to empathy is knowing, honoring, and caring for the feelings that matter to loved ones—similar to stepping into another person's shoes. This kind of recognition is vital to feeling loved. Lovers report that they finish each other's sentences. Childhood chums become friends for life because of shared experiences that still delight them.

The second step is being able to acknowledge what's in the heart and mind of someone else. An Aspie might be able to repeat a story from childhood or be able to pick out an appropriate birthday present, but it's decorum that means everything. Reciting an embarrassing childhood moment at a funeral, or giving the same gift as in a previous year might be frowned on by others. Empathy then is the ability to read the current context appropriately and respond with respect and love.

> **The second step [to empathy] is being able to acknowledge what's in the heart and mind of someone else. . . . Empathy then is the ability to read the current context appropriately and respond with respect and love.**

The third step is even more difficult for Aspies. It requires having self-knowledge. Empathic individuals know how they feel in relation to others. They hold constant how they feel and think, while they plumb the depths of the other person. Empathic people know that understanding the mind of another is not tantamount to agreeing with their beliefs or principles.

EmD-Zero people believe that to voice their understanding means they are indicating agreement. To them, apologizing equates to admitting wrongdoing and having the intent to harm. Aspies fail to process that if they employ empathic listening, they're showing they value another person's existence.

The argument for self-knowledge

In struggling to contain her meltdown, Bianca had indicated the desire to be free of her self-inflicted torment. At first, she'd blamed me for her distress. She'd wanted to punish me for somehow letting her down.

As Bianca had matured, she'd needed to find ways to cope without my help. She'd realized that Mother couldn't always be alongside. Plus, Mother had been proven fallible.[38]

How can Bianca conquer this task of growing up and taking responsibility for the outcome of her EmD-0 life?[39]

We've seen her induce physical pain to interrupt her destructive attack: When she'd yanked out a hunk of her hair, endorphins (the body's natural pain reliever) had flooded her system, helping to calm her down. But that was not truly empathy.

---

[38] I was fallible in the sense that I could not always take away Bianca's pain. Like all teenagers, she had to come to the realization that her mother cannot make her life. Growing up requires individuation and independent thinking. Without empathy, Bianca relied too heavily on me. Eventually that system had to break down.

[39] I recommend coaching to help young adults with Aspergers learn the tools they need to function independently. I call these aids ROE, or Rules of Engagement. It is far easier for autistics to learn rules than to consider how their behavior affects others. If Bianca had accepted coaching, she could have learned to measure her emotions and practice self-interventions that were less volatile. For example, Bianca could have assessed, or her mother could have asked, how distressed she was at any time, based on a 1-5 intensity scale. Next, Bianca could have turned to a list of alternative behaviors (a time out, listening to music, taking a walk, drawing) to reduce her anxiety. John Gottman, a psychologist in Seattle, Wash., has his patients wear pulse meters. He instructs them to take a break with one of their personal calm-myself-down behaviors when their pulse rate is greater than 100.

When you have empathy and act empathically, self-knowledge develops plus you know where you stand. We compare how feelings and thoughts affect us and others. Through this back-and-forth reasoning, dialog and debate we define who we are.

Absent the wiring for empathy, autistics resort to a rigid sense of morality to guide them. Rules and structure make sense and feel safe to them.

The variable emotionality of those with empathy makes no sense to Aspies. According to "Star Trek's" Mr. Spock, "Humans are illogical." Aspies would agree.

Meltdown or temper tantrum?

I'd like to step aside for a moment and help you understand the difference between a meltdown and a temper tantrum. While temper tantrums are a behavior typical of young children who have not yet learned to regulate their emotions, meltdowns are a symptom of Autism Spectrum Disorder (ASD).

Meltdowns are not developmentally normal and cannot be resolved with psychological behavior management strategies (such as placing the child in time out). The cause of meltdowns is an overly sensitive nervous system that periodically gets overloaded and erupts like a volcano, flooding the individual with extremely painful feelings. I heard one Aspie describe the meltdown he'd had in an airport as the sensation of a burning band of fire encircling and squeezing his head.

A meltdown's frightening thoughts also cloud judgment. Bianca, at times like these, had threatened to kill herself or demanded that I do so. As you saw with Bianca's meltdown, she could only disrupt her tirade by yanking out her hair. She must have had some intuitive awareness that she could not think straight unless she caused herself the kind of pain that releases endorphins.

I'd been working in my yard when I got the call from the triage nurse at SW Washington Medical Center (in Vancouver, Wash.). She told me that the police had brought Bianca to the emergency room. I was only to learn the whole horrible story once I got to the ER. Fortunately, I was only 15 minutes away. (This was in 2003 during my marital separation.)

> She must have had some intuitive awareness that she could not think straight unless she caused herself the kind of pain that releases endorphins.

The girls had been staying with their father that weekend. With Phoebe off with soccer friends, Bianca had been alone. A meltdown ensued. Inexplicably, in the middle of Bianca's obvious strife and pain, Howard had decided to leave Bianca by herself and attend a party with his girlfriend, Susan Keller.

Howard made a grave error leaving his autistic child alone in a strange apartment instead of calling me; apparently, Susan thought this was reasonable, too. After they'd left for the party, the apartment neighbors became alarmed by the escalation of Bianca's bloodcurdling screams; so they called the police.

The officers were able to calm Bianca enough to find out that she didn't live alone in the apartment and that she had her father's cell phone number. They called Howard, who was half way to the party by then (about 30 minutes away).

When they asked Howard to return home and care for his distraught daughter—instead of complying—he gave them an improbable excuse: He was too far away to come home and it would be very late in the evening before he would be returning. This, even though the police told him that they couldn't leave Bianca alone because of her extreme distress and would have to take her to the hospital. At the ER, the triage nurse also tried calling Howard: Again, he declined to return for his daughter.

As Bianca's meltdown cleared a bit and she became calmer, she was able to tell the nurse that her mother was nearby, only 15 minutes from the hospital. When I got the call, I dropped my garden tools and rushed to the hospital, not even stopping to wash my hands.

I had no idea what to expect when I got to the ER. Thank goodness, the nurses were experienced in managing patients with autism. Bianca seemed to be in good shape in spite of the meltdown. She was eating a snack and sipping 7-Up when I found her sitting in an unlocked "mental health" room.

As I arranged for Bianca's release, the nurse took me aside to speak privately out of Bianca's earshot. This was when I learned how she had come to be at the hospital and how Howard had abandoned his child. The nurse whispered, "You know, it concerns me that Bianca's father has no understanding of how to handle your daughter when she is having a meltdown. It is very odd that he refused to come to the hospital. I am worried that Bianca is not safe in his care. Are you aware of this problem?"

Wow! Years ago I had been a child protective services

caseworker. I'd had to ask the very same questions. It had been tough: I hadn't wanted a parent to feel accused of failing to protect their child while, at the same time, I'd had to determine if they understood the dangers. Now, the nurse was just doing her job, and thank goodness she took it seriously.

"Yes," I told her. "This is why I am divorcing Howard. Thank you for being there for Bianca. I appreciate it." I wanted to get out of that hospital though. I wanted to get Bianca home and settled down from this nightmarish experience.

I can certainly understand why meltdowns are confusing to neighbors and the police. I was soundly criticized many times by total strangers when Bianca erupted into a meltdown in public.

Not infrequently, I'd had to rescue her from school when a teacher, or even a school counselor, felt threatened by her rages. Even Vancouver Prosecutor Josephine Townsend had hurled accusations that my daughter's autistic meltdowns were somehow my fault.

After all the years of living with Bianca, all the special education services and mental health treatment, it still hadn't occurred to Howard that his daughter was disabled! Why couldn't he get it? Empathy Dysfunction?

I called Howard to tell him that I was taking Bianca home. He seemed unconcerned. Again, I heard him say that everything had been fine when he left her and that things had been blown out of proportion.

How could I leave my precious and fragile child in the care of this man? How could he have no understanding of his daughter's disability? If he hadn't intended to care for her, wanting to attend the party instead, why hadn't he at least called me?

Why had he insisted on the fiction that Bianca had no special needs when we went to court for our divorce? Had he been more concerned about avoiding child support payments than with the welfare of his daughter?

Living with this abuse left me shell shocked for years. It was so very painful to: endure Bianca's meltdowns; be unable to help my daughter when she suffered; and endure the total disregard of a father for his daughter.

Utterly rejected

Whether or not Bianca has reconciled her EmD-0, I have no idea: She decided to cut me off entirely 11 years ago. I've had absolutely no contact. I used to send her emails and birthday gifts. I've sent her money and tickets to events that I thought she would enjoy.

My outreach dwindled to the occasional card when I got nothing back. Eventually, I stopped trying to contact her. I learned through the grapevine that Bianca no longer considers me her mother. One of her last communications to me was a hateful letter in which she called me a "fuckwit." Aspies are very creative at making up words.

This rift came about on the heels of a trip to Hawaii. I'd taken Bianca and her sister to Kauai to celebrate Bianca's graduation from high school. (Bianca received a Special Education Diploma because of her autism.)

It had been a struggle to keep her in school. Often, I'd completed her homework for her. I'd hired many tutors, nearly every one quitting in a huff when Bianca harangued or threw books at their head. I'd been called to school many times to help teachers with Bianca's meltdowns. In spite of their special education training, these teachers hadn't hesitated to call me in a panic when they'd felt threatened by Bianca. One school psychologist had called campus security when Bianca had refused to leave her office peacefully.

When Bianca officially graduated, I'd been so relieved: I'd wanted to celebrate. I hadn't thought about whether or not Bianca would like an exotic trip to Kauai. I'd wanted only to share a beautiful experience with both of my daughters. That just hadn't been in the cards.

Bianca was frightened the entire time we were in Kauai. She was so distressed that she screamed every day. She was so loud that our hotel neighbor called security. When we were in the airport and heading home, I temporarily misplaced her passport. At this, Bianca screamed uncontrollably. The airport was on a security Yellow Alert already; hence I'd been terrified that we'd be held for questioning.

When all of us were finally on the airplane, I gave Bianca a Klonopin to help her sleep during the return flight. What a nightmare the entire trip had been.

Once safely home in Vancouver, I called Bianca's father and begged him to take Bianca for two weeks, so that my other daughter, Phoebe, and I could have a respite. Howard lived 10 minutes away yet hadn't had a visit with either of them for two or three years. He'd always had excuses, but this time he agreed.

I'd felt a hint of suspicion when Howard had been so cooperative; with good reason, it would turn out. Within a couple of days, Howard sent a fax telling me that he and his new wife, Susan, were on a trip outside the United States and unreachable by phone or email. They'd left Bianca in the care of their house sitter!

In his fax, he said that he hadn't told me he was leaving the country because then I would have spoiled his vacation. (Yet another example of this man's coercive control.)

I was beside myself with fear about Bianca's well-being. I worried that she must feel utterly rejected. As soon as I'd read his email, I'd driven to Howard's house to try to speak with Bianca. There was no answer when I knocked on the door. Within a few minutes, the police arrived and told me that the house sitter had called them.

Apparently, Howard had left instructions with the house sitter to call the cops immediately if I showed up. The officers advised me to leave, or be arrested for trespassing.

How would Bianca know that: I still loved her even though I'd needed a break from her; it was sadistic for her father to leave her in the hands of a stranger; she was being used as a pawn by her father to punish me for our divorce; and the situation was devastating for her sister, too?[40]

How would Bianca possibly know how to repair the emotionally damaged relationship with her mother? She wouldn't, couldn't—instead believing that I had rejected her, wrecking our relationship. Period.

Politically incorrect

Several years after Bianca had left, I read a police report received as part of a public records request during one of my many legal battles. It stated that Howard had called the police shortly

---

[40] When Howard cut me off from seeing Bianca, he also cut off Phoebe. Bianca never contacted either of us after that. Years later, Phoebe saw Bianca at Clark College in Vancouver. She called me in a panic, not knowing what to do. Phoebe had said, "Bianca is in the student union, and I don't know if I should try to talk with her." I'd asked Phoebe if she wanted to approach her sister, and she'd said that she did. So I'd encouraged her to go to Bianca. When Phoebe approached Bianca and spoke to her, Bianca got up and ran out of the cafeteria.

after Bianca had started living with him. According to the report, Bianca had been in the middle of a meltdown. Howard had told the police that she suffered from Asperger Syndrome. He'd been frightened when Bianca had threatened the family and herself.

She'd told her father that she had hidden knives throughout the house and planned to use them. Reading this long after, I'd still felt horrified—yet relieved—that the police had not arrested her. I was sad that neither Howard nor Bianca had called me. I could have helped: I could have at least explained to the police that Bianca needed mental health services for extremely depressed people who also suffer from Asperger Syndrome. But they hadn't called me.[41]

Howard and Bianca continue to foster the fiction that I am somehow responsible for her mental illness. Having little or no empathy had set the stage for father and daughter to harbor a hostile and destructive attitude.

When I read about mass murders committed by young men with Asperger Syndrome, I have to admit that I get it. I know that: it is politically incorrect to say so; there is no evidence that autistics are more at risk for committing these crimes than anyone

---

[41] It had to have been incredibly frightening for Bianca to have her father call the police when she was having a mental health emergency. Even worse was to have totally unprepared and armed police officers confront her unusual behavior. There's an officer who wants to help prepare members of law enforcement for situations like this. Rob Zink of the St. Paul Police Department in Minnesota, started the "Cop Autism Response Education Project" to train officers on how to interact with autistic people. Having two sons on the Autism Spectrum, Zink knows that with autistics usual police tactics can make things much worse. See Steve Silberman, "The Police Need to Understand Autism," New York Times, Sept. 19, 2017.

else; and it takes a very depressed, deranged individual to commit such heinous crimes.

I do understand how Aspies can come to hate the people who love them. I have experienced this hatred firsthand. It is chilling. I still can't wrap my head around why my child wanted to harm me. It feels like being trapped in a windowless cell where I have no way out and no one who believes me or hears my pleas.

I can relate to the parents of these hateful, depressed and mentally ill young murderers. As I'd done, these parents: had tried everything to reach their troubled child; had been in denial about the intensity of their Aspie's anger; and had wondered why their love was not enough.

Parents and family members can be lost without: an understanding of Empathy Dysfunction and all of its caveats; and the support of professionals—who should have helped the troubled offspring early on. When vindictive ex-spouses meddle, the sense of loss and confusion is magnified.

> We just need to understand the phenomenon of Empathy Dysfunction, then be willing to take on the frightening and the frightened.

Every time I read of a new horrific disaster, I want to scream like one of Bianca's velociraptors. I think we can do far, far better to help these families. We just need to understand the phenomenon of Empathy Dysfunction, then be willing to take on the frightening and the frightened.

Loving Bianca through my writing

I have many wonderful memories of my daughter Bianca. I remember:

MY DAUGHTER IS AUTISTIC

- The sweet baby I held in my arms when we met, three days after she was born, and two days before we adopted her;
- How she wouldn't fall asleep until I placed her on my chest to hear my heartbeat;
- Her singing "Big Bugs. Small Bugs," in her darling little toddler voice;
- The way she held my hand when I guided her through a strange new experience;
- When she dressed up in my cast off high heels and played "Mommy;"
- Reading books together and laughing at the dialogue;
- Taking her on school field trips;
- When she enjoyed playing with her baby sister, Phoebe;
- Girl Scouts and flute lessons;
- Adventurous trips to dinosaur museums like Drumheller, in Alberta, Canada;
- Showing her Switzerland, Italy, and Mexico;
- Trips to Disneyland;

The author's daughters, Phoebe Marshack, the toddler, at left, and Bianca Marshack, approaching school age, on the right. Here they play happily on the lawn of their home. Photo taken by the Portuguese babysitter (Maria Fattima Coelho) who later wrote to the author, recalling the loving and strong mom she had been to the girls

- Watching Disney movies like "Little Mermaid" and "Dinosaur," and being delighted by Bianca's photographic memory;
- Deep conversations when Bianca wanted to talk about something she'd heard on NPR (National Public Radio);
- Her marvelous artistic ability. I am proud to have her art hanging on my walls to this day.

There is so much to love and remember about my daughter. It's her Empathy Dysfunction that keeps us apart and no longer able to share these memories. I am left alone. How do I sustain the flame of love when it is not reciprocated?

My work as a psychologist, helping those with autism and their families, keeps me moving forward. Working out how neurotypicals (NTs)[42] can come to understand and more easily survive their lives with Aspies is my passion these days.

I have written two books on this subject, and I hope they have helped readers.

"Going Over the Edge?" is about living life with a partner who has Asperger Syndrome (ASD).

"Out of Mind – Out of Sight" is about parenting with a partner who has Asperger Syndrome (ASD).

You can order both books from www.amazon.com (USA, UK, Germany, Australia and Canada) and on my website www.kmarshack.com.

---

[42] Neurotypical," or NT, refers to those who show typical neurological behavior and development. "Atypical" loosely refers to those with some degree of Autism Spectrum Disorder.

I have created an international Internet support group for those NTs who want to connect with others who understand intimately the woes of living with autism in the family. We meet in person, online, by monthly teleconferences, and through video webinars. To learn more, go to Asperger Syndrome: Partners and Family of Adults with Asperger Syndrome (ASD), http://www.meetup.com/Asperger-Syndrome-Partners-Family-of-Adults-with-ASD/.

When I was first coming to terms with my daughter's autism, there was no one to help me. There were no books, no autism-savvy psychotherapists, and no informative websites. Feeling alone with your troubles is the worst!

Since publishing my books and starting the support group, I have heard from people all over the world who are grateful for a place to share, talk, laugh, and cry about their challenging situations.

While this type of love is not the same as holding my child, kissing away her tears, and sharing in her triumphs, it is a form of humanitarian love. It is some satisfaction. Even at a distance, connecting with total strangers who understand the complexities of Empathy Dysfunction can mean a great deal.

> While this type of love [helping others through writing and counseling about autism and Empathy Dysfunction] is not the same as holding my child, kissing away her tears, and sharing in her triumphs, it is a form of humanitarian love. It is some satisfaction.

"My Daughter Is Autistic" Highlights

1. Autistics are an example of EmD-0. They do not usually mean to cause harm but may do so because of their social missteps.

2. Parental alienation is relatively easy to accomplish with autistic children. Their inability to ascertain when they are being lied to leaves autistics vulnerable to manipulation.

3. Autism is an empathy disorder that is as frightening for the family as it is for the autistic because it feels impossible to communicate across the great divide when zero degrees of empathy is in play.

4. Meltdowns are the result of sensory and incomprehensible emotional overload. An autistic person will scream, cry, and rejects all help from their loved ones. They can act hateful and be combative.

5. Seldom can you stop the escalation of a meltdown; however, you can try doing so by using a counter-intuitive maneuver. For example, it startled my daughter when I took her picture. Somehow, that triggered her brain to return to a calmer state.

6. Sadly, the autistic may engage in self-mutilation to stop the onslaught of psychological pain during one of these disastrous declines.

7. Parents of these children often walk on eggshells to avoid meltdowns, which leaves everyone feeling alone.

8. In spite of being excruciatingly sensitive, autistics cannot speak about their feelings in relation to others' feelings. Without empathy to serve as a floodgate, emotions can spill over full force anytime.

9. Moms and dads are often unfairly blamed by others—and the autistic— for not managing the autistic better.

10. Without empathy, autistics develop a rigid sense of morality, which is at least better than the abusive self-absorption of an EmD-1.

11. Parents and partners of EmD-0 family members often have PTSD as a result of years of emotional trauma.

12. One way to survive the trauma of relationships with EmD-0 individuals is to foster your creativity outside the relationship. Develop and demonstrate your talents.

CHAPTER FIVE

Impacted by Mild Traumatic Brain Injury

"When good people consider you the bad guy, you develop a heart to help the bad ones. You actually understand them.
— Criss Jami

Empathy as it comes and goes—EmD-2

Anyone who has cared for a family member with Alzheimer's, schizophrenia, or traumatic brain injury (TBI) has witnessed the expression of empathy come and go. The unpredictability of emotions and moods is extremely stressful and frightening for caregivers and relatives: They have no means to gauge what will happen next—or where and when.

> ...caregivers and relatives... have no means to gauge what will happen next—or where and when. I have classified these people as EmD-2 since they are unable to maintain empathy on a steady course.

I have classified these people as EmD-2 since they are unable to maintain empathy on a steady course. It is akin to EmD-0 where the presence of empathy cannot be forseen; however, EmD-2 is complicated by violence to self and others. A brain injury or a brain illness is often the underlying cause.

I had long suspected that my daughter Phoebe had mild traumatic brain injury as a result of repeated sports concussions, followed by alcohol abuse.

Knowing that she was in the grip of both a brain injury and a developmental disorder (ADHD and reading disability) had made it hard for me to blame Phoebe for the lapses in judgment and her aggressive, abusive conduct. Still, I'd had to learn to protect myself during her rages and violent acting out—whether she intended to harm me or not. Never knowing when a conversation, or a day, might go south is a constant conundrum for anyone who loves someone with EmD-2.

In this chapter, I will lead you through my awakening to Phoebe's condition. Having lived with an abusive mate and an autistic older child, I'd wanted so very deeply for my younger daughter to be spared. In many ways, her empathy disorder is the most confounding and heartbreaking of all: I blame myself for failing to help her sooner.

See footnote for source attribution[43]

Getting your "bells rung"

As I start this chapter, it is Super Bowl Sunday (Feb. 7, 2016). It's been two and a half years since I last saw Phoebe and her darling little boy, Jameson: He will be three

---

[43] By Source, <a href="//en.wikipedia.org/wiki/File:Super_Bowl_50_Logo.svg" title="Fair use of copyrighted material in the context of Super Bowl 50">Fair use</a>, <a href="https://en.wikipedia.org/w/index.php?curid=49296285">Link</a>

years old in a couple of days. Gosh, I remember when Phoebe was that young.

She was such a bright, shining little one. With her broad smile, sparkling eyes, and irresistible laugh, everyone had adored her.

She was very active unlike her older sister, who could content herself with reading and drawing.

Seeing what a natural athelete Phoebe was, I enrolled her in soccer as soon as she was old enough. She excelled and truly loved the sport. Plus, the camaraderie of the game was fun for the whole family: We parents connected on the sidelines, and the girls formed the lifelong bonds of childhood teammates.

Back then, I hadn't known that head injuries could cause such severe brain damage. I'd been a watchful mother during Phoebe's games, making sure she had nutritious snacks, lots of water, shade from the sun, and rest breaks. Concerned about concussion from the start, I'd told Phoebe—and her coaches—that she wasn't allowed to do "headers."

Her coaches had just laughed at me, then given me the usual lecture: Parents were supposed to stand back and let the coach be the judge of what was necessary or not.

One coach went so far as to say, "She's not working hard enough unless she gets her bells rung once in a while!" as if head injuries were a badge of honor.

Just the same, I'd privately told Phoebe she was forbidden to do headers. It turned out I couldn't protect her from others' plays. Head injuries, I'd learned, are inherent in a fast-paced team sport.

Phoebe got her first head injury when she was 8 years old. She had just rotated in as keeper[44] and was knocked to the ground when a ball hit her squarely in the forehead. I'd sprung to my feet, but other parents signaled me to sit down, implying that Coach would take care of her.

He'd hurried onto the field and knelt down beside my prostrate daughter. The coach had helped her stand up and was about to walk her off the field when Phoebe resisted. She'd been angry and ready to take on the other team single handedly. In spite of the rule that a player must come out of the game if the coach has to go onto the field for an injury, Phoebe had wanted to remain.

The other parents and Phoebe's teammates had jumped up and cheered her determination. With a smile of approval, the coach had let her play on. I'd tried to enjoy the rest of the game, but I'd had a nagging feeling about this decision. Had it been the right thing to do?

Today's Super Bowl Fifty marks the nation's annual tribute to the billion dollar National Football League (NFL). I have just finished posting no less than three protests decrying athletes' head injuries on Facebook.[45]

No one "likes" these posts of mine. The virtual crowd wants to celebrate a big sports event with the rest of the nation—without a cloud hanging over it.

---

[44] This refers to the goalkeeper, whose job it is to prevent the opposing team from landing the ball in the goal area.

[45] Protests that in spite of the evidence otherwise: the NFL was still trying to conceal the head injury issues; and parents were still registering their children for football and soccer even though coaches were doing little or nothing to protect these young players.

The majority of Americans continue to tune in or listen to the game even though we now know that repeated concussions suffered while playing contact sports can lead to tragic and incurable degenerative brain disease. The now-prevalent chronic traumatic encephalopathy (CTE) has been known to impact boxers since the 1920s. And still, football lovers ignore the inconvenient truth about concussions and thrill in America's favorite pastime.

That puts me alone this Sunday instead of watching the game and marveling at the halftime show with friends. Alternatively, and appropriately, I am writing this chapter of warning about head injuries in youth and adult athletes.

As I browse the *New York Times* online, I see irony in the headlines.[46] There are the usual gameday articles—"Super Bowl 50: Here's How the Panthers Will Beat the Broncos," and "Recipes for Super Bowl Game Day." Adjacent headlines suggest a different kind of football story: "The NFL's Tragic CTE Roll Call" and "The NFL's Next Play: Address Brain Trauma or Fade Away."

In the *"New York Times Magazine,"* I find one especially crazy-making story, entitled, "Roger Goodell's Unstoppable Football Machine," by author Mark Leibovich. Why crazy-making? Because, after a few years of lying and covering up the dangers to players from repeated concussions, NFL Commissioner Goodell has made an about-face.

He has admitted that CTE exists and does put players at risk. As well, he acknowledges that—instead of substantially changing the game to make it safer for players—the NFL can afford to pay out millions of dollars in concussion-related

---

[46] With annual Super Bowls, there are bound to be an endless number of these stories in the *New York Times* and other news media year in and year out.

compensation! After all, he doesn't work for the benefit of the players who take the hits; he works for the teams' billionaire owners.

Since starting this chapter on Super Bowl Sunday, I have read even more stories of professional, college and even high school athletes struck down by CTE. Not just football players: Athletes in all contact sports—hockey, soccer, and baseball—are being diagnosed with CTE. It's not just concussions that lead to the disorder.

> He [NFL Commissioner Roger Goodell] has admitted that CTE exists and does put players at risk. As well, he acknowledges that—instead of substantially changing the game to make it safer for players—the NFL can afford to pay out millions of dollars in concussion-related compensation!

CTE is actually much more likely to be found in soccer players and other athletes exposed to repetitive minor hits. Instead of pointing specifically to "concussion" as the cause, this is called Mild Traumatic Brain Injury (or Mild TBI). As if there is anything mild about CTE.

In March 2016, retired soccer player Brandi Chastain announced that she had agreed to donate her brain (upon her death) to the Concussion Legacy Foundation and researchers at Boston University, the pioneers in the study of CTE. At age 47, Chastain (now a mom herself) began reporting inexplicable moments of forgetfulness. She wonders if it has something to do with her 40 years of playing sports?

When Phoebe was a child, she'd admired Chastain as a role model. For many years, Phoebe had a poster of the soccer star hanging on her bedroom wall. It is that famous photo of Chastain after her shootout goal in the 1999 World Cup final against China.

> **Many of these damaged athletes do not suffer quietly. They become violent, suicidal, and even homicidal. Sometimes, their personality shifts with little notice.**

My hope is that Chastain will become a new kind of role model for young women and mothers of child athletes.

Until Phoebe assaulted me in October 2013, I'd been in massive denial about the high probability of her having CTE. I may never know for sure about her diagnosis. Sadly, this disorder can only be diagnosed post-mortem. Former athletes may spend, and their families watch helplessly, years suffering the slow and painful CTE-induced deterioration of the brain. Many of these damaged athletes do not suffer quietly. They become violent, suicidal, and even homicidal. Sometimes, their personality shifts with little notice.

I am repeatedly traumatized when I read about the ongoing scientific advances in the diagnosis of CTE. As another season of football arrives (2017), I shudder as I read about the results of post mortem studies on athletes' brains. Take football star Aaron Hernandez. He was convicted of murder and sent to prison, where at the age of 27 he hung himself. The autopsy revealed he had a severe case of Chronic Traumatic Encephalopathy.[47]

I can't help myself from reading these stories. I feel compelled to get to the bottom of what happened to my daughter and my family. When I learned that Hernandez was so young and yet had a severe case of CTE, I just cried.

---

[47] Belson, Ken (September 21, 2017). "Aaron Hernandez Had Severe C.T.E. When He Died at Age 27." *New York Times*.

Recent research confirms that those NFL football players who developed the worst cases of CTE (as studied by the team at Boston University) had begun playing tackle football prior to age 12.[48] This is a critical time for brain development; yet children are being exposed to potential life-threatening brain trauma without regard for the consequences. Phoebe was only five when she started playing soccer.

Is it too late for Phoebe? Can my research still help her? What I do comprehend now is that Phoebe had a number of symptoms characteristic of CTE, such as migraine headaches, erratic academic performance, light-switch anger outbursts, physical violence, alcohol/drug abuse, and black-and-white thinking— good guy or bad guy, friend or foe, right or wrong— without nuance.

What had puzzled me most was her distorted and strident thinking. I'd thought Phoebe's no-compromise approach was a symptom of her ADHD. Then, I'd found research studies on empathy disorders and mild traumatic head injuries that made the connection between TBI and loss of empathy quite clear: More support for my idea of how a person lands on the EmD-2 level.

The circuits responsible for empathy are a complex system located throughout the brain. (Remember that empathy allows you to know yourself in relation to others, to put yourself in another's shoes, to know your feelings and mind as distinctive from the feelings and minds of others, and to be caring and respectful of others.)

The brain's frontal lobes are primarily responsible for our "executive functions" or adult-like reasoning. Almost all

---

[48] Belson, Ken (September 19, 2017). "Playing Tackle Football Before 12 Is Tied to Brain Problems Later." *New York Times*.

concussions involve the frontal lobes. Consider that even if your head accidently gets hit or bumped, the Jell-O-like brain inside sloshes around, hitting the front, back, top, and sides of the skull.

Phoebe's first childhood head injury may not have caused her empathy to decline, but the ensuing years of chronic mild TBI and the occasional severe soccer-caused concussion certainly sealed her fate. . . and mine.

EmD-2 explains a lot about Phoebe's downward spiral. As she had become more and more insecure, unreasonable, self-absorbed, and combative, she'd been less able to dig herself out of her problems (poor school performance, reliance on marijuana and alcohol, physical fights with boyfriends, many-many injuries, and misdemeanor arrests). I'd watched her choice of friends slip from the best and brightest to aggressive/abusive boyfriends and heroin addicts. I'd been desperate to save my daughter from self-destruction.

I did have a last chance to recover Phoebe on my birthday weekend in September of 2013. She, her young son Jameson, and I were vacationing on the Oregon coast. Thankfully, her boyfriend, Jared Glaser, had not come along, so I'd had some private time with my beautiful daughter.

At one point, Phoebe came to me in tears and asked if she and my grandson could move back home. Her relationship with Jameson's father had always been turbulent, sometimes manifesting as domestic violence. Once, Jared had threatened to kill Phoebe, but now she was more frightened for her infant son than for herself.

I held her in my arms as she cried, assuring her that I would keep the two of them safe. I was hopeful this was a turnaround. After our trip, Phoebe—like so many abused women—changed her mind and returned to Jared. She never moved back home with me. The following month, she assaulted me. I've had no contact with her since then.

My daughter has brain trauma

"Brain trauma. A combination of findings suggests past brain trauma" was Phoebe's diagnosis from the reputed Amen Clinic.[49]

The words had hung in my mind like a heavy, lumpy, water-soaked blanket after a rained-on picnic. My daughter Phoebe had suffered brain trauma, most likely from repeated head injuries while a school-age soccer player. I'd felt sick to my stomach with this realization.

With my initial read of the report about Phoebe, the tears had pumped in my chest but wouldn't surface. My mouth had been dry, my jaw tight. I'd had the sensation that a metal band was tightening around my forehead. I'd felt guilty, ashamed, and powerless. Her diagnosis had come too late. I should have done something to help my daughter sooner. Phoebe had brain trauma and was sliding downhill fast in an avalanche of symptoms.

Now, as I review the report again, I begin to process—for the first time—all that the doctor had written. His complete diagnosis explained why Phoebe had assaulted me. It spelled out why she had become so unreasonable, making dangerous choices and taking dramatic chances with her life. It made clear why

---

[49] A medical practice where biological, psychological, and social influences are integrated with neuropsychological testing, SPECT scans, and lab tests to gain an in-depth understanding of the brain. What all this reveals, leads to the creation of a tailored Amen treatment plan to help a person's brain heal.

she was choosing unsavory friends. Straight away, the report pinpointed why I was losing my daughter to alcohol and drug abuse.

The SPECT scans were taken in January 2009 when Phoebe was 18. The diagnosis shouldn't have been so startling to me since I'd been ignoring it for years. I'd continued to cling to the notion that my mothering skills and love for my daughter would help her to heal. I was wrong.

According to Dr. Anthony Bottone of the Amen Clinic near Seattle, Wash., Phoebe's succinct diagnosis was:

1. *Decreased left temporal lobe tracer activity seen with concentration.*

2. *Mild scalloping (areas of significant low bloodflow and activity) seen with concentration.*

3. *Increased tracer activity (areas of brain activity proven to be valid indicators of the general state of affairs in the brain's centers) in the anterior cingulate gyrus seen with concentration.*

4. *Brain trauma: Findings indicate decreased prefrontal pole activity and decreased temporal lobe activity.*

I hadn't wanted to read anymore, but I'd had to. I had to figure out how to protect myself from my daughter.

Repeatedly, my mind had pushed the document out of focus, requiring me to read sentences over and over to process the content. I'd felt like I would have to abandon my child to survive.

So many thoughts had run through my head: that's wrong; I am a bad mother; I didn't protect her from the head injuries. It had seemed that I would have to destroy[50] Phoebe to protect myself from things like the false arrest.

In Phoebe's report, Dr. Bottone had written:

> *"Changes in the temporal lobe contribute to problems with: mood regulation; dark thoughts; anger outbursts (often light-switch anger); reading social skills; memory; focus; concentration; and feeling spaced out."*

Oh yes, her light-switch anger. I'd been on the receiving end of that many times. (One incident that stands out happened in October 2013: Phoebe had thrown wine on me, grabbed me, and knocked me across the room into a plate glass door.) Dr. Bottone had described Phoebe as having the "bulldog mentality."

> *"When the ACG [anterior cingulate gyrus] is active then oppositional or strong-willed behavior is often seen from childhood on. Individuals may experience anxiety/depression with intense worrying. There is a tendency to black-and-white thinking with little appreciation for the nuances of different opinions. Later, this can be associated with addictive tendencies, eating disorders, and obsessive-compulsive traits. Such individuals may be able to focus*

---

[50] When I'd reread Dr. Bottone's report in the context of Phoebe's false allegations against me, I'd felt like I would have to destroy her in order to protect myself: I would have to reveal that she has brain damage, and I hadn't wanted to hurt her in that way. Mine was the classic dilemma of a codependent mom.

well on a task but are also prone to being strong-willed and not letting go of hurts easily."

Phoebe had been growing more and more defiant and unwilling to hear anything I'd said. She'd blamed me for all of her problems. She'd run away from home, abused drugs and alcohol, and engaged in promiscuity.

On the night she'd assaulted me and called the police to have me arrested, she'd crazily accused me of attempting to hurt her baby boy. When I'd tried to reason with her, she'd gone ballistic. Her inner bulldog had lashed out at me in light-switch anger.

I remember my beautiful daughter as a happy baby. She was playful and curious. Phoebe was always popular with the other children. Even the other kids' parents would comment on how much they delighted in having Phoebe visit their home for a play date.

By third grade, something was off. She'd had her first concussion playing soccer that year. Shortly after this, her school work had started to deteriorate, and the teacher suggested Phoebe needed a reading tutor. Dr. Bottone's words pierced my heart:

"Mild scalloping seen with concentration occurs when the brain, on the outside surface view, appears scalloped or dehydrated. It is often associated with toxic exposure to drugs, alcohol or environmental toxin; infection; or oxygen deprivation at some point in the past. We have also seen it in widespread trauma."

"Widespread trauma." During her years as a soccer player (and snow boarder), Phoebe had endured numerous head injuries and concussions. Her teammates had often joked about how many hits she took. The summer she was 11, Phoebe had also suffered heat stroke. It had happened during those "dog days of summer" when the winds blow hot and dry, and you can't drink enough water to keep up.

The soccer team's coach had kept putting her back in the game—until she'd passed out. Why had I let it happen? Why hadn't I protected her? Why hadn't I stood up to the coach? Where had my husband been during all of Phoebe's injuries and accidents? So many questions. So much guilt.

"You need to protect yourself"

Bill Kittleson was a paralegal for my attorney Steve Thayer[51] and responsible for putting my case evidence together to present to the court. One day, as Kittleson had walked me to his office to review his findings, he'd casually said, "It was going to happen sooner or later, Kathy."

I'd been startled that instead of talking legalese, he was addressing how all this was impacting me. Had he understood my feelings of guilt, shame, and grief? I'd looked at Bill nervously, needing some clue and confirmation from him. "What do you mean?" I'd asked.

Bill caught my glance as he'd offered me a chair in his office. He'd looked at me as if a bit surprised that I hadn't understood his meaning. After all, I am a psychologist, so I should have known what he meant, right? When he'd seen the anguished look on my face, Bill had corrected course and begun addressing me as the aggrieved mother, not as the psychologist.

---

[51] Steve Thayer defended me, in Clark County District Court in Washington, for my criminal arrest of assault against Phoebe.

WHEN EMPATHY FAILS

"Kathy, I have read all of the documents you gave us including: brain scans showing Phoebe's brain damage; police reports documenting her drunkenness and trespassing; and medical reports tracing the times you took her to the ER for treatment because she'd passed out from alcohol abuse.

I have seen the photos of your injuries when she attacked you and knocked you across the room. I believe you! Your daughter assaulted you, and that's what we will prove to the jury.

I'm so sorry for you, but you need to know this was going to happen eventually. Phoebe has been out of control for a long time. You protected her as long as you could. Now you need to protect yourself."

> **... this was a "Sophie's Choice" matter. To keep myself out of prison, I'd have to prove that my daughter was not only the assailant but potentially dangerous to others because of the extreme and unpredictable nature of her anger.**

Kittleson had understood, bringing me a great sense of relief! He'd been right: It was time to protect myself from my daughter. But this was a "Sophie's Choice"[52] matter. To keep myself out of prison, I'd have to prove that my daughter was not only the assailant but potentially

---

[52] "Sophie's Choice," is a novel and film centered on a scene at Auschwitz where a mother arrives with her young son and daughter. There a sadistic doctor (presumably the infamous Dr. Mengele), forces her to make an unbearably agonizing choice—which of her children will stay with her in the German concentration camp and which will suffer death in the ovens.

dangerous to others because of the extreme and unpredictable nature of her anger. The summer Phoebe was 17, I'd enrolled her in a therapeutic wilderness camp: I'd hoped the experience would help her curb her violence and suffocate her drug/alcohol abuse. Not so much. . . .

To help my case, Bill had asked me to document all of the times Phoebe had lost control. My list included the times she'd: clocked a high school boyfriend; been permanently banned from the bowling alley for fighting in the parking lot; stayed out all night doing drugs with friends; stolen money from me; hit me; and vomited, in a drunken stupor, all over a police officer's shoes and in the gutter.

Afraid that Phoebe would puke in his car, the officer had instead called me to pick her up and take her to the hospital instead of locking her up.

As a teenager, she'd also skipped school and sometimes remained away from home for days. Another of her boyfriends had disappeared after being arrested on a parole violation during a fight over Phoebe. I'd later learned he was a registered sex offender.

I was left facing an unbearable choice: my survival or my child's.

The night it finally happened

On Oct. 23, 2013, I was working late as usual. (Twelve-hour work days became the norm during my marital separation and divorce. The additional income was essential to raising my special-needs adopted children; keeping my psychology practice afloat; and paying the many attorneys defending me from bogus arrests, the property dispute, and my divorce.)

I worked from home most of the time: I'd usher out my last client about 6 p.m., then use the next three or four hours to answer email, make chart notes, pay bills, return calls, and eat some dinner before falling dead asleep.

On this particular night, I had just settled down to another lonely meal at the computer in my home office with a half glass of red wine and a plate of fresh grilled asparagus for my dinner. (It wasn't exactly a balanced meal, but it was quick and easy. I'd learned to be efficient with my time, so most of my meals were grilled, nuked, or dished out of a deli box.) I'd put some garlic and butter on my asparagus so that it would be more like a treat.

Before I could begin my meal, Phoebe, then 23, showed up unannounced. She'd shunned me in recent weeks in response to a miscommunication she'd determined to be my fault.

Here's how that had played out. Phoebe had wanted me to babysit my grandson one evening, so that she and Jared could go bowling. I love my little grandson and never refuse an opportunity to babysit, so of course, I was excited to get home to meet them. I'd been running five to ten minutes behind schedule. When I'd gotten home, Phoebe, the baby, and Jared had been there and already left without waiting for me.

I'd called Phoebe right away, but she'd been angry and insulting. Haranguing me, she'd stated that her time was valuable—and that she didn't have to accommodate me. When I'd suggested she return with the baby since she was only five minutes away, she'd screamed, "I don't have to obey you anymore," then hung up.

My heart had been heavy and sad. Making it worse made no sense, so I'd put down the phone, effectively giving in to Phoebe's abuse again. Then, I'd done my best to let it go.

Now, here she was. Phoebe came up the stairs to my office, carrying the sleeping 8-month-old Jameson in his car seat. She sat down on the couch next to my desk and placed the baby between us. I reached down and gently lifted one of his baby hands. My heart filled with love when his sweet little fingers wrapped around my index finger. I watched, enjoying the sweetness of my dozing grandson. When I glanced up, I saw Phoebe smiling, too.

No longer angry with me, the reason for her visit soon became apparent. She wanted money. "Mom, I need more money for school," she said. I'd encouraged Phoebe to attend community college, hoping this would settle her down and help her find a career path.

Jared is not able to support his family. He doesn't drive and has a "less than honorable" discharge from the Army, which prevents him from working at anything other than part-time minimum-wage jobs.

Phoebe drives him to and from work in the car I bought for her. Otherwise, Jared gets around town on his skateboard. It falls on my daughter to care for herself and her child. It lands on me to be backup for all of them.

I quickly assessed how best to respond, saying, "I want you to be careful not to spend all of your college funds on remedial classes or recreation. I saved that money for your college, but it won't last if you spend it when you don't really need it. Can you get a job, so that you can pay for some of your expenses?"

Phoebe had already failed several classes, hence was no longer eligible for many grants or loans and was on academic probation. Although she has average intelligence, her learning disabilities, ADHD, and apparent TBI impede her efforts to learn.[53] It has always been like this for Phoebe. I'd enrolled her in an

---

[53] Phoebe is equipped to be successful academically with some supports for her disabilities. IQ is different than disabilities. One can have normal intelligence and yet be challenged by disabilities.

alternative high school[54] to reduce the academic demands on her. She'd made it to graduation because I'd helped with most of her homework.

"There's nothing I can do about it, Mom," she explained. "I don't want Dad to know that I failed some classes, or he will want his money back. I just need to get through this quarter with good grades; then I can get myself back on track." Phoebe seemed sincere; still, I worried she didn't know how to get back on track.

She was digging herself in deeper and deeper with her dad. She'd been paying for school supplies and tuition from her college fund, then dropping out of the classes yet giving Howard the receipts for reimbursement. Sooner or later, he would figure out she'd been double-dipping.

"Well, it's important you understand this money will not last forever," I said. Next, I sounded a warning, "I saved enough for you to go to four years of college. There's not enough to also cover living expenses for you, Jared, and the baby—especially if you keep dropping your classes. You need to consider your plans."

Phoebe agreed that she would be careful, so I decided to give her more money. I still controlled the college fund at Phoebe's request: She worried that she might not be able to say, "No," to Jared if he insisted she access it as a means of supporting themselves. Relentlessly, he reminded Phoebe that college was a waste of time. He was doing just fine without an education, he claimed. Yea, right!

I believe it had been a good choice when Phoebe decided to have me manage the money, don't you? On the other hand, I

---

[54] An alternative school generally refers to private and public school programs designed for underachieving students at risk of school failure.

wonder how many times she fooled me into giving her the money, only to have her use it on anything but college.

Like a light switch

After the college and money discussion, I'd paused to take a sip of wine and eat a bite of asparagus. I found the courage to take another tack with my daughter. Since things seemed to be going well, I thought maybe, just maybe, Phoebe would be willing to help repair the damage done to our relationship during our argument a few days prior.

"Phoebe?" I asked, watching the look on her face change from smiling to suspicious. "I'd like to talk about how it hurts me when you yell at me and hang up on me. On Sunday night, I was just a few minutes late getting home, but you decided that I had done something wrong. I'm your Mom. I am here for you in so many ways, like helping with college. I'd just like you to be more respectful."

The anger danced in her eyes, but she kept quiet until I finished. Then she made this emphatic announcement, "I'm not going to apologize to you. You just want an apology!" At this point, Phoebe's EmD-2 sounds like the narcissism of EmD-1.

"No, no, honey," I responded. "I don't want an apology. I want an understanding."

I hoped that she would accept my motherly guidance. I'd thought it was a chance worth taking. I felt my chance slipping away, and I started to worry. I'd taken the risk that I still had some leverage with my daughter; that she loved me and wanted to maintain a decent relationship.

Phoebe's voice got louder as she took the defense, "I don't owe you an apology! You were late. And when you called me and demanded that I come back, I told you I wouldn't do it. So you got

> It's tough to reason with someone engulfed in black-and-white thinking like those with brain trauma. Phoebe's EmD-2 mind sees only right or wrong. Anyone who opposes her is wrong and evil.

mad and yelled at me. So I hung up on you."

It's tough to reason with someone engulfed in black-and-white thinking like those with brain trauma. Phoebe's EmD-2 mind sees only right or wrong. Anyone who opposes her is wrong and evil.

"Wow!" I'd said, incredulous. Foolishly, I'd continued trying to reason with my raging child. "That's not how I remember it at all. Please give me a break here. I'm your mother, and I love you and Jameson. I help you with all kinds of things. I bought you your car and the car seat, and other things for the baby. I've. . ."

Now in a tirade, Phoebe broke in. "It's always about the money with you. You expect me to be grateful that you buy me things. Just because Joyce and Jeff (Jared's parents) aren't rich, you think you're better than them. I'm not staying here if you keep this up. I won't apologize, and you can't make me!"

I barely got the next words out of my mouth, "Phoebe, be reasonable. We're a family, and families fix these things." Phoebe would have none of it. She stood up, grabbed the baby carrier, and stormed out of the room. She slammed my office door so violently that it shook the room even knocking some of my office knick knacks to the floor.

The ability to regulate her feelings abandons my daughter when she's feeling overwhelmed or threatened. It's likely that when she'd arrived earlier, she'd wanted, on some level, to repair "us." She hadn't come by just for money.

Nevertheless, my pressuring her to grow up and requesting that she be kinder to me had been too much for her fragile ego.

She'd blown apart any semblance of maturity. Even though she is a mother, Phoebe was incapable of perceiving that her mother was trying to help both daughter and grandson.

I sat frozen in my chair, my glass of wine still in my left hand. I heard the interior office door slam. Phoebe's violent outburst had stupefied me. When I noticed the shattered chachkies on the floor, the result of Phoebe's rashness, I had the frightening thought that she and the baby might not be safe on their drive home.

I imagined them involved in a horrible blind-rage-caused car crash. I hurried over to the door, pressed the lever with my right hand, pulled the door toward me, then stepped into the doorway. On my right, I saw the baby sitting in his baby seat on the floor at the top of the stairs, which alarmed me all the more. I imagined both of them tumbling down the stairs.

"Phoebe wait!" I said. "It's not safe. Wait, wait. . . ."

Before I could finish my sentence, Phoebe slapped my left hand and splashed the glass of red wine all over my white shirt. She screamed at me to, "Stop it. You're going to spill wine on the baby!"

Somewhat dazed, I looked in the direction of Jameson, who was now crying. His sweet little eyes fixed on me imploringly. There was no way I was going to spill wine on my grandson. Besides, Phoebe was the one who'd splashed it all over me, the carpet, and the walls. She was out of control.

I knew this feeling: the quiet, the stillness, the slow recognition that I'm under attack. I was incapable of responding. In this confrontation, the attacker was my child, and I had no desire to defend myself as I had with Esther. I held my breath.

Phoebe continued the assault. She grabbed my upper arms and shoved me back into my office, slamming me up against the

> I lost my balance and slid down the glass to the floor. When I tried to get back up, she shoved me down again. Slowly, my hands went up in front of my face to protect myself from her. I reached to pull her hair but missed.

glass door to the deck on the opposite side of the room. I lost my balance and slid down the glass to the floor. When I tried to get back up, she shoved me down again. Slowly, my hands went up in front of my face to protect myself from her. I reached to pull her hair but missed.

She seized both of my arms and pushed me down a third time, smacking me against a cast iron end table. As I struggled to regain my footing, Phoebe started dragging me like a rag doll. I fell on the couch with Phoebe on top of me. I was beyond terrified. Phoebe was 40 years younger and 75 pounds heavier than me. With my hands and arms pinned and no way to defend myself, I turned my head . . . and bit Phoebe in her left forearm.

Fighting back and fighting mad

The anger was rising in me. How dare she attack me! How dare she turn her rage on me just because her life is a mess! How dare she expose her son to this violence—the same style of violence she'd used to lash out at me for years.

The bite must have stunned Phoebe as well. She let go of me and ran out of the room. Jameson was still crying at the top of the stairs. She grabbed the handle of the car seat and rushed down the stairs with him, clumsily smacking the walls to reach the garage door. She screamed at me, "You'll never see Jameson again!"

After all the years of putting up with so much while protecting her from herself, I snapped. I roared at her, "Get out!

Get out you little bitch!" With that, Phoebe slammed the garage door and was gone.

I was furious. I had loved and protected this child from the moment I first held her in my arms, even before we adopted her. I'd assumed that her hostile acting out and violent temper tantrums were the result of growing up in a divorced family. I'd reasoned that she took out her frustrations on me because as "the Mom" she expected me to make it all right. But I couldn't make it all right. Not now. Not anymore. Phoebe would have to do the work herself.

The moment I'd bitten her arm, I'd felt the anger repressed all those years pour out of me. No more excuses for Phoebe. No more taking the blame for my child's Empathy Dysfunction. I was done! But the night's drama wasn't. The already horrible night was about to become outrageously awful.

Another night in Clark County Jail

After the incident, Phoebe had tried calling me several times, probably when she'd realized the significance of what she'd done. (People with EmD-2 can come to their senses from time to time). I finally texted her to leave me alone until the next day. Then we could talk.[55] Instead, Phoebe wound up calling the police on me.

> **No more taking the blame for my child's Empathy Dysfunction. I was done! But the night's drama wasn't.**

---

[55] I'd told Phoebe that we would talk the next day to work things out; instead, she'd called the police and had me arrested. Months later, in deposition, she'd even stated that she'd expected to talk with me the next day to resolve our problems.

WHEN EMPATHY FAILS

Jared Glaser is the abusive boyfriend of the author's daughter Phoebe Marshack and father of Phoebe's young son. His pastime is target shooting in the woods with assault rifles. Hostile, angry, and threatening, he, showed up (with Phoebe and the baby) at the author's house demanding to be let in the night of the altercation between Phoebe and the author in 2013.

First, undeterred, Phoebe and Jared came back to the house. I refused to let Jared in: like I could trust an angry, abusive boyfriend who target practices in the woods with assault rifles. (Especially after he'd said, "Kathy, let me in. I won't hurt you.")

Looking back, I acknowledge that I should have been smart enough to reach out to friends for moral support after the night's ordeal. I'd been keyed up; all I'd truly wanted was to go to bed and let sleep take me away from it all. I'd turned on the TV, and by the light of the flickering screen, I'd fallen asleep.

I'd barely dozed off when Vancouver beat cop Jamie Haske and her partner were at my doorstep, repeatedly ringing the bell and aggressively shining flashlights in my windows. I should have ignored them: But no, I'd thought I could reason with them. After a decade of being bullied by the Vancouver police, I don't know why I'd believed for a second that they would listen to me

Phoebe's police call was going to make things a hundred times worse. My mom instincts kicked in. I wanted to prevent Phoebe from further damage and trauma. I pulled a hoody over my pajamas and answered the door. I took my cell phone along to show the officers my earlier texting interaction with Phoebe. I'd hoped that evidence would help them comprehend the depth of her problems. I didn't want her arrested for assaulting me.

The male officer shined his flashlight in my face and began peppering me with questions the instant I opened the door. He accused me of being drunk and attacking Phoebe. When I protested, he threatened to charge me with resisting arrest.

I'd tried explaining that my daughter is a troubled young adult who is very dependent on me. I'd tried explaining that Phoebe has a drinking and drug abuse problem and that I am always bailing her out of trouble; I'd tried explaining that I am a mom dealing with a special needs child who makes poor choices. I'd shown them my wine-soaked clothes and the bloody cut on my wrist. I'd begged them, "Please don't do this. It will destroy my daughter!"

It had been for naught. The cops spun me around, handcuffed me, marched me across my lawn barefoot, and stuffed me into the police car. I'd wound up spending the night in Clark County jail and hiring a criminal defense attorney to the tune of about $7,500. Seven months later, I was acquitted of all charges on the grounds of self-defense.

During this time, a restraining order was in force against me, so there had been no channels for my daughter and I to attempt to reconcile. Hence, I'd been unable to share the holidays with her or celebrate my grandson's first birthday.[56]

Mom always said to "sore [sic] with the eagles"

While I'd sat in jail, Phoebe had been busy concocting a story to cover her tracks. Her EmD-2 status left her unable to consider the damage she was about to cause with her selfish attempts to turn friends and family against me.

First, she'd called my trusted secretary, Michelle, to let her know she would not be coming back to work. (I know what you are thinking. Yes, I'd hired Phoebe to do odd jobs for me, so that she and the baby would have money for food, gas, and car insurance. Call me the crazy, over-protective mom that I am!) Michelle had received the call while sitting in front of the Vancouver Courthouse parking lot, trying to figure out how to get me out of jail.

Second, Phoebe had texted her cousins John and Keely to advise them that I had attacked her without provocation. Keely had responded in disbelief, saying that she was envious of Phoebe for having a mom who would do so much for her—especially considering the toll Phoebe's bad judgment had taken on her mom. That was when Phoebe "unfriended" Keely on Facebook.

In her call with the distressed Phoebe, Keely had even brought up the time when Phoebe and Jared had bought alcohol on a family camping trip, then traded it to a couple of teenagers

---

[56] I heard indirectly about Phoebe shortly before Christmas 2016. I'd gotten a call from a collection agency looking for Phoebe regarding a bill she had failed to pay. I could honestly tell the collector that I had no idea of her whereabouts. I'd felt an odd sense of sadness that she was having trouble, and I couldn't help her. I guess it's a mom thing.

for pot. (Phoebe and Keely had kept this incident secret from me at the time.)

Third, Phoebe posted a string of messages about the assault to Facebook, ironically revealing her confusion over whether I was her hero or her assailant. Below is a sad demonstration of her brain-damaged thought process as she'd attempted to find meaning in her tormented mind.

> "The incident that happened Wednesday with my mom, I believe happened for a reason. . . . On the way to school Wednesday morning a bald eagle flew over my car. My mom used to always tell me to sore [sic] with the eagles. So I think that was gods [sic] way of saying "Phoebe, it's time for you to stand up for yourself and spread your springs [sic] and fly away!" And that's what I did. I stood up for myself and flew away while being attacked!!"

In the months I'd awaited adjudication, I'd dug into the research on brain injuries. (Research and writing help me to stay sane when dealing with the chaos created by those with empathy disorders.) I'd learned everything I could about concussions, TBI, CTE, and their intersection with empathy.

Interestingly, the October that Phoebe had assaulted me, the PBS series "Frontline" aired a special titled, "League of Denial: The NFLs Concussion Crisis." Just days after my release from jail, I'd watched it on Netflix. Tears had streamed down my face as I'd learned yet more about the NFL cover-up of the tragic brain damage caused by football.

I followed up by reading everything I could find on the subject, including studies published by Dr. Daniel Amen in the mid-nineties. He'd been studying retired NFL players for years to understand the effects of football on their brain health.[57]

In 1999, when my eldest daughter, Bianca, was in middle school and falling apart—and I could find no local child psychiatrists or psychologists equipped to help her—I'd flown Bianca to Newport Beach in California to meet with the famous doctor. Although he had not yet had the research to identify what would later be diagnosed as autism, Amen had diagnosed Bianca as having severe anxiety. Bewildered for years about how to help Bianca, I had been so relieved to have something to work with after she saw him.

It hadn't been until Phoebe was 18 that it had finally occurred to me to ask Amen to help her, too. I believe such a serious lapse in my vigilance to care for my girls' special needs is indicative of how embroiled I'd become in defending myself in a hostile divorce as well as in surviving slander, lawsuits, and stalking.

The scans of Phoebe's brain that the Amen Clinic had done in 2009 had shown the indelible ravages of widespread brain trauma. By 2013, his work had gained real traction: It had given me something to hope for. . . a cure for TBI.

In the "Journal of Psychoactive Drugs," (Feb. 1, 2013), Amen published a study entitled, "Reversing Brain Damage in Former NFL Players."

---

[57] To read Dr. Daniel Amen's NFL player report findings and see images from brain scans, visit https://www.scribd.com/mobile/document/123297016/Amen-Clinics-Retired-NFL-Players-Brain-Study

Amen's researchers had used SPECT[58] and other neuropsychological tests to measure blood flow in the brain plus cognitive functions (mood, memory, language, attention, information speed, and accuracy).

Following their initial testing, the NFL players in the study had followed Amen's brain-healthy protocol: a special diet, exercise, limited alcohol, no smoking, lots of sleep, and a fistful of vitamins, minerals, and brain boosters, such as fish oil and Gingko. After six months of treatment, the results had shown significant increases in cognitive scores, blood flow, and the self-reported symptoms of mood, memory, and motivation.

On the Amen Clinic's website, Amen posted this message regarding his study.

> *"I hope this message finds anyone who played contact sports like football, hockey, soccer, boxing so they can find help because their degenerative conditions can be reversed."*

As wonderful as this news was, I'd wanted to yell something else from the rooftops, "What about the moms, Dr. Amen?" What about the moms like me who have been assaulted by their children and even arrested? How do we benefit from brain scans, then the cure, if we are powerless to get our loved ones into treatment?

There is so much more to treating TBI than getting a SPECT scan and taking brain support supplements. The families are victims, too, traumatized by the destructiveness of Empathy Dysfunction.

---

[58] To view Dr. Daniel Amen presenting a TED Talk about the most important lesson learned from studying 83,000 brain scans, visit http://youtu.be/esPRsT-lmw8

The mother-daughter love that was

Mommy!
Thank you doesn't cut it. It's not enough to tell you how thankful I am to have you as a mom. You helped me be able to walk across the stage & graduating. You're the best. I LOVE YOU!
Phoebe (the little engine that could)

CLASS OF 2008!

The author and her youngest daughter, Phoebe Marshack, had a strong and loving bond before the ravages of Traumatic Brain Injury (TBI) took hold of Phoebe in her early twenties. Here, on high school graduation day, Phoebe accepts a warm hug from her mom —who she also chose to shout out on her mortar board. At right is a post-graduation thank you note from Phoebe to her mom that expresses gratitude to a mom she genuinely loves and admires.

For years, I'd been my daughter's hero, teaching her the value of soaring with the eagles. This, I know she knows. It's true that brain injuries have robbed Phoebe of her empathy. Still, I believe that on some deeper level, she knows the truth and will, in time, do the right thing for herself, her son—and her mother.

"Mild Traumatic Brain Injury" Highlights

1. The frightening thing about EmD-2 is that their empathy comes and goes, so you never know whether or not they are connecting with you.

2. EmD-2s can also be violent. It is not just their empathy that comes and goes, but other emotional regulatory functions as well.

3. Mild concussions and head injuries associated with contact sports, such as football, hockey, and soccer can lead to TBI and, eventually, CTE, which is incurable and can be fatal.

4. No helmet exists that can protect the soft, Jell-O-like brain from being damaged inside the skull when it is bashed in an auto accident, a football tackle, or a frontal collision with a goal post.

5. Symptoms may point to your loved one suffering from mild TBI or worse, but you no longer need to remain in the dark about treatment. Dr. David Amen has pioneered the use of brain scans and holistic treatment that looks very promising.

6. The tragedy of having a family member with EmD-2 is that you may never get them back. Without proper treatment, people with these brain injuries can become so unreasonable and belligerent that you have to keep your distance to stay safe.

7. Codependency results when you keep trying to protect your EmD-2 loved one. Making excuses for their conduct will not help. They need medical treatment.

CHAPTER SIX

On Becoming a Warrior Matriarch

"A family can be the bane of one's existence. A family can also be most of the meaning of one's existence. I don't know whether my family is bane or meaning, but they have surely gone away and left a large hole in my heart."

— **Keri Hulme**

How it begins—EmD-3

Empathy Dysfunction Type Three, or EmD-3, is represented by brain disorders such as ADHD, addiction, or bipolar disorder. Empathy can be dialed up or down in EmD-3 individuals: This is determined by whether or not they get proper medical and psychological treatment.

> **Empathy can be dialed up or down in EmD-3 individuals: This is determined by whether or not they get proper medical and psychological treatment.**

Chemical imbalances and intermittent blood flow issues in the brain (among other symptoms—also referred to as criteria or characteristics) are at play in those with EmD-3 disorders. Treatment involves medical, psychological, pastoral, and lay support (such as AA). Frankly, managing difficult and disturbing EmD-3 behaviors is impossible without treatment.

In this chapter, I describe how one of these brain disorders, drug and alcohol addiction, starts out when a person is at the EmD-3 level. Addiction is a brain disorder that drives the behavior that confuses and confounds the rest of us. The addict's behavior may appear to be as abusive and destructive as that of an EmD-1 (narcissist or psychopath). However, with proper treatment, drug users can regain empathy and even reach the highest EmD-5 level; not so with narcissists and sociopaths. They are trapped at EmD-1.

The problem is that EmD-3 addicts must want to change. It has to be their choice: treatment (and usually abstinence) versus continuing their drug/alcohol use. If not rehabilitated, it's pretty much a given that the addiction will cause permanent brain damage. This impairment, in turn, corrodes the EmD-3's empathic prowess, causing it to degenerate to an EmD-2. Even worse: Parents with EmD-3 may unwittingly create EmD-1s in succeeding generations![59]

My father's family illustrates this decline in empathy over the generations. If you survive the emotional abuse common for those who grow up in a multigenerational family where Empathy Dysfunction runs rampant, you'll likely have an additional emotional burden: a lifetime of shame.

"Po' white trash"

As my mother told it, my father's family had been considered "po' white trash" for a good long while. I'd thought Mom was joking until I realized how terribly tragic it is to be of this ilk.

---

[59] There is evidence that addiction changes DNA, meaning the addiction-prone genes can be passed along to an active or recovered addict's children. Plus, if a child is traumatized by untreated addicts, their brains may not mature normally.

I am fortunate because I had parents who wanted to escape this lifestyle. While we'd lived humbly, my parents had emphasized getting an education as the best strategy for exiting the white lower class (for which my father got lots of ridicule from his white trash relatives).[60]

Some of us succeeded at this but not all. For example, I became a psychologist. My cousin Lila Ann owned a bar, dabbled in drug dealing, and hooked up with an ex-felon and intravenous drug user (perhaps EmD-1 and definitely EmD-3 sliding into EmD-2).[61]

I hadn't seen Lila Ann for 15 or 16 years when she showed up at cousin Frankie's funeral in October 2010. Frankie had been shot in the head by her boyfriend before he'd killed himself. I'd had no idea that Frankie even lived in the Northwest near my hometown. I learned about it when the cousins started calling after her death.

Frankie's son Leonard had been the first to learn of his mother's death when he'd stopped to visit her at her boyfriend's house. The police had already arrived. When Leonard had approached them, he'd been warned to stay out of the investigation. Then, one of the officers told him a woman had been murdered. No one had asked Leonard who he was. No one had known that the dead woman was his mother. He hadn't told them. He'd just walked away alone.

---

[60] I want to be clear that Mom's use of the terms "po' white trash" and "white trash" were not meant in a demeaning way. As a person with Asperger Syndrome, Mom wasn't trying to be critical, but to be accurate. In her autistic mind, the terms were succinct.

[61] I have changed the identifying information of the people (and certain irrelevant facts) in this chapter in order to protect the privacy of some of my relatives.

> Another oddity of families like mine: Most of its members don't consider stories like this strange. Hence, each generation recreates these tragic conditions for themselves and their children, claiming everything is fine.

I'm not sure why I went to the funeral. It seemed like the right thing to do. Frankie had died at 50, bringing the end to her miserable life. Apparently, she'd been working as a hotel maid and trying to stay "clean." She'd had a string of violent boyfriends after she'd divorced Leonard's father, Maynard, also a drug addict. Maynard had married Frankie after divorcing her older sister Dorrie shortly after Dorrie was disabled in a car accident: Maynard, the driver.

Now, Dorrie panhandles from her wheelchair on the streets of downtown Seattle, Wash. Another oddity of families like mine: Most of its members don't consider stories like this strange. Hence, each generation recreates these tragic conditions for themselves and their children, claiming everything is fine. They refuse to admit they might need help.

Lila Ann and I hadn't talked much at the funeral. She'd shown up at the mortuary chapel with her husband, Sonny, but they hadn't hung around for the service or the graveside ceremony. She'd claimed she had a lunch date with someone. Frankie's sister Dorrie had also been there.

I'd been quite surprised when I later received an email from Lila Ann. I'd thought it was going to be an apology for all of those years she'd shunned me and held me responsible for the hardships in her life. According to her, I'd been at fault for not "fixing" her addict boyfriend; and for not paying her rent when she'd been evicted: because her boyfriend had been arrested for parole violations (stealing guns, then fencing the stolen property, which he'd stored at Lila Ann's house) and been sent back to state prison.

"White trash" families can be like this. If a family member is successful, it is assumed that we will help out all relatives down on their luck. If we don't bail them out of every scrape, then we are shunned. This is probably why I kept bailing out my daughter Phoebe; it's "white trash" tradition, but no one really gets better. We just keep spinning in destructiveness and self-pity.

The way her email read, it had sounded like an apology was coming; then the tone had switched. She'd calmly explained that she hadn't talked to me at the funeral because I am a horrible person who has caused her no end of suffering. It was me, she'd said, who had brought her so much pain because I'd failed to bail her out every time she'd been in trouble. Now, she was additionally blaming me for harming her son Jimmy by turning him against her. Clearly, my cousin's empathy had significantly dialed down to EmD-1 from EmD-3.

Crazy-making stuff like this often goes on in "white trash" families like mine. My cousin Lila Ann had used her son to carry drugs for her from the time he'd been in middle school. The kid's anger and violence had turned him into such a trouble-maker that he'd been expelled from eighth grade on the last day of school. That black mark made it hard for him to even get into a high school. Somehow, in my cousin's twisted mind, this had been my fault, too.

Empathy disorders are prevalent in families where drugs and bad choices have disrupted the creation of morals[62] in the frontal lobes

---

[62] The frontal lobes are responsible for Executive Function, which is required to be a responsible adult. Morality, or moral functioning, is one of those things that develops with the use of Executive Functions, such as cause and effect, conscience and empathy.

> I want to emphasize that it's nearly impossible to help people escape from empathy-disordered families. That doesn't mean we shouldn't try to help our loved ones get well. But be prepared to save yourself and leave the others behind if you are going down with the ship.
>
> Like lone wolves, members of dysfunctional families must strike out on their own to survive and even thrive.

of the brain. It's possible that EmD-3s who are not addicted could also demonstrate a lack of conscience.

I want to emphasize that it's nearly impossible to help people escape from empathy-disordered families. It doesn't mean you shouldn't try to help your loved ones get well. But be prepared to save yourself and leave the others behind if you are going down with the ship.

Like lone wolves, members of dysfunctional families must strike out on their own to survive and even thrive. I've been able to combat the loneliness of losing my family by finding solid friends—responsible, compassionate, accepting, and empathic—who are like family to me. I call them "framily."

> Always an eager student, I've become even hungrier to learn since discovering the unequalled power that comes with knowledge. Research and wisdom together are my first line of defense in protecting myself from those with Empathy Dysfunction.

Genealogy—a back-to-the-future affair

Educating myself about new and intriguing things was another strategy that helped me survive the empathy disorders that stampeded through my life. Always an eager student, I've become even hungrier to learn since discovering the unequalled power that comes with knowledge. Research and wisdom together are my first line of defense in protecting myself from those with Empathy Dysfunction.

I delight in expanding my understanding of science, history, and literature. Most fulfilling are the times when I dive deep into my heart and soul to gain insight about myself. Breaking free of a family's crazy-making belief systems is no easy feat. I look to great thinkers past and present for guidance: I sure as hell can't rely on my forefathers and foremothers for examples of wise coaching.

After Frankie's funeral, I'd been curious about the background that had contributed to the making of my convoluted and messed up family of origin. I signed up for one of those companies that do DNA testing to help you trace your ancestry. Then, I'd created a Facebook page to share my discoveries with my kinfolk.

This experiment in genealogy proved a fascinating lesson. From Facebook posts, I discovered relatives I'd never known I had, or had lost track of. I received daily messages—mostly from cousin upon cousin—through the ancestry website. What a happy surprise it was when I learned that my American ancestors had lived in the original colonies; that means I share DNA strings with lots of people in the United States!

Some are connections I am proud to name, such as Obadiah Holmes and Chad Brown, two English Baptist ministers who helped found Rhode Island and the First Baptist Church in North America. My most famous relative is Abraham Lincoln, whose lineage traces back to a daughter of Holmes.

Most of my ancestors had been considered "white trash." It's stereotypical, but the truth is they'd settled in the backwoods of America where they'd raised their young'uns and drunk their moonshine. I even found a family branch related to a great grandfather, who I'd discovered had been a bigamist. Apparently, his "secret" family had known about us, the "legitimate" cousins[63], for generations. We hadn't known about them until they were revealed in my genealogy research.

Not long ago, I got a message from a woman who had diligently researched her husband's ancestry then come to a roadblock. Her late husband's kin could be traced to an obscure Confederate general; however, her husband's DNA did not match that of the rest of his family. Her search had dead-ended with me, supposedly a second cousin of her spouse (according to the DNA comparison done by the genealogy site).

I read her email a few times, trying to figure out how I could help her. I didn't recognize the surname, and I knew no one in Elkhart, Ind., where her husband had grown up. Then, it had dawned on me that it might be my Uncle Eugene's DNA in play.

Knowing this new finding might be a hardship for her late husband's mother or grandmother, should they still be alive, I thought deeply about how to divulge the details. Uncle Gene, who'd ended his life with a bullet to his head when he was in his early fifties, had been the philandering older brother of my father.[64] It had been my dad who'd found the body. Subsequently, he was arrested for Gene's murder until the police determined it was suicide.

Before that, my uncle had been a mediocre con artist, who had been in trouble since he'd been a teenager. Uncle Gene had married several times, leaving a string of wives, girlfriends, and progeny across the country. An independent trucker, he'd

---

[63] In hillbilly culture everyone is a cousin.
[64] As for Uncle Gene's "legitimate" family, I am not sure they would have cared about the information come to light. They'd all disowned him as adults. Some family members had even changed their last names.

crisscrossed the country many times. Indiana had been a favorite stopping place because Indianapolis was his birthplace.

Figuring that this woman deserved an answer, as sordid as it was, I'd told her about Uncle Gene. I'd told her that I would put her in touch with Gene's relatives if she wanted more help. I've never heard from her again. I assume she decided to keep Gene's secret.

Shamed by the shameless

Shaming is a technique used by all low-level EmD's; however, EmD-3s are prone to, and practiced at, doing so. Causing shame is a powerful way to subdue an opponent. It's the subtle combination of blame and shame that causes the greatest damage. Shame is an instrument of torture when a family member hurls it to destroy a loved one.

> Causing shame is a powerful way to subdue an opponent. It's the subtle combination of blame and shame that causes the greatest damage. Shame is an instrument of torture when a family member hurls it to destroy a loved one.

Most vulnerable to an EmD-3's manipulation are the very people who love them. Only EmD-1s go after total strangers. As a member of a "white trash" clan, loaded with alcoholics and addicts, I had experienced blame and shame throughout my lifetime. Therefore, I'd been primed for more when I'd met Townsend. Hurl it, she did.

As City Prosecutor, she had insisted that I meet with her in person monthly to provide my Diversion reports. Most people on a court-ordered Diversion for small offenses like mine are only required to submit a written form each month. The only thing required of these defendants is to stay out of trouble for six months. After that, the charges are normally dismissed. Townsend, it seemed, had wanted to make an example of me.

She humiliated me with her statement that "people" considered me an "angry, difficult person who has a problem with authority." In a letter that is in my psychologist Frank Colistro's file, Townsend had demanded that he be tougher on me since I was so angry and hostile. Colistro had reported back to Townsend that I was an ideal client and doing well in therapy. Apparently, his response had angered Prosecutor Townsend a great deal. Because next, Townsend shamed me with the accusation that I'd been disrespectful of her staff, saying:

> *"Her moods hinge on explosive. She can pretend to be pleasant, and when she does, she does so in a way that lets you know she is pretending. She describes herself as difficult; she agrees that she is condescending. She knows that other people describe her as difficult, but she dismisses their opinion as uninformed and unimportant."*

EmD-1s don't just tell lies about you. They are hell-bent on destroying any trust you may have with friends and loved ones.

Not only had Townsend trashed me with shaming comments, but she'd twisted the knife yet deeper by undermining a critical relationship. EmD-1s don't just tell lies about you. They are hell-bent on destroying any trust you may have with friends and loved ones.

For example, I'd asked Townsend to tell me which "people" had described me as angry, difficult, and condescending. She'd looked me in the eye and, with a total smirk, said, "Your ex-husband, Howard. I'm so sorry to have to tell you this, but it's true."[65]

---

[65] I suspect Josephine Townsend wanted Howard (my ex-husband) on

Townsend went way too far with this unethical conduct. Her pattern of deceitful and malignant attacks on me—and others— led to her dismissal as Vancouver's Prosecuting Attorney.

Even the loss of that job hadn't deterred Townsend. Years later, in sworn testimony during a deposition, she'd again tried to shame me. She had continued to claim it was absolutely true that Colistro believed the things she'd written about me in letters to him, again insisting that my psychologist had diagnosed me as a "functional sociopath." Now that's what you call a double lie; a lie about me and a lie about him. Colistro, however, continues to insist Townsend's accusation is a total fabrication.

Lies accelerate faster than a wildfire. I'd had to work at lightning speed to disprove her accusations. I'd grown tired of trying to convince Townsend of the truth. My most urgent need had shifted to protecting myself from this powerful person who wanted to raze me.

"I'm an addict"

My study of genealogy had driven home how essential it is to never trust a con artist, especially one in your own family: Loving them leaves us even more vulnerable. After surviving as many cons as I have over the years, I should have seen this one coming; however, I never give up on people, especially kinfolk. Lonesome for family, though, I keep

> My study of genealogy had driven home how essential it is to never trust a con artist, especially one in your own family: Loving them leaves us even more vulnerable.

---

her side so that he would support her bid for Superior Court Judge. At the time, Howard was the chair of the Washington Family Law Section of the BAR and had some influence.

hoping other survivors are out there who might want to reestablish our crumbling family.

It was through my genealogy Facebook page that I'd reconnected with one of my father's cousins, or rather the grandson of one of his cousins, but you know they are all cousins to me.[66] Lyle Ray was married and had two sons. I didn't know much about Lyle Ray, other than he'd professed to adore my father and mother.

He had just moved to the Portland area and wanted to get together. He said that he enjoyed the stories my mother would tell when my parents visited his family back in Michigan. He admitted that he was trying to stay clean after years as a drug dealer, adding that was why he had moved his family out west. But he told me he didn't want any favors. Nope he had a good job and he would take care of his family.

At this point, his father had just passed away from undiagnosed Hepatitis C. Lyle Ray was grieving the loss of yet another family member with a drug problem. He told me that it was time to save his children. I was sympathetic. I hoped that at least one more of my kin was making the move to sobriety.

Sadly, Lyle Ray had left his mother and siblings behind in Michigan. He and his mother were alienated over a lawsuit. Apparently, when Lyle Ray's young son, Derek, was a toddler, he'd fallen from the balcony of Lyle Ray's mother's condo and sustained serious injuries. Since his mother had refused to help with the medical costs, Lyle Ray and his wife sued her for damages.

---

[66] I have so many cousins that it's hard to keep track of whether they are first cousins or second cousins or first cousins once removed, or one of the many other genealogical configurations. Growing up in my family, everyone was pigeonholed as a cousin, auntie, or granny, depending on age—regardless of the true familial relationship.

The timing couldn't have been better for Lyle Ray and his wife, Laney Jo, to look me up. They were working hard to stay clean and sober and create some semblance of a normal life. Seeing that, I'd chosen to help by being a stable senior relative in their family's life. At least I'd hoped that would be true.

I'd enjoyed their company until we parted ways five years down the road. We'd gone camping and celebrated many holidays and birthdays together. I'd taken them to movies and given them gift cards to restaurants. Laney Jo brought the family's laundry to my house and did it to save money. That had given me a chance to cook a family meal now and then.

It was difficult for Lyle Ray to get a job that supported his family; his wife Laney Jo was unemployable because of her bad teeth and lack of education. After years making money as a drug dealer, Lyle Ray didn't really have a decent resume to offer employers. It saddened me to see them living in a dingy two-bedroom apartment, struggling to make ends meet.

I'd ignored a lot of things about the young couple: I'd wanted to believe they could do better. Again, my love and optimism set me up to be conned.

Lyle Ray and Laney Jo are representations of EmD-3. They were struggling to stay sober, but the bad choices they'd continued to make cancelled out their budding empathy. For example, years of drug use (marijuana and the prescription opioid drug OxyContin) had left them with teeth too rotten to bite into an apple or a piece of corn on the cob.

They'd rarely bathed, so had a strong body odor. I'd learned the hard way not to allow them into my hot tub unless I planned to drain it afterward. I'd thoroughly enjoyed having children in my house again. However, when the boys stayed with me for a sleepover, I'd insisted they take showers, so that they wouldn't leave greasy filth on my couches. I had willingly endured their bad teeth and poor hygiene.

During the final year of our relationship, when the three of us were still talking, they'd started borrowing money. Though they really couldn't afford it, they'd moved out of the apartment and into a little rental house. They'd wanted so much to be "normal." I'd been downsizing at the time, so they'd furnished their place with my extra furniture: a bedroom set, living room chairs, carpets, and even a bicycle.

I'd been reluctant to loan them money, especially when Laney Jo refused to work. I knew that with her bad teeth and lack of skills, getting a job would be near impossible for her. I'd caved.

Then, Lyle Ray had gotten into a fist fight at work and was fired. He'd been offered a new job the next day at another company, but he hadn't been able to pass the UA (urine analysis): He'd smoked a "bowl" after being fired. To tide them over for a couple of months, until Lyle Ray could pass the UA, I'd loaned them a few hundred dollars. They'd also applied for food stamps and medical assistance.

That loan was the kiss of death for us. Once they knew I'd give them money, they never stopped asking. Laney Jo was usually the one to ask, probably figuring I wouldn't refuse a mother. Each time, she'd promised to pay it back with Lyle Ray's next pay check.

When the amount had gotten into the thousands, she'd promised to give me their tax refund. I'd gotten creative, too, and offered them odd jobs to help pay off their debt to me: things like walking the dog and helping me move into my new house. It became the couple's habit to work a few hours, then ask to be paid for half their time—because they needed the cash. By the time they'd bounced the rent check one last time, they owed me about $3,000.

WHEN EMPATHY FAILS

The final time Laney Jo asked for money, it was by email. She'd apologized for making the "ask" again. They had needed money so badly that they'd spent the tax refund promised to me—and they were awfully sorry.

Laney Jo had assured me this would be the last time they'd ever ask: She was finally going to go to work (at a cafeteria, part time, minimum wage). Predictably, she felt justified in asking me (presumably the only one she knew who had money) for another loan.

I'd said no. Then, I'd pointed out that she and Lyle Ray, now in their forties, needed to grow up and take responsibility for themselves. I'd finally faced the truth: my beloved cousins were sliding into EmD-2, lying and manipulating to support their lifestyle.

After a couple of weeks had passed, I heard from Lyle Ray. He'd asked if he could come by for a visit to clear things up. I'd been so hopeful for a happy ending. The only thing I'd gotten from Lyle Ray that day had been a schooling session on why not to trust a family con artist—ever! Remember, even though EmD-3s can aspire to be EmD-4s and even EmD-5s, you always need to be wary of the games they play.

Lyle Ray had smiled, showing his rotting teeth and the gaping hole in the front of his mouth where he'd had a tooth pulled. "You know Auntie," he'd said, "Laney Jo's pretty mad at you for calling her a drug addict".... He'd attempted to shame me into feeling guilty. Not this time: not going to happen!...

For too long, I had allowed the confidence game to continue.

Lyle Ray had smiled, showing his rotting teeth and the gaping hole in the front of his mouth where he'd had a tooth pulled. "You know Auntie," he'd said, "Laney Jo's pretty mad at you for calling her a drug addict."

"She is, Lyle Ray," I'd responded. "She may be a recovering addict, but she is still an addict." He'd attempted to shame me into feeling guilty. Not this time: not going to happen!

For too long, I had allowed the confidence game to continue. I was no good to Lyle Ray as a patsy. He needed me to confront his addiction disease in a Warrior Matriarch manner. So I did, saying, "And it does not serve her very well to play games with me about the money. I don't appreciate the lies from either of you. You know darned well that Laney Jo abused OxyContin."

Lyle Ray hadn't blinked an eye. Addicts are like that, especially those dipping toward EmD-1 conduct. Nothing makes them mad, not even the idea of being caught. EmD3s (even those slipping into EmD-1) have a modicum of empathy that enables them to track another person's point of view.

"You got me there," answered Lyle Ray. "Laney Jo did score extra Oxy, and we'd do it together. But we don't do it no more."

> **Lyle Ray hadn't blinked an eye. Addicts are like that, especially those dipping toward EmD-1 conduct. Nothing makes them mad, not even the idea of being caught. EmD-3s have a modicum of empathy that enables them to track another person's point of view.**

Looking Lyle Ray squarely in the eyes I said, "I've tried to help you and Laney Jo and the boys, but I am no help if I just make it easier for you to be irresponsible. I can't be your back-up budget plan. You need to find another way to make ends meet."

I'd hung onto hope that my cousin would work with me; that he would trust I loved him. And I'd fervently hoped that, because he loved me, I had leverage with him.

WHEN EMPATHY FAILS

Lyle Ray had tried to look pitiful, saying, "I just can't go to the PayDay Loan people again. I just got the last loan paid off. It's a nightmare. I can't pay my rent." He'd dialed up the pressure then. "I'll lose the house. I'll have to send Laney Jo and the kids back to Michigan to live with her mother. I'll have to live in my car. I don't know what I'm going to do." He'd said all this with a straight face.

Firmly, I'd answered, "I can help you, Lyle Ray, but I won't give you money anymore. Let's sit down and look at a budget for you. I can help with a grocery card now and then, but no cash." I'd taken out a piece of paper from my kitchen desk and started jotting down numbers. If Laney Jo kept working, they could make it, but there was no room for anything extra. I even calculated their cigarettes into the budget.

When I'd asked Lyle Ray how much he spent on his pot habit, he'd told me he was getting it free. "No need to put that into the budget," he'd offered. For a brief moment, it had appeared that cousin Lyle Ray was willing to cooperate, possibly turning his EmD-1 conduct into EmD-3. (Of course, I'd been alarmed that he'd been getting his pot for free.)

"Take this plan to Laney Jo; then we can talk some more. What do you think of it?" I'd asked. Lyle Ray had smiled at me, then said, "Auntie, I gotta get home to watch football." Clearly, the concept of choosing to do the right thing had been insincere.

I knew there was no longer any point to the discussion, so I folded the piece of paper with the proposed budget and handed it to

> He'd shrugged his shoulders in resignation and said, "Auntie. I'm an addict. It's just the way it is." The jig was up. Lyle Ray had recognized there was no point in trying to con me anymore.

Lyle Ray. "Think about it, honey. There are options for you. Take this home to Laney Jo, then get back to me." I'd smiled at him and held an ounce of hope.

He'd given me a sad little grin. It told me that he knew we were through—as in through for good. He'd shrugged his shoulders in resignation and said, "Auntie, I'm an addict. It's just the way it is." The jig was up. Lyle Ray had recognized there was no point in trying to con me anymore.

Sadly, he didn't take up my other option, which was to get professional treatment for his addiction. I'd made that offer when he was 16 and as a result been cut off for years. His mother had tried to shame me when I'd made that offer to help, saying I was interfering with her family. At least Lyle Ray hadn't continued with the shaming this time. Instead, he'd quietly walked away.

Sinking to a new low

That was the last time I saw Lyle Ray. I have no idea how things are going for him and his family. However, I did hear from his 14-year-old son Derek shortly after I'd refused to loan them anymore money.

In a text, Derek had demanded that I apologize to his mother for all the ways I'd wronged her. For good measure, he'd also attempted to shame me with a line that stated: No one in the family liked me.

I'd tried to be gentle with him since he'd been a young teen then. I had

---

Derek's text message to me [including an image of Syndrome, the villain in the film, "The Incredibles"] read, "You dense motherfucker." His intent had been to shame me. This response showed that his parents had indeed deteriorated to EmD-1, taking along the next generation.

apologized for making him feel bad, but I'd refused to take the blame for his parents' lying and manipulation. I'd hoped Derek could understand there might be more than one side to the story.

True to form, he'd sent a "white trash"-style text and photo as his send-off. It featured a picture of Syndrome, the evil villain in the animated film "The Incredibles." Syndrome's mission was to kill all of the superheroes in the world. Derek's text message to me read, "You dense motherfucker." This response to me showed that his parents had indeed deteriorated to EmD-1, taking along the next generation.

In Greek mythology, Sisyphus, a proud and deceitful king, was punished with the eternal task of rolling an enormous boulder up a hill over and over again. His constant struggle not to be overtaken by monster stone is considered a symbol of the daily challenge addicts and alcoholics face to maintain their sobriety.

In many ways, EmD-3s are more dangerous to us than EmD-1s. Narcissists and sociopaths are at least consistent in their self-absorption, lack of remorse, and trickery. In an odd way, you know where you stand with an EmD-1. It is the inconsistency of EmD-3s that leaves us vulnerable to ongoing abuse. They can be brilliant, funny, and caring. When they fall off the wagon, then apologize and return to recovery, we are accepting and encouraging. We want them to succeed.

The moment another's success is more important to you than it is to them, you are in grave danger. This behavior is called codependency, and it's a signal that you have become crucial to the addict's or Em-3's downward spiral. Do not linger in or around this abnormal symbiotic relationship.

Years ago, a client of mine who had 15 years of sobriety clarified why recovery for addicts (and other EmD-3s) compares to the mythical Sisyphus endlessly[67] rolling the same boulder uphill again and again. This client had called me up short when I'd offered platitudes about staying sober and living a fuller life. I would say things like "it is what it is; just keep working at it, and you will see." I'd missed that he'd had to start at a simpler level. This is what is meant by the slogan "One Day at a Time," a cornerstone of Alcoholics Anonymous (AA) and other 12-step recovery programs.

> **To stay safe, stay clear of narcissists and sociopaths. When you love an EmD-3 or addict, you must step aside, allowing them to help themselves. They will get well and stay sober—or not. It's up to them, not you!**

"Hear me, Dr. Marshack! You have no idea what it is like to wake up each morning not knowing for sure if you are truly in touch with reality," he'd said with the same resigned look I'd seen on Lyle Ray's face that last time we'd talked.

To stay safe, stay clear of narcissists and sociopaths. When you love an EmD-3 or addict, you must step aside, allowing them

---

[67] In Greek mythology, Sisyphus, the king of what is now Corinth, was punished for his self-aggrandizement and deceitfulness by being forced to roll an immense boulder up a hill only to have it repeatedly roll back, then be pushed up again for eternity.

to help themselves. They will get well and stay sober—or not. It's up to them, not you!

It may seem counterintuitive to hold back, but the truth is—your help will cripple them. Until an EmD-3 or addict has a reason to behave differently, they will stay suspended in their empathy disorder. Detach from—and love—them from a distance. Do not attempt to rescue EmD-3s by doing things for them they should be doing for themselves.

The love of a Matriarch Warrior

When young Derek chose a super villain to represent his anger in his hateful text he was aligning with the "wrong side" just like his parents, grandparents, and countless generations of our "white trash" clan. Since his auntie represented as a superhero, he'd used Syndrome—whose mission was to destroy genuine superheroes—to irk me.

In her role as resilient matriarch, the author recalls feeling like the fearsome Xena Warrior Princess, who was also portrayed as a fiercely protective mother. In the fantasy TV series featuring Xena, she is often seen protecting her young daughter, Eve, during heated battles.

It seemed like I'd crossed a war zone to protect family and fight for the greater good. In a surreal way, I'd felt like the fantasy heroine Xena Warrior Princess[68], who is both a mom and a warrior.

I may be the strongest, most resilient matriarch Derek will ever know, but that wasn't enough to pull him from a life filled with EmD-s. It's been painful knowing his "clan" of choice is made up of drug addicts. I can only hope that transformation is ahead for him.

I shut down the family Facebook page when I gave up the desperate search for kin with an ounce of empathy. I'd found instead, troubled, manipulative people who are experts in blame and shame. Many of these newfound relatives have pressured me outright to surrender to their unreasonable demands.

No dice. I am done and gone with cons!

"Warrior Matriarch" Highlights

1. EmD-3 behavior can appear to be as manipulative and destructive as that of an EmD-1. However, with proper treatment for brain chemical imbalance, EmD-3s can maintain relatively normal empathy.

---

[68] "Xena: Warrior Princess" is an American fantasy television series that aired in syndication from 1995 until 2001. It has been praised by critics for its strong female protagonist and has since acquired a strong cult following, attention in fandom, parody, and academia. The narrative follows Xena, an infamous warrior, on a quest to seek redemption for her past sins against the innocent by using her formidable fighting skills to help those who are unable to defend themselves. All the while keeping her young daughter safe.

2. If the EmD-3 (drug addict or bipolar) does not choose to get medical and psychological help, they can deteriorate to EmD-2 (i.e. brain damage), or worse (EmD-1), conduct;

3. EmD-3s have inherited their disorders: It is not hard to spot the genetic link in the family tree. Sadly, these problems tend to be carried into one generation after another, causing no end of havoc and tragedy in their relationships.

4. Because EmD-3s use blame and shame to manage loved ones, the survivors must rebuild their destroyed self-esteem.

5. Survivors in these families need to strike out on their own to create a life free from Empathy Dysfunction. Reluctant to leave the family they love, survivors must remain confident they can build a "family" of healthy, loving people able to reciprocate empathy.

6. Typically, EmD-3s tend to abuse the family and con loved ones out of money, which they use to support their destructive lifestyle. Because you love these folks, it's natural to want to help them. However, the codependence of accommodating their every need will only backfire, hurting them, and you, even more. It has to stop.

7. The untreated EmD-3 will inevitably fail in many ways, including parenting. Their children will be brought up bereft of a conscience. And so it goes on.

CHAPTER SEVEN

How Mob Mentality Materializes

"I don't even call it violence when it's in self-defense. I call it intelligence."

— Malcolm X

When a neighborly chat won't work

Normally, Emd-4s are good neighbors, and you have little to fear. Should you have a disagreement, it is usually settled satisfactorialy over a cup of coffee or tea. EmD-4s, however, can easily be whipped into a mob mentality by EmD-1s, the type who play on ignorance and fear or encourage underhanded greed. EmD-4s can be malevolent when played by an EmD-1.

When EmD-4s don't stop to consider unintended consequences, they can be swept into a frenzy at the hand of a convincing EmD-1—especially one who has status and power. This kind of "lazy" reasoning can harm others while leaving the EmD-4 stuck in a false belief and susceptible to a mob mentality's pressure.

You may want to refer back to the *Prologue* and *Appendices* where there are details about elements of the conspiracy. The maps included will help you navigate the storyline. This chapter and *Chapter Eight* take you on a deep dive into the actual events that lead to the mob mentality. Here's where you'll find the evidence for the True Conspiracy Theory. Listen up; it gets complicated.

I have previously described a situation in which my neighbors at Steamboat Landing (next door to where I lived) put up a Wanted Poster of me at their private community's front gate. At face value, their HOA Board had accepted statements made by my tormentors (Don Morris, Melanie Mooney, and Joseph and Julianne Leas).

According to those four, I was a dangerous and crazy woman guilty of assault and trespass. Their coup de gras: the claim that my psychology patients, who I saw in my home office, were also a threat to their community.

Without any attempt to fact-check or hear my side, the HOA Board morphed into a mob. They downloaded my picture from the Internet and posted it in public with a defaming notice. Long after the incident, that HOA was forced to pay me a settlement for its libelous act. To this day, many of my former neighbors can't shake believing the distorted, untrue assertions leveled at me. As outrageous as this conduct was, it pales in comparison to what I will describe in this chapter.

Layers of lies and power plays fostered this mob mentality. If it had been two neighbors bickering over a property line, the issue could have been worked out pretty quickly even if lawyers were involved. In my case, the pivotal players came from a veritable "Who's Who" list in our small Washington town of Vancouver: the Mayor, the City Manager, members of the City Council, the City Attorney, the local newspaper owner, the auto sales tycoon, and a venerable train company.

There was no way this dispute was going to be resolved with an over-the-fence casual, but candid, conversation. Too many influential people and politicians, neighbors and others had a stake in the outcome.

> ... people in power must be held accountable for their actions just like the rest of us. In fact, I believe that public employees and others with clout should be held to a higher moral standard because their actions impact the greater good—sometimes dramatically.

Even more pertinent here is that people in power must be held accountable for their actions just like the rest of us. In fact, I believe that public employees and others with clout should be held to a higher moral standard because their actions impact the greater good—sometimes dramatically. What is a smallish EmD-4 (-) action (such as the wanted poster at SBL) can turn into nightmarish mob destruction when powerful people turn a blind eye to their empathic responsibilities. Some of the power brokers in Vancouver are EmD-1s, but most are hard-working, good people at heart. However, even EmD-4s will engage in malevolent conduct when they are under the influence of ignorance, fear, or greed.

Believe in nice

It was 2004 when Jim Jacks, Vancouver Citizen Advocate, Code Enforcement Officer Richard Landis, and Josephine Townsend, Vancouver City Prosecutor, conspired to write the libelous and fateful memo about me. Politicians, civic leaders and well known local citizens (such as car sales magnate Dick Hannah and newspaper publisher Scott Campbell) were lobbying to increase the value of riverfront properties.

These wealthy neighbors of mine had the beauty of the Columbia River in the front yards of their multimillion-dollar homes; however, they had to endure the trains (and the noise from train horns) that ran along the river corridor (40-50 trains a day). This did not help the value of their already-expensive homes.

The movement of 40 to 50 Burlington Northern Santa Fe Railroad (BNSF) trains through the author's neighborhood each day prompted the Steamboat Landing residential community and other neighbors to push for a Train Horn Noise Quiet Zone (THNQZ) designation in order to maintain the worth and saleability of their multimillion-dollar estates and riverfront land.

BNSF attempted to take away this right of passage in order to remove the last obstacle—the author—to the THNQZ. Next, BNSF insisted that to use her right of way, the author would have to buy liability insurance at a premium of $50,000 a year plus maintain the crossing.

The barely visible stop sign shown above is to the right of the stretch where the author's deed guarantees her right of way across the tracks.

They generated a plan for a Train Horn Noise Quiet Zone (THNQZ)[69] taxing authority (to tax the neighboring property owners), then pushed it through the Washington State

---

[69] A "quiet zone" is a railroad grade crossing where trains are prohibited from sounding their horns in order to decrease the noise level for nearby residential communities. This is aimed at the routine horn blasts required by the Federal Train Administration at public crossings. The train horns can be silenced only when other safety measures compensate for their absence.

Legislature—complete with a first-of-its-kind Local Improvement District (LID) for train quiet zones.

That had set the stage for spending millions of dollars of Washington taxpayers' money to cover the costs of feasibility and engineering studies, tax planning, and community meetings.

The Quiet Zone proponents used a mob of City Attorneys, City Planners, and City Engineers to negotiate with Burlington Northern Santa Fe Railway Co. (BNSF), the Federal Railway Administration (FRA), the City of Vancouver, and the homeowners who stood to benefit.

Ultimately, legislation was drafted to allow The Quiet Zone (it passed the Washington Legislature in 2009). It included a new twist: Property taxes of all homeowners living near the tracks would increase to fund the project. I lived along those tracks, too, but not in some megamillion-dollar home. I'd objected to the tax proposal. It hadn't mattered: The trap to make me comply with their wishes had already been set—back in 2003.

Years before I'd even known about the THNQZ project, and well in advance of being run through the mill of law suits and neighbor harassment, Code Enforcement Officer Richard Landis had started action to revoke my home occupation permit (2004). After 20 years of peacefully working from my home office, I was told that my family therapy practice was—supposedly—endangering my neighbors.

Landis had recently revoked the home occupation permit of another small home based business nearby. He was systematically clearing the path (south of the tracks) of objectors to The Quiet Zone. I hadn't understood exactly what Landis was up to then; but I'd known that I had to stand my ground against his cease-and-desist threats.

It is telling how easily the police were drawn in by Landis. In an email to Vancouver Police Commander Dave King, Landis had said, "I have an extensive file on Kathy if you want to see it." I'd had no idea that the City of Vancouver was stalking me and using the police to shake me down!

Please note, during the early years, 2002 to 2005, when Landis began his campaign to bury me, I was already at the center of several disconcerting legal actions, including: my antagonistic divorce; an assault charge; my neighbors' land use suit; and fighting

Townsend, who was trying to revoke my Diversion agreement (detailed in *Chapter One*). All I needed was one more onslaught from the mob's arsenal.

Much of the information about this period I learned years later when, in connection to my conspiracy lawsuit against Vancouver and my neighbors, I made a public records request for any information associated with my name. It was incredible the amount of data city employees had collected on me—literally, dozens of bankers' boxes filled with documents, including my emails to Jacks, other civic leaders, and my attorneys.) The reasons for this voracious tracking will become clear as I lay out *Chapters Seven and Eight*. Essentially, I was at the center of a perfect storm generated by tempestuous egocentrics raging at me from all directions.

In deposition many years later, even more was revealed. Vancouver employee Brian Carlson had been the liaison between the City and the residents in the prospective Quiet Zone area. He'd testified that Dick Hannah (the Pacific Northwest auto tycoon) had hosted meetings (at his multimillion-dollar home on the river) for private individuals and government officials to discuss furthering the Train Horn Noise Quiet Zone (THNQZ).

It seems that during Hannah's secret "public" meetings at his house the conversation had frequently turned to "what to do about the Kathy Marshack issue." I was never invited to attend. So much for government transparency.

On the other hand, Landis arranged for me to be part of a 2005 train-related conference call arranged by a BNSF attorney. The other conference call participants were: my lawyers, a City Attorney, a City Planner, Landis and several other officials connected to The Quiet Zone issue.

There was a brief introduction by the BNSF attorney, Shana Druffner, who seemed sensitive to my desire to continue my psychology practice out of my home. After that, Landis blurted out, "But I thought you wanted me to shut down all of the businesses along the train tracks!"

"Oh Mr. Landis," said the Texan BNSF attorney diplomatically, "we wouldn't want to interfere with Dr. Marshack's business. We are here on this call today to discuss how to make safety at our train crossings a priority." However, Druffner didn't sound sincere to me. Rather, it sounded like she didn't want it to get out that BNSF, the City, and my neighbors were conspiring to remove my opposition to the safety problems associated with the THNQZ.

And they were using Landis to help them come after me. Years later, in 2009, when I poured through the bankers' boxes of stuff the City had sent over, I found numerous emails between Landis and Druffner, *(See fig. A.10)* discussing how to clean up my supposed "non-compliance." All the while in Texas, Druffner handled all of her business by phone and email, craftily playing both sides against each other.

A little bit of history might help you understand the relationship between my business license and the Train Horn Noise Quiet Zone (THNQZ); and why the city and BNSF wanted to eliminate my legal rights. I had a deeded property right granted to my predecessor by the train company in 1908. I was the only one in the neighborhood with this deed, which permited me to cross the tracks to get to and from any part of my land. *(See the Prologue and Appendix figs. A.2, A.3, and A.4 to view my 1908 Right of Way Agreement with SP&S Railway as well as maps of the contested areas.)*

The deed was explicit. Not only had I been granted access to and from my home, but the train company had also promised to build and maintain the private crossing associated with the access. This meant BNSF was obligated to uphold my deed in spite of their desire for a Quiet Zone.

The train the mob wanted to silence with a Train Horn Noise Quiet Zone—even as it rapidly approached the author's unsafe train crossing shown in the foreground.

What does my crossing deed have to do with a federal permit for a THNQZ? To save expense, the crossing to my house was ignored by the Quiet Zone planners. I questioned this error at a planning commission meeting I attended in 2005. At that time, I was told that because the train crossing near my house was a "private" crossing the law allowed the THNQZ to go through without upgraded crossing equipment near my house. Really? I watched children stand on the tracks on the lookout for their school bus and yet there is no safety equipment required? Not even a warning blast from the train?

As with my neighbor's lawsuit regarding my river easement, I started doing some historical research. Not only did I pull up my old train crossing deed, but located maps showing the construction of the track, starting in 1906. I talked with surveyors and found old photos from the period. This evidence proved to be invaluable in bolstering my rights to a safe train crossing.

I also emailed the Federal Railway Administration (FRA) to learn more about the process for securing a permit for a Train Horn Noise Quiet Zone (officially called THNQZ). I had a chance to meet the local representative of the FRA in August 2009 at the party celebrating the new permit. The mayor was present along with many other officials and civic leaders. When I mentioned my concerns to her, the THNQZ began to unravel.

For example, after the representative of the FRA visited my crossing the day after the party, she was shocked to learn these three things. First, the Quiet Zone committee had submitted permitting documents to the Feds and neglected to mention my train crossing at all. They didn't even put it on the map of the designated Quiet Zone.

Second, when the FRA representative checked the statistics on this little "private" crossing, she discovered that it is considered one of the most dangerous crossings in Vancouver.

Third, she realized that because I operated a business south of the train tracks that my crossing was considered a "private crossing serving as a public crossing."

This last point pushed it over the edge. Because I operated a business out of my home (my psychology practice), the crossing would have to be upgraded with safety equipment. Now I understood why Landis came after my home occupation permit!

This legal mumbo jumbo had BNSF, the City of Vancouver, and the THNQZ proponents backed into a corner: As long as I held a business license, and an ironclad train crossing deed, the Quiet Zone initiative could not move forward. First, the City and BNSF would have to agree to upgrade the safety features of my existing—and ancient—BNSF train crossing. *(See the photo in this section.)*

With all that my neighbors, the City, and BNSF had to gain, why hadn't they all agreed to just fix it? Yes, that would have cost more money, but if they truly supported safety along this dangerous stretch of track, why would they fight me? Instead of being reasonable, a campaign of harassing me—an unimportant nobody living in a modest 1953 ranch house in a neighborhood of wealthy homeowners—was launched in earnest.

Landis helped by threatening to take away my business license. Townsend aided by attempting to revoke my diversion; thus sending me to jail and eliminating my business that way.

BNSF had continued its attempts to take away my deeded right of way across the tracks. They'd begun insisting that to use my right of way I'd have to buy liability insurance at a premium of $50,000 a year.

It took eight years (and tons of money) for the players to agree to upgrade the safety features at this single-lane train crossing. BNSF's only solution: install LED-lit stop signs! No crossing guards. No train horn. No bells. No lights, or any other signaling device. Just a couple of light-up stop signs on a major BNSF railroad track with 40 to 50 trains a day, traveling at 60 miles per hour, moving passengers and cargo between Chicago, Ill., and Portland, Ore.

Oh yes, before I forget: Why did I call this section "Believe in nice? Because, ironically, that's the slogan Hannah uses to promote his string of successful car dealerships. Most people consider car dealers untrustworthy; I presume Hannah developed this slogan to distinguish himself from the crowd of disreputable car dealers in Oregon's Portland Metro area.

The safety "measures" at the unsafe crossing near the author's former home are shown here: a solar panel to light the Stop Sign at night; the "private" Rail Road Crossing sign; and, at the bottom where it is less visible,, the Train Horn Noise Quiet Zone sign added after the Zone was approved.

"Nice" is hardly the way he and local government officials treated me. Hannah was the host of meetings where I, and my rights, were discussed. Since City employees as well as the Vancouver Mayor attended, these were essentially public meetings that required notifying the public about time and place.

In fact, my attorney had asked the City Attorney's office to send me notices of all public meetings having anything to do with the THNQZ. You guessed it, I was never notified nor did I ever see a posted notice. There was no attempt to negotiate with me in a respectful manner.

Hannah knew full well that decisions about my property—and me—were being made clandestinely. His behavior was that of an EmD-4 (-).

"Call Richard Landis"

More than anyone, news publisher Campbell should have adhered to the ethical responsibility to present unbiased reporting; yet he used his influence for personal gain. From 2003 to 2012 he published front page stories about my divorce, my arrests, and my struggles with the neighbors over property issues, always casting me as the problem.

His editors sent reporters to photograph my court proceedings. *The Columbian* newspaper had even lined up and run a story to discredit the value of my property when I'd tried to sell and leave the area. The content was hardly newsworthy, and many readers wondered why he'd allowed it. Campbell, also one of my neighbors, had been harboring an ulterior motive.

When BNSF had tried to make me buy insurance to use the train crossing, I'd innocently pointed out that the old county road all of us, including the Campbells, lived on was still, technically, a public right of way. Surely, I could not be considered responsible for maintaining BNSF's privately-owned train crossing when it serviced a public road (the Old Camas Highway).

Once the road's public classification had been revealed, Campbell wanted to keep it quiet. He didn't want to risk that this caveat would draw more people to travel the road in front of his mansion, making it less desirable. As it turned out, he'd been desperate to protect the value of his property. He'd needed to sell it as quickly as possible; hence my claim about the old county road being public had to be quashed. I guess he thought casting doubt on me through his newspaper was the perfect ploy to protect himself.

Campbell had just fallen on hard times. It was the height of the recession, shortly after the 2008 housing bubble burst; yet it seemed like he'd been the last to register that the print news industry was near collapse. During the time Campbell supported the Quiet Zone initiative (2003 through 2014), he'd foolishly built a lavish building for his family-owned newspaper.

Then, as his business was failing, the housing bubble burst. This left Campbell with an expensive home worth far less than it had cost to build. No matter the sorry state of the housing market, he was forced to sell that home to pay business debts—a court-imposed requirement to qualify for reorganization bankruptcy for Campbell's flailing newspaper.

All of Campbell's behind-the-scenes machinations finally came to light in August 2009, a year and a half after having made yet another public records request of the City. I obtained copies of all documentation on all matters related to me, my family, and my property.

I also got copies of Campbell's personal correspondence (from his attorney) involving anything to do with the Old Camas Highway, the THNQZ, and me. Because Campbell involved himself in the Quiet Zone fracas, his attorney had to turn over some very incriminating emails written to City officials with notes in Campbell's own handwriting.

I discovered Campbell's handwritten notes (not legally considered confidential) from a private meeting he'd had with Mayor Tim Leavitt to discuss the legitimacy of my claim about the old road. This is when Campbell learned he was going to need more documentation to strengthen his case against me regarding both the existence of the Old Camas Highway and my right to use the road to get to and from my house. In the margin of his notes from this meeting, Campbell had scribbled, "Call Richard Landis."

Supposedly a low-level public servant (He worked in Code Enforcement.), Landis shows up numerous times in this book. He was involved in many nefarious hustles to harm me—as evidenced in public records, such as Landis' emails and Code Enforcement logs, depositions, and court proceedings. For a list of Landis' activities regarding my easements alone *(See fig. A.9, "Alternative Facts")*.

In addition, the records held proof that Landis had sent several memos to Campbell containing information that he hoped could be used against me. But that's not all. Here's a short list of Landis' despicable activities. He'd:

1. Helped Townsend try to revoke my Diversion agreement by issuing bogus citations concerning my home business license, my parking, my dog, my fence, and so on.

2. Worked with BNSF to further the Quiet Zone initiative by attempting to shut down my business.

3. Wrote reports for the City Attorney's office that stated he'd investigated the old road and found no evidence it had "ever been public." In actuality, the old county road had been

commissioned in 1852 under the Territory of Washington's government.[70]

4. Conjured up official-looking letters on City letterhead; letters that questioned the legitimacy of my deeded property rights.

5. Investigated my daughters' school records. I was terrified when he'd postured dragging my children into the fray.

6. Told the Steamboat Landing HOA that they could build a fence in the middle of my easement to prevent me from using it.

7. Spent nearly a year's worth of the City's Code Enforcement budget trying to have me punished for parking my motorhome on the gravel driveway next to my garage.

8. Withheld significant evidence in response to my public records request. This included the Townsend/Jacks-conceived memo and the videos taken by Don Morris, who was one of my stalkers *(more about this in Chapter Eight)*.

---

[70] Over the years, Landis asserted several qualifiers about the River Easement road and the Old Camas Highway. He said that: my deed was "vague;" the Old Camas Highway (OCH) had never been built; the OCH was my neighbor's "private driveway;" there was an underlying easement on my property for a County road but it was not the OCH; there was no survey to show whether the OCH was north or south of the train tracks; and the OCH was "never a public road." In other words, Landis kept coming up with ways to interfere with my rights by making contradictory statements about the old roads.

Owen, Pat

From:	Owen, Pat
Sent:	Wednesday, September 01, 2004 2:10 PM
To:	Landis, Richard
Cc:	Chumbley, Traci
Subject:	"144th Court" south of Evergreen Hwy

Tracking: Recipient Delivery
Landis, Richard Delivered: 9/1/2004 2:10 PM
Chumbley, Traci Delivered: 9/1/2004 2:10 PM

See exhibit of site below.

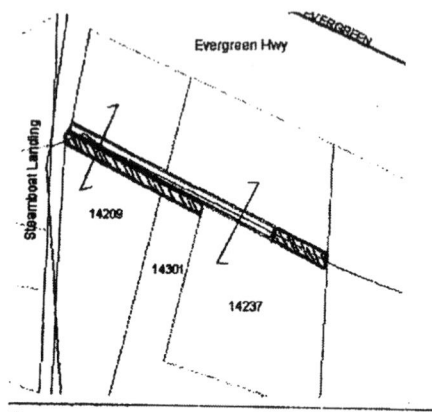

[site diagram showing Evergreen Hwy, Steamboat Landing, parcels 14209, 14301, 14237]

The areas outlined in red and blue are easements for ingress and egress, (private roads).

The deed for 14237 SE Evergreen Hwy, owner Kathy Marshak, contains a paragraph stating:
"TOGETHER WITH an easement for ingress and egress over and across a strip of land 30 feet in width, as said roadway now exists, leading from subject property to the "Steamboat Landing" as well as leading over and across that tract of land described as the "Old Camas Highway".

Hoping this answers the question of status of this property. Let me know if there are additional questions.
Thanks, Pat

Patricia (Pat) Owen
Right of Way Services/Records
City of Vancouver
Transportation Services
1300 Franklin - PO Box 1995

9/22/2004

See Fig. A.11 for samples of the in excess of 60 pages of correspondence about the author's property between Landis, Owen, and others in 2004.

In this and communications that followed, Enforcement Officer Richard Landis inquires about the current status of the author's easements and Old Camas Road history.

It is revealing when Pat Owen, working in the Transportation Services Department, questions why Landis is interested in the train crossing and the old road when neither falls within the purview of his job.

The other thing indicative of Landis' meddling in areas where he had no business: The fact that Assistant City Attorney Allison Chinn redacted sections of Landis' and Owens' correspondence. Supposedly, the blacked-out portions contained confidential information provided by City Attorneys.

HOW MOB MENTALITY MATERIALIZES

Honestly, I am not making this stuff up. Occasionally, an honorable City employee would question Landis' actions. In the spring of 2004, my new neighbors, Joseph and Julianne Leas, had challenged my easement to cross their property to the river road. I'd then contacted Pat Owen, a Vancouver employee who worked for Transportation Services and handled rights of way records.

When I'd asked Owen for access to public records on my property and the county roads in our area, she responded, "Oh, it won't take me any time at all to get you those records. I just pulled them last week for Richard Landis." I'd never met Landis at that point.

Why was he checking up on my property rights? Who'd asked him to do so? Owen had also wanted to know and sent Landis an email on Oct.13, 2004. She'd asked, "Since this is a private civil dispute—should the City even be involved?" Landis told her that BNSF and City Attorney Jim McNamara needed the records to clear up my claim that the Old Camas Highway was a public right of way past Campbell's house. Landis also told Owen that BNSF wanted a conference call to clear up the matter of the old road.

By then, the Leas and neighbor Mary Kellogg had joined forces to sue me over the river easement road. Landis was busily talking with lots of people about me, the easement lawsuit, and the Quiet Zone: These things fell well outside his purview.

The Landis-caused chaos enabled Campbell to cast me in a highly unfavorable light. He'd managed to have his private meetings with the Mayor about protecting his property. I'd been denied access to Leavitt every time I'd asked, dating back to the time Jacks had written a libelous memo about me.[71]

---

[71] In an email follow-up to his 2004 memo, Jacks assured the Mayor and

Campbell finagled a deal for the City to buy his newspaper building, essentially bailing him out of debt. (Vancouver paid $18.5 million for Campbell's building in 2010, far less than Campbell's asking price of $41.5 million). It became the posh headquarters for the Mayor, the Council, and City Hall.

After getting assurances from Leavitt that no one (me), and no road or right of way issues would get in his way, Campbell was able to sell his house to David Lindsay. He bought the home with written assurances that Campbell would pay for any problems caused by the county road issue. Lindsay promptly tore up the Old Camas Highway in front of his house and built a wall—still standing today—preventing my secondary access to the main road (S.E. Evergreen Highway).

It fell on deaf ears when I tried explaining to city officials that my neighbors and I needed a secondary access due to safety issues south of the train tracks. I even had a fire department evaluation *(See fig. A.6)* that determined it was unsafe to block the Old Camas Highway. In the report, Fire Captain Mike Berg stated:

> *"I might suggest we advise the property owners on this road we cannot meet time response guidelines into this area for fire or medical responses and also let their fire insurance companies know that we as a Department cannot operate with our normal fire ground operations and expect larger fire damage due to extreme fire access problems for both equipment and personnel due to the limitations of the road and surrounding trees and vegetation or we accept the possibility that we most likely will damage rigs in this area."*

City Council that I would not attend their "open" City Council meetings to discuss my concerns.

The Scene of the Crimes
the New City Hall in Vancouver, Wash.

Initially owned by Scott Campbell, the building was designed to house his newspaper, The Columbian. Personal and business financial woes during the Great Recession forced him to sell. Campbell sold it to the City of Vancouver for a song.

City Hall was where Jim Jacks, the City's Citizen Advocate (although he worked against the author rather than for her), wrote the libelous email about the author and circulated it around the building. He'd blindly believed falsehoods about the author as told to him by Vancouver City Prosecutor Josephine Townsend and Code Enforcement Officer Richard Landis, who also worked at City Hall. Other "mob" members at City Hall included the Mayor and some members of City Council

Thus began the conspiring against the author by Vancouver employees and her neighbors. She later sued Vancouver for conspiracy and defamation. The City settled with her for $75,000 as "recompense" for more than a decade of hell at the hands of its staff.

The action was illegal: Never were proper permits issued to alter a federally-protected wetland adjacent to a natural pond and stream. I couldn't get the City of Vancouver to acknowledge the violation.[72]

I sued Lindsay for violating my right to use the road (Old Camas Highway); without unlimited funds to go after this multimillionaire, I'd had to settle. Lindsay paid me $50,000 to go away. I paid the law firm for two of the three attorneys involved $25,000. (My title company paid the third attorney.)

Campbell certainly seemed like an EmD-1 because his actions were unethical. However, for most of his life, he had been a good citizen, even a philanthropist (ironically serving on the board of an environmental group trying to save Columbia River Chum Salmon habitat). No one had ever accused him of causing trouble for anyone.

He may not have been considered the best businessman after investing more money into his failing newspaper; however, I can understand his desire to save his family's legacy, a three-generation Clark County institution.

On the other hand, Campbell had been quite willing to use his considerable influence and alliance with Landis to throw me under the bus. This level of behaving badly is EmD-4 (-).

"All the best"

Jacks was not famous or wealthy. As far as I can tell, he functioned as a rather uninspired EmD-4(-). Nevertheless, he caused severe harm to my family. He would turn out to be quite the fabricator.

---

[72] The paper trail is thick with evidence documenting these behind-the-scenes negotiations.

Naively, he'd followed Townsend's deceitful description of me and the events, never stopping to question disparities in the evidence that had evoked his boss, City Manager Pat McDonnell, to tell Jacks to get to the bottom of my complaint in the first place. (As it turned out, Jacks had never even opened the file about me that Townsend was supposed to have shown him.) Jacks served as an unwitting tool for Townsend and other power brokers in Vancouver.

EmD-4s are easily frightened, and Jacks was no different. He hadn't even had the courage to admit or correct his incompetent actions when later deposed about his actions.

Even so, I felt sorry for this man in a way. He'd lost his budding political career (He'd been elected to the Washington State Legislature in 2010 after his stint as Vancouver Citizen Advocate.) and left the state of Washington in disgrace:

In March 2011, four months after being re-elected to represent Vancouver's 49th District, Jacks unexpectedly resigned. This followed on the heels of the City's discovery of his years-old, but nonetheless libelous, memo about me. On April 23, 2011, *The Columbian* ran an article with this Jacks' quote, "I resigned because I'm an alcoholic."

I hadn't felt too sorry, though, when during deposition, Jacks had rejected his chance to come clean and rectify the great wrong he'd done to me by writing his libelous memo. Had he taken that opportunity to be transparent and honest, he would have become an EmD-5 hero. Instead, Jacks had choked and fled. (I tried to teach my children that an apology for a wrong doing is only a start.

(I tried to teach my children that an apology for a wrong doing is only a start. Correcting the error is critical, particularly if you have harmed another person.)

Correcting the error is critical, particularly if you have harmed another person.)

"All the best!"[73] was how Jacks had signed his defaming letter to McDonnell—guaranteeing the content was factual. If you think about it, that salutation in this context is an immature message, no different than Hannah's sales slogan, "Believe in Nice." Platitudes mean nothing when they aren't backed up with truth, integrity, or courageous action.

Jacks had been the first hire by McDonnell to serve in the brand new role of Vancouver Citizen Advocate (or ombudsman). Jacks, a young married father, must have been proud of his accomplishment. McDonnell had probably regarded the fresh-faced fellow with the charming smile as the ideal person to hear public complaints; then help citizens resolve issues by guiding them through the maze of City government.

Jacks kept meticulous records of these interactions and his efforts to aid. What I later read in his logs revealed how this man (at Townsend's behest) had sought to destroy my reputation, setting the course for the next decade of my life.

First, Jacks crafted the entire memo to McDonnell from falsehoods told him by Townsend and Landis. In deposition, Jacks admitted never opening my Diversion file; yet his memo had included quotations supposedly taken from that file. Also in deposition, Jacks referenced nonexistent reports from my psychologist and court appearances that had never happened. He

---

[73] The terms narcissist and sociopath are actually traits of diagnosable personality disorders. They are not diagnoses per se. Neither is the term "functional sociopath," actually a diagnosis. It is a term entirely invented by Jacks. I primarily use the terms narcissist and sociopath to describe qualities among those with EmD-1. However, other EmDs can demonstrate narcissism and sociopathy from time to time.

only reported what Townsend and Landis had told him was in my files. If he had only opened the file, he would have seen none of these supposedly incriminating documents actually existed.

From Landis, Jacks had heard concocted stories about my failure to comply with City codes over the years and the subsequent warnings I'd been given. None of it had been true. Townsend, in her deposition, confirmed that Jacks had never read the file. She admitted that her boss Ted Gathe (Vancouver's Chief Attorney) had told her to *show* Jacks the file. Townsend had literally done as directed and held the record in the air in front of Jacks. Then, she'd proceeded to tell Jacks her interpretation of its contents.

One of the most harmful lies Townsend told Jacks: that I'd been diagnosed as a "functional sociopath." Jacks didn't question this outlandish lie and dutifully recorded it in his report to the City Manager. Although Jacks was the Ombudsman (i.e. citizen helper) for the city, he reported directly to the city manager, Pat McDonnell instead of sending anything to me, the citizen who asked for help.[74]

Nor did Jacks: verify any statements made by Townsend or Landis; check court records; read Landis' Code Enforcement file; speak with my psychotherapist; ask me to address the issues (one of the roles of an ombudsman); give me a chance to defend myself; or inform me there even was a report in which I was the subject. And yet he sent off the report to McDonnell calling it "factual information."

---

[74] The Ombudsman should represent the citizen and investigate the matter at hand. He should contact all parties in an unbiased way. Instead, Jacks tipped my opposition off to my complaint and allowed them to concoct a story to cover themselves.

Apparently, dispensing with me had given Jacks an opportunity to further his political ambition in the State Legislature—where he happily did the bidding of The Quiet Zone folks. It was Jacks who pushed through legislation that allowed residents along the river (including me) to be taxed specifically to support the creation of a Train Horn Noise Quiet Zone.

> **Apparently, dispensing with me had given Jacks an opportunity to further his political ambition in the State Legislature—where he happily did the bidding of The Quiet Zone folks. It was Jacks who pushed through legislation that allowed residents along the river (including me) to be taxed specifically to support the creation of a Train Horn Noise Quiet Zone.**

Jacks' fame and fortune were cut short when I sued the City of Vancouver in 2008, then, in 2009, discovered the libelous memo he, Townsend, and Landis had fabricated. Some of the power brokers (including Gathe, whose wife would later be appointed to fill Jacks' vacated spot) were worried that Jacks, now a State Representative, had become a liability.

Astonishingly, in the middle of a legislative session, Jacks abruptly turned in a handwritten resignation letter and dropped out of sight for several weeks. (Jacks was replaced in the Legislature[75] by Sharon Wylie, Gathe's wife. Wylie, who was first appointed to Jacks' spot, went on to be elected to the seat in 2011.)

---

[75] When a vacancy in the Washington State Legislature occurs, the Board of County Commissioners where the vacant seat is located has the responsibility to select a replacement. The State Central Committee of the political party that last held the seat must submit a list of three candidates to the Commissioners. A selection must be made within 60 days of the vacancy. The person appointed will hold the seat until his or her successor is elected at the next general election.

I'll discuss more in the *following chapter* about how Townsend and Landis functioned as EmD-1s; but this is a good place to remind you of the fundamental difference between EmD-4s (Jacks, Campbell, and Hannah) and EmD-1s (Townsend and Landis). All five were enmeshed in lies and cover-ups that severely damaged others, but their motivations were different.

Hannah used his influence as a wealthy Vancouver resident to further his private agenda to have a Train Horn Noise Quiet Zone (THNQZ) in place since it would enhance the atmosphere in his backyard (hence help enhance the value of his home, i.e. personal gain). He wasn't concerned about the tax cost to the landowners near the tracks. Nor was Hannah concerned about crossings remaining safe with a THNQZ in place. Without a horn to sound a warning of approach before reaching track crossings at dangerous spots—the safety of others would be sacrificed.

I am not sure if Hannah asked the City for favors, but he was allowed favorite status. My rights were violated because City officials gave him—but not me—a private audience.

Making The Quiet Zone happen might have been Campbell's original goal, but that shifted when his business deteriorated and the housing market crashed. Under severe financial pressure and powerfully motivated by fear, Campbell violated the ethical code of a newspaper publisher to save his home as well as his new building. He broke the rules and called in favors with the Mayor and Landis: He wanted them to keep me distracted with other problems—which Landis and Townsend happily did.

Campbell had to have known, especially being a third-generation newspaper man, that what he was doing—embedding with public officials and taking a public stance on issues that impacted him personally—was underhanded and unconscionable. His goals were to save face and survive financial woes.

The all-too-trusting Jacks had been in way over his head all along. It doesn't appear that he'd knowingly lied until his deposition almost a decade after the memo affair had taken place. When asked then if he still believed what he'd written in the memo about me, Jacks said, "I had no reason to believe it wasn't true."

With all that had come to light in the years after he'd composed that fateful memo, Jacks must have seen that he'd been conned by Townsend and Landis; however, typical of EmD-4s (-), he wouldn't admit it. A main factor in his injurious actions had been: to please others, who could, in turn, help him advance in his career.

What motivated Townsend and Landis to haunt me? As far as I know, neither of them: received money for lying; got a promotion; or curried favor with influential people. Their underlying motivation may never be completely clear to me. However, their lies did stir up a lot of trouble for many people, not just me (i.e. many of the players in this book).

My suspicion is that being EmD-1s, they just plain got a kick out of messing with people and watching them suffer.

Police: political pawns or peacekeepers?

In 2016, came the killing of five Texas police officers while they were protecting protesters in a peaceful Dallas march for Black Lives Matter. In the aftermath, Dallas Police Chief David Brown said, "We're asking cops to do too much in this country" ("Tampa Bay Times," July 11, 2016). That comment really struck a chord with me.

I'd had to deal with Vancouver cops for years. I'd witnessed them being duped into

> I'd had to deal with Vancouver cops for years. I'd witnessed them being duped into brokering the nefarious games played by my neighbors, politicians, and influentials.

brokering the nefarious games played by my neighbors, politicians, and influentials. Local law enforcement hadn't been up to the challenge: They were used every bit as much as Jacks had been.

It was the Vancouver officers' failure to question orders—hence falsely arrest me—that brought so much harm to my family, beginning in 2003. I cannot forgive law enforcement for that; or Landis for repeatedly misinforming the police about my property rights. This didn't seem like "asking cops to do too much" to me.

Long after Nichols had confirmed my rights, the police were still under the impression that my movements on the easement road were restricted. My attorney and I met with East Precinct Commander Rick Smith and gave him copies of court orders affirming my easement rights. Because of Landis' misinformation, Smith remained unconvinced.

Instead, he listened to the complaints of the folks at Steamboat Landing, the same people who'd been forced to pay me defamation damages over the Wanted Poster incident. Smith rationalized that he'd taken no action against the illegal fence builders, because he'd followed the lead set by a public servant (Landis). It was Landis who had advised SBL to build a fence in the middle of the old road in the first place: He claimed the police had authorized it. If a City official had taken this stance, then it must be advisable, according to Smith.

By then, my immediate neighbors had begun mixing it up with the police. Morris (the one who'd stalked me) had planted rebar stakes—like impalement devices—into the easement road to the river, and even into the river bank and beach sand, which is illegal according to the US Army Corps of Engineers.[76] (I will write more about Morris in the *next chapter*.)

Morris had even claimed to the police that these stakes were survey markers (which he and the police referred to as "assessment stakes") that denoted the limits of my easement. Further, Morris had falsely claimed that a washed-up tree stump indicated the western-most boundary of my easement. Remarkably, the foolish police had believed Morris. When I complained about Morris to Smith, the commander responded with this email:

> *"Sgt. Knotts and Lt. King sought verification regarding your ability to use the easement and walk to the beach. They told your assistant that you, in fact, had access to the beach via the easement, but that you needed to restrict your movements on the beach from the tree stump to the assessment stake."* (July 5, 2006 email).

By 2007, Morris had been found guilty of contempt and been court ordered to remove the dangerous rebar stakes. The spring runoff into the Columbia had washed the tree stump downriver. Nichols once again restored my property rights. He also found my neighbors in contempt for violating my rights and his court orders.

I had no faith that the police would protect me. By then, Morris and his wife had assaulted my daughter Phoebe and me. Contractors working for Lindsay had slashed my tires. People at

---

[76] The entire Columbia River is federally protected up to the high water mark on the riverbank.

Steamboat Landing continued to call the police whenever they saw my daughters or me at the river.

One neighbor, Merilee Amy, had chased my daughter Phoebe off the river easement road, threatening her with a shovel. Amy had been planting pumpkins in the middle of the road as a means of destroying it when Phoebe happened by.

Each and every time the police had arrived, it had been me they'd confronted and questioned—and three times arrested. Not once, did law enforcement offer to protect me or investigate the accuracy of the neighbors' accusations. Once I realized the police believed the fabricated Townsend/Jacks report, their failure to act on my behalf made sense: The cops hadn't had the wherewithal to do their job when faced with someone they believed to be a functional sociopath.

Lt. Dave King had been promoted to East Precinct Commander after Smith left for another job. This was long after I'd won lawsuits against my neighbors and they'd paid fines for contempt. Still, in 2007, King believed he had to protect the community from me.

My chiropractor, a kind man with no idea how crazy everything was, decided that he could help me by contacting a friend of his on the Vancouver Police force, West Precinct Cmdr. George Delgado. The following is the email exchange between commanders King and Delgado.

WHEN EMPATHY FAILS

From: Delgado, George
Sent: Friday, June 08, 2007 12:34 PM
To: King, Dave
Subject: Neighbor Problem

Hi Dave,
My Chiropractor (a Friend) just called to tell me about a problem one of his clients is having with a neighbor. They live near a walking path that leads to the Columbia River (Steamboat Landing). Apparently, one of the families is harassing the children of the other family, to the point of assaulting them. Would you be able to give them a call and evaluate the situation? I do believe the address is in East Precinct. The person to contact is Kathy Marshack 909-7687. The address is 14237 SE Evergreen Hwy.

Thank you,
George

Message: RE: Neighbor Problem
RE: Neighbor Problem
From: King, Dave Date Friday, June 08, 2007 1:36 PM
To: Delgado, George
Cc: Kistler, Nannette; Chapman, John
Subject RE: Neighbor Problem

We are aware of the situation. I will call you and advise what the real problem is.

> *I am acquainted with Kathy Marshack as is the City Attorneys Office(all the City Attorneys) City of Vancouver Code Enforcement, County Government, Dept of Ecology, Army Corps of Engineers, City Transportation Dept, Burlington Northern Railroad, Steamboat Landing Property Owners Association, Judge Nichols, County Recorders Office, County Building Department, Evergreen School District and numerous lawyers. Kathy has been advised not to trespass on SBL property in the future or she is subject to Criminal Trespass.*
>
> *Dave*

Earlier, in February 2007, *The Columbian* newspaper's investigative reporter Stephanie Rice had made a public records request of King. She'd asked for the log of all police calls regarding my neighbors—including those with Campbell (her boss), his wife, and me. Rice even threatened legal action in her email to King:

> *"Please be advised that I am prepared to pursue whatever legal remedy necessary to obtain access to the requested records. I would note that violation of the open records law can result in a fine of up to $100 for each day that I am denied access. Litigation costs, including reasonable attorney fees, may also be awarded."*

I don't know what Rice was hoping to find, or related to which case. Nor do I know what she ever did with her findings. Perhaps she never got to the bottom of the story, or chose to ignore what she'd discovered—or her boss Campbell killed the story. He was, after all, a pivotal player in it.

At this point, I had just been exonerated, once again, from a false arrest. Apparent-ly, Rice hadn't found it newsworthy to report that her boss had been involved in a scandal to deprive me of my rights, which had led to my false arrest for trespassing.

The story of my exoneration from that trumped-up accusation by the prominent Campbell certainly seemed newsworthy. To this day, that story has never appeared in his newspaper. I can't help but wonder if, feeling cornered and afraid of being called out for lack of ethics, Campbell somehow forced Rice to go silent.

Even with my exoneration, King had continued to harbor the belief that I was the "real problem." It meant nothing to him that I'd been found innocent and that my neighbors had admitted to assaulting and stalking me.

It is very frightening when cops, with all of their

> **Even with my exoneration, King [a Vancouver Precinct Commander] had continued to harbor the belief that I was the "real problem." It meant nothing to him that I'd been found innocent and that my neighbors had admitted to assaulting and stalking me.**
>
> **It is very frightening when cops, with all of their weaponry and combat training, are duped; hence turning on an innocent citizen. With the police on the side of my accusers, is it any wonder their mob mentality grew stonger?**

weaponry and combat training, are duped; hence turning on an innocent citizen. Law enforcement officers do, after all, vow to protect the citizenry and to work to uphold rights for the greater good in the Officers' Pledge or Creed:

"I, do solemnly, sincerely and truly declare and affirm that I will faithfully discharge the duties of the office of constable with fairness, integrity, diligence and impartiality, and that I will uphold fundamental human rights and accord equal respect to all people, according to law."

With the police on the side of my accusers, is it any wonder their mob mentality grew stonger?

The terror of being cyberstalked

For nearly a year, I received hate email from a man I didn't know. He'd said his name was Steve Kappler. I'd replied to one of his emails and asked him to stop the abusive communication. That had only egged him on. He'd possessed quite a bit of knowledge about me, my family, and the neighborhood dispute. It was alarming to think that he'd been observing us, and I hadn't known.

When the stalker mentioned my daughter Phoebe, fright took over. I reported the stalking to the police. As usual, I was brushed off. On July 5, 2006, Smith wrote, ". . . there doesn't appear to be any articulated threats or harassment issues contained within the postings."

WHEN EMPATHY FAILS

Below are excerpts from emails sent to me from Kappler.

"Your daughter is a retard!"
"Get real and get help nutzo!"
"SBL is trying to get rid of you for being a pest, like a bug who needs swatting."
"Lady get it through your head, we all know that you and your retard of a daughter are nuts!"
"No not a rebel, just a psychopath!"
"As a person who claims to be helping people, you yourself need help. You are as close to a sociopath as they come!"
"Your daughter Phoebe is mentally slow. That is why your secretary takes her to school for ½ days."
"You are like a roach. You scurry when the lights get turned on."
"I will be here with the truth, as presented by the courts and the police. Not presented from your warped and screwed up skull."
"Prying eyes are all around you. Keep up the lies and I will keep up with the real truth."
"How many times must you be told to stay away. You have been banned by that community, must feel good."
"It is such a pleasure being able to call you out and call you what you are . . . a liar."
"In my opinion you are crazy. . . you are truly evil and a horrible person. When your professional colleagues hear about your actions, and they will, I hope they will take your license away from you."
"I look forward to you being in jail for what you have done, you deserve to be."

HOW MOB MENTALITY MATERIALIZES

> **"Lady get it through your head, we all know that you and your retard of a daughter are nuts!"**
>
> [—excerpt from cyberstalker's email to the author]

The emails were frightening regardless of Smith's opinion. Furthermore, the police had just arrested me for trespass—because I'd used my legally deeded easement to walk to the river. I was furious that I was being stalked, threatened, and denied my rights.

Since the police, once again, had denied me protection, I hired a private investigator who specializes in cybercrime. Within a few days, he discovered that the emails were being sent from the stalker's workplace, an office at Sysco Foods near Portland in Oregon. The sender turned out to be Ken Morris, the nephew of my disturbing neighbor Don Morris.

I turned the information over to the Vancouver police. This time, they deemed it a crime since Morris was using an alias to disguise himself. He was charged with the crime known as the gross misdemeanor of cyberstalking.

When Morris was arrested at his apartment, he, ironically, blamed writing the hateful emails on his empathy: Angry with me for standing in the way of his family's goal to develop their property, Morris said he'd sent the emails to help his clan silence me and scare me away. He even told police about the times he'd spent at his grandmother Mary Kellogg's house—his relatives all laughing about me and the trouble they'd caused me. Morris believed that I deserved his abuse because I was evil; that was his justification for haranguing me with monstrous emails.

He seemed unaware that I had lived peacefully next to his grandmother for 20 years and still had legitimate legal rights to use the real estate easement; or that Nichols had recently upheld those legal rights. Morris wasn't arrested until a year after he'd started the stalking. By then, his family members had been found guilty of contempt of court for their own outrageous conduct toward me.

The lie that just won't die

From the time the harassment at the hands of neighbors and City officials began, it took more than five years to unearth the infamous Jacks' memo that had been circulated through City Hall with the intent of taking me down. My conspiracy lawsuit against Vancouver had been filed in 2008 along with another public records request. It was an entire year and a half before those documents were delivered to my attorney Dan Lorenz, who promptly sent them my way.[77]

Just leaving on his vacation, Lorenz had instructed me to let him know if I came across anything important. He was in Turkey when I found the damning Jacks' memo. Thrilled with my discovery, I sent Lorenz a text message right away.

Finding and reading that memo left me shocked, thrilled, and relieved simultaneously. It explained the terrible disrespect, unfair treatment, and lack of justice I'd been experiencing for years. The relief came from hoping Jacks' memo would be the smoking-gun. Perhaps, after igniting years of suffering and the

---

[77] Lorenz had actually made several public records requests starting in 2006, but none produced the Jacks' report until 2009. In Chapter 8, "Just Plain Mean," I will explain the cover-up that kept Jacks' defaming memo about me secret for years.

loss of my family, the memo could now be used to set things right with my daughters. Sadly, that would not happen.

It was also puzzling that the memo—extremely damaging to the City government and to the employees who had conceived, written, and circulated it—had been so easily discoverable all along. (You need to know that previously the Jacks' memo had been wiped clean from the files of Landis, the Mayor, and the City Manager. Someone had failed to purge the memo from Jacks' files). I couldn't wait for Lorenz to return from his vacation and make contact with Assistant City Attorney Allison Chinn, who was handling the Conspiracy lawsuit for Vancouver.

When he did ask Chinn about the memo, Lorenz thought she might be open to settling the lawsuit, considering there was now proof of the City's serious crimes against me. To his amazement, Chinn said she believed the shameful letter to be factual.

Chinn told my attorney that she could prove this because there was evidence in my Diversion file that supported what Jacks had written about me. Did it never occur to Chinn that Townsend and Jacks had lied—especially when Townsend had been forced to resign, or be fired, in 2005 for similar misconduct in another case?

To prove that Townsend had lied to Jacks about me, Dan provided Chinn with evidence from my psychologist, Frank Colistro, Ed.D. It included my entire medical/psychotherapy file. The reports within showed the only diagnosis ever noted was major depression. In an affidavit, Colistro had stated:

> "At no time have I ever diagnosed Dr. Marshack to be a sociopath or functional sociopath. At no time, have I ever believed that she would be unable to recognize or accept responsibility for her actions. At no time did

I ever have concerns that she should not be treating others or that she was in no condition to be seeing patients herself.
"*At no time did I ever indicate or even suggest any of the foregoing to Ms. Townsend. Any such assertion on her part is a total fabrication.*"

Chinn didn't answer Lorenz's phone calls or emails for months. Then, in December 2009, she admitted that my Diversion file had been inexplicably shredded and was unrecoverable! In lawyerspeak, that meant there was no way to prove the file had or hadn't contained the damning documents Townsend had alluded to.

(This file was the folder Townsend had waved in front of Jacks, saying it held proof I was a functional sociopath. It was that statement by Townsend that had ignited the decade-long cascade of traumatizing harassment, stalking, lawsuits, and false accusations.)

I now have an abundance of evidence that I am not a functional sociopath. This includes: copies of court records showing that I was involved in a property dispute not lengthy criminal proceedings; statements from plenty of witnesses that attest to my character; and Landis' records, which prove I was not cited for any code infractions until the year the Train Horn Noise Quiet Zone initiative took off.

None of this had mattered to anyone but me. Nor had it mattered that soon after I'd filed a lawsuit against the City of Vancouver, a city employee shredded my Diversion file, illegally destroying evidence.

"Mob Mentality" Highlights

1. When a reasonable discussion with an EmD-4 fails to resolve a problem, protect yourself from possible reprisal.

2. When normally well-intentioned EmD-4s are under the influence of ignorance, fear, or greed, they can turn against you. Don't get paranoid, but stay alert.

3. Be creative in resolving problems with EmD-4s. They succumb to fear, then anger, so keep your channel to God clear and remain neutral.

4. Government transparency does not exist. Never assume a government employee at any level (County Clerk, City Attorney, members of Law Enforcement) will help you. Instead, help, and protect, yourself by doing your own research.

5. Everyone has an angle, even your friends and your attorney.

6. Just because an EmD-4 does the right thing by you, it doesn't mean they'll keep it up.

7. Once an EmD-4 lies, it often becomes a pattern because consistency is comforting, even when it steals the truth.

8. Karma can be harsh. Do not engage in lies or corruption. Avoid liars and corrupt people; they are likely to turn against you if it suits them.

9. Cops can be bamboozled. They are best at arresting criminals like bank robbers and murderers, but they are out of their element when it comes to taking a stand against local politics and pressure from influentials.

10. Once a lie about you has been around for a while, you will never live it down. Don't bother. Rebuild your life elsewhere.

CHAPTER EIGHT

Just Plain Mean

"People tend to think of psychopaths as criminals. In fact, the majority of psychopaths aren't criminal."

— **Robert D. Hare**

Why me?

While whirling in the eye of this perfect storm of Empathy Dysfunction my situation had appeared, and felt, unbelievably chaotic. In hindsight, and similar to the way physicists describe the birth of the Universe, both form and order had been present all the time.

BREAKING NEWS

Jim Jacks forced from Washington Legislature for 'inappropriate behavior' toward female staffer in 2011

Jim Jacks is a prominent player in this book, especially in this chapter where I discuss his damaging lies, falsifying of facts, and other henchman activities. Literally, as we were going to press with "When Empathy Fails," the Associated Press broke the news that the reason Jacks had left the Washington Legislature, four months into his second term, was not the result of alcoholism but because of bad behavior toward a female colleague. https://www.seattletimes.com/seattle-news/politics/reports-of-sexual-harassment-surface-against-2-lawmakers-in-olympia/ This revelation of an even more malevolent predatory nature sinks Jacks to a much lower level on the Empathy Dysfunction Scale.

See the Afterword for the US~Observer (November 2017) article written by the author in response to the breaking news about Jacks' fall from grace in the Washington State Legislature.

> **None of my experiences would have been worth it if I hadn't been inspired to create the Empathy Dysfunction Scale (EmD).**

This delicate balance is established by the victim and an out-to-get-you person; the kind who, in my case, had the precise timing, plentiful motivation, and the money and power to manipulate things to go their way. Unfortunately, I'd been the victim.

In this chapter, I pull together the loose ends of the story that resulted in the title of this book, "When Empathy Fails."

No one, including me, had seen the whole picture in enough detail to avoid serious errors. I survived because I am smart, alert, and persistent. I think this book will help you do even better than I did, should you find yourself in the crosshairs of an EmD-1.

None of my experiences would have been worth it if I hadn't been inspired to create the Empathy Dysfunction Scale (EmD).

I may have lost my family, but I found a new meaning in the trauma. I needed this incredible mix of mental, emotional, and physical assault in order to gain a deeper perspective on the range of empathy and Empathy Dysfunction that exists in the world.

That led to the epiphany that a sort of empathy thermometer might help people like me avoid snares concocted by EmDs. My EmD Scale is the result. I know that my simple little EmD Scale[78] is only the beginning, but I am offering it as a start for

---

[78] This EmD Scale has not yet been validated through research. I am presenting it to you on face value. Similarly, the famous psychologist Abraham Maslow introduced his hypothetical theory about what motivates people in 1943 long before it was validated. This is how research often starts... with an observation.

JUST PLAIN MEAN

```
-----Original Message-----
From: WebResponse@ci.vancouver.wa.us [mailto:WebResponse@ci.vancouver.wa.us]
Sent: Saturday, September 04, 2004 8:25 PM
To: jim.jacks@ci.vancouver.wa.us
Subject: Loss of Livelihood

First Name: Kathy
Last Name: Marshack
Phone: 360-256-0448
Email: kmarshack@kmarshack.com
Subject: Loss of Livelihood
Comment: Dear Mr. Jack,

I am having a problem resolving some problems with the City and thought I would appeal to
you for help. The situation has grown way out of hand and no one is listening. It seems
that there are solutions that are reasonable and fair but I cannot get anyone to listen. A
friend suggested that I contact you to see if you could step in and help.

First, Code Enforcement has decided to fine me for operating my psychology practice in my
home. I have had my office in my home since 1987, prior to the City incorporating my area.
When the City incorporated I sent in all of the necessary paperwork to get my City
business license and home business permit. No problem. I thought everything was fine until
this year. A new neighbor moved in in April 2004 and within three weeks filed a complaint
against me. The Code Enforcement Officer Richard Landis determined that I was violating
the city codes by having my secretary on the premises, even though the current code allows
for one employee. I informed the City in 1997 that I had an employee and was still granted
a home business permit, so I never thought I was in violation. However, Richard Landis
says that even though I told the City and I even wrote a letter to that effect in 1997, I
was still in violation. He fined me $250.00 and it was upheld by the City Hearings
officer, Mr. Epstein. I would like your help in clearing my record on this account. I
have been an honest business person for 25 years and never had a problem such as this.
I simply do not understand why I would be fined for being honest and not bothering anyone.

Secondly, I am in the middle of a dispute with this neighbor over easement rights to the
river. I suspect her complaint to the City on my business license is part of the dispute,
rather than a real grievance. We live near the Columbia River and have a common road to
our houses and a common easement across another neighbor's property so that we can access
the river. This neighbor has determined just after she moved in that I do not have the
right to the easement. In fact, she secured a permit from the City to build a gate to
block my access to the river. When I explained that I have a deeded access to the river
as do 13 neighbors total, she filed her complaint against me. I tried explaining to Mr.
Landis that the business complaint really grew out of this real estate issue, but he would
not listen. He investigated the situation and decided that I do not have such an easement.
It is clearly stated in my property deed. In fact, it is clearly stated in the deeds of 12
other neighbors. Why Mr. Landis got involved in the property dispute I do not know. And
why he considers the property dispute part of the investigation of my home based business
I do not know either.

The third issue is that I recently ended a very difficult marriage to a local divorce
attorney. Even though my ex-husband knows all of the judges in town, I could not get the
divorce moved out of the county for over a year, because Diane Woolard agreed to hear the
matter. Diane is a friend of my husband and clearly in a conflicted relationship, but she
would not recuse herself from the case, even though every other Judge on the Clark County
Bench recused themselves from the case. Needless to say I had to endure a year of biased
decisions on her part which eventually culminated in my arrest. I was able to work out a
diversion agreement with the City Prosecutor Josephine Townsend which would end in 12
months, sometime next year. However, now that the City has fined me for the home business
permit issue, Ms. Townsend has decided to revoke the diversion plan because she says that
I have committed a crime. She is asking for jail time because I was fined $250.00 for my
home business permit.

I need your help to straighten this out because I cannot afford to shut down my practice
over this. I am a single parent of two teenage daughters. One of my daughters is autistic
and requires a lot of supervision. She is homeschooled and because of her emotional
problems I need to be close to help her. If I cannot work at home, I cannot easily
support my family. First, allow me to continue to work from my home as I have done for 18 years without incident. Secondly, allow the
neighbors to use their deeded access and develop a neighborhood agreement to that effect.
Unfortunately the City Mediation Services has decided that our problem is too big for
them. But it seems such a simple solution.

I know that you may hear a lot of complaints and cannot get to all of them, but I am
desperate here. I cannot afford to stop supporting my family and if Richard Landis has his
way, I will be totally shut down. I have also contacted Councilman Larry Smith at the
advice of a friend and sent an email to Royce Pollard. Please help me correct this
injustice. It seems that certain city officials are going off without reason.

Thank you,

Kathy J. Marshack, Ph.D.
Licensed Psychologist
(360) 256-0448; 360-253-3810 home
www.kmarshack.com
www.entrepreneurialcouples.com
```

(See fig. A.7)

Shown at left is the author's original 2004 email to Vancouver Citizen Advocate, Jim Jacks. In it, she'd asked for his help in dealing with Vancouver Code Enforcement Officer Richard Landis, who was trying to revoke her permit to operate a business out of her home. As well, the author had asked for Jacks' assistance in negotiating with City Prosecutor Josephine Townsend, who was trying to revoke the author's Diversion plan because she'd been fined $250 for supposedly violating what was her legal business permit. To review the wording of the letter. Jacks subsequently forwarded this letter to his "partners in crime" Josephine Townsend and Richard Landis with nary a word of response to the author about her concerns.

those who want to take understanding Empathy Dysfunction a step further. We know very little about empathy: I hope my new Scale will contribute to the effort to comprehend its many facets.

As for City Prosecutor Josephine Townsend, Code Enforcement Officer Richard Landis, and Don Morris—all EmD-1s—I want you to better understand how they think, not just what they did. If you come away believing they were "just plain mean," then you may miss the keys to protecting yourself. I now see many of the mistakes I made.

If you are the target of an EmD-1, you will pay a price. My goal is to help you evade, or recover from their abuse a lot faster than I did. I'd had no mentor to guide me through the storm. I'd had noble and loyal friends, a few honest attorneys, and the brave staff of the *US~Observer,* who reported and published some of my story.

Before I go on, I want to clarify that even though this story is personal, it's not all about me. For example, Townsend, and Landis have caused trauma to others, too. Since the *US~Observer* investigated and published much of my story, I have heard from many people who have been abused by these two.

Inevitably, we ask, "Why me?" Was it because I am a fighter? Was it because I happened to live next door to Don Morris' elderly mother, Mary Kellogg? Was it because I'd recently divorced a local divorce attorney? Was it because I questioned authority? Was it because I am a mom? Who knows?

I don't believe that "Why me?" thoughts serve a worthy purpose. A better option is to take on the challenge when life hands you a nasty surprise. Things will seem less desperate if you embrace the fraudsters' actions as a cruel reality; then turn the troubles into a miracle. Otherwise, you will become one of the many hapless victims.

"The" memo

I alluded to the libelous memo written in 2004 in *Chapter One*. Throughout, I have used excerpts from it to highlight how the actions of those with EmD-1 can trigger EmD-4s to develop a mob mentality mindset.

Now seems the time to show you the entire memo written by Jacks with the malicious encouragement of Townsend, and Landis. It was written a few days after I'd sent a request to Jacks asking for assistance in dealing with a couple of rogue Vancouver employees. Read these two emails (mine and Jacks'). Let the meaning of these outlandish lies sink in. They are the hallmark of EmD-1s. Damaging behavior like this just gets worse when people do nothing to end the lies or derail the trauma these liars cause. It has to stop!

On Sept. 3, 2004, I'd written what I think you'll agree was a forthright and reasonable webmail to Jacks. *(See fig. A.7 to view the text of the author's letter to Jacks in larger format.)*

That same day, Jacks forwarded my entire email to Townsend and Landis without contacting me first. His introduction was brief and quite cavalier. His memo is shown on following page.

Jacks' log notes show that he did have conversations with Landis and Townsend. Later (in deposition), I learned that Jacks never even reviewed the files these two had compiled on me. He simply took their word on what the files contained.

On Sept. 7, 2004, Jacks wrote his response to my request, but he did not bother to send it to me. He sent the defaming memo only to his immediate boss, City Manager Pat McDonnell, declaring it to be factual.

Jacks never consulted me about the accusations. He never talked with my neighbors or any witnesses (including the psychologist who supposedly diagnosed me). He never shared his quasi-investigation with me.

```
Jacks, Jim

From:        Townsend, Josephine
Sent:        Tuesday, September 07, 2004 8:22 AM
To:          Jacks, Jim; Landis, Richard
Cc:          Hoggatt, Judy
Subject:     RE: Loss of Livelihood

Jim,
```

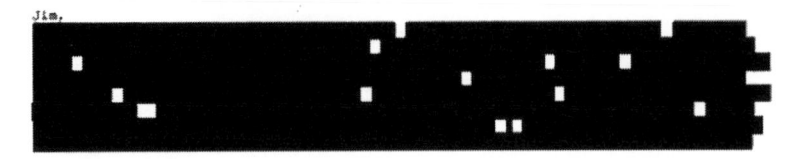

[redacted]

```
Josephine C. Townsend
Vancouver City Prosecutor
210 E 13th Street, P.O. Box 1995
Vancouver WA 98668-1995
Voice 360-696-8251
Fax 360-696-8250
josephine.townsend@ci.vancouver.wa.us

Confidentiality Notice: This e-mail may contain confidential and privileged information.
If you have received this message by mistake, please notify me immediately by replying to
this message or telephoning me, and do not review, disclose, copy or distribute it. Thank
you.


-----Original Message-----
From: Jacks, Jim
Sent: Tuesday, September 07, 2004 7:44 AM
To: Landis, Richard; Townsend, Josephine
Cc: Hoggatt, Judy
Subject: FW: Loss of Livelihood

Greetings Richard and Josie,

Please see below and then call me. Thanks!

All the best,

Jim Jacks
Citizen Advocate
City Manager's Office
360-696-8139
```

Note that where Vancouver Citizen Advocate Jim Jacks tells recipients Josephine Townsend and Code Enforcement Officer Richard Landis to "see below," Jacks is referring to the accompanying letter he had received from the author asking for his help. Her letter to him is shown on the previous page. In forwarding the author's letter to Townsend and Landis, Jacks was informing the very two people named in the author's complaint! Jacks never responded to the author. Note also that Townsend's response to Jack's was redacted. This is the first in the chain of emails that led up to the fateful 2004 email in which Jacks claimed that the author was a "functional sociopath." Jacks' actions set off a reign of torment and terror inflicted by City officials. To read the full text of Jacks' defaming email (See Fig. A.8)

On Sept. 9, 2004, McDonnell sent the memo to the Mayor and two City Council members. About 25 minutes later, Jacks sent the same defaming memo to Townsend and Landis with the message, "As soon as I connect with Ms. Marshack it will be case closed on this end."

In this secret memo, I was accused of being a functional sociopath with explosive anger management problems. Then, I was described as "resentful of authority and thinks that society's laws do not apply to her." With the encouragement of Townsend and Landis, Jacks implied that I could not be trusted to tell the truth about anything; therefore, I should not get any help from him with my complaints.

Two days later, out of the blue, I was sued over the easement by my neighbors Joseph and Julianne Leas and Kellogg.[79]

Jacks' title then was Citizen Advocate. That, too, was a lie: He made not one move to help me, the Vancouver citizen who had filed the grievance against two city employees.

---

[79] The purpose of the lawsuit was to gain Quiet Title to a river easement that was deeded to me when I bought my house. The Leas, Morris, and Kellogg hoped to extinguish my right to use a road to the river, so that they could make more money developing their riverfront properties. (Quiet Title is a lawsuit to settle a dispute over who has title to real property.)

Below is Jacks' fateful defaming memo about me (*See fig. A.8*):

Jacks, Jim

From: Jacks, Jim
Sent: Tuesday, September 07, 2004 3:50 PM
To: McDonnell, Pat
Subject: RE: Kathy Marshack's contact with the City

Greetings Pat,

You asked for factual information relating to the Kathy Marshack situation. Basically she wants (1) the City to reverse the Hearing Examiner's decision, (2) take her side in an easement dispute with her neighbors, and (3) the City prosecutor's office to keep her on a Diversion agreement with the Court even though she has violated it.

(1) Home Occupation Permit Violation
Ms. Marshack resides and works as a licensed psychologist from 14237 SE Evergreen Highway, just east from Steamboat Landing. This house (and others) is accessed by a private drive which crosses the railroad tracks. In 1999 there was an accident involving a car and a train at this private crossing.

Ms. Marshack's neighbor's house has a circular driveway that is frequently used by her clients. Both the current owners of the house and the previous owners have complained to Code Enforcement regarding excessive traffic to the business.

After investigating, Code Enforcement eventually issued a citation which she then appealed. The Hearings Examiner date was August 12, 2004 and she was represented by legal counsel.

The Hearings Examiner decision found that:
Ms. Marshack never had a legally established business because she never obtained a home occupation permit from the County, even though she operated a business from 1987 to 1996.

In 1997, the City advised her that she needed to apply for a home occupation permit. She did obtain one. However, she has failed to comply with it because of her employee. Since 1997 she has been told four times that the conditions of the permit did not allow nonresident employees in R-10 zoned areas. The Hearings Examiner denied her appeal on August 30, 2004.

I talked at length with Code Enforcement staff and I am confident that they gave her every reasonable opportunity to come into compliance. Ms. Marshack chose not to comply with the home occupation permit. She has had numerous opportunities to apply for a variance but has refused to do so. Her diagnosis (explained below) illustrates why.

(2) Easements
Ms. Marshack and her neighbors have a number of easement access issues in contention. These are civil matters and do not involve the City.

(3) Arrested During Divorce
During the course of her divorce, Ms. Marshack was arrested in October 2003 for criminal trespass, malicious mischief, and assault for an incident that occurred at her husband's law office. There was a significant amount of property damage. She attacked her husband's secretary (who was NOT involved with the divorce) and broke her right hand, gave her a black eye, bruised her right foot and right thigh. I have personally seen the photos from the court file of the property damage and the injuries to the victim of the assault.

Because she had no prior arrests she was put on a diversion program. Her conditions included participating in 26 weeks of anger management treatment and having no legal violations of any kind during her 12 months on diversion.

Marshack - Citizen Advocate Office - 000042

Jacks' letter continues on following page

JUST PLAIN MEAN

Continuation of Jacks' letter from previous page

The Hearings Examiner decision found that:
Ms. Marshack never had a legally established business because she never obtained a home occupation permit from the County, even though she operated a business from 1987 to 1996.

In 1997, the City advised her that she needed to apply for a home occupation permit. She did obtain one. However, she has failed to comply with it because of her employee. Since 1997 she has been told four times that the conditions of the permit did not allow nonresident employees in R-10 zoned areas. The Hearings Examiner denied her appeal on August 30, 2004.

I talked at length with Code Enforcement staff and I am confident that they gave her every reasonable opportunity to come into compliance. Ms. Marshack chose not to comply with the home occupation permit. She has had numerous opportunities to apply for a variance but has refused to do so. Her diagnosis (explained below) illustrates why.

(2) Easements
Ms. Marshack and her neighbors have a number of easement access issues in contention. These are civil matters and do not involve the City.

(3) Arrested During Divorce
During the course of her divorce, Ms. Marshack was arrested in October 2003 for criminal trespass, malicious mischief, and assault for an incident that occurred at her husband's law office. There was a significant amount of property damage. She attacked her husband's secretary (who was NOT involved with the divorce) and broke her right hand, gave her a black eye, bruised her right foot and right thigh. I have personally seen the photos from the court file of the property damage and the injuries to the victim of the assault.

Because she had no prior arrests she was put on a diversion program. Her conditions included participating in 26 weeks of anger management treatment and having no legal violations of any kind during her 12 months on diversion.

The Hearings Examiner's decision constitutes a violation. Ms. Marshack has a court date on September 29th. It is likely that she will be moved off the diversion program and convicted. Contrary to her assertion, the prosecutor is NOT asking for jail time. The conviction will likely mean that she will lose her license to practice as a psychologist.

Ms. Marshack's Diagnosis
Ms. Marshack is a licensed psychologist. She is also undergoing counseling as a client with a licensed psychologist. During the course of the legal proceedings Kathy Marshack's counselor shared with the court and city prosecution staff that in his professional opinion "Ms. Marshack is a functional sociopath." This basically means that she has no regard for other people and has no remorse for her actions. She has "explosive anger management problems." She is "resentful of authority and thinks that society's laws do not apply to her." He also believes that "she should NOT be a practicing psychologist."

Summary
Ms. Marshack is articulate and lucid. She presents what appears to be an organized case. However, there is little that we can do to help her.
(1) She has participated in the Hearings Examiner appeal process and we cannot reverse his decision
(2) The easements are a civil issue between private parties.
(3) She will be treated like any other person in the criminal justice system on a diversion contract.

All the best,

Jim Jacks

Marshack - Citizen Advocate Office - 000426

Jacks had sent the memo to Townsend and Landis and asked for their review before he sent it on to the Mayor, City Manager, and members of the City Council. Landis said, "Good to go."[80]

Townsend's response was redacted from her file by the City Attorney's office. They maintained that she was providing legal consultation to Jacks; hence her response was confidential. I have never seen what she actually wrote to Jacks about me.

> "Greetings Richard and Josie Please see below and then call me.
>
> All the best,
> Jim Jacks,
> Citizen Advocate
> City Manager's Office
> 360-695-8139"

Clearly, Landis and Townsend knew Jacks' letter was full of falsehoods. These public officials didn't bat an eye when they dropped it.

Several more entries in Jacks' log confirmed that he'd made contact with a number of people at City Hall and given them the "facts" about me. On Sept.10, 2004, he'd told his superiors, "I had a conversation with Kathy Marshack this afternoon. It went pretty well. I am confident that she will NOT contact the media over the

---

[80] Notice that in his letter, Jacks wrote that I was "articulate" and "lucid," seemingly shocking behavior for someone he claimed to be a functional sociopath. From then on, no matter how articulate and lucid I was in defending myself, City officials viewed Jacks' opinions as evidence of my sociopathy.

weekend or come to the Council meeting on Monday." In short order, Jacks and his superiors dispensed with me—and my rights.[81]

Virtually nothing in Jacks' memo was truthful. For example, Landis told Jacks that he'd had numerous complaints from my neighbors at the time (Jody Campbell and the Leas) as well as from my previous neighbors (Kathy VanAtta and Kevin and Kathy Burton) about my home-based business. Yet, there were no records whatsoever of previous complaints about my home-based business—or anything else—on file with the City.

Landis' Code Enforcement log shows that I'd had no complaints in 20 years. That clean slate went south the day Jody Campbell called Code Enforcement on me. Between that and my opposition to the Train Horn Noise Quiet Zone (THNQZ) initiative, complaints about me were filed in earnest.

According to Jacks, I was given four warnings to come into compliance but had refused. In truth, the Code Enforcement and Planning Office records show that I made calls, wrote letters, and hired an attorney to help rectify the perceived problem—that my home-based psychology business was disturbing my neighbors.

Jacks cemented this defamation by saying, "Ms. Marshack chose not to comply with the home occupation permit. She has had numerous opportunities to apply for a variance but has refused to do so. Her diagnosis (explained below) illustrates why."

It is inexcusable that he failed to tell me about these accusations and that I wasn't allowed to defend myself.

---

[81] I had not seen these documents until 2009, five years after they'd been written—even though I'd made a public records request when I'd first sued the City in 2008. The City responded by saying it had been determined that Townsend's emails were confidential, so they "redacted" them. Hence, I have never seen what she wrote to Jacks.

Jacks went on to defend his actions by introducing a totally unrelated case. The one where Townsend had falsely accused me of assaulting my ex-husband's secretary Esther Burns, giving her a black eye and breaking her hand. Actually, Esther had assaulted me when she'd grabbed my arm and shoved me into a wall. In self-defense, I'd hit her while trying to break free. Esther had not sustained a broken hand. The altercation landed me behind bars.

Townsend was the Prosecutor who offered me the option of a Diversion program instead of a jail sentence for my alleged criminal action. One of her terms forced me to pay Esther's medical costs, which totaled $58.06, hardly the cost of treating a broken hand.

Jacks had never done a proper investigation. He had not read the files or paid heed to exonerating evidence. Instead, he'd believed the words of liars. It is inexcusable that he failed to tell me about these accusations or allowed me to defend myself.

Five years later, when I finally saw what Jacks had written, my children and I had already suffered irreparable damage. I'd been forced to fight for my psychologist license, my property rights, my children's safety, and my freedom—all without knowing the content or context of the rumors about me.

I won back everything except my good reputation. As neighbor Amber had put it in 2014, I am still considered an undesirable liar who causes problems for people. It might as well have been written in stone. This is the lie that ultimately drove my children away.

Increasing lies and run-up pressure

Landis and Townsend, essentially being used as tools by Campbell and the Quiet Zone Committee did not let up on me. They amped up their lies to pressure me to stop my protests.

Although Townsend had failed in her bid to have my Diversion revoked, she persisted in harassing me. She wrote letters to my psychologist, telling him that: I was angry and condescending to her staff; my moods hinged on explosive; and I had no respect for authority.

Questioning my mental stability, Townsend had the audacity to tell my counselor that our sessions had been a waste of time. She contacted my divorce attorney and told him that I was a terrible mother and that the only reason my children had any problems (disabilities) was because of me. *(See fig. A.13)*

When stories about Townsend's unethical treatment of me emerged in the *US~Observer,* questions arose. One of her Court-assigned clients subsequently had concerns about Townsend as her defender. In a follow-up email to that client, Townsend had lied again, saying, "The u.s. observer is a web cite set up by a former criminal defendant [the author] I prosecuted." The client had then sent Townsend's vindictive email to the *US~Observer* and to me, asking for clarification. Ed Snook, the owner and publisher of the *US~Observer,* published a scathing denial confirming that he had never been prosecuted by Townsend.

Townsend also accused me of writing an anonymous blog that exposed her various unethical and criminal actions. Flailing, Townsend even had her attorney send me a cease and desist demand letter for the blog. I wasn't behind the blog. It was written by a local attorney who'd decided to expose Townsend and even filed a complaint against her with the Washington State Bar Association.[82] (My attorney Dan Lorenz had filed an informal

---

[82] Many years later, in deposition, Townsend reiterated these unfounded allegations. She maintained that I was the owner and editor of the *US~Observer*—roles filled by publisher Edward Snook. For an

complaint with the BAR in 2005 when she'd been hounding me about negating my Diversion agreement *(See fig. A.13)*.

To avoid being fired by her boss, Chief City Attorney Ted Gathe, Townsend was forced to resign as City Prosecutor. She was investigated and censured by the Washington State Bar Association for withholding "exculpatory" evidence that would have exonerated a defendant in another of her cases.

As a result, Townsend was placed on a Bar Association brand of Diversion for two years. During that time, she was required to have her work supervised by an appointed attorney. When the Washington Commission on Judicial Conduct learned she had concealed the Bar Association's disciplinary action, Townsend was compelled to resign her position on the Washington Commission on Judicial Conduct as well. (Yes, miraculously, she got herself appointed to the commission even though she had been adjudicated for unethical conduct).

Townsend has run for office many times, most recently, in 2014, for Clark County Prosecutor. In each election, Townsend's unethical conduct and disrespect for the law have been spotlighted by her peers, opponents, and the press. She has consistently polled as "unqualified" in integrity by her peers in the Vancouver Bar Association. Remarkably, when this book was published in 2017, the woman was still a licensed attorney.

Landis continued to haunt me. When he'd failed to get my home occupation permit pulled, he turned to discrediting me with my neighbors and various government agencies.

---

excellent review of Townsend's ethical violations read, "In Townsend's resume, disputes over integrity, mismanagement," by Paris Achen. Sept. 14, 2014, *The Columbian*, Vancouver, WA.

He wrote memos wrongfully stating that my easement rights did not exist. He researched my children's school records to discredit my comments that my girls had disabilities; that required tutors and other related services to be conducted at my home.

He encouraged residents of Steamboat Landing to erect a fence in the middle of the old road to block my river access (and called it a "police line"). Then a sign was posted at the river's edge that referred to the City Code regarding trespassing. SBL took credit for posting it.

The "no trespassing" sign hung on the makeshift fence in the middle of the author's legitimate easement. The fence and sign were the work of the Steamboat Landing Home Owners Association. It was one of many easement wrongdoings at the hands of the author's neighbors.

The most egregious of Landis' offenses was hoodwinking my immediate neighbors into stalking me: He'd encouraged them to take secret photos and videos of my family, my guests, and me.[83]

Landis had insider influence and happily used it against me every chance he could. Because he was the Vancouver Supervising Code Enforcement Officer, Landis was the designated Code Enforcement Officer for other city, county, state, and federal agencies as well.

That meant Landis was the one directed to investigate when I'd complained to the Washington State Department of

---

[83] All of this is documented in Richard Landis' deposition, emails, and Code Enforcement logs.

Ecology about the fence my neighbors had erected in a federally protected wetland and into the river itself.

To cast doubt on my veracity, Landis sent the state ecology officials copies of *The Columbian* newspaper articles about my arrests. Then he lied to the Department of Ecology, saying that the Vancouver Police had authorized the fence as a temporary police line to prevent me from trespassing.

Legally, I couldn't actually have been arrested for trespass since I had a legitimate easement and the Court had upheld it. But Landis and the police were convinced I was lying about it.

The truth: The police had not authorized the fence and had no legal authority to do so. Furthermore, I'd had a court order granting me the right to use the newly-fenced-off road and beach since being sued over my easement rights by Kellogg and the Leas. They'd paid it no heed, forcing me to sue them for contempt: Two years later, in 2008, Washington Superior Court Judge John Nichols, who was presiding at my civil suit, ordered the fence on my easement to be removed, by Don Morris who colluded with SBL in installing the fence in the first place.

The illegal "fence" that stretched from the author's easement, a protected wetland, into the Columbia River. Code Enforcement Officer Richard Landis lied to the Washington State Department of Ecology when he told them the Vancouver Police had authorized the fence as a temporary police line to prevent me from trespassing. A judge later ordered it removed.

JUST PLAIN MEAN

Stooping to a new level of "low," Vancouver Code Enforcement Officer Richard Landis fought to get the author's home business permit declared void because of the "parking issues" it supposedly evoked. He encouraged her neighbor Don Morris to take photos of cars (and their license plates) at the author's house to use as evidence—even if that meant stalking her. Photo at left shows parking available for guests and clients in the author's roomy driveway. Note that in this photo, the Leas' home is slightly visible behind the trees. The photo to the right shows that there's parking space aplenty in front of the author's garage.

WHY DID STEAMBOAT LANDING RESIDENTS HANG THE WANTED POSTER ON THE PRIVATE COMMUNITY'S FRONT GATE?

THE SBL HOME OWNERS ASSOCIATION SHARED OWNERSHIP OF THE EASEMENT ROAD TO THE RIVER, AS COMMON PROPERTY WITH MARY KELLOGG. THEY WERE AFRAID THE PUBLIC WOULD DISCOVER THE RIVER ACCESS AND USE IT IF MY EASEMENT RIGHTS WEREN'T SHUT DOWN. WHILE I DID NOT OWN THE PRIVATE ROAD, I HAD A DEEDED EASEMENT RIGHT TO USE THE ROAD TO THE RIVER. NINE NEIGHBORS HAD THIS SAME RIGHT GRANTED IN THEIR DEEDS.

ALTHOUGH MARY KELLOGG SUED ME TO TAKE AWAY MY RIGHT TO USE THE RIVER ACCESS ROAD, HER SON DON MORRIS HANDLED THE LAWSUIT FOR HIS MOTHER.

DON MORRIS STOOD TO GAIN A GOOD DEAL OF MONEY WHEN HE INHERITED HIS MOTHER'S ACREAGE ALONG THE PRESTIGIOUS RIVERFRONT.

AS RESIDENTS OF SBL, MORRIS AND HIS WIFE MELANIE MOONEY STIRRED UP THE RESIDENTS OF THAT COMMUNITY: PEOPLE RESIDING IN SBL BECAME SO AFRAID OF ME THAT THEY CALLED THE POLICE NUMEROUS TIMES WHEN THEY SAW ME USING THE EASEMENT.

THE POLICE INVESTIGATED EACH AND EVERY TIME—ALWAYS ASSUMING I WAS THE OFFENDING PARTY.

In April 2004, the two years spent litigating my hostile divorce came to a close. Within that time, I had been falsely arrested, then placed on Diversion for two years—unless I committed a crime[84] within that period. Then, out of the blue other legal issues surfaced.

A few weeks later that spring of 2004, Landis came after my home occupation permit. Next, Townsend issued a revocation of my 2004 Diversion agreement (related to my 2003 arrest) on the premise that the citation regarding my home occupation permit status was considered a "crime." By September, I had new neighbors (the Leas), and they were suing me over my easement rights. These attacks were demoralizing and put me at a disadvantage with my neighbors.

For the next few years, my neighbors had unlimited access to Landis, who'd handled their every complaint. An email sent to Landis by the City Accounting Department on Feb. 22, 2006, stated that my parking case, pushed so hard by Landis, had cost the City half of the Code Enforcement budget for the year.

That cost was for citations against me for parking on my own property![85] The Leas and Don Morris had been his

---

[84] Diversion is a common practice in municipal courts that handle small crimes and misdemeanors. Typically, the defendant agrees to forego the right to a trial in exchange for an agreement to have their arrests expunged after a period of time, during which they cannot commit any major crimes. In my case, the Diversion was for two years (later reduced to 12 months) and included anger management treatment.

[85] The fact that I parked my cars and RV on this old gravel driveway also came under fire. This driveway—established before there were building codes in the County and prior to the City incorporating my section of the county—was in place before I bought the house and was used as such by its two previous owners. Clearly, I was not in any violation of any codes. No matter, the City forced me to pave the graveled area with asphalt.

accomplices: The three of them had provided Landis with dozens of secret photos and videos of me, my daughter, and our dog, the landscapers, my fence, and the people who visited me—plus their car's license plates.

Vigilante justice

As the inflammatory rumors about me pervaded City Hall, the Police department, then my neighborhood, generally level-headed EmD-4s started feeling justified in persecuting me.

This photo shows the bizarre poster David and Martha Lindsay (buyers of the Campbell home) used to assert their right to block the neighborhood road: The Mob Mentality phenomenon unleashed. The Lindsays' behavior was shut down, and they eventually paid me a settlement of $50,000, but the belief that I was a functional sociopath persisted.

This bizarre gun-shooting-range poster reads, "Nothing Inside-Worth Dying For." It was put up by David and Martha Lindsay (buyers of the Campbell home) to assert their right to block the neighborhood road: mob mentality unleashed.

The sign is on the eastern end of the Old Camas Highway. The Lindsays paid the author a settlement of $50,000 for blocking her road access.

Steamboat Landing HOA was forced to pay the author $25,000 for defaming her when they displayed the Wanted Poster and blocking my road access.

Remember Vancouver Police Cmdr. Dave King? In his 2013 deposition, he seemed surprised when reading the documents proving my legal right to the easement. Until then, he'd never read any of my many emails—which had court orders attached. He'd chosen to continue the malignant gossip by telling Vancouver Police Cmdr. George Delgado that I was the real problem.

Is it any wonder my neighbors had felt entitled to inflict vigilante justice with Landis and the Vancouver Police on their side? Don Morris and Melanie Mooney (husband and wife), for instance, had perceived themselves as enormously empowered.

On the evening of July 4, 2006, Morris aggressively approached me as I walked home from the river with my guests. "Hey Bitch!" he yelled. "I've just been writing down the license plate numbers of the cars at your house. I'm gonna have you and your friends all arrested for trespass. Are you ready to spend more time in jail?"

Earlier that night, a small group of my friends and some teenage friends of my daughter Phoebe had built a fire on the beach and set off fireworks to celebrate Independence Day—a family tradition. We loved watching the fireworks explode, lighting the night sky and reflecting on the water.

Being on the beach July 4 and Christmas day were so important to my family that Judge Nichols had granted me exclusive use of the beach on those days. His intent had been to help me avoid confrontations with my nasty neighbors. Nevertheless, Morris and Mooney spent that Independence Day patrolling the beach. The couple built their own huge bonfire close to mine and heckled my party-goers all evening.

What else happened that night? Mooney went so far as to tell a teen using my easement that he was trespassing, then smack him on the leg with a red-hot poker from her nearby fire!

WHEN EMPATHY FAILS

As we were leaving the beach, my friends Mick, Andy, and I had to walk past the Mooney bonfire. That's when Melanie confronted us. Waving that fiery poker, she'd demanded, "Are you Kathy?"

I responded, "Leave us alone, Melanie. We're just trying to go home."

The next thing I knew, she grabbed my wrist, trying to shake my flashlight loose. Then she bit me! The pain made me scream, "She bit me!"

I pulled loose from her grip and turned to catch up with Mick and Andy, who were a couple of steps ahead of me. Hearing me scream, Phoebe had rushed from the beach to help me. I assured my small band that the incident was over and continued toward my house in the dark. Mooney did not pursue us. Phoebe rejoined her friends on the beach.

As we'd approached, my house, Morris had come from around the side of the Leas' house, from the direction of my house: He had been taking notes of my guest's license plate numbers. He walked right toward me on the river easement road we shared.

What else happened that night? Mooney [She and her husband Don Morris were my hostile neighbors.] went so far as to tell a teen using my easement that he was trespassing, then smacked him on the leg with a red-hot poker from her nearby fire! That's when Mooney confronted us. Waving that fiery poker, she asked, "Are you Kathy?"

I'd responded, "Leave us alone, Melanie. We're just trying to go home."

The next thing I knew, she grabbed my wrist, trying to shake my flashlight loose. Then she bit me!

. . . . and it was I who was cited for Assault 4.

I was startled to see him there—and scared when he confronted me. I was already in shock from being attacked and bitten by his wife. When Morris said, "Hey, Bitch!" I looked right into his eyes and reflexively started to walk toward him. It was eerie, and I'd felt caught in his hateful hypnotic spell. Everything shifted into slow motion (just like it had when Esther had assaulted me and would be later when Phoebe's anger of betrayal turned ugly).

Mick grabbed my arm, saying, "Let it go, Kathy. Let's just go home." She put her other arm around me and gently guided me away from Morris. My hand was throbbing from the bite wound.

At home, people were gathering in the kitchen. Someone said, "You should call the police, Kathy." I declined. I'd had too many run-ins with the Vancouver Police, and none had ended well. No matter how many times I'd been harassed, stalked, and assaulted, the police never believed me. In fact, one of the police sergeants had told me that if I called the cops again for protection, he would arrest me for false reporting.

One of my guests was my friend Jody, a nurse. She looked at the human bite on my hand and said, "Well, you should go to the hospital, Kathy. I think you're okay, but you might need a tetanus shot."

The phone rang. It was Phoebe's friend Cassie. She quickly explained, "Kathy, Phoebe's crying. The police are here on the beach, and they are threatening to arrest Phoebe as an accessory to an assault. They say she's lying about the thing with Mooney and trying to protect you. Can you come back?"

I sprang into action as did my friends. We'd made it halfway to the beach when we met Phoebe and the police. I walked to my daughter and hugged her as she cried into my shoulder. Speaking softly, I said, "It will be okay, honey. They don't want you. They want me. You'll be fine. I'll handle this."

Officer Jason Calhoun came over and ordered me to leave Phoebe's side.

His words, were, "You are interfering with a police investigation and telling your daughter what to say. Stand over here." Pointing to a spot a few feet away, he threatened to arrest Phoebe as an accessory to my "crime."

Andy spoke up to the officer, saying, "She's comforting her daughter. Leave her alone." But it did no good. Officer Calhoun and his partner were busily taking notes and getting ready to arrest me—again.

In the early hours of July 5, the "investigation" was completed, and it was I who was cited for Assault 4. Within a few days, Vancouver Prosecutor Kevin McClure added new charges: stalking, criminal trespass, and lying to the police.

This time, I wasn't going to be railroaded into accepting Diversion or some plea bargain. I went to trial, which was finally held in February 2007. After Mooney had admitted assaulting me, the jury found me "not guilty" of assault.

The stalking charge against me was dismissed before trial when, during a separate trial for contempt of court, Don Morris had admitted to stalking me. He had hidden, unbeknownst to me, in the bushes and trees near my house, during the week of June 5, 2006.

When there's an arrest and a release on bail—there's generally need of a bail bondsman to pledge money as a guarantee the accused will appear in court. Quite unexpectedly, the author found herself in need of help from the Vancouver business pictured, following one of her arrests. She was eventually exonerated.

JUST PLAIN MEAN

> The handwriting of Don Morris as it appeared on the envelope filled with stalking videos that he delivered to Vancouver Code Enforcement Officer Richard Landis. Morris had taken more than 50 videos of the author, her family, friends, and clients.
>
> This piece of correspondence was marked into evidence at Code Enforcement where Landis gave it an ID file number and logged the videos in as evidence against the author. This provides further proof that Landis knew the whereabouts of the damaging videos all along. This caught him in a lie.
>
> Morris' mission was to prove that business and personal activities at the author's home endangered his neighborhood. Once Landis had the videos in hand, they landed on the desk of Planning Officer Chad Eiiken. In turn, Eiken sent the author a letter—drafted by Landis and approved by City Attorney Charles Isely—about her permit.
>
> These pivotal videos remained secret even after the author's public records request to access all evidence against her. Nor were the videos entered into evidence for the author's court case that resulted from her July 2006 Assault 4 arrest for attacking Morris' wife Melanie Mooney. (Mooney later admitted it had been her who had attacked the author, not the reverse.)

Secretly, he'd taken more than 50 video clips of my guests, clients, their cars—and me. The unscrupulous Morris conducted more video stalking after the July 4 altercation. He filed a petition *(See Chapter Nine, "Cyberstalkers conjure their victims as wrongdoers" section)* against me with Code Enforcement. Morris included a CD of his video clips to prove his (false) complaints that my psychology practice was endangering the community.

In his letter to Landis, Morris had requested revocation of my home business permit,stating that I was endangering his elderly mother next door as well as other neighbors, and they ". . . should not be exposed to her mental health patients."

Morris' videos remained hidden in the office of City Planner Chad Eiken—where Landis had left them. Only days before my criminal trial, had Morris confessed to having taken the videos. This reversal forced McClure to dismiss the stalking charges against me. However, the Prosecutor decided to pursue the cooked-up assault charge.

When the jury was deliberating on the assault case, Morris, Mooney, Kellogg, and their family members sat in the courtroom holding hands and praying for my conviction: This, even though the stalking charges had been dismissed, and Mooney had admitted assaulting me. These people inexplicably still believed I was dangerous. None were arrested for their crimes against me. It seemed that, in Vancouver, it was perfectly acceptable to treat me with total disregard.

Flat out obstruction of justice

You may well wonder why it took five years for me to discover the Jacks/Townsend/Landis libelous email, especially since my attorneys made several public records requests. Yes, several requests were made in accordance with the law and duly filed with the Vancouver Records Clerk, and the Clark County Sheriff's Department (for copies of police reports).

Because the City and County governments did not respond to these requests, or denied them, on Nov. 20, 2006, two of my attorneys, Therese Lavallee and Daniel Lorenz went so far as to serve a Subpoena Duces Tecum on Raylin McJilton Vancouver Records Clerk, ordering her to **appear in person with all documents.** The subpoena stated:

(This verbiage was included in a subpoena for the Vancouver Records Clerk to appear in person with all documents encompassed by the author's lawyer's repeated public records requests. She did not comply.)

"You are required to bring any and all records, complaints, reports, phone logs, written reports, telephone contact information, emails, making allegations against Kathy Marshack or her residence address of 14237 SE Evergreen Highway, Vancouver, Washington."

"You are required to bring any and all records, complaints, reports, phone logs, written reports, telephone contact information, emails, making allegations against Kathy Marshack or her residence address of 14237 SE Evergreen Highway, Vancouver Washington."

McJilton failed to produce the Jacks/Townsend/Landis email (written Sept. 7, 2004). Nor did she produce the 50 video clips taken by Morris or his accompanying log. Morris had turned these videos over to Landis in June and July of 2006. Instead, she sent 35 complaints (with 20 photographs) filed by Joseph and Julianne Leas as evidence that my home business permit should be revoked.

Was this evidence cherry-picked to throw my attorneys off the track? Remember, by November 2006, the Jacks/Townsend/Landis memo defaming me had been circulating through City Hall for more than two years. Also, by this time I had been arrested for video stalking Morris (July 4, 2006) even though McClure had no evidence (and never did) to support the charge. Morris' report to the police was all he'd had to go on.[86]

---

[86] Don Morris told the police that a neighbor saw me videotaping at a specific date and time when it so happened that I'd actually been in a dental chair getting implants. It never seemed to matter to the Vancouver Police that Morris was untruthful.

Lorenz had been making public records requests since March 13, 2006, but always got the runaround. Assistant City Attorney Charles Isely responded April 4, 2006, with a bill for $13 to supply 14 photos and a partial copy of Landis' Code Enforcement Log. Isely ended his letter with this comment:

> **Lorenz [the author's attorney] sent public records requests repeatedly throughout 2006, 2007, and 2008. Instead of being transparent, the City and County had continued to stall.**

"Unless I hear differently from you, I will consider the enclosed materials as completely fulfilling your public records request."

No, it was not completely fulfilled. Not by a long shot. On Dec. 6, 2006, at the trial of Morris, Mooney, Kellogg, and the Leas for contempt of court after violating my rights to use the roads to the river, Morris had admitted taking more than 50 secret videos of me, then turning them over to Landis (July 2006), along with several still photos and a written log of the times and places he'd monitored my activities as well as those of my family and clients.

During the court lunch break, Lorenz went to Isely's office to demand the evidence he had repeatedly requested, especially now that Morris had confessed to video stalking me. Within the hour, Isely appeared in court with the videos. He'd found them on the desk of Eiken, who had received them from Landis.[87]

---

[87] On July 31, 2006 Chad Eiken, Planning Review Manager for Vancouver, wrote a letter informing me that he had received new inquiries from my neighbors about the status of my home occupation permit. He did not share the complaints, nor the videos. Apparently, he'd long kept these documents buried on his desk. That's where the documents were discovered Dec. 6, 2006, when my attorney Dan Lorenz demanded them from City Attorney Charles Isely, and, when Isely did not comply I filed a complaint with the BAR about Isely. *(See fig. A.13)*

Now that he knew City attorneys, Code Enforcement officers, and a City Planner were hiding evidence, Lorenz sent public records requests repeatedly throughout 2006, 2007, and 2008. Instead of being transparent, the City and County had continued to stall. For example, this note came from Assistant City Attorney Judith Zeider on July 18, 2008:

"The report you request pertains to an open and active investigation in which enforcement proceedings are contemplated, and is therefore exempt from disclosure at this time."

The Clark County Sheriff's Office Public Disclosure Supervisor, Carolyn Demme, repeatedly denied Lorenz' requests for police reports with the excuse that all information was to be sent to Judge Nichols (who was handling the property litigation with my neighbors over the roads): He would then decide if we could see it.

In exasperation, Lorenz finally wrote a letter to Judge Nichols on Aug. 14, 2008, asking for help to get the records that I was legally entitled to. Still nothing: The Judge still did not have the records either, no matter what City/County employees had claimed. Lorenz started his letter to Judge Nichols thusly:

"I wanted to bring to your attention the problems I have been experiencing in attempting to get records from the City of Vancouver relative to ongoing conflicts involving the parties to this litigation. Enclosed please find a series of letters responding to public records request, including the request for information regarding an assault by Melanie Mooney of Dr. Marshack on June 16, 2008." (See fig. A.12)

Not until August 2009, when Assistant City Attorney Alison Chinn finally sent over the infamous Jacks/Townsend/Landis memo, and other documents showing the City's obstruction of justice, did I finally find the defaming email smoking gun. Sadly, it's likely the only reason Chinn included the libelous memo is because she believed it was "factual." That's what she told Lorenz when he called her in September 2009 after he returned from his vacation.

Chinn didn't apologize for hiding the memo for five years. She didn't excuse Jacks' behavior for failing to share his findings with the citizen who requested help. She didn't attempt to resolve this grievous injustice. Nope. Instead, she defended Townsend, Jacks, and Landis, stating that since the City of Vancouver had shredded Townsend's file on me, they could not provide the evidence that proved or disproved the defaming memo had ever existed.

Are you a just a little bit suspicious that Landis was behind this cloak and dagger espionage? Let me walk you through a few of his emails during this time, so that you can see how this EmD-1 created chaos within the legal system.

About an hour after Jacks sent him a copy of my request for help, Landis sent the defensive email shown below to Jacks. In it, Landis denies that he is interested in my river easements, even though we now know he was clearly deep into research on the old roads and my right to use them.

Further, he gives himself away when he mentions that he is checking with Burlington Northern and Santa Fe Railway (BNSF)

From: Landis, Richard
Sent: Tuesday, September 07, 2004 8:57 AM
To: Jacks, Jim; Townsend, Josephine
Cc: Hoggatt, Judy; Sharp, Jodie
Subject: RE: Loss of Livelihood

Jim, we have more law firms involved in this than I care to guess. Our involvement is strictly about the Home Occupation and any adverse affect it has on neighbors. The easement issues are civil and I have told her attorney that time after time. Our case file is a public record and anyone may look at it. We have received a technically complete application, however we are trying to resolve some discrepancies and hear from Burlington Northern on the private railroad crossing and whether they have or will permit the business that uses the private railroad crossing.

-----Original Message-----
From: Jacks, Jim
Sent: Tuesday, September 07, 2004 7:44 AM
To: Landis, Richard; Townsend, Josephine
Cc: Hoggatt, Judy
Subject: FW: Loss of Livelihood

Greetings Richard and Josie,

Please see below and then call me. Thanks!

All the best,

Jim Jacks
Citizen Advocate
City Manager's Office
360-696-8139

About an hour after Jim Jacks sent him a copy of the author's request for help, Landis sent this defensive reply. In it, Landis denies that he is interested in the author's river easements, even though he's been researching rights to use old roads like the Old Camas Highway fronting the author's stretch of land in Vancouver.

about my right to use the train crossing, as if that has anything to do with my home occupation permit. But of course, Landis is quite concerned about the Train Horn Noise Quiet Zone (THNQZ) by then.

By mid-July 2006, Morris had turned over the videos, written logs of his stalking activities, and a petition signed by other neighbors he had coerced into joining the mob. Landis turned the videos over to Eiken along with a letter he had drafted for Eiken to send. All went to Isely for approval (according to emails in the stash Chinn sent to Lorenz in 2009).

Here's how it had played out:

- **July 28, 2006 (Friday 10:57 a.m.)** Landis sent an email to Code Enforcement Officer Tammi Neblock, stating, "Tammi, here is the draft for Chad to sign to Marshack, play with it as you see fit."

- **July 28, 2006 (Friday 12:41 p.m.)** Neblock sent the letter back to Landis with this cheery missive, "I made some changes, see what you think. Thanks!"

- **July 30, 2006 (Sunday 10 a.m.)** Isely sent the letter back to Landis under the subject "Home Occ Warning Letter."

- **July 31, 2006 (Monday)** Eiken mailed me the warning letter with formal copies to Landis and Isely, as noted under his signature line.

- **Aug. 2, 2006 (Wednesday)** Eiken's letter was blind-copied to the office of Miller, Nash Law Firm, the lawyers representing my adversarial neighbors (Leas, Kellogg,

Morris, and Mooney). I did not discover that City employees were secretly sending my correspondence to my neighbors and their attorneys until I got the complete records request in 2009.

- **Aug. 10, 2006 (Monday)** I finally received the Landis/Eiken letter. It was delayed in reaching me because Eiken did not use my mailing address; hence it had been returned and rerouted.

By the time of the Lorenz' and Lavallee subpoena for all records (Nov. 20, 2006), Landis, Eiken, Nebloc, and Isely all knew about the stalking videos and other documents provided to Landis by Morris. Worse, Morris' attorney Steve Turner had not turned over these documents as required by law when his clients were subpoenaed. This all came to light at the Dec. 6, 2006 contempt hearing when Morris admitted taking the videos and giving them to Landis.

How did Landis manage this deception? According to the emails, Landis received a copy of the subpoena sent to McJilton, so he knew full well he was to turn over Morris' tapes and logs, plus his own files. Instead, on Nov. 22, 2006, he sent this email to Nebloc (Meyer, her new name), Eiken, and McJilton:

> *"Per the subpoena received they want all e-mails that pertain to Kathy Marshack or her property at 14237 SE Evergreen Highway. I can only retrieve the last 30 days of e-mails deleted. If you any e-mails still on*

> *file please provide them to Raelyn McJillton not later than 28 November."*

By August 2009, when I finally got the public records (at least I assume I got all of them), I was amazed at the volume of documents the City had collected on me and my activities. It has literally taken me years to extract all of the corruption and cover-ups in these files.

As I take one more pass through the evidence for this book, a wave of sadness passes over me. I wonder how things would have turned out differently had I known about the Jacks' memo in September 2004. If I had, I could have defended myself and stopped the malicious gossip. In that scenario, I wonder how the police would have handled the scene the night that Melanie Mooney assaulted me (July 4, 2006). Would they have arrested Mooney instead of me? I wonder if Morris would have faced misdemeanor charges for stalking me if Landis had turned the videos over to the police?

The saddest thoughts are for my children. If I had known the truth way back then, when they were still living with me, could we have gone back to a normal life? Would they still be calling me "Mom"?

> **The saddest thoughts are for my children. If I had known the truth way back then, when they were still living with me, could we have gone back to a normal life? Would they still be calling me "Mom"?**

The truth or the "take?"

One of the tenets behind EmD-1 conduct is that the truth doesn't matter. What counts with EmD-1s is the "takeaway," or the "take;" in other words, what they believe to be true.

Townsend sabotaged me by telling Jacks that I was a "functional sociopath," and Jacks "took" it to be the truth. Landis created a host of lies to undermine me. He "took" the stance that he had an extensive file on me, neglecting to mention that it contained nothing incriminating.

Morris wove a tale of deceit that many others "took" as truth, which allowed him to stalk and assault me with impunity.[88] For example, he convinced the police that a driftwood stump on the beach was a bona fide survey marker. The absurdity of that claim defies reason.

Even Phoebe was "taken" in by the lies: She told my secretary and her Facebook friends that I had "a record," meaning that I'd been convicted of multiple crimes. My daughter, troubled as she is, succumbed to the very EmD-1 logic used by Townsend, Landis, and Morris.

To this day, I have not been convicted, save for a parking ticket. Although I have fended off multiple attacks by vicious EmD-1s, my reputation as a "crazy dangerous bitch" endures.[89]

Chairman of the Board

Evidence to the contrary, my nefarious reputation was "taken" for granted by the inattentive and unaware EmD-4s. Let

---

[88] I will explain shortly the assaults I endured from Don Morris, for which he was never arrested.

[89] The "Bitch" epithet was used frequently by Morris. He screamed those vicious words at me on the night of July 4, 2006, as I'd returned from the beach and again later that night. As I'd hurried along (on our shared easement to the river) to rescue my daughter Phoebe, who'd been stopped by the police for being on the beach, Morris had yelled, "Lock up the bitch." The officers had seen no need to insist Morris stop yelling at me and calm down.

me introduce you to a pair of them. Toni Montgomery, the former President of the Steamboat Landing HOA, was the one who saw fit to post my photo alongside disparaging words on SBL's front gate.

Brian Carlson, (the City employee who acted as City/Community Liaison for establishing the Train Horn Noise Quiet Zone), met privately with all of my neighbors and took up their gossip. Lighthearted exchanges, like those between Montgomery and Carlson, kept the rumors alive.

> From: Toni [mailto:teddybear.bandt@comcast.net]
> Sent: Monday, March 31, 2008 9:09 AM
> To: Carlson, Brian
> Subject: Re: yesterday's meeting
> Thanks for the reply.
> I am checking with all others to see if Wed. @4 would work for them. I am tied up with the Marshack Vs City of Van. newest lawsuit on Tuesday. Would you please buy her house!
> Toni

> RE: yesterday's meeting
> From Carlson, Brian Date Monday, March 31, 2008 9:14 AM
> To 'Toni'
> Cc
> Subject RE: yesterday's meeting
> OK thanks Toni. I'll save Wed for a meeting. I'll also bring $1 as a down payment on that house!

I bet you have been thinking, "Why on earth didn't she sell her house and get out of there?" I did try many times. When I'd figured out the neighbors' harassment motive was their desire to develop their riverfront properties—I'd offered to sell to them. Over a 10-year period, beginning in 2004 when Don Morris and Leas had begun harassing me, I enlisted the aid of five realtors. Each time, the lingering litigation was problematic, and the various real estate agents soon tired of showing my house.

Plus, getting me out of their hair wouldn't result in the be-all and end-all solution to the easement issue for Kellogg or the Leas. My easement rights would pass to the next owner of my home and property, who might also object to relinquishing their easement rights. It had been very clear that Kellogg, Morris and the Leas wanted the easement obliterated.

If the neighbors had wanted me to sell, why had they sabotaged the possibility by broadcasting that I was "One crazy lady" on www.rottenneighbor.com? Who would want to buy a house where neighbors make nasty comments about each other? Neither my litigious neighbors nor I were able to sell our properties.

As the litigation dragged on, I'd watched my neighbor Mary Kellogg's developers come and go. The builders' signs would go up, and they'd start to work the property—until realizing their progress would be limited. (I assume the developers had been lied to by Morris and the Leas. Once the developers got wind of what was going on, they'd pull their crews and drop out—just as Kresa had when he couldn't sway me on the road and easement.)

In 2011, Kellogg's realtor Susan Gustafson (Windermere Realty) complained to my attorney: Gustafson said she was going to sue me since I insisted on interfering with the sale of the Kellogg property.

In an email to Gustafson, I offered to talk to her about her concerns. Of course, I denied interfering with their attempts to sell. I summarized the litigation I had with these neighbors, explaining that I was the prevailing party.

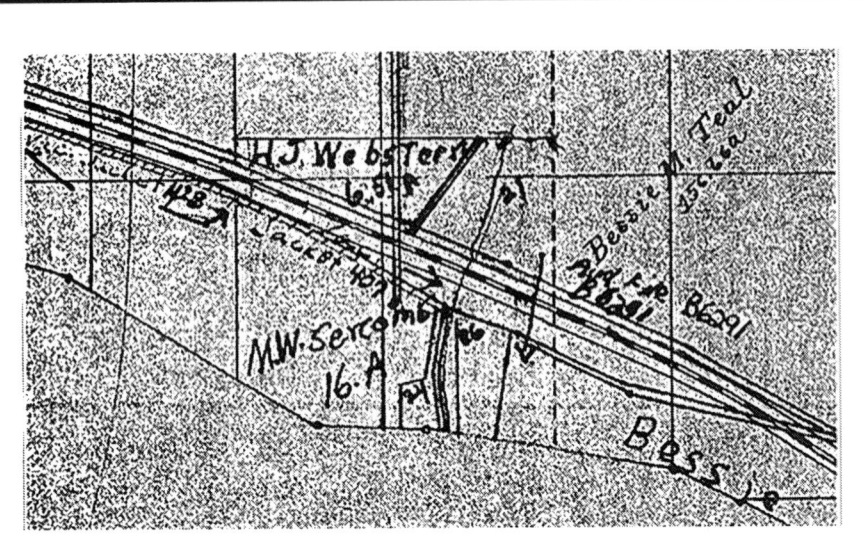

At right, notice the arrow pointing down. The road to the left of the arrow, along Sercomb's and Webster's land, was vacated in 1931; to the right, where the author's home was, the road was never vacated; hence was still public when the Lindsays tore it up then buit on what had been the road.

(There were two "roads" at the heart of the conflict with Kellogg, the Leas, and I. The east to west Old Camas Highway is where my house was. The river easement road goes north to south at the west end of the Old Camas Highway. My deed said that I have the right to travel along the Old Camas Highway to the river easement and thence to the river.

The Old Camas Highway had never been vacated—a road vacation is a legal term referring to decommissioning a public right of way, allowing it to revert to the landowner adjacent to the old road. With a deaf ear to that fact, the City of Vancouver determined that the small stretch of the highway from my house to the easement belonged to Kellogg—even though her house was not on the road, and mine was.)

I wanted Gustafson to understand that my neighbors had been court ordered to pay me damages and to cease all harassment—which now appeared to include sending a Realtor to bully me.

I told her that I would hold off involving my attorney until she and I had spoken directly. Gustafson refused to respond. Instead, she contacted my lawyer again, and complained that I was a liar. She told him emphatically that when I'd contacted her by email, she'd felt stalked and raped. Gustafson also affirmed that she had consulted the Windermere attorney about suing me, which she never had. Nor did she ever follow through and sue me.

In 2012, Morris found a developer for his mother's riverfront property: Kent Kresa (retired Chairman of the Board of General Motors).[90] Kresa conducted a feasibility study for most of a year. Sometime that summer, Kresa sent a messenger, surveyor Nin Beseda (who had been involved in the property dispute for years and knew full well about my rights), to my home to advise me that Kresa's crew would be cutting down some of my trees and removing landscaping to make room for widening and upgrading the road that went by my house and to the river.

I vehemently objected to his proposed action and total disregard of my rights. What had engendered him to make the unilateral decision to invade and damage my yard?! Again, I found myself defending my property rights.

I directed Beseda to tell Kresa he couldn't make a move without considering my legal rights. I dragged out copies of

---

[90] Kresa had been Chairman of the Board for General Motors when the auto industry was bailed out by the U.S. government. He sold his Beverly Hills mansion in 2013 for $27.5 million. Kresa prides himself on his Donald Trump-style philanthropy and negotiating abilities. To me, it was more like he was bullying me to sell low. It didn't work.

court orders, settlement agreements, my deeds, and the 1984 road maintenance agreement that required full agreement by all neighbors before the road could be modified.

The wealth of legal documents stumped Kresa for only a couple of days. Then, a manila envelope addressed to me showed up under the trees at the end of my driveway. Inside was an offer to buy my house. It was an option I thought just might work.

Kresa's offer was a bit lower than the market value, so I sent a counteroffer, which he rapidly refused. The phone message from his real estate agent (I have the recording still.) was priceless. "Mr. Kresa won't pay another dime for a road." The speaker went on to say that I had until Thursday that week to change my mind; or else Kresa would pull out of the entire neighborhood development deal.

A road? They wanted my home of 30 years, so they could claim rights to the Old Camas Highway in front of it? I wasn't offended. I was encouraged. This was proof of the land grab motive I had suspected for a decade. Neither Kresa nor his agent understood that I didn't care one iota if my neighbors could sell their properties or not. I let Thursday come and go. Kresa's contractors' trucks left. The "for sale" and "custom builders" signs were pulled up.

The neighbors spent several months stymied by my refusal to acquiesce and sell. As expected, Morris ramped up the intimidation. Early one morning, after I had left the house, he brought in his workmen to destroy my roadside landscaping, which included 60- to 70-year-old rhododendrons. By the time I got home, the "evidence" had been chipped and hauled away.

Another time, my secretary had called to alert me that Morris was heckling the crew I'd hired to prune a large tree in my yard—25 feet from his mother's property line. Coincidently,

JUST PLAIN MEAN

As expected [after I'd refused Kresa's offer to buy my house], Morris ramped up the intimidation. Early one morning, after I had left the house, he brought in his workmen to destroy my roadside landscaping, which included 60- to 70-year-old rhododendrons. By the time I got home, the "evidence" had been chipped and hauled away.

Another time, my secretary had called to alert me that Morris was heckling the crew I'd hired to prune a tree in my yard—25 feet from his mother's property line. Coincidently, the Comcast cable crew had been there at the same time to lay a cable to my house. Morris had stood in the rain, threatening to dig up the cable. Worse, he'd threatened to kill my yard crew.

Morris had assaulted me more than once (one time hitting me in the head from behind and knocking me to the ground), threatened to kill my dog, and all but run down my daughter as she walked our family dog. So I took him at his word when he claimed that he would harm my workers. "Keep those Wetbacks off my property," he'd demanded.

My secretary called the police, who, typically, did nothing. I resorted to an alternate plan: I contacted a real estate attorney. I asked him to take over and get the deal done.

It had been plenty obvious that Kresa wanted the property. Why else would he have: had a yearlong feasibility study done; put in a long gravel access road across my neighbor's property; trenched for utilities; and started negotiations with Vancouver and the train company to widen the railroad crossing?

A year later (2014), just after settling my conspiracy lawsuit with the City of Vancouver for assisting my neighbors in their land grab; and being cleared of the assault charges falsely made by Phoebe, I sold the house to Kresa for $600,000. (The worth had been $900,000 before the lawsuits deflated its value and the housing bubble burst.) Two years after that, Kresa tore my former home down to make way for his multimillion-dollar custom dwellings.

Postscript

It remains incomprehensible to me why these EmD-1s, Townsend, Landis, and Morris, sought to destroy my life. There were far easier ways to negotiate a Train Horn Noise Quiet Zone and riverfront development.

If they had sought my cooperation at the start, these things most likely could have been settled 10 years earlier and at much less cost. I must keep reminding myself that EmD-1s create chaos for the sole purpose of destroying a life and watching as their evil meddling and manipulation unfold. That is their only motivation.

I wasn't their only victim. The actions of Townsend, Landis, and Morris also confounded other neighbors, City Hall officials, the newspaper's owner, the Vancouver Police, and the BNSF train company. The threesome whipped people—Mooney, Kellogg, the Leas, the City, Campbell, and many neighbors—into a frenzy. Collectively, this cost these Quiet Zone proponents hundreds of thousands of dollars.

All three of these EmD-1s walked away unscathed. Townsend continues to practice as an attorney in Vancouver. Landis is retired and collecting a pension from the City of Vancouver despite his considerable wrongdoings. Morris collected his inheritance when he sold his mother's property. My attorneys settled with all of the parties to the easement dispute—Leas, Kellogg, the City of Vancouver, Morris, Lindsay, and SBL—one at a time.

For me, it wasn't so easy. I sold my house and moved out of the state to start fresh; but my relationship with my daughters had been irreparably damaged. As I have said before, it was just too hard for my vulnerable and disabled children to suffer with and stand by their mother during the abuse dished out by Townsend, Landis, and Morris

It's been over a decade since I've seen Bianca and four years since I've seen or talked to Phoebe. In 2005, when Bianca was living with her father, Howard, she'd threatened to kill him or herself. The police had been called. Three days later, Bianca wrote me a goodbye message. In it, she referred to me as a "liar," "a fuckwit," "a hypocrite," "an asshole," and "a half-insane wounded animal." She ended her email like this:

> *"Enough is enough. I no longer have any ties to you except for a lifetime of bad memories. I denounce you unfit for fondness or rememberence. Your presence is a bane upon my life. Now I shall remove it. Goodbye Stranger. It was not nice knowing you."*

You can imagine how frightening it was to receive this email. I couldn't be sure how suicidal my daughter was. Apparent to me was Bianca's anguish. She'd been suffering from an Autistic meltdown and had turned to blaming me for the tragedy in our lives. As far as I know, both girls feel similarly about me. I don't believe she truly hates me, but I do know that Bianca suffers.

I have recovered my life in most ways since I left Vancouver. I have a new home, new friends, and creative professional work. No longer do I jump out of my skin when I see a police car or get an official-looking letter from a government agency.

Survive and conquer the EmD-1s: That I did. It's the anguish of daughters lost that still stripes my life with struggle. I suspect this will last the rest of my life.

"Just Plain Mean" Highlights

1. Don't ask, "Why me?" Instead, take on the challenge to stop the liars.

2. Don't go after every lie. EmD-1s are masters at lying and creating chaos. Take the time to build your case. The truth is your best defense even when finding it takes a while.

3. Where are you most vulnerable? That's where you will be attacked. Being a mom was my soft spot, so the reprehensible bullies came after my children.

4. One particularly powerful tactic of EmD-1s is to demoralize their victim. Much like the coercive control seen in abusive situations, EmD-1s isolate their victims from social support. Keep your social circle strong.

5. In any violent encounter, always call the police first. Whoever calls first is considered the victim by the police.

6. In spite of your constitutional rights, if you are arrested (even under false allegations), the reality is that you will have to prove your innocence. This is frightening and can be costly.

7. If you are innocent, my personal recommendation is to consider whether settling for Diversion or taking a plea is advisable in lieu of defending yourself at trial.

8. Of course, you should consult an attorney about your options. Reckon with the fact that agreeing to "lesser" charges or Diversion may leave you in legal limbo.

9. Trust your intuition about unethical people. When you have a nagging negative feeling about someone, your presentiment is probably correct. Stay the course even when others question or disagree with your sixth sense.

10. Don't expect a happy ending. You may be able to stop the EmD-1s, who are essentially crooks busy stealing your life, loves, character, and hope. Know that what you can't stop is the unrelenting hurt EmD-1s level at your heart and soul. Above all, remember that we human beings have incredible resilience.

CHAPTER NINE

In the Cross-hairs of Cyberattackers

"The world is not fair, and often fools, cowards, liars and the selfish hide in high places."

— Bryant H McGill

On being cyberattacked

America's 2016 presidential election brought the public an increased awareness and much deeper look into the scope of international cyberattacks. It exposed political candidates' vulnerability to the kind of computer hacking that gathers email addresses; then takes advantage of that data to spread personal and confidential details to the public.

Worse, nefarious individuals (EmD-1) used the stolen information to spin untrue stories about candidates. Former U.S. Intelligence Chief James Clapper told Congress in early 2017, that the infiltration was much more dangerous and widespread than the illegal release of emails: The hackers had also disseminated "classic propaganda, disinformation, and fake news" (*New York Times* Jan. 5, 2017).

U.S. lives were put in direct danger when this material was exposed on WikiLeaks[91] and similar websites.

---

[91] Founded in 2006 by Julian Assange, WikiLeaks is an international non-profit organization that publishes secret information, news leaks, and classified media from anonymous sources.

As if this isn't enough, the American public is assaulted daily with new revelations about how vulnerable we are to hacking, disinformation, and fake news. In September 2017, Facebook revealed that it had sold ad space to Russian operatives; therein the spies posted fake news stories adverse to presidential candidate Hillary Clinton.

Further, the Russians strategically created several fake Facebook accounts that looked like those of ordinary American citizens. These fake Americans posted links to the false news stories, spinning out the web of lies farther and farther. With the popularity of social media, such as Facebook and Twitter, these fake stories very quickly went "viral."[92]

Even worse for our peace of mind the Russian trolls created Facebook pages to encourage divisiveness in communities. For example, in May 2016 they created a fake Facebook page called "Heart of Texas" encouraging demonstrators to show up at the opening of a library at a Houston Mosque. They also created a fake Facebook page "United Muslims of America" encouraging local Muslims to come out and protect the Mosque. Angry people did turn out for the event. Like a horrible reality TV show, these Americans had been duped into creating a fight on camera.[93]

Sure, cyberespionage has been going on awhile, but it's become far easier for the average person to use it to evil ends. A savvy social media user—especially one with a grudge—can ignite a vicious firestorm of slander, bullying, overt and covert threats, and online stalking.

---

[92] Vaidhyanathan, Siva. (September 8, 2017). "Facebook Wins, Democracy Loses." *New York Times*.

[93] Manjoo, Farhad. (November 8, 2017). "What Reality TV Teachers Us About Russia's Influence Campaign." *New York Times*.

The poster in the above photo was the result of a cyberattack—one of many—by my Vancouver neighbors. For more than a decade, I endured this level of cyberevil from private citizens and public officials.

Neighbors downloaded my photo from my website, then added it to a defaming poster at the front gate of their private riverfront community. The information on the poster is false. It states that there was a restraining order against me. There was no restraining order. It was the opposite: I had a court order barring them from publicly discriminating against me. No matter. My neighbors had come after me anyway, costing me thousands of dollars in attorney fees plus untold damage to my reputation.

The libelous scroll-like poster put up by my Steamboat Landing neighbors during their reign of harassment. It read, "SBL Homeowners —Kathy Marshack, who lives east of this community, is not permitted on SBL property at any time. A restraining order has been filed on 7/6/06. If you see Ms. Marshack in SBL, do not approach her! Immediately call the Police."

I was not a threat to these righteously indignant people in the usual ways. I am not famous. I don't have a lot of money. I am not running for political office. But I did stand in the way of influentials who wanted to develop property along the Columbia River, at the expense of community safety, by trying to skimp on proper train crossing guard gates. They used the same unethical cybertactics pointed out by Clapper—propaganda, disinformation, and fake news.

Some of these cyberattacks I've explained in previous chapters. Here, I am offering you a new way to look at how insidious this virtual espionage can be. Defending yourself from these invisible and hard-to-trace onslaughts is tough.

Unable to rely on the police (or, in a broader sense, national intelligence agencies) to protect me, I'd been utterly on my own. Here is what I learned and how I survived.

A reputation under fire

Writing was one way I distracted myself from the pain of victimization. I was excited to meet with my writing partner, Gary, each month to share progress on my book, "Going over the Edge? Life with a Partner or Spouse with Asperger Syndrome." Gary helped me to see the value in turning my energy—borne of frustration with unfair deals, libel, and slander—toward a humanitarian cause.

I could help an underserved mental health population by writing a book for and about couples and families stressed out by caring for loved ones on the Autism Spectrum. It was cathartic, too, as I came to terms with the Autism in my immediate family.

It never occurred to me that this labor of love would create hostility in the Autism community. Before I'd even published the book, I'd had to defend

The cover of the author's book, "Going over the Edge? Life with a Partner or Spouse with Asperger Syndrome," which provides tools to help manage a relationship where autism is in play.

myself to the Oregon Board of Psychologist Examiners. A New Hampshire woman, Kathleen Seidel, founder of the website www.neurodiversity.com[94] filed a complaint. First, she'd sent me an email complaining about the pre-publishing announcement for the book on my website.

Next, she'd demanded that I cease publication. Her complaint to the board had stated that my book was "discriminating against a protected class" (Autistics and those with Asperger Syndrome). Further, she'd claimed that I was not competent to write such a book. Remember now; she'd filed the complaint before the book published.

It took a year (and more legal fees) to have this bogus complaint dismissed: It was "determined" that I am a well-trained and licensed psychologist, who is competent to write on this subject. The book was published in 2009 despite the trouble Seidel had caused. It became a bestseller for my small publisher, Autism-Asperger Publishing Company. (The book's success paved the way for my second book on the subject, "Out of Mind-Out of Sight: Parenting with a Partner with Asperger Syndrome," published in 2013.)

Still, the cybersmear campaign started by Seidel had ramped up after her formal complaint. An attorney in Canada

---

[94] Neurodiversity is the idea that neurological differences, like autism and ADHD, are the result of variation in the human genome. Traditionally, these conditions were viewed as medical and psychological pathologies. Research has shown this to be untrue even though autism and ADHD are genetic anomalies and considered developmental disorders. These differences are the result of genetic predisposition and environmental interaction not disease or injury. To learn more about Seidel, please read her bio on WikiPedia https://en.wikipedia.org/wiki/Kathleen_Seidel.

sent an email warning me that I was being targeted by a group determined to keep my "Going over the Edge" book from being published or distributed. The attorney had also been targeted by the group (www.aspiesforfreedom.com) because of her work exposing autism as a factor in some high-conflict divorces.

When I checked out the website, I discovered an extended chat about me. Several people had suggested ways to:

- Infiltrate my computer to destroy my data (hacking);
- Smear me with false complaints (propaganda);
- Mount a campaign to prove that I was Autistic and struggling to accept that by writing the book (disinformation).

I found one positive chat from a young man, who had contacted me via email, pretending to request professional services for his autism. He reported back to the chat room that I'd seemed supportive and professional and that perhaps the group chat participants were wrong about me. Sadly, they swiftly pounced on him, describing my caring response as mere pity rather than genuine concern for his welfare.

In spite of this cyberespionage, I moved ahead with publication of my book; however, publisher Keith Miles had become nervous about backlash. To help allay the fears of any paranoid Aspies who thought I was out to get them, he turned to autism specialist Stephen M. Shore, Ed.D. An internationally-known and well-respected author and university professor, Shore (diagnosed with Autism Spectrum Disorder, or ASD), agreed to write the foreword to my book. As well, the professor's wife (who is not autistic), Yi Liu Shore, wrote a testimonial for the back cover.

"With vivid examples drawn from years of professional practice and life experience, Dr. Marshack expertly guides the reader towards success in marriage when Asperger Syndrome is present. Full of practical tips, the major lesson learned from this book is that learning [how to] to interface between the different 'operating systems' of Spectrum and non-spectrum partners leads to better communication with greater mutual understanding and satisfaction. Highly recommended to all seeking to learn more about Asperger Syndrome and long-term relationships."

— Yi Liu Shore

Alas, this would not be the end of the cyberattacks on me or my book. It was a prospective Amazon buyer of my book in the United Kingdom who tipped me off to trouble this time. He sent me an email, saying that he was looking forward to reading my book; however, he thought the price of 149.50 British Pounds (equal to $193.63 US) was excessive.

Sure enough, someone had infiltrated Amazon and changed the price, not just in Britain, but around the world. In Canada and the United States, the cost had been altered to $199.95. In Germany, it had switched to 172.50 Euros (equal to $187.95 US). The actual price was $19.95 US.

It took months to resolve this problem. . . . Each time the sky-high price was corrected by Amazon, the hackers replaced it with a ridiculous cost.

world. In Canada and the United States, the cost had been altered to $199.95. In Germany, it had switched to 172.50 Euros (equal to $187.95 US). The actual price was $19.95 US.

It took months to resolve this problem: No one at Amazon believed there'd been any hacking. No one (not even my publisher) would acknowledge that I was the victim of a smear campaign involving cybercrime.

Each time the sky-high price was corrected by Amazon, the hackers replaced it with a ridiculous cost. Or, they used another illegal tactic to sabotage book sales, such as changing the publication date to the distant future. They did everything they could to make sure my first book about Asperger Syndrome would not sell, hoping to cause me to fail as an author.

Eventually, I was able to convince the European book distributor to take me seriously. He asked Amazon to implement website safeguards that thwarted the hackers.[95]

I am happy to say, the false allegations were cleared up, and the cyberattacks have stopped. "Going over the Edge?" has sold by the thousands all over the world. As an outgrowth, I hold teleconferences and videoconferences for members of my non-profit Meetup group, Asperger Syndrome: Partners & Families of Adults with ASD.

And, I have a thriving private practice that serves those on the autism Spectrum as well as non-Spectrum clients who have autistic loved ones. As different as they are, the two populations

---

[95] My ex-husband, Howard Marshack, also tried to stop distribution of my book. He sent an email threatening to sue if I published the book and in any way implied that he has Autism Spectrum Disorder. This, along with the cyberattacks at Amazon, occurred at the same time I was fighting for my sanity—and my rights—against neighbors and the City of Vancouver.

have one thing in common: They want the help of a professional psychologist who understands their unique life.

Disinformation defined

The term "disinformation" is a quirky bit of jargon that I first heard when Clapper discussed it with the U.S. Congress. It's a type of propaganda that consists of lies and misleading information. "Disinformation" sort of sounds correct; however, when you tease it apart, you find kernels of truth that fail to hold the lies together. Disinformation—illogical, targeted, and covert—is purposefully generated, planted, or disseminated to twist the truth and bring harm.

For example, early in the smear campaign orchestrated by my neighbors and city officials, a man named Stan[96] had created a website using my name, (www.kathymarshack.com), in order to malign me. Although the site was taken down (after more than a decade), one of the false things he stated there was that I had been arrested during my divorce; which was accurate, though misleading, because the charges had been dismissed. Stan was trying to protect himself from accusations of child sexual abuse that had been revealed to and reported by me.

This guy became furious after his wife told me he'd been downloading child pornography and mixing it with photos of their preschooler. She'd found a portable hard drive of child pornography—with a gun on top of it—hidden in the ceiling of her husband's

---

[96] Stan is not his real name.

office. By law, I am required to report suspected child abuse, so I did.[97]

The FBI got involved because the allegations were about interstate sex trafficking.[98]

They were unable to prove the charges because of an "investigative technicality" that prevented them from using the evidence on the hard drive. When Stan's wife had decided to divorce him, he came after me for revenge.

On his website (www.kathymarshack.com), Stan belted out blame, insisting that I'd caused the divorce. This is classic disinformation. He'd made false accusations about me to distract from the real issue—his arrest for trafficking in child pornography.

My divorce-related arrest had nothing whatsoever to do with this man's guilt or innocence. He took a smidgen of truth about me (that I'd been arrested) and spun it into false evidence in an attempt to prove I was a terrible psychologist responsible for his divorce.

For more than a decade, Stan paid for the URL www.kathymarshack.com. I have no way of knowing how much harm the website caused me. A few clients have told me their friends warned them about me after Googling my name. What the potential clients found on Stan's website, however, had sparked more intrigue than fear.

---

[97] As a psychologist, I am considered a "mandatory reporter," thus legally obligated to report suspected child abuse to the authorities. I do not have to prove it. Proof is left to the police and the courts. The law expects professional psychologists to be more alert to child abuse potential and to protect the child by reporting even suspected abuse.

[98] Child pornography is illegal in any form, such as downloading it onto a secondary hard drive and hiding it in the ceiling, and by anyone who is connected with it

Occasionally, new clients have mentioned that after viewing Stan's fake news website, they'd felt encouraged to see me. His site was bizarre and obviously the work of a deranged person. His rantings convinced potential clients to work with me, precisely because I was a psychologist tough enough to withstand Stan's cyberattack.

Did you know that you don't own the rights to your name? Anyone can establish a website with your name, then use it to attack you or broadcast their version of facts about you.

Or, call them alternative facts, a phrase coined by U.S. Counselor to the President Kellyanne Conway to describe and defend demonstrably false statements.[99] Disinformation is protected free speech and at the same time damning and immoral.

By the way, I recently Googled the status of www.kathymarshack.com and found that Stan had closed this website and that the URL for the website (i.e. my name) was available for purchase. I guess Stan gave up cyberstalking me. I thought about buying back the domain name to control the use—and misuse—of my name on the Internet.

However, when I saw the price, I decided against it. The value of www.kathymarshack.com is currently listed on Dynadot is $1,399 a year, which is considered a premium price. (Dynadot offers domain registrations, renewals, and transfers. Through its domain marketplace, customers can bid on domains due to expire

---

[99] U.S. Counselor to the President Kellyanne Conway introduced the term "alternative facts" to defend President Donald Trump's fabrication that the size of his inaugural crowd exceeded that of former President Obama. She was wrong: President Trump's event was roughly one-third the size. See January 22, 2017 *New York Times*, https://www.nytimes.com/2017/01/22/us/politics/president-trump-inauguration-crowd-white-house.html.

or place a backorder for domains pending deletion. They can also bid on domains put up for auction by current owners or sell domains to potential buyers.)

A premium price? I assume that means my namesake is a hot property. Who says cybercrime can't be amusing?

Cybercrime at City Hall

Throughout the book, I have discussed the damage caused by the disinformation concocted by City Prosecutor Townsend, Citizen Advocate Jacks and Code Enforcement Officer Landis. In Citizen Advocate Jacks' secret and malicious email memo to colleagues and law enforcement, he'd reported what he deemed "factual information." In truth, Jacks had presented alternative facts and outright lies, based on hearsay received from Landis and others.[100] He had done no investigation of his own to support his claims.

Relying only on what Townsend had told him, Jacks wrote that I couldn't be trusted because I'd been diagnosed by my psychotherapist as a "functional sociopath." He added that my psychologist had testified to this supposed fact in court (another lie promulgated by Townsend).

Of course this was not true. My dear psychotherapist had never testified against me (or ever testified in a Vancouver court). He had offered an affidavit for my lawsuit against the City verifying that Townsend's accusations were a total fabrication.

---

[100] Landis defended his intrusion into my life with the same "factual information" excuse. He maintained that it had been his duty to investigate every complaint against me. Never mind that the complaints had been a form of harassment.

Plus, my psychologist's therapy records showed that I was depressed and fighting to protect myself and my children—nothing more.[101]

The clandestine memo had been cleverly crafted around some grains of truth. At first blush, the outlandish allegations about me seemed credible: I am a psychologist. I was arrested. I was involved in a lawsuit, although Jacks failed to mention that I was the respondent, not the moving party, and I had never been found guilty of anything because all false charges were dismissed, and eventually I won every matter in court.

Fast and furious: That's how Jacks' disinformation gained ground. He'd written that there had been numerous neighborhood complaints about my psychology practice over the years (because he accepted what Landis told him about me but never read Landis' file either): Not so. Not a single complaint had been made during the 20 years I'd lived in my home. The complaints began when new neighbors (some of the riverfront development fans) had sued me.

Jacks added that Landis had worked with me to correct my supposed transgressions and found me too uncooperative. That's so untrue: I had never met Landis before he sent me a citation demanding that I fire my secretary and shut down my office. Jacks had emphasized that my supposed diagnosis as a "functional sociopath," proved I was an angry, manipulative woman who had no respect for legal authority and basically couldn't be trusted. In his memo, Jacks had gone on to assure everyone at City Hall that

---

[101] I was able to see my therapy records because the City Attorney handling the lawsuit subpoenaed them. They also got to see that there was no diagnosis in Dr. Frank Colistro's records, except that of depression due to fighting off multiple cyberattackers.

he had dispensed with me: I wouldn't be bothering them again or showing up to complain at City Council meetings.

Once the malicious email got around, it gathered momentum. My neighbors were emboldened to post the wanted poster at their front gate. They filed numerous complaints about me with Vancouver Code Enforcement and the police. These false charges led to my multiple arrests.

> **I was jailed twice and even went to trial for a third arrest. I was never convicted of anything, but I paid a hefty price—$250,000—for attorneys to defend my innocence and have my rights restored.**

I was jailed twice and even went to trial for a third arrest. I was never convicted of anything, but I paid a hefty price—$250,000—for attorneys to defend my innocence and have my rights restored.

You might well ask why Townsend and Landis lied to Jacks. Probably, because they'd felt threatened when I'd asked Jacks, the Mayor, and City Council members for help resolving the problems I was having with the two of them.

Without facts to defend their misconduct and malicious actions toward me, Townsend and Landis came up with their remarkable story as a cover. Once launched, the disinformation spread exponentially, especially through electronic communication.

In the end, Townsend was fired and faced disbarment investigations in Washington more than once. Jacks was forced to resign as a Washington State Representative, then moved out of state. To this end, justice was served—a little bit. However, when the libelous memo finally surfaced after a public records request had been delayed five years, I'd had no recourse.

I was just starting my lawsuit against my neighbors and the City of Vancouver for conspiracy to defame me and deprive me of my property rights, it would be slow going. The libelous memo had left an indelible mark on my reputation, even though it was false.

The additional problem with disinformation is that it **never** dies. When it's of this magnitude and written by then well-respected city officials, it sticks forever. The negative gossip continued even after I'd settled my defamation and conspiracy lawsuit against the City of Vancouver. With only a few days left before moving out of the neighborhood, I'd had a garage sale.[102] A neighbor I'd never met stopped by. Her name was Amber.

She told me the tale of "this terrible woman," who had a fake professional license and had caused so much trouble for the neighborhood. I guess she hadn't figured out that I was that woman. As Amber gossiped about me—to me—my decision to move out of state to escape the ruthless EmDs in my life was further affirmed. The chat with Amber also confirmed an unfortunate truth: I would not be getting away from the story.

---

[102] If you recall, I'd decided to renegotiate the sale of my house to Kent Kresa, the developer working with the Kellogg/Morris heirs. I hired attorney Steve Morasch to finalize the sale. I made this decision after my daughter Phoebe falsely accused me of assault. Having lost the last member of my family, I thought it would be safer to leave Vancouver as soon as I had a buyer for my house. I sold it in June 2014, closed in August 2014, and moved to my new home the same month.

Cyberstalkers believe their victims are in the wrong

One of my false arrests was for stalking my neighbor Don Morris in July 2006. I was accused of taking videos of Morris and his wife, Melanie Mooney. It wasn't true and there was no supporting evidence. My supposed stalking him was one of those alternative facts Morris told the Vancouver police.

The officers, of course, had believed Morris since Jacks had already cast me as a malevolent force in the community (2004). In a cruel irony, it turned out that Morris had been stalking me. It's common for stalkers to accuse their victim of doing exactly what they themselves are doing.

In June and July of 2006, Morris had taken a series of secret videos of my family, my guests, and me. He'd hidden behind the trees or in his car, secretly recording my comings and goings. He'd videotaped things like my dog sleeping in the driveway, cars parked in front of my house, my daughter and I walking back from soccer practice, and other mundane things you might see in suburbia.

All told, there were about 50 video clips (according to Morris' courtroom testimony; Judge Nichols even watched the videos in our contempt hearing)). He submitted the videos, along

WHEN EMPATHY FAILS

The July 2006 petition signed by six neighbors to convince authorities that the author was a menace. It reads: "Kathy Marshack has taken her mental health clients onto the properties of Joseph & Julianne Leas, Mary Kellogg, & the Steamboat landing community. She has held counseling sessions on Steamboat Landing Comm. Property more than twice. Pictures attached."

with a petition signed by some of my neighbors, to Vancouver Code Enforcement as evidence that I was a menace to the community.

False evidence, like the videos, gave Vancouver City officials license to come after me with a vengeance. I was cited for:

- Having a home office without a permit: I had a permit;

- Parking my motor home on a gravel driveway next to my garage: No permit of any kind was required;

- Having no permit to use the local train crossing: I had a 1908 crossing deed from the railroad company, which is more stringent than a permit;

- Trespassing on my neighbor's driveway: I had a court order allowing me access to and use of this area, which was actually an easement.

> *Pictured are the author's car and RV as they were routinely parked in her old gravel driveway adjacent to her home and garage. No permit of any kind was required for using her private property in this manner. However, that didn't deter Code Enforcement Officer Richard Landis from insisting parking on gravel was against the law, hence a crime.*
>
> *In fact, this driveway had been established before there were building codes in the County and prior to the City incorporating her section of the county. The driveway was in place before she bought the house and had been used as such by its two previous owners.*
>
> *Clearly, the author was not in violation of any codes. No matter, the City forced her to pave the graveled area with asphalt.*

I'd known nothing of these stalking videos until years later. In 2008 I had filed a contempt motion against Morris and the rest of my neighbors because they'd continued to violate my property rights after Nichols had ruled in my favor. During the 2008-2009 court proceedings, Morris mentioned that he had taken videos of me and had turned them over, predictably, to Landis.

In spite of the several public records requests I'd made (starting in 2006), Landis kept mum about possessing the videos—ignoring my right to evidence from discovery. I was left vulnerable to false allegations of stalking Morris when, in fact, Morris had been stalking me.

It's important that you understand how the justice system "works." Even though Morris had admitted taking the videos while hiding, he was never arrested for stalking me. In no way was justice served. Instead, the Vancouver City Prosecutor dismissed the stalking charge made by Morris against me.

As Landis was fond of pointing out (in his emails), most public agencies are "complaint driven." What this means is that ruthless people can run wild with cyberattacks and false allegations, forcing you to be on the defense. Your best offense: Going after your attackers through public exposure. I will explain how later in this chapter.

More cyberstalking—yes, more of the same madness

What would you do if you:
- Received an anonymous email, referring to your 15-year-old daughter as a "retard?"
- Got an email accusing you of being a psychopath who should be driven from the community?
- Found another email message from a cyberstalker saying that you belonged in jail?
- Read an email from your stalker that he/she would make sure you lost your professional license?
- Read in the newspaper and in an email from the anonymous stalker denigrating comments about the list price of your house?

These represent some of the messages I received from a cyberstalker over a year's span (2007-2008). The stalker called himself Steve Kappler, and he sent his messages by webmail through my website. My first reaction was to reach out to him and find a reasonable solution. (As I'd attempted to do years earlier when I'd walked to a neighbor's house to speak about a misunderstanding and been accused of trespassing.)

Since my only contact with Kappler was online, I couldn't very well call him or walk to his residence. I sent him an explanatory email, pointing out that he may have only part of the story. Instead of a decent response, I got an email back that accused me of delivering lies from my "warped and screwed up skull."

Reasoning with Kappler was impossible, and I was frightened for the safety of my daughter, so I called the police. I knew getting their help was a long shot; by then the Vancouver police had warned they would arrest me if I made—what they considered— a false complaint.

Indeed, East Precinct Commander. Rick Smith denied my request for help. He told me the police didn't have the staff to trace emails even if they appeared to be threatening. In his message of July 5, 2006, which he sent to several officers including then Lt. Dave King, Commander Smith said:

> "Regarding the messages on your public website, there doesn't appear to be any articulated threats or harassment issues contained within the postings. I do NOT agree or disagree with the comments that you continue to forward to VPD. I do NOT think the comments are professional, however, there are still no threats. It appears that you have the ability to restrict or cease the comments portion until a resolution is made. However, that is under your control."

At least the Commander hadn't considered Kappler's comments "professional" in quality. Whatever that had meant, he refused to help. So, I hired a private investigator, Jerry, to track down the email stalker. Jerry is a retired Los Angeles Police Department (LAPD) detective specializing in internet crime.

Within a couple of days, Jerry located the computer where the emails had originated. And, he uncovered two suspects who regularly used that computer, which was located at their workplace, Sysco Foods, Inc. in Portland, Ore.

The stalker turned out to be Ken Morris, the 30-something nephew of my neighbor Don Morris. Jerry packaged up his research in a way that guaranteed the Vancouver Police would have to respond. A seasoned detective, Jerry was well aware of the games that go on within a police department. He knew how to bypass the folderol.

I paid his fee of $600 and called the police again as he'd advised. The officer who took Jerry's report from me turned it over to Sgt. Scott Smith, who, as it turned out, was the head of cybercrime for the Vancouver police.[103]

Smith verified all of Jerry's work, then made the arrest. Early one morning, Ken Morris opened the door of his home to find the cops waiting. Rubbing his eyes after being awakened and wearing only boxer shorts and a T-shirt, Morris admitted to the cyberstalking.

He justified his ruthless actions as helping his family. His relations, it seemed, were furious with me for asserting my right to the river easement; thus interfering with their plans to develop his grandmother's adjacent property.

Nephew Ken admitted that his Uncle Don and other family members met regularly at the home of his grandmother, Mary Kellogg, to discuss me and how to put an end to my easement since he believed I was a lying trespasser. He never used the term easement "rights" since he believed I didn't have any. Dutifully, the younger Morris had jumped in to help, using his considerable cyberstalking skills to frighten me.

---

[103] Not only does the Vancouver Police Department have a division focused on cybercrime, it seemed they indeed did have the time and staff to trace threatening emails.

Morris was adjudicated in 2008 for cybercrime, a gross misdemeanor.[104] Since he had no criminal record, he was placed on Diversion for one year. Just as the year was up, he made a Facebook "friend" request of me and signed up to follow me on Twitter. I quickly banned him from both accounts.

Again, I sought some protection from the City Attorney's office. City officials couldn't have cared less that he'd begun stalking me again. At least Sysco Foods had fired him.

Faked news

To disparage the author and discredit her publically, her bullying neighbor Scott Campbell ran this front-page fake news article in his newspaper, The Columbian. *While it did include some facts to make it appear to be "real news," important – true – details were omitted: Including the fact that Campbell had made several moves to prevent the author from using her court-ordered easement rights.*

---

[104] Cybercrime may threaten a person or a nation's security and financial health. It includes computer crime, cyberbullying, sexting, and identity theft. Research indicates the global cost of cybercrime may reach $6 trillion by 2021. There are both federal and state cybercrime laws. http://www.ncsl.org/research/telecommunications-and-information-technology/computer-hacking-and-unauthorized-access-laws.aspx

"Rumble on the River," a March 2007 front-page fake news article by Stephanie Rice, a reporter for *The Columbian* newspaper, is only one of several published in the Vancouver paper to discredit me. I'd hoped if she actually dug into the story and did some real investigative reporting, Rice would discover that I was the victim. But she never used any of the police reports to correct her misleading stories.

While Rice put in some facts to make the article appear to be "real news," she skimped on important details. She ignored the evidence she collected from her police records request, which would have cleared me. Rice completely missed the fact that I'd won rights to the easement, even though my neighbors (including her boss, publisher Scott Campbell) had harassed me.

The year after this article appeared, my neighbors were found guilty of contempt for violating my rights. Ken Morris' cyberstalking arrest came soon after. Neither of these genuine news stories made the paper. Instead, Rice repeatedly wrote stories that made it appear I'd caused the harassment.

The distorted "Rumble on the River" piece concluded with a comment from one of her sources, "The property has been for sale for so long that buyers will know something is wrong." Well, that was a no brainer!

I'd first listed my property in early 2005, shortly after the Leas moved in next door and started their campaign of harassment. My Realtor, Mike Canton of Canton Realty, had been excited to list the property for nearly a million dollars. (This had been on the upside of the housing bubble when the real estate market was still hot.)

He'd told me to start packing up: After all, he'd have my house sold within a week. Before he'd even put for sale signs in the yard, he'd been visited by Julianne Leas and Kellogg. They'd threatened to disrupt any attempt to sell my home. And they did.

Realtors and prospective buyers were confronted by Leas each time they'd tried to use the easement to show the riverfront to potential buyers.[105] I got a court order to make them stop interfering with my Realtor, but their menacing continued. Why would anyone buy a house where there were hostile neighbors like mine? My property sat there year after year as the legal battles waged on (from 2004 until I sold to Kresa in 2015).

It was evident that my greedy neighbors hoped to make a killing by developing their desirable Columbia River waterfront real estate; hence they had their sights set on my land, too. Soon after they'd sued me in September 2004, I offered to sell my property to them rather than deal with their harassment. They refused.

Instead, they did everything they could—including breaking the law—to drive down the price of my property. Too bad they hadn't been able to predict the 2008 stock market crash and how the resulting housing price plummet would impact them. Shortly after "Rumble on the River" ran, Lehman Brothers, the 100-year-old Wall Street investment bank, sold 23 offices, followed by bankruptcy the next year.

About this time, Campbell was facing a business bankruptcy–the result of miscalculating Wall Street and constructing an expensive building to house his newspaper empire. Campbell and his wife Jody were my neighbors to the east.[106] With

---

[105] My Realtors testified in court about the harassment inflicted on them by my neighbors.

[106] Jody Campbell had been the first to file a complaint against me with Code Enforcement in 2004. Code Enforcement Officer Dan Jones referred to her then as my "influential neighbor."

his newspaper failing, Campbell had been unable to pay the debt on his new building. He was forced to sell his riverfront home and property to settle his debts.

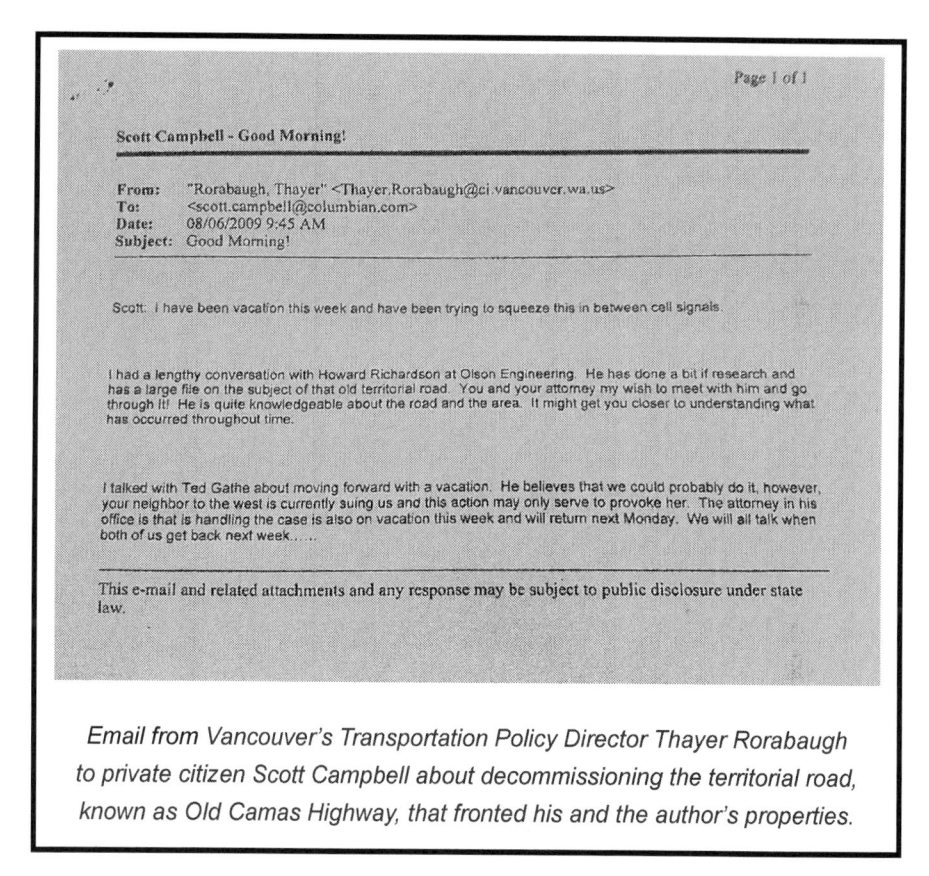

Scott Campbell - Good Morning!

From: "Rorabaugh, Thayer" <Thayer.Rorabaugh@ci.vancouver.wa.us>
To: <scott.campbell@columbian.com>
Date: 08/06/2009 9:45 AM
Subject: Good Morning!

Scott: I have been vacation this week and have been trying to squeeze this in between cell signals.

I had a lengthy conversation with Howard Richardson at Olson Engineering. He has done a bit if research and has a large file on the subject of that old territorial road. You and your attorney my wish to meet with him and go through it! He is quite knowledgeable about the road and the area. It might get you closer to understanding what has occurred throughout time.

I talked with Ted Gathe about moving forward with a vacation. He believes that we could probably do it, however, your neighbor to the west is currently suing us and this action may only serve to provoke her. The attorney in his office is that is handling the case is also on vacation this week and will return next Monday. We will all talk when both of us get back next week......

This e-mail and related attachments and any response may be subject to public disclosure under state law.

Email from Vancouver's Transportation Policy Director Thayer Rorabaugh to private citizen Scott Campbell about decommissioning the territorial road, known as Old Camas Highway, that fronted his and the author's properties.

Campbell's entanglement in controversies over the road, easement, and train horn noise had the potential to sink any offer on his home. So, he used his considerable influence with the City Attorney Ted Gathe, Vancouver Mayor Tim Leavitt, and Code Enforcement Officer Richard Landis.

I have copies of notes and emails proving these officials had assured Campbell that selling his house at top dollar would not be impeded by my claims to use the Old Camas Highway past his house, or my concerns for safety at the unguarded train crossing.

In an email exchange between Campbell and Vancouver Transportation Policy Director Thayer Rorabaugh, Campbell got personal attention regarding his request for a road vacation—a legal term referring to decommissioning a public right of way and allowing it to revert to the adjacent landowner.

To sell his house to the highest bidder, Campbell needed his property to be free of any encumbrances—like the old, but still public, road in front of his estate. All it took for Campbell to have his way was a simple request of the City Attorney and the Mayor, shown here. If only I'd received that level—any level—of help from the City.

A newspaper man, who supposedly had a journalist's ethics and moral compass, Campbell surely knew better than to curry personal favor with city officials. Using influence to gain special treatment is the kind of corruption that keeps ordinary citizens oppressed.

With the insiders' help, the Campbells got their place sold. They also struck a deal with the City to buy the new newspaper building, thus bailing the couple out of debt. The building has since become home to Vancouver's City Hall—the swank offices now occupied by the Mayor and City Council members. Coincidence? I think not. Minus this insider help, it took me several more years to sell my home and escape the neighborhood Purgatory. Kent Kresa, a developer working for these neighbors, was the eventual buyer.

Be outrageous and power down cyberbullies

Cybercriminals move fast and are smooth at covering their tracks. When you are in the cross hairs of their scope, these reprehensibles will shoot bullets of disinformation, alternative facts, and fake news at you. A detective like Jerry might be able to track down one cyberstalker; but when you are up against powerbrokers who have access to unlimited resources (government officials, wealthy business owners, and media moguls), it takes great cunning to outwit or snare them.

That's why I recommend using outrageous defense strategies. I used traditional methods of self-defense—lawsuits, counter-lawsuits, and filing complaints with government agencies. These processes are expensive, time-consuming, and produce few results (especially if you are going after powerful people).

You can bypass (or add to) these traditional methods of fighting injustice by using your Constitutional right to free speech. It's called "creative dissent" when you challenge alternative facts and disinformation by using online and other media outlets to speak the truth.

Remember, the "U.S. Constitution" protects an American's right to free speech for an imperative reason: to protect us from tyranny and from demagogues who would dismantle our hard-won freedoms. We have the right to disagree with our political leaders, even the President of the United States, if we do not believe we are getting fair treatment. And we have the right to disagree without being punished.

It was formal dissent when I filed a Land Use Petition Act (LUPA) appeal against the City of Vancouver, questioning their right to fine me for parking cars and my motor home on a gravel driveway next to my 1953 ranch house (built before there were codes for paving). I followed up my formal lawsuit with informal methods of creative dissent.

I "informally" took photos of hundreds of vehicles, including City-owned vehicles, parked on dirt, grass, and gravel around the city and county. I even found an old airplane without wings parked in a backyard. I submitted my photos to Code Enforcement as evidence that I'd been singled out unfairly. The powers that be took no action; at least they'd been put on notice that I wouldn't be "railroaded."

My photos and press releases were widely cast by a PR website that helps get a client's message to the press. As a result, I was tapped to do interviews on local television and radio networks. Most media people love a story about injustice, especially the kind about an ordinary citizen targeted by corrupt government.

One radio host, Lars Larson—amazed at the level of corruption and injustice—had suggested I make a DVD depicting my parking situation. He'd offered to do the voiceover. I was delighted to accept his generous offer.

I prepared a DVD with the parking photos, the radio interview, and the television news spots from Fox News affiliate KPTV Portland. I wrote the accompanying script for Larson, a conservative talk show host and celebrity based in Portland, Ore. Next, the DVD was mailed to every media source I thought might be interested. It also appeared for a time on my website.

My research skills played a big part in sniffing out the libel and slander. Those who use propaganda,

> **My research skills played a big part in sniffing out the libel and slander. Those who use propaganda, disinformation, and fake news don't expect you to research their lies.**

Dean Baker, the history editor at The Columbian *newspaper in Vancouver, Wash., wrote this article. It ran under the radar of the publisher, Scott Campbell, who was one of the author's opponents in her struggle to retain her property rights.*

disinformation, and fake news don't expect you to research their lies.

If you are willing to check out details and run down facts, you will find the contradictions. Some of what I discovered was historical in nature.

The history editor at *The Columbian* was fascinated by my research on the Wild West pioneers who had settled our little town. I provided him with my research findings, and he wrote an excellent piece detailing the 150-year-old story behind the old road now under dispute.

The maps, deeds, and other documents I furnished journalist Dean Baker clearly showed that an old public right of way passed right in front of Campbell's house. When he found out that I'd slipped a news story into his paper under the guise of history, Campbell must have been furious.

The research I'd conducted served double duty: I created a PowerPoint that I called "The River, the Road, and the Train." It begins in the 1830s with the development of the community of Fort Vancouver by the first British settlers (the Hudson Bay Company) and later to the first American homesteaders (i.e. Silas Maxon in 1847 the original owner of my land).

The saga moves from the steamboat era of the 1830s and the construction of the first road in the county in 1852 to the onset of the train in 1908. It closes with a look at modern times— and the crazy river easement lawsuit started by my neighbors.

For a spell, I posted the informative PowerPoint to my website. Then, I donated it to Washington's Clark County Historical Society and the Umatilla Indian Reservation. I also included the presentation and my research as part of an application to the National Register of Historic Places[107] in recognition of the first road built in the Oregon Territory (known originally as the Columbia City to Cascade City Highway and later as the Old Camas Highway). Sharing the truth in a responsible way gave me satisfaction whether or not it helped me with the legal matters at hand.

The greatest vehicle for my creative dissent was the *US~Observer*. This newspaper is committed to exposing government corruption and wrongful prosecution. The paper's mission is to exonerate innocent people. I knew I could trust them to investigate my situation and print the unbiased truth. The resulting news articles were extremely unnerving to my neighbors and officials at City Hall.

My neighbors, Joseph and Julianne Leas, upset by all of "my" media exposure, complained to Landis. He took the complaint to the Mayor's office. When Assistant City Attorney Allison Chinn saw the *US~Observer* articles she complained to my attorney Dan Lorenz, saying that by exposing City officials, I was interfering in the City conspiracy lawsuit proceedings. Politely, my attorney reminded Chinn of my right to free speech.

---

[107] When the Americans took Fort Vancouver from the British, they changed the name to Columbia City. Later, it was changed to Vancouver. The road was intended to go to Cascade City or North Bonneville, but could only make it as far as Camas. Thus it became the Old Camas Highway and appeared in my deed as such.

Of even greater interest is how the *US~Observer* coverage affected Townsend. To get even with the *US~Observer* for "outing" her elicit behavior, she'd threatened to expose the owner of the paper as a defendant she had once prosecuted—a bald-faced lie.[108]

Witnessing the impact of the media exposure, I decided on an outrageous personal action: I applied for an interim appointment to the City Council (the spot vacated by Leavitt when he'd been elected Vancouver's Mayor). My platform: I was the perfect person to clean up our corrupt City Hall because I had been victimized by City officials.

As part of my application, I submitted the libelous memo written by Townsend, Jacks, and Landis along with the evidence that it was rife with lies. I outlined the many ways their unethical actions had harmed my family and me.

All the City Council members, the Mayor, the City Manager, and other elected and administrative city officials reviewed my paperwork. No surprise, I didn't get the City Council slot; but once again, I'd made it known that I would not go quietly.

You will notice that not all of these methods brought a direct return on investment. They did advance my cause: The powerbrokers were put on notice that I would call them out and hold my government accountable for its false, unconstitutional, and abusive actions.

Creative dissent is vital to changing the institutions that condone the type of abuse my neighbors and in-cahoots officials got away with. We're living in an era when cybercrime is creating

---

[108] This bit of disinformation was exposed in a *US~Observer* column. Townsend had never prosecuted the newspaper's owner. In deposition, Townsend had claimed that I was the owner of the paper, another jaw-dropping lie.

enormous chaos and destruction for individuals (like a single, working mom raising daughters in suburbia) and for our very country.

Not everyone can stay strong through a decade-plus onslaught of lawsuits, harassment, false arrests, and cyberattacks. With persistence, you can outsmart these crooks. No one should have to go through what I did. If you do find yourself the target of cyberattacks, I hope the tools and methods I've shared will help you survive the turmoil.

"In the Cross-hairs of Cyberattackers" Highlights

1. Few laws protect you from cyberattacks. You are on your own.

2. Since many government agencies are complaint-driven, they benefit the complainer, meaning that the victim of the complaint will be investigated regardless of the truth of the complaint against them.

3. Cyberstalkers (EmD-1s) will lie about you and even accuse you of stalking them.

4. Disinformation, propaganda, and fake news can look very real. Don't be lazy and take as truth all that you read, hear, and see. Check the sources to be certain.

5. Lies by any other name are still lies. "Alternative facts" are not facts, they are lies.

6. In our modern world of the Internet, lies are shared at lightning speed, and they never die.

7. Don't think you are safe from cyberattacks because you are a "good" person.

8. As the saying goes, "No good deed goes unpunished." Whenever you take a stand for yourself or a worthy cause, be prepared for being distracted by those with intent on denigrating and punishing you.

9. Use your talents to build your resilience. God wants you to put your energy where you can make a difference, not where you can't.

10. Be selective in the lies you determine to take down. Don't go after every falsehood. EmD-1s will generate dozens to distract you and splinter your attention. Do your due diligence, then decide.

11. Use creative dissent. You are entitled to free speech and due process in this country.

12. Expose cyberabuse by notifying the media. Generally, professional journalists like covering a good story about the underdog.

CHAPTER TEN

Radiant Warrior, Resilience Epitomized

"The heart of a mother is a deep abyss at the bottom of which you will always find forgiveness."

— Honore de Balzac

The bright side of Empathy Dysfunction

Since I have emphasized Empathy Dysfunction in this book, you might think that healthy empathy (EmD-4 and EmD-5) is relatively rare. Not so! Most people function in this EmD-4 range (only a handful in the EmD-5 range).

Remember, my goal is to educate you about the dark side of Empathy Dysfunction so that you are better prepared to protect yourself from its malevolence. In this chapter, I take a detour to show you how those with empathy, both EmD-4 and EmD-5, make the world a better, brighter place.

EmD-4 represents the average person. They have abundant empathy. People trust them because EmD-4s do want to reciprocate in their relationships with family, coworkers, friends, and neighbors.

On the down side, these folks can become codependent. Because of their heightened sensitivity to others, Em-D-4s respond with care, tenderness, and nurturing—sometimes too much. Setting and keeping boundaries is not an easy thing for many EmD-4s. They react as if another person's suffering is something they should personally take on and fix. A good example of this is the terrible mistake I'd made by giving money to my cousin: As my father before me had done with his family, I fell into codependency with that loan. Dad had assumed his cousin and his wife would honor the gift. Codependent actions mean both parties lose.

> **Codependent actions mean both parties lose.**

Those with the greatest empathy, EmD-5s, do not make codependent-style mistakes. They: do have compassion, respect the rights of others, never engage in violence (verbally or physically) or manipulation. EmD-5s are good at reading others' intentions and feelings while, at the same time, holding constant an awareness of themselves as separate from others. EmD-5s can detach from the games others play yet keep constant in their love—for themselves—and others. No easy feat.

I don't claim to be an EmD-5 all of the time. Despite my many experiences with individuals who are EmD-0, -1, -2, -3, and -4, I still slip into codependency or let myself become a victim now and again. Such is life. Often, we face situations where we can choose to operate at a higher level of empathy—or not.

Choosing the higher empathy road takes courage. It is this choice to function as an entirely empathetic EmD-5 that leads to resilience and the ability to soar.

You will see how I managed to hang in there throughout the ravages I experienced at the hands of people with severe Empathy Dysfunction. I detached and turned it over to God. Believe it or not, I found that I was better for it all. To take it a step further, in an EmD-5 action, I wrote this book to help others see the way out of, or through, an Empathy Dysfunction vortex.

The liftoff dream

One morning in May 2016, I awoke from a dream that left me feeling exuberant. A premonition of sorts, the dream showed that because of my courage and resilience, I was finally and at last on the path to freedom and finding my authentic self. (This is an awareness of the true-I voice inside my head. Think of it as listening to your gut. That intuition, or feeling you get when something doesn't feel right is your genuine, or authentic, voice battling your ego.)

Or, "To thy own self be true," as William Shakespeare said in his famous play "Hamlet."

> **Or, "To thy own self be true," as William Shakespeare said in his famous play "Hamlet."**

In my dream, I was living in a small apartment in San Francisco, and I was making preparations to leave the planet Earth on my personal rocket ship. I'd decided to spend my last night on Earth giving my goodbyes to those I'd loved and who'd loved me.

I'd seen my beloved Bianca and Phoebe. The meeting had been brief and tender but uneventful. It had felt as though everything had been resolved between each of my daughters and I. Childhood friends and college buddies had met up with me. It had seemed that everyone I'd needed to see lived in

San Francisco. *(Dreams are like that, using "poetic license" to make points or offer insights.")*

Oddly, I'd spent most of the night with my ex-husband, Howard. We'd had a great time walking the streets of the City by the Bay, dropping into little bars, and laughing as we'd reminisced on our life together. As the evening had waned, I'd said, "Well I have to go now. I have to finish packing because I leave early in the morning." I'd given Howard a warm hug as I left.

When I'd gotten home, Howard had called. He'd said, "Would you like to spend some more time together tonight? There is supposed to be a fantastic meteor shower up in the mountains. Some of the fragments will get through the atmosphere and burn into the snow on the ridges and slopes, making beautiful fiery aqua-blue pools in the snow and ice. We could drive up tonight, and you could leave another day."

I'd imagined the scene, both snowy and firey, as Howard had spoken. I'd been tempted to go with him. Momentarily, I'd felt sad, thinking that I would no longer be able to enjoy the splendors of Earth: Once my rocket ship left the galaxy, I would never be able to return.

Again, I'd thought about leaving my Bianca and Phoebe, but I'd felt no regret. It clearly had been the time for me to go. "Thank you, no," I'd reluctantly told Howard. "I really don't have time. I need lots of rest for tomorrow's adventure."

Perplexed, Howard had asked, "Why are you leaving? You belong here with us." When I'd still refused, he'd offered more, "Maybe the kids and I could go with you."

I'd smiled, thinking Howard finally appreciated me, then said, "Howard, I have been preparing my rocket ship for a long time. When I found it, it needed lots of repairs, but it's ready now. And it is a rocket ship for only one person. In fact, there are many more one-person rocket ships hidden in warehouses and basements all over San Francisco. If you want to leave, you have to find one of them, repair it, then make plans to blast off on your own."

The next morning, I'd climbed into my rocket ship and started the engine. Liftoff had been gradual. My "ship" had looked like a sturdy, dark gray stealth bomber.[109] *At first, I'd been going much too slowly, and the ship had started to stall. I'd known I would fail to get through the Earth's atmosphere if I didn't take charge of this powerful rocket ship. With my right hand, I'd grasped the throttle and pushed it hard, all the way forward. As I'd heard a huge burst from the engine, I was flattened against the back of my seat.*

At last, my rocket ship had exploded through the atmosphere, carrying me into the star-studded blackness of space. Free at last from all the anchors and chains that had weighed me down for so long.

---

[109] The rocket ship in my dream was similar to the B-2 Spirit long-range strike bomber built for the U.S. Air Force by Northrop Grumman, a leading global security company.

Within each of us, there is a seed of resilience. It is in our nature, as human beings, to survive adversity. To sprout and grow that little seed, we need experiences that force us to discover what we are made of—and who we truly are. Your parents can't give you resiliency. You can't acquire it through higher education. Nor can it be developed with on-the-job training or work experience.

Our resilience expands when we face our fears and take full responsibility for finding and living our purpose. It is picking yourself up after a fall, then trying again and again until you get it right.

As my dream demonstrated, each of us must find our way solo. Your mind and soul will remain like the abandoned space vehicle—stuck—until, with 100 percent commitment, you rebuild it, which will take your blood, sweat, and tears.

Resilience does not grow without courage. We can survive almost any hardship, injustice, or treachery; but to truly express your personal blessings—your gifts and talents—you must have the courage to embrace the unknown. Being true to yourself isn't easy when there are multiple powers anxious to stop you. EmD individuals—like those in this book—wield powerful and ruthless forces.

> **Take heart: When it feels as if those negative forces are defeating you, call on your courage to blast you past your detractors on into further spiritual enlightenment. You can mark where you are on the path to enlightenment by recognizing the forces opposing you—anger, guilt, fear, deceit, confusion, and self-doubt.**

Take heart: When it feels as if those negative forces are defeating you, call on your courage to blast you past your detractors on into further spiritual enlightenment. You can mark where you are on the path to enlightenment by recognizing the forces opposing you— anger, guilt, fear, deceit, confusion, and self-doubt.

I'm about to walk you through the stretches of my journey where I discovered my courage and resilience; brought on when I faced multiple people with EmD who tried to shame me and bring harm to my family and me.

Eventually, I came to accept and appreciate that I was given the life of a warrior, with a purpose: to help people and the planet in my unique way (hopefully, through this and my other books). We are all here to make a difference by using our gifts whether they befit a warrior,[110] a nurturer, an administrative leader, a grocery clerk, an artist, or an astrophysicist.

Mine is only one story. Hopefully, I will inspire you to tell your story, too.

A brand new theorem: Dr. Kathy's Theory of Relativity

Hanging on the wall of my office where I see it every day is a quote by an anonymous author.

> *"Sometimes God calms the storm.*
> *"Sometimes God lets the storm rage,*
> *"And calms his child."*

---

[110] Like Xena, Warrior Princess, or anyone on a hero's journey, much more is required than ace fighting skills. A warrior must also have the wherewithal to stay the course and do the right thing—often against great odds and entirely alone.

For the longest time, I described my experience in Vancouver as the perfect storm, when I inexplicably found myself the object of shaming attacks on several fronts. The hits came from the Vancouver City government, greedy neighbors, cutthroat businessmen, power-hungry politicians, and a vindictive ex-spouse. Eventually, all this forced my children to leave and compelled me to endure their betrayal.

With God's help, I found within the tenacity to survive that perfect storm. I even discovered that I had a surplus of resilience: This is what has enabled me to turn the storm into something useful, what I call "Dr. Kathy's Theory of Relativity."

In 2016, "Einstein's Theory of General Relativity" was given a huge boost when the first detection of gravitational waves[111] was confirmed, proving his famous theory.[112] Remember how you can recall where you were or what you were wearing at the time of a significant event (President Kennedy's assassination, the moon landing, September 11)?

I distinctly recall that I had been travelling a freeway north to Portland when I heard the newscaster on my car radio announce this most significant scientific finding. I was thrilled! Many claim this to be the biggest revelation since the discovery that Earth is

---

[111] Two sensitive computerized detectors sensed a gravitational wave as it passed through Earth. More than 1,000 scientists worked on the $1-billion LIGO (Laser Interferometer Gravitational-Wave Observatory) experiment funded by the National Science Foundation.

[112] Einstein predicted a century ago that space and time are interwoven in the Universe with the ability to stretch, shrink, and jiggle. The proof of this dynamism came when scientists heard and recorded the sound of two black holes colliding a billion light-years from Earth. The brief chirrup provided the first evidence of gravitational waves, the ripples in the fabric of space that Einstein had calculated.

round and orbits the sun. My intuition told me this Big Reveal would be a huge turning point for me, too.

Einstein postulated that 1.3 billion years ago two giant black holes collided, sending huge shock waves through the fabric of the Universe. This impacted time and space. He theorized that these waves distorted the Universe, causing it to roll, fold, and curve, sometimes bumping into astral bodies like Earth and its sun. It also explains gravity and the reason that time is relative.

Pondering this discovery of the century (perhaps the millennium), I realized that it was time to rearrange how I'd been perceiving my personal perfect storm. I would need to switch to a vantage point where I could see my experiences as relative; then sort out the distortions in my time-space continuum.

Instead of fighting it, I decided to ride the gravitational wave that had given rise to the decade of haunting events that led me to write "When Empathy Fails." At once, my life made sense. My Big Reveal? I am no longer a victim or a survivor. I am the true me, riding wave after wave of transformation in my life. A sea change like this is what I mean by "Dr. Kathy's Theory of Relativity."

Ride the wave

My theory of relativity began to form with the first of my three arrests in October 2003. It precipitated my meeting the unethical City Prosecutor Josephine Townsend (as discussed in *Chapter One*). It was July 4, 2006, when I was arrested a second time (as described in *Chapter Eight*).

After my Independence Day arrest, I'd hired a dynamite attorney, Therese Lavallee. I wasn't taking any chances with the legal system after the travesty of my first arrest and nasty dealings with Townsend—who by then (in early 2005) had been fired as Vancouver's Prosecutor and had also faced two ethics investigations by the Washington State BAR. Townsend's replacement, Kevin McClure, was cut from the same cloth. He, too, was an EmD-1.

Lavallee had been furious when she learned McClure planned to prove to the jury that my injuries had been self-inflicted. His argument was that I'd injured myself as a method of covering up my supposed attack on my neighbor Melanie Mooney. Even more outrageous: McClure planned this strategy months after Mooney had admitted attacking me first; hence provoking my acts of self-defense.

> **I'd offered a prayer that if God's plan had me going to jail, I be given strength, courage, and protection. Because I am like Christ's Apostle Thomas, who had needed proof Jesus had risen from the dead, I'd asked for a sign that God was working behind the scenes on my behalf.**

It was February 2007 before I went to trial (for the misdemeanors of assault, trespass, stalking, and lying to the police). I'd sat in the courtroom dazed on the first day of voir dire, the method of selecting a jury. As I'd watched and listened to the process, I'd released any thoughts (delusions) I'd had about controlling the situation. I'd decided to ride the wave.

If God wanted me to go through this parody of justice, there must be a reason. I'd offered a prayer that if God's plan had me going to jail, I be given strength, courage, and protection. Because I am like Christ's Apostle Thomas, who had needed proof Jesus had risen from the dead, I'd asked for a sign that God was working behind the scenes on my behalf.

Before the proceedings began, Lavallee had asked if I was interested in playing a game of distraction to help me relax. She'd said, "Take out a piece of paper and write down the names of the jurors that you would like to be on the jury.

We get to pick only two. Prosecutor McClure gets to pick two, and Judge Melnick picks two." (In a misdemeanor trial there are only six jurors). She'd smiled at me and said, "I think it will be fun to see if I can maneuver the judge and Kevin to pick my favorites!"

She had admonished me to keep quiet and make notes on my legal pad without drawing too much attention: because Melnick had very strict rules about defendants influencing the jury. He'd already scolded me once for leaning over to ask a question of Lavallee. He'd said, "If you make any gesture to influence the jury or a witness, I will declare a mistrial!"

The author spent hours and hours in the Clark County Courthouse as her laywers tried to resolve more than 20 cases and charges --- mostly false ---brought against her between 2002 and 2014. Her life largely turned and churned based on the state of her court affairs.

I'd begun to understand why defendants interviewed by TV news reporters always look so staid, as if they don't care what happens to them. They're on air and probably petrified just as I was.

As I'd watched in awe, Lavallee deftly navigated through voir dire. In her questions to potential jurors, she'd planted seeds that could help identify which way a juror was apt to lean in my case. For example, "Do you believe you would be able to do the right thing when faced with conflicting evidence?"

When jury selection was complete, Lavallee and I looked at the names written on each other's yellow legal notepads. Our names for top choices and an alternate matched! We had picked the same six jurors! My attorney and I were on the same wavelength! That bode well, I thought.

Even more extraordinary, these were the same jurors chosen by McClure and Judge Melnick. Coincidence? I think not: This was God making good the promise to calm his child in a storm—the sign I'd prayed for. Just then—as in the frightening Russian roulette game of chance—the court clerk spun the basket of remaining candidates' names and randomly drew out one to be the alternate juror.

Yes! It was the same name Lavallee and I had chosen, independently. Hope started to grow within my heart: Despite Judge Melnick's admonition to remain perfectly still and stay neutral, I'd smiled; a small, discreet, yet grateful, smile.

> **She'd also admitted to intercepting me on the beach, threatening my guests with a burning poker from the bonfire, grabbing me and my flashlight, then biting me.**

A calm had come over me as the courtroom storm raged for three days. I rode this life wave to shore; where a verdict of "not guilty" on all counts waited. Mooney had admitted to assaulting me, proving that I'd been defending myself. She'd also admitted to intercepting me on the beach, threatening my guests with a burning poker from the bonfire, grabbing me and my flashlight, then biting me.

Her EmD-1 husband Don Morris, was caught in perjury, rendering his testimony invalid.[113] The police officers who arrested me had testified that they hadn't thoroughly investigated the situation and may have misjudged me. Even after these admissions of guilt, McClure stuck with his implausible accusation that I'd bitten myself: This, even after Mooney had confessed to biting me.

Lavallee, on the other hand, was operating at EmD-5 level, because she stayed calm, cool, and collected. She was respectful of everyone. She laid out the case against my neighbors and explained it all to me as well. This attorney treated me as if we were partners in the endeavor, not that I needed rescuing. Plus, when the verdict came in favoring me, Lavellee took no credit for the good outcome.

It wound up costing me $45,000 to defend myself from these false charges. In retrospect, I can honestly claim it was an amazing experience. It taught me to ride the waves in my life and accept my role as a warrior.

Later, Lavallee told me that when she'd left the courtroom, Howard had been there and congratulated her on the win—as if it were just another day in court with small talk between lawyers. Apparently, he had been hanging out in the courthouse to follow the progress of my trial.

He'd said nothing to me. Nor (as far as I know) did he ever bother to help Bianca see that I'd been the victim of the assault;

---

[113] Tapes of the Don Morris testimony had been played at the trial over the property dispute and in connection with his contempt of court in the civil matter. His testimony at my criminal trial was the opposite of what he had said on tape at the other trials.

hence, found "not guilty." Even so, I began to take back my life and cement the belief that I am perfect, whole, and complete just as I am.

Traveling the Relativity Universe and fighting off those who mean me harm is hard work even for a warrior. I remain a lone warrior devoted to rehabilitating my rocket ship.

Warrior in training

In front of her childhood home in Portland, Ore., the author, age 5, is dressed as a superhero protecting the baby doll in her arms. In a Back-to-the-future manner, her pose predicts the path her life will take; devotion to help others and keep them safe.

My warrior destiny was apparent even in childhood—as you can see in the photograph (taken by my proud father). I was standing in the front yard of our modest post-World War II bungalow. My baby doll was in my arms and my superhero cape over my shoulders. Even then, I'd fancied myself a protector of the innocent.

On closer inspection, you might be able to see that my T-shirt is striped with my name, "Kathy-Kathy-Kathy." Gosh, I'd loved that T-shirt and was heartbroken when I outgrew it! Several psychodynamic[114] forces contributed to my superhero persona:

---

[114] Psychodynamics is the interrelation of the unconscious and conscious mental and emotional forces that determine personality and motivation. Psychodynamic therapy, also known as insight-oriented therapy, focuses on unconscious processes as they are manifested in

- Having an alcoholic father and an autistic mother;
- Being the oldest child of two daughters;
- Growing up a brilliant child with no outlet for my talents in our "po' white trash" community;
- Achieving straight "As" in school;
- Starting a food fight to protest teacher oppression;
- Being age 22 when I divorced my first husband, an alcoholic;
- Striking out on my own to travel around Europe at 23;
- Moving to Hawaii to earn a master's degree in social work.

It isn't so much why, or even how, I became a superhero, but that I accepted the role extremely early on. I'd found myself in a world akin to that of Xena, the Warrior Princess, single-handedly fighting for truth and justice.

I've always had a feel for the underdog. My mantra is, "Free the Oppressed." Whenever I went to court during the decade I was victimized I wore, on my jacket lapel, a U.S. Army Special Forces pin with the inscription, "De Oppresso Liber."

The U.S. Army Special Forces pin the author wore to all of her court appearances. Translated from Latin, it means "to free from oppression."

Nary a soul recognized or acknowledged the pin, not even when I raised my right hand to be sworn in as a witness. I like to think everyone knew and unconsciously accepted the message

---

a person's present behavior. The goals of psychodynamic therapy are a client's self-awareness and understanding of the influence of the past on present behavior.

on the pin; after all, in a court of law, everyone is sworn to tell the truth and to uphold the Constitution of the United States of America, which promises freedom from oppression.[115]

On the other hand, it may have been that the Judge thought I was a "Monty Python" fan. (In one of the surreal "Monty Python" British comedy sketches, the peasants shout, "free the oppressed"). Either way, the pin helped me to maintain my perspective on the limits of our "justice" system.

Training in the trenches

I got much of my training to be a warrior as a young social worker for the State of Oregon, Children's Services Division (when I was age 25 to 30). Three troubling cases from that time come to mind. They had so obviously demonstrated that not even children are safe in the hands of "the system"—unless a warrior-type is willing to go all out.

- **A medical resident at Oregon Health Sciences University (OHSU) called Child Protective Services (CPS) in Portland, where I worked, to report that he had saved the life of a five year old**. I investigated. This was the third time the boy had been brought to the emergency room after ingesting his mother's tranquilizers. No one, not police, paramedics,

---

[115] Over the years, I have been given a variety of gifts representing how others see me. For example, I was given a poster of Russel Crowe sailing into danger in the movie "Master and Commander." Another friend gave me a statuette of the Elf Warrior in "Lord of the Rings" Yet another friend gave me the Green Beret pin. I've had the pin since the early eighties.

or ER staff, had thought to report it before; on the third near-death experience, this doctor thought it prudent to call.

I asked the child if he'd known the drugs would kill him, and why he kept taking them. He'd replied that he understood the gravity of taking his mother's pills. Then, he told me that he'd done so, "Because my mom told me to."

Thankfully, his mother was arrested and stripped of her parental rights. The little boy was adopted. It took a couple of years for his nightmares to stop.

- **A six-month-old child was abandoned in Portland by a trucker couple who had picked up the baby at a truck stop in Rhode Island.** As a favor to the destitute mother, the couple had offered to care for the child for a couple of weeks. Then, they'd driven the infant across the country to Oregon.

    They'd promised the mother that they would return with the baby in two weeks and hook up with her at the truck stop. They never returned, instead handing off the baby to a relative, who quickly applied for a welfare grant to care for the baby boy.

    As the social worker assigned to the case, I filed a motion for temporary custody, placed the child in foster care, then started looking for the mother (who in the interim had followed her boyfriend from Rhode Island to Texas to Michigan).

I'd had to do some "fancy dancing" along the way since the Juvenile Court Commissioner Richard Knapp ordered that the baby be returned to the trucker couple. In his twisted mind, he'd determined that Oregon didn't have jurisdiction over a child from Rhode Island. In spite of his threat to find me in contempt of court, the child remained safe in the Portland foster home.

- **A Portland foster family had a reputation for abusing teenagers placed in their care.** One of their discipline methods: grab a kid by the hair, toss him or her into the swimming pool, and hold the child's head under water.

  In addition, three foster girls reported being sexually molested by the foster father. Even more surreal, the foster mother was physically abusing her own 16-year-old-year old daughter, who was disabled with cerebral palsy.

  The teen had previously lived in foster care for 12 years because of the mother's abuse. While this child had been in foster care, her abusive mother was, unbelievably, certified by the State of Oregon to be a foster parent. I'd had one heckuva time getting protection for these children since I had to expose government complicity.

  You see, several social workers had known about the abuse and had chosen not to place children in this foster home; but they'd done nothing to shut it down. When I'd tried to expose the abuse, Multnomah County (in Oregon) Judge Kathleen Nachtigal told me—while in court—that I had become too involved, then ejected me from the courtroom.

Nachtigal had also determined that the testimony of the sexual abuse was moot since there were other foster children who'd reported they had not been abused. (What about the children who had?) Fortunately, the child with cerebral palsy was reunited with her foster family, and the abusive foster home was shut down.

Shortly after, I received a disciplinary notice from Children's Services Division. They'd determined that I was insubordinate and incompetent because I'd questioned the wisdom of the foster home licensing unit, which had certified the abusive couple.

This last case prompted me to rethink my career. After five years working for the State of Oregon, I returned to graduate school to earn my doctorate in psychology. I have worked as a psychologist ever since. But it hasn't been much easier as a psychologist in private practice.

My warrior sensitivities force me to take action over and over again. Like the time my client, an Oregon middle school choir teacher, told me she was having sex with a 13-year-old male student. I never could get the child protected. I reported to the Vancouver Police, who said it was not their jurisdiction because they didn't handle child abuse. I reported to the Clark County Sheriff, who said it was not their jurisdiction either since I worked in Washington, but the teacher lived in Oregon.

I reported to the Police in Gresham, Oregon, where the teacher lived. They told me that child abuse reports had to be filed with Child Protective Services (CPS) in Portland (my old employer). When I called CPS, I was instructed to file the report with the Gresham Police. Talk about being given the runaround! And with the well-being of children at stake!

Completely stumped, I wrote a letter (in the days before email) to the Chief of Police for Portland to complain that it was downright criminal not to take my report. Thankfully, he'd responded and ordered the Gresham Police to investigate.

Their finding? The lieutenant who'd studied the case told me that since the barely-teenaged boy "looked like a man," they'd closed the case. I was operating at an EmD-5 level here. The Gresham Police officer clearly was not.

Can you see how this early warrior training contributed to establishing the resilience that I'd had to call into play in a big way when inundated by divorce, hostile neighbors, physical assault, harassment, false arrest, lawsuits, and the loss of my daughters?

It's not just that I am motivated to confront corrupt, abusive people and systems. A warrior has to do more than just come out swinging. You also need cunning and a strategy. Without that, you end up creamed or in jail (and I've been there).

In those early days of warrior training, I'd learned to trust no one and to cover myself with knowledge—often garnered through extensive research. It is decidedly useful to be smarter, more persistent, and better prepared than the Empathy Dysfunction person you're up against.

Those with EmD rely on doublespeak and evasive manipulation to make their mark. Those tendencies leave EmDs vulnerable to being blindsided by the honest, determined, and uncompromising warrior.

Responding to the pairing of gossip and shame with robust resilience

Shaming is a powerful tool in the hands of those with empathy disorders. Even a warrior who has truth and rationality on her side can have a difficult time shaking the shame she feels. One reason for this: We keep searching for the kernel of truth in the accusations made by the person living with Empathy Dysfunction.

We have empathy, which makes us introspective; and we all have the flaws characteristic of human beings: always being late; overspending; telling occasional small white lies; being overweight; or being divorced.

Having empathy and flaws sets humans up to be nervous about criticism and to accept the burden of shame. Worse, most

> **A false witness shall be punished and a liar shall be caught.**
>
> Proverbs 19:9

The above reference to Proverbs may be Biblical in origin, but the way these words were paraphrased and used by the author's neighbors in an attempt to shame her was evil incarnate.

In the "King James Bible" and many other translations, Proverb 19:9 reads, "A false witness shall not be unpunished, and he that speaketh lies shall perish.")

people—other EmDs as well as neurotypicals[116]—believe gossip, making it nearly impossible to override falsehoods with truth.

So the cycle of shaming continues; however, if you consistently operate as an EmD-4+ or an EmD-5, you can build superior resilience in the face of gossip.

In 2005, my next door neighbors Joseph and Julianne Leas posted this Bible verse on the back window of their car, parked it facing my house and blocking the road. Over the next few days, they displayed additional posters that featured Bible verses. All this because the Leas had been furious that I'd dared to stand up for myself and my property rights.

You saw how well this worked for the Leas in an earlier chapter. They sued me: They lost in summary judgement. They sued again: They lost. They appealed: They lost. I sued for contempt of court: They lost. I countersued for damages: They lost.

Still, their shaming drove a wedge between many of my neighbors and me. By the time of my arrest two years later, their gossip and shaming were at fever pitch. Once the malignant gossip about me was circulating, the SBL community amped up its alienation efforts. Shortly after my false arrest on July 4, 2006, Mooney (my assailant) convinced her neighborhood association, Steamboat Landing (SBL), to post a Wanted Poster on the front gate of their private community *(as seen in Chapter 9)*.

The SBL Homeowner's Association's Board President, Toni Montgomery, took responsibility for the Wanted Poster. When challenged by some members of her community, Montgomery had

---

[116] Neurotypicals are not affected by a developmental disorder, such as autism, and are generally free of major Empathy Dysfunction.

defended the poster. Vancouver Police Lieutenant Dave King, she'd explained, had encouraged her to post it.[117]

According to Montgomery, the Lieutenant had also confirmed that he would arrest me if I trespassed. (He'd sent Montgomery emails to this end.) Even after the court had upheld my rights to the easement road (which crossed through SBL turf) that I used to walk to the river, Lt. King and other police officers threatened me with arrest for years.

The Wanted Poster was up less than a month. It was removed when SBL's attorney so advised them. The consequences for me and the damage to my reputation could never be undone or repaired, so I sued SBL. They paid their attorney $75,000 (according to SBL Board minutes) to handle the suit and paid me $25,000 in damages.

But the shaming had continued full force. SBL residents frequently called the Police on me. Usually, it was when an ill-informed SBL neighbor, like Patti Lightfoot, who called whenever they spied me using my easement to walk Simon to the river. A report made by Vancouver Police Officer Richard Rich, claimed that Lightfoot was so afraid of me she'd run inside her house whenever she saw me there. According to Rich, "Lightfoot said she is not afraid of many people, especially since her job is in emergency rooms, but Kathy scares her." Apparently, Lightfoot also said, "My blood runs cold when I see her face."

On July 5, 2006, several SBL neighbors signed a petition to have my business license revoked. Primary among them was Don Morris, who'd stated that I was endangering the community with my psychology practice.

---

[117] Lt. Dave King was later promoted to Precinct Commander.

To prove my supposed transgressions, he'd submitted dozens of secret videos he had taken of my daughter, my guests, my black Labrador retriever, and me to Code Enforcement. All I ever got by way of notification was a letter from the City advising me they'd received a complaint; however, it was not something I was allowed to see. It would be years before this grievance came to light: Landis kept the videos—which were evidence— hidden until Dec.6, 2006 when he was forced to reveal them.[118]

Another round of shaming came when a man, using the alias Steve Kappler, cyberstalked me. In his emails, he'd called me a "roach" and referred to my teenage daughter Phoebe as "a retard." He'd said that he was continuing to watch me secretly and would report me to the police whenever he could.

He'd said that with Steamboat Landing now involved in the neighborhood fray (over the train crossing, public road status, and my river easement), my family and I would be, thankfully, driven out. Terrified, I'd notified the police. Instead of helping me, East Precinct Commander Rick Smith had told me the emails weren't threatening—so I should handle the problem myself.

I took Cmrd. Smith up on his advice and hired a private detective to track down the stalker. It turned out to be Ken Morris, the 30-year-old nephew of Don Morris. Ken had sent the emails from his workplace, using his coworker's ID. Enraged that the Vancouver Police hadn't lifted a finger to help me address the cyberstalking, I'd demanded they make an arrest. Eventually, they did arrest Ken for the gross misdemeanor of Cyberstalking. Plus,

---

[118] On Dec. 6, 2006, Don Morris testified in court that he had taken 50 videos and turned them over to Richard Landis in June and July of 2006. Landis could no longer keep this evidence hidden when my attorney demanded the release of the videos.

Ken was fired by his employer, Sysco Food Distributors. Of course, this crazed my neighbors even more.

It was the 2004 libelous memo written by Jacks, Townsend, and Landis that fostered, then fed and spread, the alleged lies that shamed me. Why, once I'd been labeled bonkers, would City government members or police officers deign to help or protect me? It takes only one unethical, manipulative, and vindictive EmD-1 to rouse and provoke the average EmD-4 or a whole community of them. The mob mentality comes to mind.

EmD-4s lack strong interpersonal boundaries, which amplifies their codependency tendencies. Flimsy boundaries mean EmD-4s can be manipulated masterfully through fear and anger. That's how many of my otherwise-decent neighbors were turned to the side of my adversaries.

And, it's why—once their EmD-4 empathy level had gone sour—no SBL resident ever thought to question why their homeowner's association was spending time and money terrorizing my family and me over a property dispute that had nothing to do with the neighborhood at large. These neighbors were acting out of negative empathy even if, usually, they functioned as EmD-4s with an abundance of compassion.

Years later, I accepted that I was—and still am—a terrific mother. I'd provided unconditional love, healthy food, a warm home, quality education, liberal enrichment opportunities, and the best medical care available. I grieved greatly when I lost Bianca, then Phoebe. I still do; but I am no longer ashamed of losing my daughters.

Shedding the shame

Before I could understand Empathy Dysfunction and develop "Dr. Kathy's Theory of Relativity," I'd had to get past my debilitating shame. If not, I'd have been locked interminably in self-absorbed pity. Enduring attacks about my children or my mothering had been excruciating—their impact nearly impossible to shake.

Townsend told my attorney Dan Lorenz the only reason my daughter Bianca was troubled was that I was a terrible mother. Believe me, I'd felt like a terrible mother: I'd been unable to shield my children from the neighbors' beastly daily attacks. I'd felt helpless as my daughters' childhood years disappeared into my warrior-mom battles to protect us.

When even my daughters began shaming me, I'd endured the most piercing kind of sorrow. Gaining absolution, or self-forgiveness, after they'd shamed me was by far the most difficult undertaking of my life.

Years later, I accepted that I was—and still am—a terrific mother. I'd provided unconditional love, healthy food, a warm home, quality education, liberal enrichment opportunities, and the best medical care available. I grieved greatly when I lost Bianca, then Phoebe. I still do; but I am no longer ashamed of losing my daughters.

I'd protected my children from the onslaught as best I could. I never told Phoebe that Ken Morris had called her a "retard." A mother's ultimate sacrifice is to stand by her children and take the hits—even when her kids are the mudslingiers. To this day, my daughters hold me responsible for subjecting them to that tumultuous decade. They refuse to call me Mom, but I am proud to be their mother still.

I am reminded of a blog written by another shamed mother, Liza Long, following the Sandy Hook tragedy. Adam Lanza, 20, massacred 20 children and six educators, then killed himself at Sandy Hook Elementary School in Newtown, Conn., on Dec. 14, 2012. In a poignant essay, Long wrote, "I am Adam Lanza's mother." Long, however, was not Lanza's mom: Lanza had killed his mother at home before beginning his school murder spree.

What Long had meant was that she could easily have been (or become) the victim of violence as Lanza's late mother had been. Long had been trying to convey that she understood perfectly well how her mentally ill son could someday make the same mistake and kill her: Especially since he had been hospitalized more than once following a violent act.

Her impassioned plea had been to expand and enhance community services to the mentally ill. Long had implored legislators, law enforcement, and medical personnel to step up and work unceasingly to understand the toll on a single mother when raising a dangerously disturbed child.

As a single mother, I'd wept when I read Long's words. She'd taken lots of hits after bringing this painful and sensitive subject into the light. It is a no-win situation for mothers. If Long had complained that her son was dangerous, would he have gotten proper help? If she'd complained, would that have made her a bad mother? Was what happened her fault?

It is beyond cruel to try to destroy a mother like Long, or like me. On the heels of a hostile divorce, I'd struggled to raise two disabled children while in the midst of neighborhood turmoil inflamed by corrupt government officials.

Thankfully, there were a few people along the way who refused to join the mob and shame me. Oregon Superior Court Judge John Nichols was one who consistently operated at an EmD-5 level. I remember one day in court, early in 2005, when he'd taken me by surprise.

During one of our many times in court over the property dispute, and in front of my nasty neighbors, he'd warned me, "Be careful. You are a target." He'd told me to protect myself whenever

> During one of our many times in court over the property dispute, and in front of my nasty neighbors, he'd [Judge John Nichols] warned me, "Be careful. You are a target." He'd told me to protect myself whenever I used the road to the river and to take witnesses.

I used the road to the river and to take witnesses.

After that, I took my camera and copies of my protective orders whenever I left my house. With a couple of short sentences, Nichols had validated my experience and reinforced how critical it was that I protect myself. He had called out my stalkers with his sharp words. Even this had not ended, or diluted, their vendetta or their warped belief that I was evil incarnate. Still, his comments had helped me tremendously: I knew that each time I was in his courtroom, Nichols would be fair and reasonable, remaining neutral as a judge should.

On another occasion, Nichols had transformed my shame by shutting down attorney Steve Turner, who was representing one of my neighbors. As Turner had questioned me on the witness stand, he'd made the case that his client, Don Morris, was no danger to me: This, in spite of the fact that he had: video-stalked me, sworn at my children and me, hit me, and threatened to kill my dog.

Turner's argument: Since I'd stood up for myself, it had been okay for Morris to abuse me. Nichols sustained my attorney's objection to Turner's unseemly badgering of me. Turner continued to argue with the Judge about the validity of his ridiculous defense. Turner reasoned that if I could handle the Don Morris abuse, then it didn't qualify as abuse.

Nichols ended the debate swiftly, "Mr. Turner, I have sustained the objection, so please move along with your questioning. Besides, we all know that Dr. Marshack is outspoken." In a decisive move, the Judge had stripped away more of my shame and publicly established my status as an outspoken warrior.

It has been difficult to release all remnants of the shame I wore like a dense pelt for those many years. Gradually, the impenetrable fur has been shed—at a faster pace now as my reliable rocket ship carries me farther and farther away. The point of no return is mine! (This refers to gaining the deep perspective that you cannot go back and change things while also being confident that you can and will move forward.)

Most of the shame I'd felt was gone by 2014 when I sold my house and left Vancouver. Phoebe's betrayal and my third false arrest in 2013 had seemed a fitting time to finally sell to my neighbor's land developer, Kent Kresa. (You met him in *Chapter Eight*.)

Becoming a Radiant Warrior (EmD-5)

It had been the final day of my last garage sale in Vancouver when Amber had dropped by. During a lull in the sales, Amber sat down in a folding chair and chatted with me. Cheerfully, she'd said, "You know, when I saw your garage sale signs up on Evergreen Highway, I was nervous about driving down this road. There's a woman down here who is just awful."

With her bold comments, I realized that Amber was a resident of Steamboat Landing, the very neighborhood I had sued over the wanted poster. I'd looked at her then to be certain she was not messing with me. I could see she was unaware of who I was, so I'd asked, "Really? And who would that be?"

"Oh, don't you know?" Amber's eyes had widened in surprise.

"Well," I'd responded while offering her some lemonade, "I have heard things, but tell me what you know."

"Well," continued Amber as she'd leaned in to give me the dirt. "She's supposedly a psychiatrist or something, but she doesn't really have a license. She just pretends. And she has caused all kinds of trouble for us over at Steamboat Landing with her lies."

Faking concern, I'd said, "That sounds just terrible." One of my friends had been standing nearby eavesdropping on the conversation. She'd looked worried for me, like at any minute Amber would catch on. I'd been concerned, too, since my name and the words "licensed psychologist" were clearly visible on my home office door. Amber hadn't connected the dots.

Gossiping on, Amber had said, "Yeah, well it's over now. She's been shut down, and we won't be hearing from her again. Too bad though, that you're moving. It's nice to have a great neighbor like you living down here where it's been such a nightmare. In fact, if you'd like to join the Fourth of July block party over at Steamboat Landing, let me know. We would love to have you."

Amber had given me her email and phone number, then left with a smile. All the while, my friend Julie had stood there filled with dread about the outcome. "How could you keep a straight face, Kathy?" Julie had asked me with an expression of awe.

I'd broken the tension with a quip, saying, "I'm Wonder Woman!" Julie had started to laugh. "After all," I'd said. "Wouldn't it be a kick in the pants to attend a Fourth of July party with the neighbors who had me arrested on Independence Day eight years ago?" We were still laughing so hard tears were streaming down our faces as the next garage sale customers arrived. No shame now. Just freedom. And a lot of laughs.

Taking full responsibility for myself and trusting that God is with me every day in every way makes it possible to go it alone. There are still days I miss my children and my darling little grandson. There are days I feel like the lonesome warrior; sometimes there is no one to wipe away my tears of sadness.

I also believe that I have reached the point of no return regarding shame. I am moving on (in my rocket ship), with the EmD-5 tool of resilience—and without those low-level EmD folks who shamed me. Resilience plus awareness will keep me free of others who have clutches like my naysayers in Vancouver did.

Besides, I regularly receive reminders that I am a Radiant Warrior. Recently, I got a text on Mother's Day wishing me a happy holiday. The message read, "You deserve a great Mother's Day!" I didn't recognize the sender's phone number, and it certainly wasn't from one of my shunning daughters.

Thinking that it was a mistake and meant for another mother, I sent back a carefully worded response, urging the sender to recheck the intended phone number. I didn't want another mother to miss out.

The message had been meant for me. The sender was a young man, a 20-something client of mine (about the same age as my daughters). He'd responded, saying that the message was meant for me because he thought my children darned lucky to have me as their mom. (He hadn't known of my estrangement from my girls.)

"Dr. Kathy's Theory of Relativity" would suggest that the young man was correct. In a Universe where time and space are relative, there are still some who call me Mom.

"Radiant Warrior" Highlights

1. EmD-4s have empathy and can reciprocate in their relationships. However, they are not always clear about their psychological boundaries and can be manipulated or become co-dependent, taking on the responsibilities of others. Don't fall into the trap of doing for others that which they should be doing for themselves.

2. EmD-5s are those angels among us who have Radiant Empathy. They hold dear the thoughts and feelings of others while staying true to themselves.

3. Choosing to function at an EmD-5 level is important. From this fully empathic place, you can better make the courageous choice to develop your resilience—a much-needed characteristic in becoming your authentic self.

4. "Dr. Kathy's Theory of Relativity" describes the process of accepting the storms caused by those with Empathy Dysfunction: Riding the waves of transformation created by these gales; then, coming out the other side a better person—a person who is perfect, whole, and complete as is.

5. You are a not a victim. Nor are you merely a survivor. As you ride the gravitational waves of transformation rippling through the Universe and your life, you will become more adept at trusting the Universe to guide you.

6. Develop your warrior skills if you can. People with Empathy Dysfunction rely on double-talk and manipulation to control others. EmDs become off-kilter and vulnerable when an honest, well-prepared warrior shows up.

7. Shame is a powerful tool that can sack you for decades if you let it. No one has the right to judge you even if you make mistakes. Accept—and honor—yourself by acknowledging your accomplishments and the beautiful, loving soul that resides within you.

8. Along the way, you will meet Radiant Angels, who will remind you of your value. Join their ranks!

CHAPTER ELEVEN

In Conclusion

How I Survived the Decade-long Perfect Storm and Learned to Dance as It Raged

> *"I distracted myself from the fear and terrorism by thinking about things like how the universe began and whether time travel is possible."*
>
> — Malala Yousafzai

The witch-hunt that led to something good: creation of the Empathy Dysfunction Scale

I was the subject of a witch-hunt. This phenomenon may have taken hold in Salem, Mass., during the 1600s, but it was alive and well in Vancouver, Wash., where, in the 21st century, I was considered the witch by private citizens and government bodies.

In my intolerable marriage, my children and I were oppressed and abused every single day. For the sake of our safety and sanity, I'd decided to strike out on my own. I'd had no idea how divorcing a local divorce attorney, in a relatively small town, could trigger a barrage of unscrupulous attacks from several quarters.

Like sharks, the opportunists took advantage of both my precarious situation (juggling too many responsibilities while threatened from all angles) and my mother's instinct to protect my children. I'd been terrified and confused when I was initially harassed, stalked, sued, assaulted, and falsely arrested. Naively, I'd played into the hands of these sharks: all low-level—and influential—EmDs. I lost some battles with them and gained deep scars in other skirmishes. By and by, my warrior instinct kicked in, and I discovered I had a store of resilience.

As awful as it was to live through the devastating storm of onslaughts when the waves parted, I'd envisioned a way to transform my suffering into something dynamic, the Empathy Dysfunction Scale.

The many roles I'd played during this storm—mother, psychologist, neighbor, friend, advocate, protector, defendant, model citizen, American—provided multiple perspectives on the games played by those with severe Empathy Dysfunction. My resilience and inner guidance system revealed how I could partner the personal and the professional to aid other EmD victims.

In this final chapter, I share the ways I managed to keep my sanity and conquer my fears as the depth of my strength, love, and wisdom was revealed.

- I learned a lot about EmDs and developed the EmD Scale, which is the underpinning of this book.
- I found the courage to face my accusers.
- I endured the betrayal of friends and neighbors who I had known for years.
- I learned to be resourceful, discovering court evidence that surprised my attorneys.

CONCLUSION – I SURVIVED THE PERFECT STORM

- I found the strength to carry on even when I had little energy left.
- I became a financial wizard as I juggled multiple attorneys and three credit cards.
- I ran interference for Phoebe; such as the time, when the Camas Police called me to rescue my drunken daughter.
- I comforted Bianca when her autistic meltdowns were the worst.
- I managed to keep working as a psychologist because, apparently, I have the stamina of a warrior.

You may never be the prey in an EmD storm or scam, but you have, or will, come face to face with one of the pernicious EmD types described in this book.

The truth is, sometimes, people **are** out to get you: Be prepared. Use my experiences to help you navigate the unruly world of Empathy Dysfunction

If you are suffering at the hands of someone with severe Empathy Dysfunction, you may not think, or feel, that the Universe is on your side. You may not believe that you have the resiliency to bounce back from the EmD's covert and overt attacks. I didn't believe it at first either. In each preceding chapter, you've seen me find a means to survive the perfect storm.

Below are some tips that have helped me. My prayer is that my ability to sustain during a 12-year storm will help you through your personal perfect storm. I hope you will take note, then recognize when to use the tips. Let them serve as your shield when you take the dare and fight the bullies, and the other empathy-lacking, hostile, and self-centered people in your life.

Tip One: Keep your channel clear

This tip came to me in the first year of my perfect storm; however, I didn't learn to use it well until much later.

Keep your channel clear. Simple? Not when you are under siege, tired, and frightened.

I have sound insight and intuition. I trust my hunches most of the time. Admittedly, I am inconsistent about activating my inner guidance system to keep my channel clear.

Why not use the system more often, more deliberately? Instead of delighting in an occasional coincidence, or praying for help when you are desperate, why not daily ask for spiritual guidance (through prayer, mediation, journaling, or a brisk walk through the woods)?

In the spring of 2004, my neighbor Julianne Leas had threatened to have me arrested for trespassing on my easement, which passed by her house. Leas' hostility was extreme, but I hadn't had a clue that her rancor would kindle the formation of a spiteful mob focused on bringing me down. Her threat did, however, provide me with an insight that would serve me and steady me in the coming years.

The Portland, Ore., billboard that featured the road sign for homes along S.E. Evergreen Highway in Vancouver, Wash., the troubled street where the author lived: And where she was stalked and hounded by neighbors who coveted her property for the building of more high-end homes.

CONCLUSION – I SURVIVED THE PERFECT STORM

Not long after, at the end of a work day in my tiny Portland office (I saw clients there as well as in my home office in Vancouver.), I'd had a few minutes to spare before leaving for home; so I'd sat down on the couch to meditate on the problem of my neighbor's threats. Closing my eyes, I'd asked, "Should I sell my house and leave the problem behind?" For good measure, I'd asked God to provide a sign that would help me know what to do.

When I'd opened my eyes, there had been no big revelation, but I had felt like there was an answer coming. Feeling calmer, I'd grabbed my purse and briefcase and headed to my car for the trip home.

When you put a question, or a prayer, to the Universe, God gives you the answer you need—if you are ready to see it and translate the meaning. A few minutes into the drive, I'd been startled to see a giant new billboard with an advertisement for a real estate company (shown above) that showed my street sign, S.E. Evergreen Highway front and center! I knew this was my "sign" from God. Although I couldn't be certain of the meaning of this sign.

How was I supposed to interpret God's message: Was I supposed to list my S.E. Evergreen house for sale; or not sell because I was already living where I belonged? It's circular, pondering reasoning like this that tangles the mind.

> **When you put a question, or a prayer, to the Universe, God gives you the answer you need—if you are ready to see it and translate the meaning.**

Ironically, it hadn't mattered if I did or didn't sell. Shortly after this, the neighbors leveled a real property lawsuit against me, suspending any hope of selling and escaping. I'd remained there 10 more years. When I did sell, it was to Kent Kresa, the land developer who represented the Kellogg heirs (Don

Morris and his siblings). My house then sat vacant for two years until 2016 when Kresa tore it down to make way for the construction of luxury homes.

Still bewildered by the growing mob that was after me, it had taken a couple more years for me to observe another, more subtle, message from the Universe on the same billboard. Along the bottom of the billboard framing the sign, right in the center and directly under the SE Evergreen Highway street sign was the name of the company that owned the mega outdoor ad space, "Clear Channel." Those two words crystallized the real meaning in the sign from God: I must keep my channel clear! So must you!

Navigating this wild ride on Earth is not easy if we rely solely on logic and reason: The real answers to life's mysteries are seldom found there. When you keep your channel clear through meditation, prayer, or a gratitude journal, you are more apt to find the truth that exists outside the limits of our narrow time/space continuum here on earth. Clearing your mind allows answers—even to your deepest dilemmas—to flow through to your consciousness.

I'd used the clearing-the-channel method after my daughter Phoebe assaulted me, and I'd been arrested. Phoebe had been at my home with my infant grandson when, somehow provoked, she'd slammed me up against a plate glass door. She'd justified her behavior with the lie that I'd been drunk and attacked her for no reason.

I could defend myself against this false accusation: For example, the police breathalyzer had clocked me at .02 Blood Alcohol Level (BAC), which is what you might find after ingesting cough syrup. The legal intoxication limit is .08 BAC. Plus, I was bleeding and had bruises all over my arms where she'd grabbed me and shoved me into the door.

CONCLUSION – I SURVIVED THE PERFECT STORM

My injuries had been irrelevant to the arresting officer Jamie Haske. The incident landed me—not Phoebe—in the Clark County Jail. Police generally first accept the word of the accuser and arrest the accused. Later the attorneys work it out. Plus, the Vancouver Police had, years before, determined to arrest me whenever they got the chance. This, because of the libelous "functional sociopath" sabotage at Townsend's hand.

As I'd lain, dismayed, on the metal cot in my cell, I'd puzzled over why Phoebe would have made up such an outlandish and outright lie. I'd had a lot of time for contemplation as the tedious hours in jail dragged on. No answer had come to me—until a few months later when I was diagnosed with severe glaucoma.[119]

During my in-jail meditations, I'd received some nudges from the Universe to take better care of the "physical" me. Post-jail, I'd made a few health appointments, including one for an eye exam, something I hadn't taken care of in three years.

When the glaucoma problem surfaced, lots of pieces had fallen into place. Glaucoma can cause the loss of peripheral vision, which explained my tendency to bump into things or inadvertently brush items off a table. Worse, I'd fallen down the stairs three times over the course of the perfect-storm decade. Phoebe's false allegation had prompted me to clear my channel and see an ophthalmologist.

Another cleared-channel eye opener for me—realizing what may have been behind my daughter's betrayal. Could Phoebe have noticed my glaucoma-caused clumsiness and mistook it for drunkenness?

---

[119] Glaucoma is an eye disorder characterized by increased pressure within the eyeball. This damages the optic disc, impairing vision and sometimes progressing to blindness.

Could she have instinctively struck out at me when she believed her baby was in danger? I can only hope that Phoebe will manage to clear her channel, too, and realize that there's been a terrible mistake. She doesn't have to choose between her child and her mother: She can love us both.

Keeping your channel clear is not: looking for answers; making goals; or counting coup. It is centering within your internal and sacred place. It is putting aside your beliefs about right and wrong, good and bad. It means that your logical/rational mind is at rest, allowing another part of you to emerge. It means that you are letting love guide you.

Tip Two: Just keep going

My dear friend and psychologist, Frank Colistro, kept me going during the years I was under attack. One day, in his inimitable way, Frank had comforted me with the mock-Latin proverb, "Illegitimi non carborundum." It means, "Don't let the bastards grind you down." Frank's sardonic way of saying things always brought me perspective.[120]

> One day, in his inimitable way, Frank [the author's psychologist] had comforted me with the mock-Latin proverb, "Illegitimi non carborundum." It means, "Don't let the bastards grind you down."

I'd invoked that pseudo proverb the day I was served with papers stating City Prosecutor Josephine Townsend intended to revoke my Diversion Agreement. If this agreement were to

---

[120] I would highly recommend that each and every one of you find a savvy psychologist to be your guide when dealing with severe EmDs. Therapists are trained to help you reframe your terror into insight and to help you develop a successful game plan.

be revoked, it could be perilous: I could lose my professional psychology license and go to jail.

I was already tangled in a painful divorce plus being sued by vicious neighbors over an easement. Now, in hopes of retaining the Diversion Agreement, I would be forced to defend myself and protect my family from new false allegations.

When my attorney Bob Yoseph told me Townsend was on the warpath and would stop at nothing to crucify me, I'd been bewildered and frightened. He hadn't understood why she was angry with me, but he told me she had a reputation as a "bulldog" who would not stop until she destroyed her target.

This is typical of EmD-1s, such as Townsend. I'd wanted only to run and hide. Instead, and with God's aid, I'd repeated those three words, "Illegitimi non carborundum," like a mantra and ratcheted up my courage.

I wanted to hide away, but the following Sunday, I went to church alone. (If nothing else, go to church and ask God for help!) It was a beautiful, sunny spring day. The worship service should have been inspiring. Everyone was kind and supportive, having known me for years.

Nevertheless, when I got home, I still felt desolate. I could have gone into the garden and enjoyed the sunshine while I weeded and mowed the grass (something I actually enjoy). For some reason, I chose to go to the basement and clean out old files. I felt safer underground, in the dark and away from prying eyes. The children were taking care of themselves quietly in their rooms, which meant I could be miserable in private.

I opened the file cabinet that housed important papers, like the mortgage,[121] life insurance policies, and the children's adoption records. My intent was to clean out files now obsolete—a mindless task I hoped would be a distraction and free of emotion.

Running my hand along the tabs in the packed drawer, my thumb stopped at a file I didn't recognize. In my ex-husband's handwriting, the label read, "Lester Kellogg's Maps."

Curious, I stopped cleaning to read the contents. I'd never seen it before. Inside was a treasure trove of documents that would ultimately seal the fate of my litigious neighbors (Mary Kellogg, who was Lester's widow, and her accomplices Don Morris, Melanie Mooney, and the Leas) as well as the Train Horn Noise Quiet Zone Committee.

Howard had neatly organized the papers, which included deeds to my property going back to 1864. That was the year President Abraham Lincoln had authorized a "patent deed"[122] to the original homesteader, Silas Maxon.

I found 1906 maps drawn by the early train company, Spokane-Portland-Seattle Railway (SP & S), when they'd first purchased the right of way to build a stretch of railroad track across my property. Next, I discovered a 1908 deed from SP & S that granted my predecessor (and therefore me) a perpetual easement across the train track. The easements to the river

---

[121] I'd already found the mortgage papers housed here after I'd been confronted by Joseph and Julianne Leas, who'd accused me of trespassing. That was the juncture where I'd retrieved the property description that granted me an easement past the Leas' house. I'd made a copy for Leas, but it hadn't mattered. Julianne continued to call me a liar.

[122] A land patent is an exclusive land grant made by a sovereign entity (proprietary landowner) with respect to a particular tract of land.

and across the properties of Kellogg and the Leas' were well documented: They were at least 150 years old. It was a stunning discovery! My spirits lifted.

All this would prove decidedly useful to my attorney (at that time Zach Stoumbos). Particularly, since my neighbors had been making a case that the easements and roads in question had never existed except in my mind; hence, their suing me for trespassing across their private driveways.

These old documents would also prove useful a few years later when Vancouver Code Enforcement and BNSF (the current train company) harassed me no end over my legal right to use the rail crossing. As the Quiet Zone advocates gained ground, I'd demanded the track crossing be upgraded to improve safety. With that, their harassment of me had increased in frequency and severity.

Howard's handwriting on the tab of this file had confirmed he'd known about my right to the easements all along. And yet, he'd tried to convince my attorney that he had no recollection of the property rights. The file name suggested that Mary Kellogg and her family had known their lawsuit was bogus from the start. Amazing.

To be honest, when I'd first found the mystery file, I hadn't been clever enough to put all of this together—the depth of Howard's betrayal for instance. But it had given me renewed hope on that gloomy Sunday. Faced with no alternative except to quit life (which of course is not a reasonable choice), I'd decided to just keep on going: Even though I hadn't known where I was going exactly.

I'd been glum to be sure, but I'd also been resolute: These ruthless EmDs would not keep me from believing that my life had merit. My life mattered so much that I'd been led to attend church, so that I might sit and communicate with God. At the moment I decided to take action to help myself, I'd inadvertently opened a channel to the Universe.

> I'd been glum to be sure, but I'd also been resolute: These ruthless EmDs would not keep me from believing that my life had merit.

Accepting the Universal truth that I am worthy in God's eyes had paved the way for me to miraculously find the file that would prove my innocence in all instances involving my easement and the train crossing. The bastards would not grind me down.

Tip Three: Stop! Do anything else!

The axiom, "If you keep doing what you've always done and expect different results, it's insanity," certainly holds true in relationships with EmDs. This saying is similar to the tenant, "Just keep going," but involves clearing your channel by engaging in a different action even if it seems to be irrelevant.

> The axiom, "If you keep doing what you've always done and expect different results, it's insanity," certainly holds true in relationships with EmDs. This saying is similar to the tenant, "Just keep going," but involves clearing your channel by engaging in a different action even if it seems to be irrelevant.

The painful truth is that feelings of distress impede our ability to recognize what we should do next. If no one is listening to you or helping you fix the problem, stop the useless flailing around and take a different tack.

Before I'd fully understood that I was dealing with several low-on-empathy individuals, I'd felt very sorry for myself. I'd tried

CONCLUSION – I SURVIVED THE PERFECT STORM

several rational problem-solving approaches with my ex-husband and adjacent property owners: I'd offered to mediate with Howard and to sell my house to the hateful neighbors. It hadn't mattered. They'd wanted a fight that would bury me financially, and it nearly did.

Finding the old deeds in the basement had been a Godsend. My curiosity aroused, I embarked on a historical investigation even though I hadn't been sure my findings would be terribly useful.

It had provided me with a different, and distracting, path to follow. I found more related old documents, such as deeds, maps, photos, newspapers, even old silent movie documentaries, as I'd searched the Internet, the County Surveyor's Office, the Oregon Historical Society, the Clark County Historical Society, and the U.S. Army Corps of Engineers photo library.

Eventually, I was able to piece together a detailed history of the area where I lived—Township One of the Oregon Territory. When I'd noticed that my deed mentioned the right of travel to the steamboat landing, (as if anyone travels by steamboat on the Columbia River anymore), I began checking into old shipping companies.

> **In it [the PowerPoint presentation entitled, "The River, the Road, and the Train"], I summed up how the West had been won by wily, ruthless, white American settlers. (Many likely plagued with severe Empathy Dysfunction.)**

I'd also been eager to trace the origin of the Old Camas Highway, my access route to the steamboat landing, according to my deed. That detail led me to research the area's land development by the first American settlers. I found the 1908 SP & S Train Company deed that granted me a perpetual right of way to any part of my land. That steered me to pursue

A modern-day barge, operated by Shaver, the one company that converted to diesel sternwheelers and remains as the only original steamboat company operating on the Columbia River

the history of trains in the Territory.

At first, some of what I learned hadn't appeared relevant to my perfect storm of a life. As I'd hoped, however, the research kept my mind occupied and provided relief from my incessant worry about the pickle I was in.

Here's some of what I discovered.

The old road I lived on had been the first road built in the county (1852-1857). Maxon had been in the militia and helped his brother, Captain Hamilton Jordan Goss Maxon of the U.S. Cavalry, to massacre whole villages of Native Americans. Silas had been present at the first hanging in the Oregon Territory when—in

Much of the research the author did to prove the easement rights to her property were still valid—even though originated in the long ago—happened here at the Clark County Historical Museum in Washington State. She brought her findings together in a PowerPoint presentation called, "The River, the Road, and the Train," which she donated to the Museum.

In the process of searching the archives, she developed strong investigative reporting skills.

CONCLUSION – I SURVIVED THE PERFECT STORM

a complete travesty of justice—five Cayuse Indian men had been hung for war crimes.

Territorial Water Rights from long ago had allowed the easement to the river in the first place: Because farmers could not be cut off from water or water transportation.

The circa 1917 Interstate Bridge (carrying Interstate 5 traffic over the Columbia River) had been approved by Clark County Commissioners—before the advent of automobiles around 1909—to connect Vancouver and Portland. The original records refer to it as a "wagon bridge."

In time, the roads, bridges, and trains made steamboats obsolete. However, one company (Shaver) converted to diesel sternwheelers (and tugboats), evolving into the Shaver Barge company. It is the only surviving steamboat company on the Columbia River and still carries shipments up and down the River.

The view from the author's former home along the Columbia River in Vancouver, Wash. Such a peaceful scene; yet access to the river was at the heart of the bullying inflicted by her land-grabbing neighbors.

I brought all of my research together in a PowerPoint presentation entitled, "The River, the Road, and the Train." In it, I summed up how the West had been won by wily, ruthless, white American settlers. (Many likely plagued with severe Empathy Dysfunction.)

I donated the PowerPoint to the Clark County Historical Society and the Umatilla Indian Reservation—much to the chagrin of my neighbors. They wanted to keep these facts under wraps. The local newspaper, *The Columbian*, ran the story "Right of Way" about my findings."[123] The piece must have infuriated the paper's owner, Scott Campbell, also one of my neighborhood enemies.

Another idyllic scene from the author's former home as one of the Columbia's few remaining passenger steamboats, the Queen of the West, passes by. It paints a scene from another era—the one when in-perpetuity deeds to the author's land and river access were set in stone.

While digging into this research, I also began another "do anything else" project: genealogical research. I discovered my colonial roots in Rhode Island where two of my ancestors, Obadiah Holmes and Chad Brown, had signed the petition to King Charles to create the colony of Rhode Island and Plymouth Plantation. In addition to Holmes and Brown, there were eight other signatories including Thomas Olney.

One of Olney's descendants, B.T. Olney, had travelled west and homesteaded the land next to Maxon's (mine during the perfect storm years and earlier).

---

[123] Baker, Dean. (February 15, 2006). "Right of Way." The Columbian. Vancouver, Wash.

CONCLUSION – I SURVIVED THE PERFECT STORM

That meant Campbell's home was on one of the Rhode Island founder's descendants, the B.T. Olney Donation Land Claim[124] of all places. I love stumbling across these little bits of coincidence. Of course, scientists will tell you that there are only six degrees of separation among any of us—and that's what generates fortuitous things like this.

"Six degrees of separation" is the theory proposed in 1929 by the Hungarian writer Frigyes Karinthy in the short story, "Chains." In 1967, psychologist Stanley Milgram proved the theory that anyone on the planet is connected to any other person on the planet through a chain of acquaintances that has no more than five to seven "intermediaries" (people in-between).

All of my sleuthing through dusty files and brittle, yellowed papers had proven useful. First, it helped my attorneys show the Court that the history of my property rights went back to Territorial Law and couldn't be swept under the rug. Second, my fascination with the research had helped me keep my mind off of the nasty people incessantly harassing me. Third, and most important, my research helped me to recognize the bigger picture—that we are all connected, and we should honor those connections.

Nobel Peace Prize winner Desmond Tutu summed it up beautifully:

"God created us for fellowship. God created us so that we should form the human family, existing together because we were made for each other. We are not made for an exclusive

---

[124] The Donation Land Claim Act of 1850 was a U.S. federal statute enacted by Congress to promote homestead settlement in the Oregon Territory.

self-sufficiency but for interdependence, and we break that law of being at our peril."

Tip Four: Embrace your worst fear

One of my worst fears became the namesake for chapter one, "No One Calls Me Mom Anymore." For years, I'd wanted to organize these stories into a book. I'd known at some unconscious level there was something important to tell readers. However, I'd remained impeded because I kept ruminating on all of the terrible things I had gone through and was going through still.

Finally discerning that concentrating on what was wrong was compounding my misery, I experienced a dramatic shift in attitude. In spite of this realization, I continued struggling to find a way to integrate all of the stories I wanted to tell into a meaningful book. One evening, I had the epiphany that I needed to embrace my very worst fear if I was to break through the writer's block.

> **One of my worst fears became the namesake for chapter one, "No One Calls Me Mom Anymore."**

Drifting off into my nightly contemplation (a type of meditation), I'd asked the question, "What's your worst fear, Kathy?" Almost immediately the answer came to me word for word: No one calls me Mom anymore. I was stunned by that revelation. Abruptly, my worst fear had crystallized: I would never see my children again; never again experience the joy of being their mother and a grandmother; and never again hear them call me Mom. This primordial fear had kept me stuck in unremitting grief for years.

> **Finally discerning that concentrating on what was wrong was compounding my misery, I experienced a dramatic shift in attitude.**

A wave of relief passed through me the instant I acknowledged this fear. I finally knew what was bothering me deep down inside: Stifling fear that my children and I would never reconcile. I don't like that prospect; however, the Universe has helped me to see that the sum of my life does not depend on my children—notwithstanding how important they are to me and how valiantly I have fought for them.

My motherly love and devotion were what my neighbors, Townsend, and ex-husband all used as a wedge against me. Even my daughters have used my love for them to shame me.

When you are willing to embrace your worst fears, you are far less apt to be controlled by cold-hearted shame-and-blame EmDs. If you are ready to embrace your fears: not just face them, but embrace them, you can get a handle on your life. Don't allow your fear to mask a painful truth. Remember, the truth will set you free.

In my case, creativity had been unleashed: The concept of the Empathy Dysfunction Scale had come tumbling out of my unconscious once I'd identified and faced down my most severe fear. With a jolt, I'd recognized that all of my perfect storm episodes had been tied together by Empathy Dysfunction! I had to write about it. I had to.

Tip Five: Forgive yourself

Another aspect of embracing your fear is self-forgiveness. This might be your most sturdy shield against selfish EmDs. When the idea that God loves you, no matter what mistakes you have made, becomes one of your core values, you have the power of the Universe on your side. Let me show you how this worked for me shortly after I got out of jail for assault the first time in 2003.

Trying to lighten my mood, I'd purchased a lottery ticket using my jail ID numbers. A couple of days later, I placed the UPC number on my ticket into the lottery scanner at the local Fred Meyer grocery store. Lights flashed this message on the screen, "You're a winner!" (I only won $6, but the message was priceless).

The Universe-is-on-my-side story gets even better a year or so later. I'd been deep into surviving the City Hall, community, and ex-husband harassment when I received a call from Joy Darlington, a freelance writer and editor. She'd interviewed me a couple of years prior when writing a story for "Dance" magazine about entrepreneurial couples, something I have written about extensively.[125] This time, Joy was calling to ask me to write a chapter in the book, "Sixty Things to Do When You Turn Sixty,"[126] which she was co-editing.

I was flattered that she'd thought to include me alongside famous people, such as author and humorist Garrison Keillor and leading feminist/activist Gloria Steinem! Joy brushed my modesty aside, saying, "I

Author Dr. Kathy Marshack presenting former President Bill Clinton with an autographed copy of "Sixty Things to Do When You Turn Sixty" at a 2007 fundraiser for then presidential candidate Hillary Clinton.

---

[125] (1998). "Entrepreneurial Couples: Making It Work at Work and at Home." Palo Alto, California: Davies-Black.

[126] (2006). "Sixty Things to Do When You Turn Sixty." Portland, Maine: Ronnie Sellers Productions.

know you have a story in you." My contribution to the book is the chapter, "Go Directly to Jail," which has been very well received by the media—if you care to search it on Google.

But wait, there's more. On April 17, 2007, through a series of improbable events, I attended a fundraiser in Lake Oswego, Ore., for Hillary Clinton's first presidential campaign. The guest speaker was former President Bill Clinton.

Knowing that Hillary was turning 60 that October, I'd grabbed a copy of the book as I headed out the door to attend the event. I autographed it with a birthday message to her. At the party, I expected to be lost in the shuffle of wealthy and influential guests. Amazingly, I met President Clinton and personally handed him Hillary's present![127]

These good things had somewhat offset the deluge of complaints and debasing messages I'd been receiving. They hadn't totally freed me of my shame, but the winning lottery ticket, commissioned chapter, and Clinton handshake had spiked my confidence enough for me to embrace my fear and step into the storm. I became more resilient and less vulnerable to the attempts at humiliation.

---

[127] A friend of mine told me he was going to the fund raiser because the host had invited him. I asked if I could go along, which required an FBI clearance. In spite of all of my trouble with the Vancouver establishment, I was granted a clearance and was allowed to attend. Only VIPs were allowed to personally meet President Clinton. I had written VIP on my paper name badge as a joke; but the assistants at the party took it to mean I was invited to a personal meeting with him. So I was able to personally hand him Hillary's present.

Tip Six: Do a little bit more

Back in 2001, right after 9/11, I'd done a radio interview to offer psychological advice on how to handle the frightening aftermath of America's first real brush with terrorism.

Having no substantive life experience on this subject, I'd used a familiar and effective technique: I cleared my channel to the Universe. That exercise helped me give listeners what would turn out to be a prophetic tip: "Do all that you can, then do a little bit more." This sound bite (more fully explained in *Chapter One*), aired over and over during that traumatic time.

I'd had no idea then how powerful this insight would be: It has served me well as a survival tool. You, too, will find the dynamic potential—and gain internal strength—in this tip when you stand up for yourself, speak out about what you believe in, and reach out to others who need you.

A day doesn't go by that I don't receive a loving message from someone, a friend, a client, or a reader who appreciates my work. It pleases me to know that I have helped, and continue to help, people on their personal and spiritual journeys.

This also fills me with joy, because my intent was "to do a little more," to help. I never dreamed I would author two books about autism plus this book about how to survive the torment of hurtful, hateful, harmful people and public officials. Nor did I set out to invent the Empathy Dysfunction Scale.

My first, tentative steps to "do a little more" led to my writing the book, "Going over the Edge? Life with a Partner or Spouse with Asperger Syndrome." I knew that my personal experience with autistic family members was important to share with those living in a similar situation.

CONCLUSION – I SURVIVED THE PERFECT STORM

Much has been written about autistic children, a little about autistic adults; but what about the many neurotypical (NT)[128] family members who care for them? My book, published in 2009, was intended to aid the often overlooked NTs who do the caring.

My next little bit more was to offer a free support group for those neurotypicals in the Portland, Ore., area. I paid a few dollars to sponsor the group on www.meetup.com, a social networking site. At first, we were a smallish group that gathered for lunch once a month in Portland. Slowly, the group grew. To my surprise, the need for NTs to come together for conversation and support quickly outpaced the initial NT lunch group.

Between 2009 and 2017, we grew into a worldwide group of more than 2,000 members. We meet in person, online, through teleconferences and videoconferences. If you are an English speaker and need this type of support to shore yourself up, you are certainly welcome to join.

---

[128] Neurotypical, or NT, is the term used to describe those who do not have autism and do have functional empathy. The wives, husbands, mothers, fathers, siblings, and significant others of those on the Autism Spectrum generally fall into the EmD-4 (high empathy) category.

Membership is free. More information is available at my website www.kmarshack.com.

The success of the Meetup group and "Going over the Edge? Life with a Partner or Spouse with Asperger Syndrome" (a best seller for the publisher, AAPC), led me to author a second book, "Out of Mind—Out of Sight: Parenting with a Partner with Asperger Syndrome," which published in 2013.[129] Here I wrote about discovering the premise of Empathy Dysfunction. I hadn't yet put together the pieces of the puzzle that would lead me to envision the EmD Scale.

There is yet another exciting development from doing all that I can and a little bit more: The books and the Meetup group have taken on lives of their own. My fledgling effort to guide and validate NTs who live with Aspies has spread around the world.

Members from many countries have started face-to-face NT support groups. Plus, I've heard from several graduate students and universities planning to publish research on the subject of NTs in relationship with those on the Autism Spectrum

You may well ask: What does writing books about NTs in relationship with Aspies have to do with surviving threats from EmDs?

First, writing the books, hence creating something of value, kept my mind off the destructive forces surrounding my family and me.

Second, during those years of writing, I got clearer about empathy and Empathy Dysfunction, which are spelled out in this book.

---

[129] Both of my books on Asperger Syndrome and neurotypicals are available at www.amazon.com.

Third, I cleareded my channel and found my new mission: Partnering with the Universe in a deliberate effort to create a meaningful contribution to the world. You, too, may be destined to create or perform great things (large or small) when you do all you can— and a little bit more—to survive another's Empathy Dysfunction.

Tip Seven: You are enough

This last tip is probably the most significant. When I say, "You are enough," I mean that you can trust yourself completely because you are perfect just as you are no matter what others think. It took me years to comprehend this three-word philosophy. Before I could believe that about myself, I'd had to incorporate the other six tips into my life.

> **When I say, "You are enough," I mean that you can trust yourself completely, because you are perfect just as you are.**

I don't mean the outward you (or the you that you present to others), but the Divine You (or the Deeper You); the You who knows the genuine You; and the You who believes in your meaningful connections with the Universe. When you trust your Deeper You, fear will vanish.

I'd gotten this message through a dream shortly after Howard and I had separated. Before falling asleep, I'd said a prayer that asked the Universe to settle things (I call it Karma) between Howard and me. It was beyond time for us to be free of each other. Once asleep, I'd had a dream within a dream multiple times.

The dream sequences captured me in amazing feats of strength, courage, and endurance. In the back-to-back dreams. I had:

__#1.__ Found myself climbing tall mountains of ice and snow. A fierce wind had whipped around me in an attempt to tear me off one of the tall frozen peaks.

__#2.__ Showed up in my dream as a medieval soldier, riding a horse and fighting deadly battles with only a sword to protect myself.

__#3.__ Swum through frigid waters, watching as my ship sank.

__#4.__ Gripped the outside front edge of a roller coaster car, hanging on precipitously as it dropped madly down a metal hill. My hands kept slipping, and I'd screamed in terror to the two men inside the car. "Help me! Help me! I'm going to die!"

They laughed at me, as if hanging off a rocketing roller coaster car was normal. One of them was my friend Dave. The other was someone I believed to be God's representative (a spiritual teacher I had been following at the time. Dave looked right at me, gave a hearty laugh and said, "Don't worry. You're not going to die." Awakening in the dark of the dream, I'd found myself in yet another dream.

__#5.__ Stood alone in the middle of a huge arena as the house lights came up. People all around were applauding and cheering for me. They seemed happy and incredibly joyful—but at my expense. "What the heck?" I asked myself, confused. "Was this all a test of some kind? What was I supposed to do now?"

"Kathy, Kathy," I heard my name called from far up in the bleachers. Dazed, I turned toward the voices. At the far end of the arena, in the cheap-seat corner, I spotted my friends, calling me to

join them. "Come on up," someone urged. "We want to party!" They seemed remarkably happy for me.

Methodically, I made my way up the stairs to them, no joy in my heart. "It just figures," I thought. "That's where I belong, up in the nosebleed section." I was disgusted with myself for choking and screaming for help in the previous roller coaster dream.

When I got up there, it was clear my friends were impatient with me for taking so long. "Hurry up, Kathy. We've got presents for you," Dave's wife, Bobbi, said. Handing me a slice of cake, she added with exuberance, "Come on, come on! Isn't this great?" I still felt glum, but the idea of presents gave me a burst of energy and enthusiasm.

"But I failed," I whined to Bobbi.

"You didn't fail, silly," she said with delight in her voice. "You did great. You even got a gift from God. Open it. Open it!" Bobbi was so excited that she could hardly contain herself. She handed me a square, white, linen-like envelope like the formal ones used for wedding invitations and graduation announcements. On the front, in pencil, all caps, was one word, "GOD."

Nervously, I turned the envelope over, unsealed the flap, and shook out the contents, a folded note, and a keychain. As I held the empty keychain in my hand, turning it over and wondering what it meant, Bobbi urged me to read the letter. "Come on! Read it," she insisted. Everyone had crowded around. They, too, were excited to find out what God had written to me.

I unfolded the paper, but my eyes could not read the note. "I can't; I can't read it," I said plaintively, turning to Bobbi in despair. What an epic fail to be unable to read God's personal note to me! By now, I was aware I was dreaming, but I wasn't awake. I couldn't wake up yet: I had to read the letter from God first.

Bobbi, the sweetest friend one could have and an unabashed lover of God, smiled, then gently and patiently encouraged me. "Kathy, just ask God to read it to you."

And so I did. Instantaneously, God responded, "I am your partner." Everyone was speechless.

Me? I foolishly argued with God, exclaiming, "Oh no! You're not my partner. I'm your servant!"

How on earth could I have rejected God's gift? What a twit I'd been to look a gift horse in the mouth. God, of course, overlooked my ignorance. Lovingly, but firmly, He retorted, "No, Kathy. I am YOUR partner," with the emphasis on YOUR.

Finally awake, I realized that I have mighty connections of my very own.

While it took me many years to fully understand and apply the lessons in this dream, I finally accepted that God is my partner—which I would need reminding of many times in the coming years.

God's gift of a key chain symbolized the foundation for the rest of my life. It would be up to me to fill it with the keys to truth, strength, love, wisdom, and the great many other life lessons that await. Because God is my partner (and yours), we are co-creating my life (and yours). It can be no other way.

Sometimes, you can afford to be a lover. Sometimes, life demands that you be a warrior. Whatever is required of you during your time on Planet Earth, believe that **YOU ARE ENOUGH.** You have all of the resources (or keys) within to tackle any problem whether it involves Empathy Dysfunction or not.

This book, "When Empathy Fails," is a key for your keychain. Having read it, you now know things the average person does not. This kind of insightful knowledge is the best kind of gift—except for a keychain from God.

Postscript: Another letter from God

I was nearly finished writing this book when I received an eye-popping surprise of a letter in the mail. It was from the Rev. John J. Boyle of the Archdiocese of Portland's Department of Canonical Services/Tribunal (a Catholic Church court). The letter, dated Oct. 16, 2016, started simply enough:

"As you may know, your former spouse, Howard Harvey Marshack, has asked this Tribunal to look into his former marriage with you to establish whether or not it is possible for him to enter into a new marriage in the Catholic Church. I am writing to ask for your assistance in this matter."

Nothing much astonishes me these days; but as I held the letter in my hand, I found myself looking inward to see how I was thinking and feeling about this request for an annulment.[130]

---

[130] When a Catholic marriage is annulled, a Church tribunal declares that a marriage thought to be valid according to Church law actually fell short of at least one of the essential elements required for a binding union. Those elements are: the spouses are free to marry; they are capable of giving their consent to marry; they freely exchange their consent; in consenting to marry, they have the intention to marry for life, to be faithful to one another and be open to children; they intend the good of each other; and their consent is given in the presence of two witnesses and before a properly authorized Christian minister.

I didn't feel surprised, or hurt, or annoyed. Nor did I feel indifferent—if indifference is a feeling. There was, though, a hint of something familiar, an unidentified emotion not quite within my grasp. While considering the oddness of the request—Howard is Jewish, and I am not Catholic (I supposed his current wife is Catholic.)—I had an "aha" moment that revealed a missing piece of my story. You may not believe it, but Boyle's letter warmed me, and I smiled as my grateful heart opened to accept this second God-sent gift.

> **What greater blessing than to receive a letter from God (through God's emissary, the Rev. Boyle)? This time, I didn't question God's gift. I made it mine.**

Yes, I am a warrior, and that has made a huge difference to my success in a life rife with EmDs. The most valuable resource in my warrior tool kit is surrender. When you can finally let go of your worries, and hand them over to God for good, you will be set free from the ravages of Empathy Dysfunction.

Know that even when you "walk through the valley of the shadow of death,"[131] you needn't be afraid: You are not, and never will be, alone. God is with you, guiding you, protecting you, partnering with you through every curve and straightaway during your wild, roller coaster ride on Earth.

I have plenty of evidence that God is with me—the selection of a perfect jury in my assault and trespass trial; meeting Laura, the smiling addict, while in jail; discovering the stashed-away legal documents that swayed legal battles my way; and finding hidden life messages on a towering billboard.

---

[131] Taken from the 23rd Psalm by King David during a time of doom and gloom. (Ps23:4,ESV)

CONCLUSION – I SURVIVED THE PERFECT STORM

That accustomed feeling I'd had while reading the Archdiocesan letter from the Adjutant Judicial Vicar? It was the whisper of God reassuring me that He is with me 24/7 every day of my life.

What greater blessing than to receive a letter from God (through God's emissary, the Rev. Boyle)? This time, I didn't question God's gift. I made it mine.

EPILOGUE
BraveHeart

"We must let go of the life we have planned, so as to accept the one that is waiting for us."

— Joseph Campbell

How many attorneys did it take?

Sixteen attorneys; that's how many. Over a period of 12 years, that's the number I hired to protect myself against the machinations of Vancouver City employees, greedy neighbors, the local newspaper owner, and a vindictive ex-husband. In addition, I appeared before eight judges in that time period.

All told, I was involved in more than 20 legal matters (divorce, lawsuits, harassment and contempt orders, false arrests, stalking protection, City code violations and licensing board complaints). I even had to hire a lawyer to help clear up my credit score, which sunk two levels, from "exceptional" to "fair" (650) because of a maleficent medical billing collector.[132]

---

[132] Fisher's Landing Physical Therapy in Vancouver, Wash., overcharged me for my daughter Phoebe's physical therapy following surgery on her ankle. I disputed the charges, and showed Fisher's two audits from my health insurance provider that documented the erroneous charges. Instead of correcting this, Fisher's turned my account over to a collection agency. It took me three years to get this straightened out and my credit score reinstated even though I'd been guilty of nothing.

EPILOGUE – BRAVEHEART

I was utterly stunned when I counted up the attorneys who were involved during this 12-year fight for my family, my rights, and my freedom. I hadn't really thought about the growing number of attorneys in my life at the time I'd hired each one. I'd only known that I desperately needed protection. In the heat of battle, there had been no time for second thoughts: only action.

> ... I spent $564,744 on legal fees from 2002 to 2014. ... I collected $125,951 in settlement damages... Let that sink in. This is the price of justice in America. The lawyers get their exorbitant cut, and clients—already victims—like me get to make payments on horrendous legal debt. And that leaves a good many of us struggling to clean up our credit score—if we can.

When I made the list of attorneys for this book (at the request of my editor), even I didn't believe the sum; but it's true. Counting up the attorneys and judges made me wonder what this had cost altogether. Honestly, I'd never added it up before. I think I would have been too horrified and scared to persevere in taking care of the mess(es) I was in.

To pay these attorneys, I'd worked 10-12-hour days and cut anything extra from my household budget—such as piano lessons for the girls (and sadly my time with them). I'd borrowed on credit cards and refinanced the house twice in order to pay the lawyers.

I had at least one certified public accountant (CPA) advise me to file bankruptcy, but I hadn't listened. I'd pressed on through. This is the nature of courage. Bravery requires that you put fear aside and do what you have to do, one step at a time and often alone.

Here's the incredible bottom line: I spent $564,744 on legal fees from 2002 to 2014.[133] This amount doesn't even include the half a million dollars (or more) my title insurance company paid attorneys Zach Stoumbos and Dan Lorenz to handle the lawsuits against my neighbors for the easement dispute.

Nor does it count the amount the title insurance company paid Lance Brooks to handle my lawsuit against David and Martha Lindsay for blocking my access to the Old Camas Highway to my east—which happened to be my alternative exit route in case of a fire. In fact, Stoumbos told me that the litigation over my easements was the most expensive lawsuit in Clark County History![134]

I collected $125,951 in settlement damages from those EmD neighbors and the City of Vancouver.[135] Let that sink in. This is the price of justice in America. The lawyers get their exorbitant cut, and clients—already victims—like me get to make payments on horrendous legal debt. And that leaves a good many of us struggling to clean up our credit score—if we can.

Another costly piece: Mick Seidel, who took my case even though he considered it worth very little, believed I would not be

---

[133] The lion's share of legal fees goes to the attorneys. The rest pays paralegals, court reporters, hired experts, filing fees, and miscellaneous office charges, such as making copies. The client pays for all of it.

[134] If all of my legal fees cost this much, what do you think it cost the other side(s)?

[135] Although I actually settled for $265,000 in damages from Julianne and Joseph Leas, Don Morris and Melanie Mooney, Mary Kellogg, Ken Morris, Steamboat Landing, David and Martha Lindsay, and the City of Vancouver, my lawyers took $139,049 of those settlement fees.

able to convince a jury that I'd been significantly harmed. He'd agreed that the conduct of City employees had been atrocious. Yet, he'd opined that—because I had survived and "appeared" unscathed physically or medically (i.e. not in a coma or a wheelchair)—a jury would reason that I had incurred no lasting damage; hence side with the City.

Seidel was honorable in that he took the case to conclusion. On my behalf, he accepted a settlement offer from Vancouver for $75,000. Of that, I paid him $67,849. Seidel walked away with more than 90 percent of my settlement funds. That boils down to my receiving $7,151 as "recompense" for the more than 10 years of hell at the hands of Vancouver.

Plus, many indirect costs grew from the legal debt. For example, during this span of time, when I was age 52 to 65 (typically prime earning years), I was unable to contribute one red cent to my retirement account. I am self-employed, so no one was contributing to that account but me (and a smidgen from Social Security).

Howard had demanded half of my retirement savings when we'd divorced since he had saved nothing for himself (even though I'd implored him to do so). In truth, he hadn't needed any retirement money from me. When his father died the year after our divorce, Howard inherited millions.[136] All this means that I will be working (Don't get me wrong, I love my work and am quite capable of continuing it for years) for a living until I'm in my eighties, or I die.

Going through the exercise of enumerating my attorneys for the book, the enormity of what I went through took on new meaning. Finally, I gave myself credit for having weathered—and survived—the perfect storm. I don't think too many people would have had the stamina to do that.

As I'd fantasized when I was a little girl, I became a superhero albeit unintentionally. I earned my stars, or rather, my cape, by surviving all of these things and more. For another perspective on what occurred and what I endured, I've provided a by-the-numbers list *(See fig. A.15)*.

When I see this list in its entirety, I don't think it's bragging to describe myself as "BraveHeart." Without my resilience, intense love for my children, strong sense of justice, and fighting spirit, I wouldn't have made it through to the safe side.

If this book is to be of help to others in similar situations, I must be honest. You will need to rise to the occasion(s) in your own life, too. There's no hiding. It takes tremendous courage and resourcefulness to do what I did. Furthermore, rebuilding a life following this type of devastation requires a brave heart.

It requires that you know—beyond a shadow of a doubt—that you are worth it, even when your loved ones forsake you. It demands that you know others need you to be all that you are capable of being; so that you can help guide them to the next step in their own hero's journey.

---

[136] Howard Marshack shared the wealth with his sister, Susan (now deceased), and brother, Richard.

The overpowering loneliness

Because I am BraveHeart and have grit doesn't mean I feel no pain. It can be unbearably lonely in my world. I suffer from Post-Traumatic Stress Disorder (PTSD). One way that it manifests: I become alarmed when I perceive my new neighbors as being even slightly thoughtless or unkind. It's a kind of unhealthy hyper-vigilance often impossible to shake.

I only feel safe after I am inside the gated parking lot of the marina where I now live, and after the locked gate to the houseboat ramp clangs shut behind me. For good measure, I installed computerized locks on the doors of my new house.

My dog, Simon, helps me feel comfortable in our new home on the river. He loves his daily walks along the river bank. Of course, he can't pass up an opportunity to splash into the water. As a black Lab, Simon manages to take my mind off my worries with his perennially puppy personality.

The author's ever-loyal black Labrador retriever, Simon, named after the roguish hero Simon Templar in the TV series "The Saint," popular in the 1960s. Here he enjoys sunning himself after a swim near her new marina home on the stretch of the Columbia River running through Portland, Ore. On the Empathy Dysfunction Scale, Simon is 100-percent Radiant Angel (EmD-5).

When night falls, I am comforted by the blanket of dark, watery silence that surrounds my new home. When I fall asleep, it is by the illumination of battery-operated candles that provide just enough light that I don't feel totally alone in the dark. Hearing the muffled sleep sounds of my "pack," the dog and three cats, beside me invariably takes the edge off of the aloneness.

I have gone on to make new friends who are very dear. I treasure those who have the courage to keep reaching out to me. Since I continue to work long hours, they are patient about finding time for us to spend together.

Do I need to work so much? I convince myself that my finances require it after being inundated with the legal bills from 16 attorneys. Remember, by the end of my perfect storm, I'd spent more than $550,000 on legal fees.

It could be true that work keeps me feeling safe as well. I am good at what I do. I have achieved a modicum of success as a psychologist and author. At work, I am not alone, and I am appreciated.

When a child client snuggles with my dog and is, for a moment, comforted from the pain of his parents' hostile divorce, I am also comforted.[137] When an adult client sheds tears of relief to have finally found a psychologist who understands, I feel understood. When a male client with Asperger syndrome opens his heart to the tragedy of life without empathy, I share the pain of love lost.

In these moments, I 'm not alone. In fact, I feel more connected to the powerful and benevolent spirit of the Universe.

---

[137] My dog, Simon, accompanies me to work most days unless I take him to doggy day care to play with his pals.

I am ever so grateful for the work that allows that spirit to flow through me to others.

Who am I if no longer Mom?

How it was before conspiracy stole the loves of her life

The author with her daughters, Bianca (right) and Phoebe (center), relaxed and happy on a California beach in 2003. She recalls what a wonderful time the three of them had, travelling through national parks (Sequoia and Lassen), playing at amusement parks (Disneyland, Universal Studios, and Sea World). While on their vacation, Phoebe attended a camp to help with her learning disabilities—which her father refused to help pay for. It was a special trip for all.

Two months later, the author was falsely arrested for assault. Jim Jacks' defaming memo brought the storm raining down on her and the girls a year later (September 2004). By October 2005, Bianca had gone to live with her father. She hasn't been seen by the author since.

As I have documented in this book, I am a victim of lies. I don't mean little white lies. I mean big mortal-sin, criminal, unfixable lies. The worst and most painful lie is the one about my mothering. I am a victim of Parental Alienation Syndrome (PAS), which also fuels my PTSD. For more detail on PAS, see *Chapter Three*.

It is a destructive tactic used against a parent and his or her children to emotionally and physically undermine their parent-child relationship. The greatest tragedy in my life has been losing my children to the turmoil that came with the unbelievable lies told about me.

Who am I if not Mom anymore? I am certainly more than a victim of lies just as I am more than a victim of parental alienation. I am BraveHeart. If my children showed up at my house today, I would welcome them with open arms. I would ask for their forgiveness, and I would forgive them.

I would open my grandmother closet and bring out toys for my grandson. If they never show up again, I will grieve: But I will carry on, continuing to live my life fully one day at a time. I hope God finds this solution good enough.

An epilogue is another beginning

An epilogue is supposed to tell the reader what happened after the story in the book ends. In a way, I began the book with the epilogue by using the title, "When Empathy Fails." But the subtitle is the real epilogue isn't it: "How to stop those hell-bent on destroying you." That's what I did, and so can you.

In August 2014, I sold my Vancouver home and moved back to Portland, Ore., along with Simon and my two cats.[138] I have, at last, found peace in my lovely marina home on the Columbia River. It is a magical place; a cluster of modest floating homes upriver from Portland sheltered by a small wild island.

I kayak every day in the summer—right from my backdoor. Simon, my black Lab, absolutely loves his daily explorations, chasing geese and herons, and, of course, going for a swim. I have three cats now, having acquired Seven of Nine a year after I moved in. She was an abandoned kitten when I found her along a

---

[138] I say I moved back because I was born and raised in Portland, Ore. After 30 years in Vancouver, I was ready to reboot my life back in my hometown.

highway in Portland. She has a favorite spot on the deck where she watches the fish.[139]

My favorite times of the day are the moments I stop to take in the breathtaking view from the walking ramp to the marina. When I return from work, I park my car in the upland parking lot, grab my belongings, and head to the west gate of the marina. I press the gate code and swing back the heavy metal gate to the ramp. Once through the gate, I enter another dimension.

As in the Panamanian jungle with Iker, I am surrounded by Mother Nature, a world of sky-gliding herons, honking geese, diving ducks, glorious bald eagles soaring high and free, diving osprey, jumping steelhead, tail-smacking beavers, and playful otters. The beauty and serenity here feel like a well-deserved hero's welcome—every day. I am, finally, home, my soul serene in this tranquil place. Each day, I take it all in—the sights, sounds, smells—and count my blessings.

Just about the time I start to succumb to grief over the loss of my children, I am reminded of the importance of sharing the Empathy Dysfunction Scale with others. I would never have put the pieces of it together if I hadn't been rejected, harassed, assaulted, sued, and stalked. Because my long journey with

---

[139] I have given all my pets names that represent power, wisdom, and brave hearts. Simon Templar is named after the fictional character, a kind of roguish hero, in "The Saint." My two Russian blue kitties are named Neo and Trinity after the fictional duo who try to save the world through love in the science fiction movie "The Matrix." Seven of Nine is named after a "Star Trek: Voyager" television series character who is born human (Annika Hansen), assimilated by the Borg as a child, then escapes being a Borg Collective drone in order to recapture her humanity. In the show, Seven of Nine subsequently joins the USS Voyager crew, becoming a "good guy."

EmDs molded me into BraveHeart, I know the importance of warning others about how to protect themselves from emotionally dysfunctional people bent on destruction.

Even before this book was published, Laura, another writer, gave me this unsolicited and much appreciated feedback. It proves that I am on target with the Empathy Dysfunction Scale and my mission to spread its use.[140] Interestingly, Laura is also on the Autism Spectrum, a topic I have written about extensively.

Below are some excerpts from Laura's email letter. To view in its entirety, *(See fig. A.16.)*

To: Kathy Marshack
Subject: Thank goodness I've read many parts of your book!

Kathy,
"I just had a "rider from hell" experience while out Ubering around, and I have to thank you for letting me in on your journey in developing the EmD book. She was just like that woman you described in the "No Disney Cruise" chapter [the Introduction].

When I arrived, with my cute little PT Cruiser that meets all the requirements as an UberX car, and even has a hatchback,

---

[140] Laura makes her living as an Uber driver while working on a master's degree in design and development of online workplace educational materials. In what spare time that leaves her, she writes engrossing science fiction.

she showed up with a bike, two saddlebags, a pizza box and a dachshund.

She tried to get her bike in the hatchback, and of course, it didn't fit. She mentioned that it was a very small space, and I pointed out that this would have been even more of a problem in a sedan. She wanted me to lift the back end of the bike because she's a small woman and was having a hard time.

While I was maneuvering the bike and the seats around, her pizza fell all over the front seat. Her dog was wet (hot day, understandable), and the little guy ended up sitting with her on the front seat, which was all that was left for the two of them....

She ate one of the Almond Rocas I happened to have in one of my drink holders, then told her dog he couldn't have chocolate. Instead, she tried to get him to eat some duck she had with her, but he wasn't interested.

Nor had he been regarding the chocolate though she seemed to want me to think he was; then, essentially blaming me for not keeping my Cruiser dog safe, she claimed to be worried that the easily available chocolate could harm him....

When we arrived at the destination, she let her dog run into the street, so I grabbed the leash and brought him back for his own sake, not hers. I'm sure she would have loved the sympathy she would have derived if he'd been run over....

As someone with an ASD, I struggle with my understanding of other people, sensitive to the fact that I often misinterpret their behaviors, even more so than the average person....

If I hadn't read that section of your book, as well as many of the others, I'd have been second-guessing whether she was intentionally making me extremely uncomfortable or not. I felt like I could see, from what you'd described, how she

> *was calibrating me, finding my sensitive places, and applying pressure..*
>
> *I'd been able to see where this woman could have been intentionally working me over. That was enough for me to keep her at arm's length without feeling any sympathy or guilt for not helping her any more than I did....*
>
> *Namaste,*
> *Laura*

"When Empathy Fails" is so much more than the tale of a trashed mom. I hope my triumphant story helps you as it did Laura. I want to give you the knowledge you need to thwart low-level EmDs, like Laura's Uber passenger, when they insinuate themselves into your life.

No need to make all of my mistakes to acquire these skills. I've done that for you and documented the course corrections. Now it's up to you to be the hero in your own life story.

AFTERWORD

"Silence encourages the tormentor, never the tormented."
— Elie Wiesel

Breaking News

The following *US~Observer* article was written by the author in response to the Nov. 2, 2017, *Associated Press* story (http://www.latimes.com/sns-bc-wa--sexual-harassment-capitol-20171102-story.html) that broke the news about Jim Jacks' alleged sexual misbehavior during his abbreviated time as a State Congressman. The story was picked up by several local (http://nwnewsnetwork.org/post/former-staffer-says-washington-house-failed-protect-her-sexual-harassment-lawmaker) and national news outlets, including the *Seattle Times*, the *Chicago Tribune*, and the *Los Angeles Times*. Jacks is one of the two main figures in her book "When Empathy Fails."

#MeToo Jim Jacks

Former Washington Rep. Jim Jacks is seen in this 2009 Washington Legislature photo. Jacks abruptly resigned his seat in March 2011.

[As published in the *US~Observer*]

Jim Jacks forced from Washington Legislature for 'inappropriate behavior' toward female staffer in 2011

By Kathy J. Marshack, Ph.D.

Nov. 2, 2017. "Amid the flurry of news stories regarding sexual harassment by celebrities, such as Harvey Weinstein, Kevin Spacey, Louis C.K., and others, I was listening to an OPB newscast and heard a familiar name, Jim Jacks. Next, the reporter briefly discussed Jacks' 2011 dismissal from the Washington Legislature for inappropriate behavior. I knew that name. Hearing it made my stomach lurch."

I was dumbstruck when I heard (and read a release from *The Associated Press*) that Jacks was among the current pack of predators being called out (as published in the LA Times and Chicago Tribune). I'd known that he had walked off the job as a Washington State House Representative in 2011 without explanation—except for a handwritten note faxed from an Oregon hotel (to House Majority Leader Pat Sullivan). What I didn't know was that he'd been forced to resign for "inappropriate behavior" toward a young female staffer (verified this week by the Washington State Democratic House Majority Leader Pat Sullivan).

A month after Jacks' inexplicable departure, an unremarkable tidbit had been published in Scott Campbell's Vancouver newspaper, *The Columbian*. Interviewed by *The Columbian's* Editor Lou Brancaccio, Jacks supposedly admitted to alcoholism and said he was taking time off from politics to resolve his personal problems.

Rumors had surfaced among the Vancouver locals who knew Jacks: They'd suspected he was canned for sexual misconduct; especially since they saw him drinking in local establishments. None of this was reported at the time. In fact, Brancaccio reported that Jacks was not guilty of any misconduct, and he encouraged readers to support Jacks on his journey to recovery.

This week (six years later), Sullivan confessed to hiding this truth for those many years. His excuse: The female staffer involved was reluctant to go public at the time. If that was true, why did Sullivan think it timely to reveal this secret now? Could it be that Jacks' improprieties were about to surface anyway, and it would be politically expedient to admit the truth first? (But that is another story).

Gossip? Or is there more?

Before you write me off as pedaling salacious gossip, let me remind you that back in 2004 Jacks was part of a ring of three Vancouver government employees, who set out to destroy me with a defaming memo defining me as a "functional sociopath" who'd been diagnosed by psychologist Frank Colistro, Ed.D. At the prompting of Vancouver's then City Prosecutor Josephine Townsend and Code Enforcement Officer Richard Landis, Jacks had been the one to write that damaging and untrue memo. He sent this libelous memo to the Vancouver City Manager, Mayor, and City Council . . . but neglected to inform me of his action. Thus I had no recourse to protect myself.

Not only had he lied to the others about my diagnosis, he'd declared that I had no respect for the authority of the court and believed that the state's laws did not apply to me. He suggested that Dr. Colistro had found me to be an angry and abusive person. According to Jacks, I was destined to lose my license as a psychologist for all of my supposed and absolutely fabricated wrongdoings.

None of this was true, and Jacks' lies about me were categorically denied by Dr. Colistro. Still, his single untruthful memo set off a decade-plus witch hunt that cost me half a million dollars in legal fees; many emotionally frightening nights; and the loss of my children. I was able to sue the City of Vancouver for this malicious defamation (and won a small settlement), but I will never be able to reclaim the life I had as a mother to my children. Jim Jacks stole that from me just as he stole peace of mind from his more recent victim.

What does the #MeToo phenomenon have to do with it?

What does the #MeToo phenomenon have to do with me and my encounter with Jim Jacks? When the stories started to tumble out about the sexual exploitation of women by powerful men in Hollywood and business, the #MeToo Tweet went viral on Twitter, Facebook, and other social media. I could relate. Like most women, I have had many an encounter with a male boss who crossed the line. Some would call these micro-aggressions, but they nevertheless left me speechless and afraid.

There was:
- The elementary school principal I worked for as a school social worker, who would stand and watch me walk up the stairs.
- The eighth grade teacher who kept me after school so that, once alone, he could stroke my hair.
- The boss who stared down my shirt and asked if I was wearing a bra.
- The grad school professor who singled me out in public for "driving him wild."
- The groping and leering I endured on the subways and trains of Europe.
- The times that men exposed themselves to me in public, going so far as to offer me money for sexual acts.

AFTERWORD

- The time a strange man followed me to my hotel on the beach at Waikiki and tried to get into my room.
- Even my first encounter with a sexual predator was frightening. I was only five when a man offered me candy, and asked me to climb into his car.

Jim Jacks is not guilty of sexual misconduct with me; nonetheless, he damaged me badly with his unconscionable lies. Hearing the new and appalling stories of others who have suffered predation, a floodgate of emotion about betrayal and destruction overcame me. Not only is Jacks guilty of defamation, he's guilty of never giving me a chance to defend myself (just as many women suffer in silence about their sexual assaults).

The Jacks' abusive memo was kept secret for five years until I discovered it in a public records request I made of the City of Vancouver in 2009. I was shocked and overwhelmed to find that exonerating piece of evidence. I imagine Sullivan, coming forward six years after Jacks' "inappropriate" behavior with a State Capitol staffer, is feeling shock waves of his own. He covered for Jacks and contributed to harming the young woman he assaulted by silencing her complaint.

It is the silence that kills one's spirit. As for me, I won't be silenced anymore about Jacks or the rest of the scoundrels in Vancouver, Washington. Victims shouldn't have to stand by watching their abusers and others cover up these injustices.

If you've had similar experiences with Jim Jacks, who now works at Portland State University in Oregon, I'd welcome hearing from you at— #MeToo Jim Jacks, editor@usobserver.com

How to stop those hell-bent on destroying you

I have written about people like Jacks in my soon-to-be-published book, "*WHEN EMPATHY FAILS: How to stop those hell-bent on destroying you.*" In fact, Jacks is one of the two people figuring most prominently in the stories I tell. But I think I have been too easy on Jacks. Like so many survivors of abuse, I've tried to see him as less despicable than he really is.

Why? Because it somehow makes me feel a little safer in the world. That is, if it wasn't that bad, or if it was just a mistake (even a terrible mistake), or if there had been something I could have done differently. . . then I could feel just a bit safer in an unpredictable world where there really are people hell-bent on destroying you, just like Jacks did to me.

It really is even worse than that actually. Sometimes there is a mob of conscienceless people who are working together to destroy you. Think about how it worked in my case. As Vancouver Citizen Advocate, Jacks set me up to lose my freedom, my property, and my children with his malicious memo.

The next year, he was elected to the Washington State House of Representatives. As a newly- minted legislator, he did the bidding of Vancouver's power brokers and helped to pass legislation for a Train Horn Noise Quiet Zone (THNQZ) in our neighborhood.

Because of my so-called sociopathy (a completely unfounded rumor that had spread like wildfire through political crowds, civil servants, and neighbors), no one would listen to me about safety at the train crossing near my house. Without the train horn, cyclers, motorists, and pedestrians using the railroad crossing would have little warning of an approaching train; hence, be in great danger of being hit by the train.

The greedy neighbors also felt justified filing false complaints against me with Code Enforcement in order to push forward the revocation of my business and professional licenses. Without my ability to work, I would have been totally crushed and eventually been forced out of their way. That was just what the heartless land developers wanted; then they could make millions on waterfront real estate development. There's more to this story, but I think you get the picture (and it is more fully explained in my book).

Author: Kathy Marshack

I will not be silenced

In light of this breaking news Jacks' story, I can now let go of my self-deception and be more clear-eyed about who Jacks really is, a man fully without empathy and dangerous to others. Clearly, Jacks abused his power as a legislator. He lied to the press when he resigned. Plus, he has done nothing to correct the grave damage he caused me by writing the defaming memo.

He'd had a chance to come clean when he was deposed by my attorney in 2013. At that time, Jacks was asked if he actually believed what he had written about me (considering he'd never actually investigated the lies, instead, trusting what others had said). He'd been shamefully cool. Without so much as an embarrassed downward glance, he'd said, "I had no reason to believe it was untrue."

When empathy fails, and power is in the hands of those without a conscience, they plow a wide swath of destruction. Even after all of my study of and experience with real-life scoundrels, I'd given Jacks too much credit. I'd let him silence me and I'd been fooled by yet another unredeemable person with severe Empathy Dysfunction. Don't let this be you."

---

*Kathy Marshack, Ph.D., is a Portland Psychologist and investigative reporter for the **US~Observer**. Her forthcoming book "When Empathy Fails: How to stop those hell-bent on destroying you" will soon be featured in the **US~Observer**.*

Note from the Publisher of the *US~Observer*: We at the *US~Observer* recognize that there is a great deal more to investigate on this breaking news story. For example, we have questions about why the Democratic Majority Leader chose this moment to reveal the truth about Jacks? Why Jacks was replaced at the state legislature by the wife of Vancouver's Chief City Attorney? Why the city of Vancouver suppressed the defaming memo about Dr. Marshack in the first place and still tries to cover it up? Why former City Prosecutor Townsend was fired and then inexplicably offered a financial settlement to leave quietly? With

AFTERWORD

all of the outrageous evidence against Jacks and the others, why did Dr. Marshack's attorneys settle her case for a pittance instead of going to trial? We have a great many more questions that will be investigated because like Dr. Marshack we don't believe victims should be silenced. --- Edward Snook.

APPENDIX

"It's easier to fool people than to convince them that they have been fooled." -

- Mark Twain

DOCUMENTS, REPORTS, CORRESPONDENCE

Herein are documents and maps that prove
the author's land claims and
expose the many lies drummed up and spread
by her greedy harassers in hopes of forcing her off her land.

Figs. A.1 through A.16 follow

APPENDIX

EmD Assessment Tool

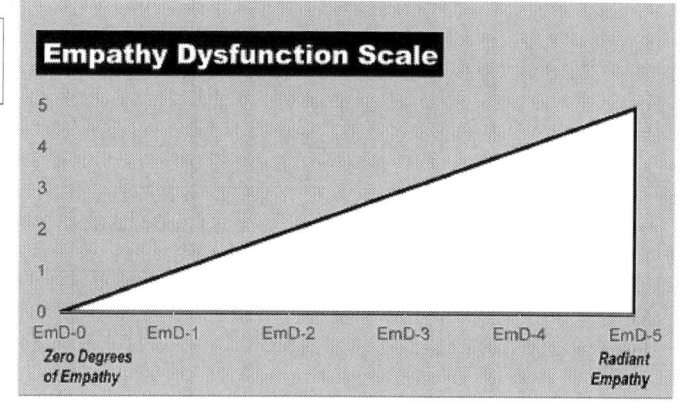

Fig. A.1

Empathy Dysfunction Scale

EmD-0 — Zero Degrees of Empathy
EmD-5 — Radiant Empathy

Originated by Dr. Kathy Marshack

Understanding the Varying Degrees of Empathy in Humans

EmD-0 **Zero Degrees of Empathy**—struggle to understand the empathic reciprocity of normal communication, but they are not out to get you. Deep down, they have a moral code; or they can be taught about morality. *Examples: autistics and young children.*

EmD-1 **Self-Absorbed individuals**—only interested in their own agenda; hence usually cause serious harm. It only takes a single EmD-1 to destroy everything their victim has worked for. *Examples: narcissists and psychopaths/sociopaths.*

EmD-2 **Organic Brain Injury/illness**—unpredictable mental functioning that creates chaos in their lives and the lives of their caregivers and loved ones. *Examples: the mentally ill and traumatic brain injured (TBI).*

EmD-3 **Controllable Mental Illness**—can function at much higher levels of empathy if their disorders are treated with medicine, psychotherapy, and psychosocial education. Otherwise, their empathy is intermittent, depending on their stage of illness. *Examples: alcoholics, addicts, and those with bipolar disorder.*

EmD-4 **Basic Good-enough Empathy**—psychologically unaware yet good citizens and neighbors most of the time; however, they are prone to gossip and codependency. *Examples: unless asked to do more than they desire, most are trustworthy.*

EmD-5 **Radiant Empathy**—fearless individuals with empathy fully functioning nearly all of the time. They have clear boundaries for themselves and others. *Examples: the devoted friend who accepts all of your flaws; the 88-year-old man who plants saplings for future generations; the Medal of Honor winner; the woman who fights for those who are disenfranchised; and the mother who always forgives.*

Copyright Kathy J. Marshack, Ph.D. 2017

Following the epiphany moment when the idea to rate levels of Empathy Dysfunction came to her, the author developed the EmD Scale. It provides a simple and straightforward way for you to get a general idea of the depth and constancy of a person's empathy—or lack thereof. When you've pinpointed a level, refer to the chapter that focuses on that type of empathy to learn more.

WHEN EMPATHY FAILS

Fig. A.2 1908 Crossing Deed granted by Spokane, Portland and Seattle Railway Company. It established the right to a safe train crossing to and from the author's Vancouver property in perpetuity.

Date: April 24, 1908. Filed: May 9, 1908 at 2:05 P.M. Book "71" Pg49s

Ack'd: " " " Before Robert A. Webster, Notary Public (s) for Washington, residing at Vancouver in said State (Clarke County.) By Clara Ryan.

" " " " Before Robert A. Webster, Notary Public (s) for Washington, residing at Vancouver, in said State (County of Clarke.) By B. A. Randall and Grace E. Randall.

Witnesses: Robert A. Webster, (only one)

Grantors: B. A. RANDALL (no seal)
CLARA RYAN (no seal)
GRACE E. RANDALL (no seal)

Grantee: SPOKANE, PORTLAND AND SEATTLE RAILWAY COMPANY, a Washington corporation,

Instrument: Special Warranty Deed (Correction.) convey and warrant.

Consideration: $1.00

Description: The following described real estate situate in the County of Clarke and State of Washington, viz: A strip of land one hundred feet in width, being fifty feet in width on each side of the center line of the railroad of said Railway Company as now located, staked out and to be constructed over and across the following described tract of land, to-wit: Beginning at a point in the center of what is known as Douthit Creek, said point being nineteen chains and fifteen links North and two chains and seventy-two links west of the southeast corner of the S. D. Maxon Donation Land Claim in township one north of range two east of the Willamette Meridian, and running thence east two chains and seventy-two links to the east line of said Donation Claim, thence south on said line to the north bank of the Columbia River and to the south-east corner of said claim, thence with the meanders of said river south 87° west nine chains, thence south 86° 2' west nine chains, thence north 79° 30' west two chains and ninety-two links to the south-east corner of the A. B. Pillsbury tract, thence north sixteen chains and fifty-five links to the center of the County Road; thence south 64° 45' east along the center of said County Road sixteen chains and thirty links to the southeast corner of the B. E. Randall (now Stowell) tract, thence north 15° 20' east along a ditch five chains and seventeen links to a stake in Douthit Creek, thence with said Creek about north 25° east to the place of beginning.
Said consideration also being in full settlement of all claims and demands for damage sustained by reason of the loca- (see sheet no.2)

46

See the following page to view the remainder of the 1908 Crossing Deed shown here.

Fig. A.2 Continued from previous page - *1908 Crossing Deed granted by Spokane, Portland and Seattle Railway Company*

(sheet No. 2 of Book "75" Pg. 49.)

tion, construction, maintenance and operation of said railroad, on, over and across said described land.

The grantors are to be permitted to extend and maintain two lines of water pipe across said strip of land, the same to be laid and maintained under the supervision of the Railway Company and subject to its customary regulations.

The Railway Company to provide a suitable private grade crossing for the use of grantors at some practicable point so as to give the grantors access to their land upon either side of said strip.

This deed is given to correct error in description in that certain deed given May 3d, 1906 by the grantors herein to said Portland and Seattle Railway Company and recorded May 5th, 1906 at page 129, book 61, Deed Records of Clarke County, Washington.

TO SHOW EXCEPTION: TITLE NOT FOLLOWED HEREIN

WHEN EMPATHY FAILS

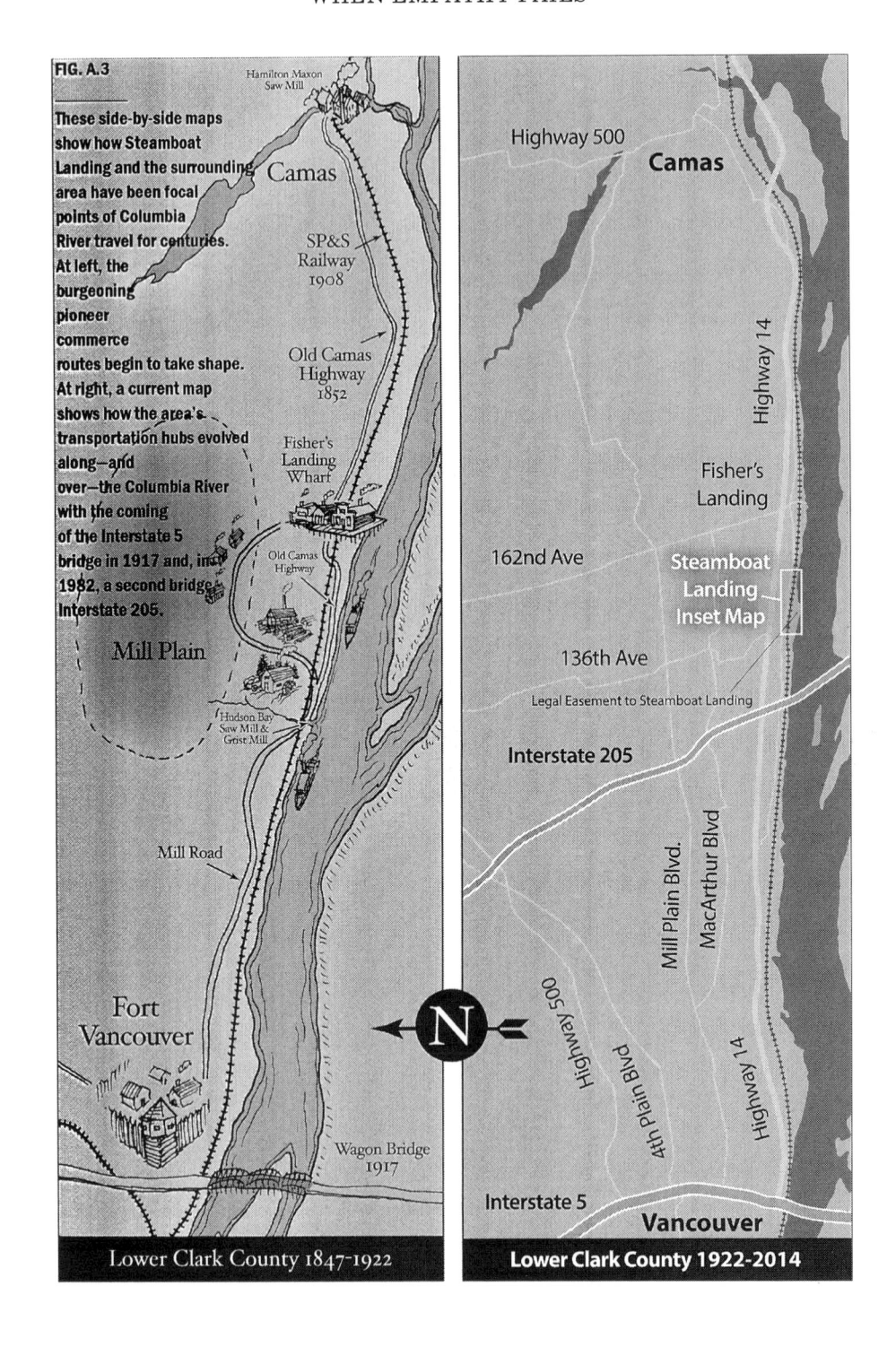

FIG. A.3

These side-by-side maps show how Steamboat Landing and the surrounding area have been focal points of Columbia River travel for centuries. At left, the burgeoning pioneer commerce routes begin to take shape. At right, a current map shows how the area's transportation hubs evolved along—and over—the Columbia River with the coming of the Interstate 5 bridge in 1917 and, in 1982, a second bridge, Interstate 205.

Lower Clark County 1847-1922 | Lower Clark County 1922-2014

APPENDIX

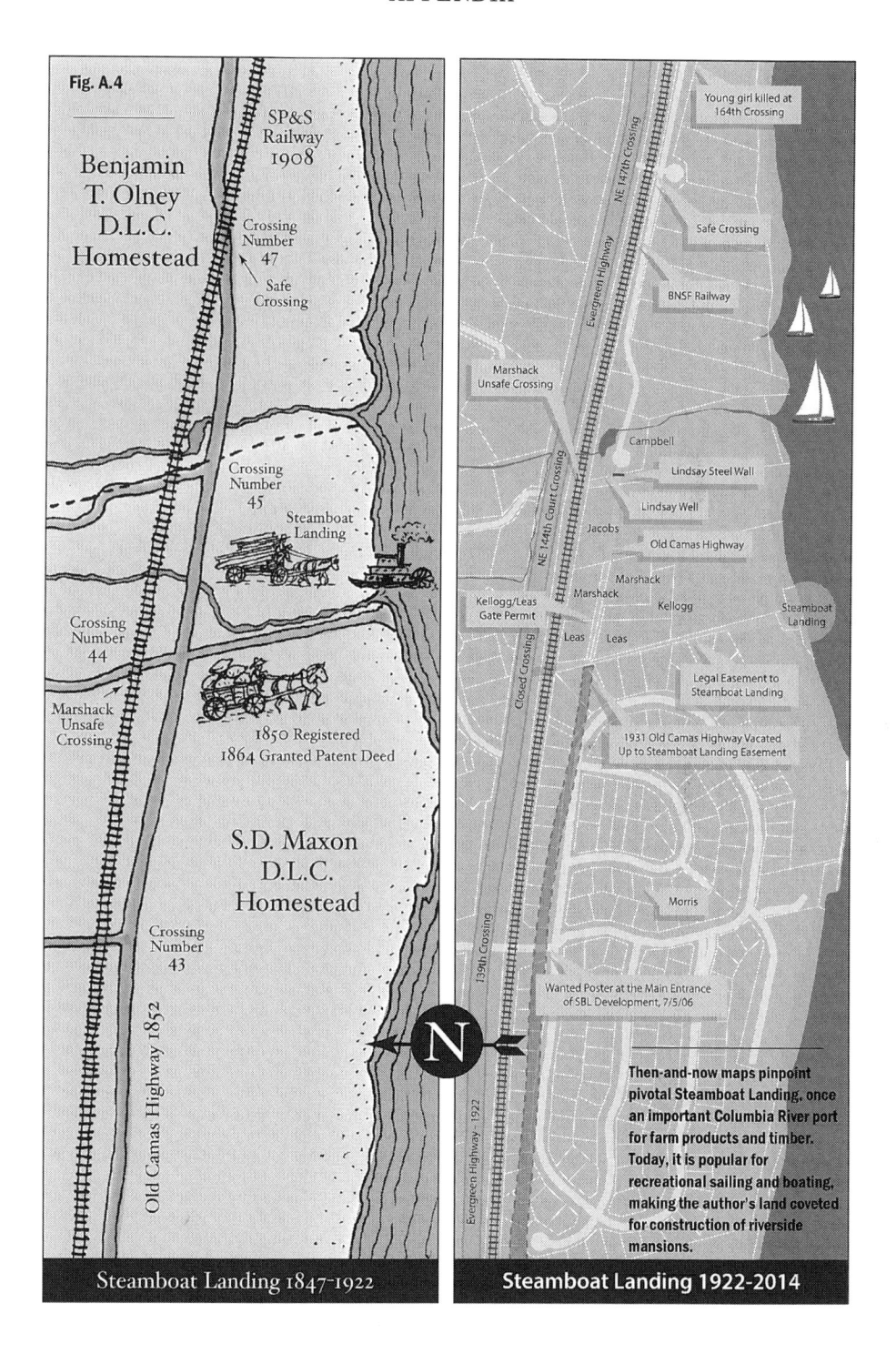

Fig. A.4

Steamboat Landing 1847-1922

- Benjamin T. Olney D.L.C. Homestead
- SP&S Railway 1908
- Crossing Number 47
- Safe Crossing
- Crossing Number 45
- Steamboat Landing
- Crossing Number 44
- Marshack Unsafe Crossing
- 1850 Registered
- 1864 Granted Patent Deed
- S.D. Maxon D.L.C. Homestead
- Crossing Number 43
- Old Camas Highway 1852

Steamboat Landing 1922-2014

- Young girl killed at 164th Crossing
- NE 147th Crossing
- Safe Crossing
- Evergreen Highway
- BNSF Railway
- Marshack Unsafe Crossing
- Campbell
- Lindsay Steel Wall
- Lindsay Well
- NE 144th Court Crossing
- Jacobs
- Old Camas Highway
- Marshack
- Kellogg/Leas Gate Permit
- Closed Crossing
- Marshack
- Kellogg
- Steamboat Landing
- Leas Leas
- Legal Easement to Steamboat Landing
- 1931 Old Camas Highway Vacated Up to Steamboat Landing Easement
- Morris
- 139th Crossing
- Wanted Poster at the Main Entrance of SBL Development, 7/5/06
- Evergreen Highway 1922

Then-and-now maps pinpoint pivotal Steamboat Landing, once an important Columbia River port for farm products and timber. Today, it is popular for recreational sailing and boating, making the author's land coveted for construction of riverside mansions.

From: Phoebe Marshack
Sent: Sunday, July 31, 2005 9:12 PM
To: Kathy Marshack
Subject: i love you

Fig. A.5

Loving note Phoebe sent to her mom in the summer of 2005 after her older sister left home to live with their father

Mommy,

i just wanted to tell you that i love you and i thank you in every single way for everything you've done for me.

you've been a strong person for who knows how long and i admire that. i admire you all together. i know when i was younger, i didnt understand things very well but having to grow up with a father and a sister with AS and then gettin myself into a relationship that turned out to be a mess just made me a more mature person. in ways most of my friends are more mature than me because they dont have ADHD but in other ways im the more mature one. and i always will be. i just wish i wasnt such a stress mess and get all these migraines. i just wish i could teach myself how to relax and not worry but i cant.

still today, im a huge stress-mess. but knowing more about why i grew up the way i did and having a mom like you has made me more of a successful person in many different ways. no one but you understands what ive been and still am going through and at times as you can see i just hate it and cant take it anymore. i wish i had a father like a lot of my other friends have whos there for me and i know i can count on but i dont. i have a screwed up father that i wish never got the label of being my dad. i know that what i wrote back to him was pretty strong and harsh but its only the truth about how i feel toward him.

i know that bianca can be a loving and caring person at times but at other times, we both just wanna shoot ourselfs because shes so difficult. shes your daughter and my sister. i know i say harsh things toward her but thats how i really feel. but on top of it all, i still love her even though shes NEVER been a sister. because shes ur daughter, seeing her throw her life away like this and making all these bad choices, hurts you deep inside because i know you would spend every penny to help find the right medication for her to make her happy. and i know you would spend a lot of your time doing her work for her so she could pass school. and helped her out and you've been there for her for the past 18 years. we all know that even thought in return she treats you like shit, you always have and always will love her and will care and worry for her.

but remember that one thing you told me when we were on our vacation in Hawaii. NOT TO LET YOU GET WEAK! no matter how much it hurts you and your heart to see those nasty notes from her, you HAVE to stay strong mom you just HAVE to. because in the end, everything will happen for a reason!! its so nice here at home without the screaming and yelling daily and i would like to keep it that way. thats one of the big things that made me get sooo stressed out.

but just know, even if i am only 15 years old, i will ALWAYS be here for you mommy. i love you to pieces and im a lucky girl to have such a great mother like you. we will both get through this. I PROMISE! just keep your head up and think all positive thoughts.

Love always and forever,
Phoebe Irene Marshack #19

I LOVE YOU MOMMY!

APPENDIX

Fig. A. 6
Report from Vancouver Fire Marshall that lines out the nature of the lack of fire safety at the author's home (and her neighbors) after David and Martha Lindsay took the liberty of blocking access to and tearing up the still-public Old Camas Highway where it fronted their home. This destroyed the ability of fire fighting equipment to get to and from the author's home quickly— via a safe train crossing— in case of fire or medical emergency, especially in winter when her train crossing was often impassable.

Message: FW: Test Railroad Crossing in 89 area
FW: Test Railroad Crossing in 89 area
From Landis, Richard Date Friday, February 18, 2005 8:44 AM
To ; Isely, Charles
Cc
Subject FW: Test Railroad Crossing in 89 area

From: Gentry, John
Sent: Friday, February 18, 2005 8:39 AM
To: Landis, Richard
Cc: McCoy, Dan
Subject: FW: Test Railroad Crossing in 89 area
Richard,
Captain Berg provides us with a veteran firefighter and officer's analysis of the situation.
John

From: Berg, Mike
Sent: Thursday, February 17, 2005 3:14 PM
To: McCoy, Dan; Furrer, Andy; Murray, Kevin; Gentry, John
Cc: Sott, Terry; Miletich, Tom; Senchyna, Mike
Subject: RE: Test Railroad Crossing in 89 area
John:
We went down and checked this address out today - we have had an issue with road in the past and
got no resolve - the railroad crossing poses no problem to speak of for the engine (it would be nice to
be a little larger) - but we have a major problem with the road way itself once the engine gets across
the tracks - you have an immediate right or left turn depending on the address you are going to - the

house on the left is very new (the guy that owns the Columbian news paper just built this monster) this
roadway is VERY narrow and has rockwork built up that is an issue - the road that goes to the left is a
little more difficult turn with the large trees it takes some maneuvering to get the engine headed to the
west which is where the rest of the houses are - adding to the degree of difficulty heading to the west is
file:///C|/Documents%20and%20Settings/vincigk/Desktop/New%20Folder/0107815.html (1 of 3) [5/21/2009 3:09:23 PM]
Marshack - Emails – 002984
that this is a very wet area (in a normal year) and this road has no room for error but the trees and
vegetation most likely would keep you on the road surface itself - also towards the end where you think
you have reached the last house (at least by appearances) if you check further you will find that what
appears to be a circle driveway is really also to right a circle that brings you to another drive that goes
around what appears to be the last house and heads south towards the river and if you follow this it
brings you down to another house that is actually on the river (you are not able to see this house from
the original road way or drive that has all the large trees by the railroad track) - while there is a red
district 5 house number sign that has an arrow built into it showing the house road direction in all
appearances you would assume the number would be for the house that appears to be the last house
on the drive (the lady at this house point out the other house to us today - news to me) - the issue we
had here before was that we damaged the rig in getting out of this drive on a medical call years ago
and people got paper work in there files - it is actually harder to get out than to get in as the last turn
with the rock work and trees make this a 3 person maneuver with major engine work - as I stated we
went down there today and it is sunny and bright and we still had a very hard time and still put a large
smug on the side of the engine in turning to get out that is going to require a least an hour of waxing
and such, night time we are going to damage rigs as happened before - even trying to back all the way

APPENDIX

out is hard because of the last turn and the rock work over the wet land access bridge (culvert) this
drive needs work to make this more emergency response ready - I know there isn't much we can do as
this is a private road but I might suggest we advised the property owners on this road we can not meet
time response guidelines into this area for fire or medical responses and also let there fire insurance
companies know that we as a Department can not operate with our normal fire ground operations and
expect larger fire damage due to extreme fire access problems for both equipment and personnel due
to the limitations of the road and surrounding trees and vegetation or we accept the possibility that we
most likely will damage rigs in this area.
Mike Berg Station 89

From: McCoy, Dan
Sent: Tuesday, February 15, 2005 8:07 AM
To: Berg, Mike; Furrer, Andy; Murray, Kevin; Gentry, John; McCoy, Dan
Subject: FW: Test Railroad Crossing in 89 area
John... I will pass this on to the captains of 89 and they can sort out who gets to go to the location and
figure it out... thanks, dan

From: Gentry, John
Sent: Monday, February 14, 2005 4:09 PM
To: McCoy, Dan
Subject: Test Railroad Crossing in 89 area Dan,
The owner of the house at 14237 SE Evergreen Hwy is claiming that her private railroad crossing is

file:///C|/Documents%20and%20Settings/vincigk/Desktop/New%20Folder/0107815.html (2 of 3) [5/21/2009 3:09:23 PM]

Marshack - Emails – 002985

actually at public road. One of the points of contention is whether or not the crossing and access road
is adequate to allow fire apparatus to reach her house. Could you ask one of the Captains at 89 to take
their rig down and see if they can make it to her house? The crossing is on the south side of the Old
Evergreen Hwy across from SE 144 Court.

By the way the light in the first picture is a train. Their speed limit in that area is 60 MPH.

<< File: 14237 SE Evergreen Hwy 007.jpg >>
<< File: 14237 SE Evergreen Hwy 010.jpg >>

John Gentry
Lead Deputy Fire Marshal
Vancouver Fire Department
900 W Evergreen Blvd
Vancouver, WA 98660
Phone: 360-759-4405

file:///C|/Documents%20and%20Settings/vincigk/Desktop/New%20Folder/0107815.html (3 of 3) [5/21/2009 3:09:23 PM]
Marshack - Emails - 002986

APPENDIX

Fig. A. 7

2004 letter the author wrote to Vancouver Citizen Advocate Jim Jacks. In it, she requested his help in dealing with Richard Landis and Josephine Townsend—the same two people Jacks would wind up conspiring with to "legally" bully her.

Dear Mr. Jack:

"I am having a problem resolving some problems with the City and thought I would appeal to you for help. The situation has grown way out of hand and no one is listening. It seems that there are solutions that are reasonable and fair but I cannot get anyone to listen. A friend suggested I contact you to see if you could step in and help.

"First, Code Enforcement has decided to fine me for operating my psychology practice in my home. I have had my office in my home since 1987, prior to the city incorporating my area. When the City incorporated I sent in all of the necessary paperwork to get my City business license and home business permit. No problem. I thought everything was fine until this year. A new neighbor moved in in April 2004 and within three weeks filed a complaint against me. The Code Enforcement Officer Richard Landis determined that I was violating the city codes by having my secretary on the premises, even though the current code allows for one employee. I informed the City in 1997 that I had an employee and was still granted a home business permit, do I never thought I was in violation. However, Richard Landis says that even though I told the City and I even wrote a letter to that effect in 1987, I was still in violation. He fined me $250.00 and it was upheld by the City Hearings officer, Mr. Epstein. I would like your help in clearing my record on this account. I have been an honest business person for 25 years and never had a problem such as this. I simply do not understand why I could be fined for being honest and not bothering anyone.

"Secondly, I am in the middle of a dispute with this neighbor over easement rights to the river. I suspect her complaint to the City on my business license is part of the dispute, rather than a real grievance. WE live near the Columbia River and have a common road to our houses and a common easement across another neighbor's property so that we can access the river. This neighbor has determined just after she moved in that I do not have the right to the easement. In fact, she secured a permit from the City to build a gate to block my access to the river. When I explained that I have a deeded access to the river as do 13 neighbors total, she filed her complaint against me. I tried explaining to Mr. Landis that the business complaint really grew out of this real estate issue, but he would not listen. He investigated the situation and decided that I do not have such an easement. It is clearly stated in my property deed. In fact, it is clearly stated in the deeds of 12 other neighbors. Why Mr. Landis got involved in the

property dispute I do not know. And why he considers the property dispute part of the investigation of my home based business I do not know either.

"The third issue is that I recently ended a very difficult marriage to a local divorce attorney. Even though my ex-husband knows all of the judges in town, I could not get the divorce moved out of the county for over a year, because Diane Woolard agreed to hear the matter. Diane is a friend of my husband and clearly in a conflicted relationship, but she would not recuse herself from the case, even though every other Judge on the Clark County Bench recused themselves from the case. Needless to say I had to endure a year of biased decisions on her pat which eventually culminated in my arrest. I was able to work out a diversion agreement with the City Prosecutor Josephine Townsend which should end in 12 months, sometime next year. However, now that the City has fined me for the home business permit issue, Ms. Townsend has decided to revoke the diversion plan because she says that I have committed a crime. She is asking for jail time because I was fined $250.00 for my home business permit!

"I need your help to straighten this out because I cannot afford to shut down my practice over this. I am a single parent of two teenage daughters. One of my daughter's is autistic and requires a lot of supervision. She is homeschooled and because of her emotional problems I need to be close by to help her. If I cannot work at home, I cannot easily support my family. The solutions seem fairly simple to me. First, allow me to continue to work from my home as I have for 18 years without incident. Secondly, allow the neighbors to use their deeded access and develop a neighborhood agreement to that effect. Unfortunately the City Mediation Services has decided that our problem is too big for them. But it seems such a simple solution.

"I know that you may hear a lot of complaints and can't get to all of them, but I am desperate here. I cannot afford to stop supporting my family and if Richard Landis has his way, I will be totally shut down. I have also contacted Councilman Larry Smith at the advice of a friend and sent an email to Royce Pollard. Please help me correct his injustice. It seems that certain City officials are going off without reason.

"Thank you,
"Kathy J. Marshack, Ph.D.
Licensed Psychologist"

APPENDIX

Fig. A. 8

The libelous 2004 memo written about the author by Jim Jacks with the aid of Richard Landis and Josephine Townsend.

Jacks, Jim
From: Jacks, Jim
Sent: Tuesday, September 07, 2004 3:50 PM
To: McDonnell, Pat
Subject: RE: Kathy Marshack's contact with the City

Greetings Pat,

You asked for factual information relating to the Kathy Marshack situation. Basically she wants (1) the City to reverse the Hearing Examiner's decision, (2) take her side in an easement dispute with her neighbors, and (3) the City prosecutor's office to keep her on a Diversion agreement with the Court even though she has violated it.

(1) Home Occupation Permit Violation
Ms. Marshack resides and works as a licensed psychologist from 14237 SE Evergreen Highway, just east from Steamboat Landing. This house (and others) is accessed by a private drive which crosses the railroad tracks. In 1999 there was an accident involving a car and a train at this private crossing.

Ms. Marshack's neighbor's house has a circular driveway that is frequently used by her clients. Both the current owners of the house and the previous owners have complained to Code Enforcement regarding excessive traffic to the business.

After investigating, Code Enforcement eventually issued a citation which she then appealed. The Hearings Examiner date was August 12, 2004 and she was represented by legal counsel.

The Hearings Examiner decision found that:
Ms. Marshack never had a legally established business because she never obtained a home occupation permit from the County, even though she operated a business from 1987 to 1996.

In 1997, the City advised her that she needed to apply for a home occupation permit. She did obtain one. However, she has failed to comply with it because of her employee. Since 1997 she has been told four times that the conditions of the permit did not allow nonresident employees in R-10 zoned areas. The Hearings Examiner denied her appeal on August 30, 2004.

I talked at length with Code Enforcement staff and I am confident that they gave her every reasonable opportunity to come into compliance. Ms. Marshack chose not to comply with the home occupation permit. She has had numerous opportunities to apply for a variance but has refused to do so. Her diagnosis (explained below) illustrates why.

(2) Easements
Ms. Marshack and her neighbors have a number of easement access issues in contention. These are civil matters and do not involve the City.

(3) Arrested During Divorce
During the course of her divorce, Ms. Marshack was arrested in October 2003 for criminal trespass, malicious mischief, and assault for an incident that occurred at her husband's law office. There was a significant amount of property damage. She attacked her husband's secretary (who was NOT involved with the divorce) and broke her right hand, gave her a black eye, bruised her right foot and right thigh. I have personally seen the photos from the court file of the property damage and the injuries to the victim of the assault.

Because she had no prior arrests she was put on a diversion program. Her conditions included participating in 26 weeks of anger management treatment and having no legal violations of any kind during her 12 months on diversion.

Marshack - Citizen Advocate Office - 000042

The Hearings Examiner's decision constitutes a violation. Ms. Marshack has a court date on September 29th. It is likely that she will be moved off the diversion program and convicted. Contrary to her assertion, the prosecutor is NOT asking for jail time. The conviction will likely mean that she will lose her license to practice as a psychologist.

Ms. Marshack's Diagnosis

Ms. Marshack is a licensed psychologist. She is also undergoing counseling as a client with a licensed psychologist. During the course of the legal proceedings Kathy Marshack's counselor shared with the court and city prosecution staff that in his professional opinion "Ms. Marshack is a functional sociopath." This basically means that she has no regard for other people and has no remorse for her actions. She has "explosive anger management problems." She is "resentful of authority and thinks that society's laws do not apply to her." He also believes that "she should NOT be a practicing psychologist."

Summary

Ms. Marshack is articulate and lucid. She presents what appears to be an organized case. However, there is little that we can do to help her.
(1) She has participated in the Hearings Examiner appeal process and we cannot reverse his decision
(2) The easements are a civil issue between private parties.
(3) She will be treated like any other person in the criminal justice system on a diversion contract.

All the best,

Jim Jacks
Citizen Advocate
City Manager's Office
360-696-8139

Marshack - Citizen Advocate Office - 000043

Fig. A. 9

One Man's
ALTERNATIVE FACTS
And The Damage They Did

A Timeline Showing Richard Landis' Involvement in "The River, the Road, and the Train"

Vancouver Code Enforcement Officer Richard Landis had his hand in nearly everything that transpired over the 12 years I was hounded by my neighbors, City Hall, and the Vancouver Police. Landis lied, manipulated, withheld information, and generally went after me every which way he could.

It was the ferocious "alternative facts" that Landis fed neighbors and City Hall that gave him such sway. Without his covert help, the players in my story would have had a much more difficult time trying to destroy me.

On the other hand, because Landis left a trail, although much of it was hidden, detoured, or destroyed, this telling timeline has evolved. It provides a marvelous window into the mind of a man who has no conscience (EmD-1) and only objective: to cause harm.

This timeline is a synopsis of Landis' activities and is based on actual documents from the public records. Every item on this list is backed by a recorded document (i.e. email, letter, court document, and even Landis' own Code Enforcement logs).

I've started with some historic documents that reveal the underpinnings of Landis' game plan. If it weren't for these, the realities about the River (the easement road), the Road (the Old Camas Highway), and the Train (originally the SP&S), may never have come to light. Most of these archived materials were located at the Clark County Historical Society and the Clark County Surveyor's Office.

The maps and agreements for these old routes, which grew out of pioneer commerce, date back more than 100 years. Much to his chagrin, Landis would learn that these old contracts and deeds were still as valid as the day they were originally signed and dated.

Much to his chagrin, Landis would learn that these old contracts and deeds were still as valid as the day they were originally signed and dated.

Even with these plain-and-simple old legal records providing solid evidence about my property rights, Landis had charged in with all his might to derail my fight for those rights. He got away with it all.

My rights and their history

Let's follow the "dots" as Landis tries to carve out his own version of my property rights—largely to facilitate the implementation of a Train Horn Noise Quiet Zone (THNQZ)—and is foiled by these five maps and documents. His name may not appear in each of the incidents in this telling list, but his fingerprints are embedded there nonetheless.

APPENDIX

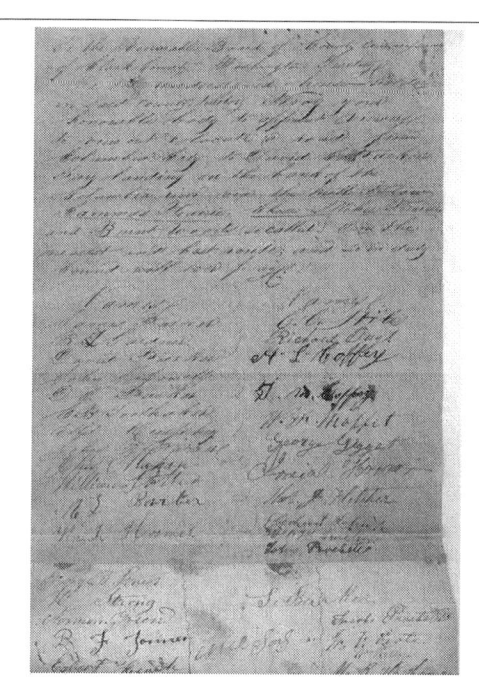

#1

In 1851, several settlers in Clarke County* (including **Silas Maxon**, the original owner of my land) petitioned the newly formed American territorial government to create a road, which would later be called "The Old Camas Highway." Turns out, the old road described in my deed was the first American road "viewed out," surveyed, and constructed in Clark County. I found this document in a drawer in the basement of the Clark County Surveyor's Office.

---

* What is now known as "Clark" County was spelled as "Clarke" County in early documents.

The petition was signed by these early pioneers and reads: *"To the Honorable Board of County Commissioners of Clark County, Washington Territory; We the undersigned householders in said county and territory, pray your honorable body to appoint viewers to view out and locate a road from Columbia City to David Parker's Ferry Landing on the bank of the Columbia River, via the Mill Plain, Cammas Prairie, Close Illihee Prairie, and Burnt Woods (so called), on the nearest and best route; and so in duty bound will ever pray."*

(By the way, when the Americans took over the area from the British, they changed the name of the town from Ft. Vancouver to Columbia City. A few years later, it was changed again to Vancouver. By 1857, the county road is documented on a survey map running from Vancouver to Camas.)

WHEN EMPATHY FAILS

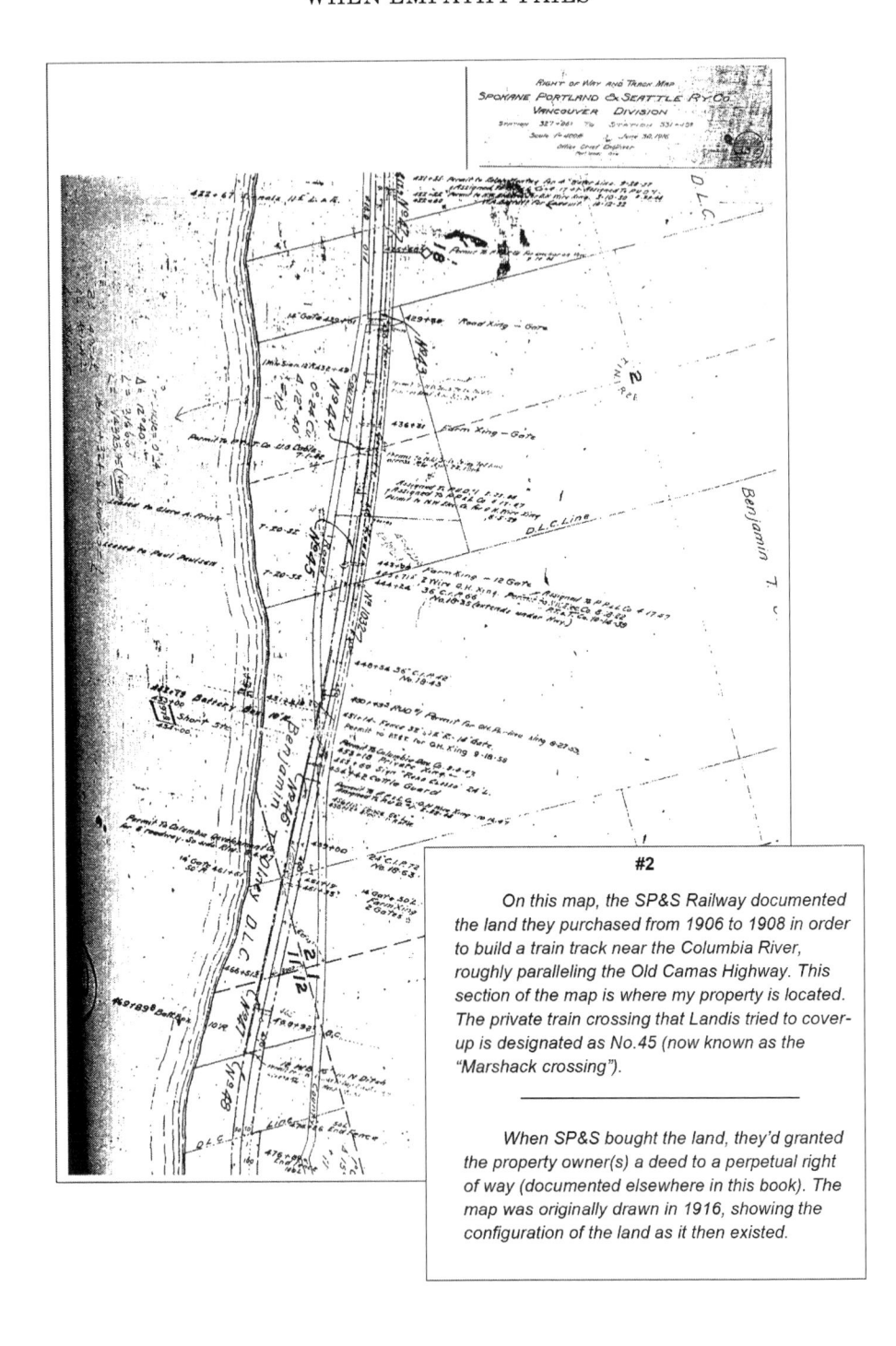

#2

On this map, the SP&S Railway documented the land they purchased from 1906 to 1908 in order to build a train track near the Columbia River, roughly paralleling the Old Camas Highway. This section of the map is where my property is located. The private train crossing that Landis tried to cover-up is designated as No.45 (now known as the "Marshack crossing").

When SP&S bought the land, they'd granted the property owner(s) a deed to a perpetual right of way (documented elsewhere in this book). The map was originally drawn in 1916, showing the configuration of the land as it then existed.

APPENDIX

Date: May 3,1910. Filed: Oct.7,1910 at 4:20 P.M.Book "85"Pg.61.

Ack'd: " " " Before H.W.Arnold Notary Public (s) for Clarke County, State of Washington,residing at Vancouver,therein.

Witnesses: H.W.Arnold, N.E.Bennett.

Grantors: CHARLES W. LAVER (s) and KEZIAH D. LAVER (s) his wife.

Grantee: MATILDA A. DUBOIS

Instrument: Quit Claim Deed. Remise,release and forever quit-claim.

Consideration: $1.00

Description: All our right,title and interest in and to the following described premises, namely: The undivided one fourth interest to the following. Begining at a point N.75°15" W. (9179) Nine and 79/100 chains from the point where the East line of the S.D.Maxon Donation Land Claim intersects the Columbia River, thence S.6°45' E. to low water mark in the Columbia River, thence following low water mark down stream (125) one hundred and twenty-five feet thence North 6°45" W (1.70) one and 70/100 chains thence N.75°15" East (125) one hundred and twenty-five feet more or less to a point, thence S.6°45 E to the place of begining. Also Begining at the North East corner of the above described land and running thence South 75°15" W. tracing the North line of said land (30) thirty feet, thence N. 6°45" E to the County road thence Easterly along said road (30) thirty feet, thence S 6°45" W to the place of begining.

(Here follows rough plat of same)

#3

This 1910 Quit Claim deed describes not only the river easement but the county road known as Old Camas Highway. In many of the old deeds, surveys, and historic documents, the Old Camas Highway is referred to as the "old county road" or the "Columbia City to Cascade City Road." The facts set forth in this Quit Claim have been verified by several surveyors over the years.

#4

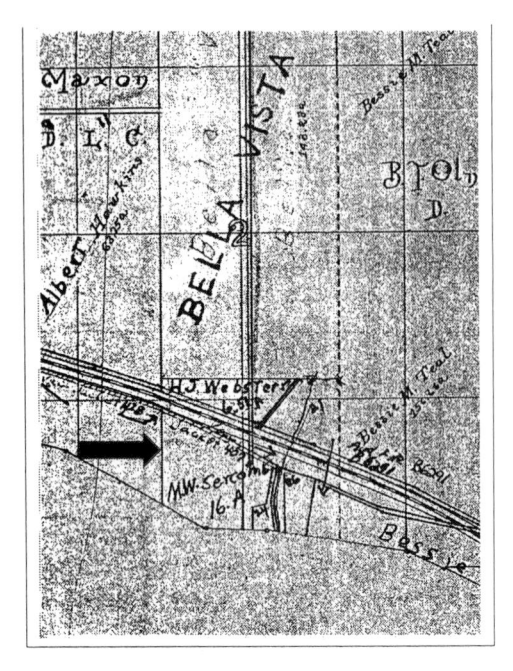

By 1936, Hattie Webster had requested road vacation of the Old Camas Highway that bordered her property. The road had no longer served a public purpose after 1922 when the Evergreen Highway was developed north of the train tracks.

Hence, the Old Camas Highway had been returned to the property owners who'd petitioned the county. Note that this is the last road vacation order recorded for the Old Camas Highway.

Notice the "vacation jacket" hash marks on the map: They show the road as vacated only to the west of the river easement under fire by **Landis**.

The road to the east, which runs along my property as well as the properties of **Joseph and Julianne Leas, Mary Kellogg, Mary Jacob,** and **Scott and Jody Campbell,** was never vacated and was technically—and legally—still a public right of way at the time of our heated dispute.

APPENDIX

#5

My ex-husband, **Howard Marshack**, and I bought our little piece of paradise near the Columbia River in 1984. It was a 1953 ranch house situated between the train tracks and the river.

Never could I have foreseen that this purchase would come to be at the center of the perfect storm of shaming, and stalking that landed me in court several times—and in jail on three occasions.

We settled in, started our family, remodeled, and spent many happy hours playing at the river with our children.

Below is the wording from the explanatory memo about my easement sent to **Richard Landis** by Roads and Rights of Way Clerk **Pat Owen** just prior to my request for the same document on Sept. 22, 2004.

Clearly, it proved that I had an easement to the river. **Landis** had been privy to this information even before he'd started investigating me and my neighbors had sued. That certainly had not stopped him from trying to prove otherwise!

The deed for 14237 SE Evergreen Hwy, owner Kathy Marshack, contains a paragraph stating: *TOGETHER WITH an easement for ingress and egress over and across a strip of land 30 feet in width, as said roadway now exists, leading from subject property to the "Steamboat Landing" as well as leading over and across that tract of land described as the "Old Camus Highway."*

WHEN EMPATHY FAILS

The modern-era timeline below documents how Landis tried—in no less than 69 covert and once-removed ways—to subvert historical and legal documents in an effort to pursue the establishment of a Train Horn Noise Quiet Zone (THNQZ) in my neighborhood—and to protect the property of my neighbors Scott and Jody Campbell.

(I have not included the actual documents for the rest of the timeline since they are in the form of emails or letters. However, they are available upon request from the City of Vancouver. As Landis is fond of saying, "They are all public record.")

---

1. **1992,** memo written by then Assistant City Attorney **Ted Gathe** advises the Vancouver City Council on the legal technicalities for vacating an old territorial road.
2. **Jan. 29, 2004, Jody Campbell** (neighbor and wife of newspaper owner **Scott Campbell**) calls my office to complain that she is going to report me to Code Enforcement for running an illegal business from my home.
3. **Feb. 8, 2004,** I attend the first neighborhood **THNQZ** meeting. In attendance are politicians, City employees, civic leaders, and representatives from Burlington Northern and Santa Fe Railroad Company **(BNSF)** and the Federal Railroad Administration **(FRA)**. Noted in their presentation is that the City started the process for a Quiet Zone in June 2001.
4. **Feb. 11, 2004,** Vancouver Code Enforcement Officer **Dan Jones** starts the investigation of **Jody Campbell's** complaint. He informs my secretary that I do not have a home occupation permit and am operating illegally.
5. **Feb. 18, 2004, Jones'** log shows that my permit was found. He writes in his log, "no violation."
6. **Feb. 24, 2004, Jones** decides to do a "re-inspection" for some reason, but still finds no violation and closes the case.
7. **May 20, 2004, Jones** emails City Council Member **Pat Jollota** to inquire about the steamboat landing described in the Marshack Chicago Title report. Jollota is also a retired curator for the Clark County Historical Society and has written several

APPENDIX

books on the history of Clark County.[1] Jones mentions that he is inquiring for **Richard Landis**. No other complaints are filed against me at this time, yet Landis remains curious about my property rights.

8. **May 21, 2004,** Landis reopens my Code Enforcement case even though his log shows there have been no further complaints. He faxes me a citation, alleging that I am in violation for not having a legitimate home occupation permit and violating City codes for home based businesses. He fines me $250 and demands that I fire my secretary and resolve the problem by June 30, 2004.

9. **May 24, 2004,** Vancouver Planning Office grants a permit to **Mary Kellogg** and **Dr. Joseph and Mrs. Julianne Leas**. The permit is to build a gate blocking my access to the Old Camas Highway and the river easement. It states: "Gate will not block legal access to other properties."

10. **June 15, 2004,** Landis prints GIS (online Government Information System) reports for my property as well as those of the **Leas** and **Kellogg**. He handwrites in the margin a notation that there are old property descriptions of "two roads."

11. **July 14, 2004,** Landis sends a letter to my attorney **Mike Wynne,** stating that my easement rights are "vague," and that he intends to pursue a complaint against me with **BNSF**. He also admits investigating my children's school records.

12. **Aug. 17, 2004,** Landis prints more GIS records for the properties on 144th Court. These neighbors have easement rights similar to mine in their deeds (10 of us did). Landis' log indicates that he called these property owners to inquire about their easement rights.

13. **Aug. 31, 2004,** Landis writes to **BNSF** Safety Manager **Steve Mills** complaining about my unauthorized use of the train crossing.

14. **Aug. 31, 2004,** neighbor **Don Morris** sends a letter to **Landis** complaining about my use of the Old Camas Highway. Morris insists that I am endangering his aging and blind mother **(Kellogg)** as she walks across the train tracks to get her mail. He also claims that his mother owns the Old Camas Highway.

---

[1] In 2004, Dan Jones of Code Enforcement wrote to Museum Curator Pat Jollota, asking, ". . . In 1929 where was Steamboat landing geographically located? . . .As curator of the museum I thought you may have had some type of historical documentation. . . .I'm asking for Richard Landis who has a case, that this information would help with. :) dj. " Jollota's response was, "Dan, there were several of them [river landings], many of them were so-called 'mud landings', the boat simply nosed into the mud and loaded or unloaded."

WHEN EMPATHY FAILS

15. **Sept. 1, 2004, Pat Owen,** Vancouver Roads and Rights of Way Clerk, sends **Landis** information that he requested regarding the property descriptions for all of my neighbors and me.
16. **Sept. 3, 2004,** I send an email to Citizen Advocate **Jim Jacks** requesting help with two rogue City employees, **Josephine Townsend** and **Richard Landis**. Specific to Landis, I complain that he has accused me of trespassing when I have easement rights.
17. **Sept. 7, 2004, Jacks** forwards my complaint to **Landis** and **Townsend**. Landis replies to Jacks by stating that he is not concerned with my easement rights; he is only conducting an investigation of my home occupation permit.
18. **Sept. 8, 2004,** the **Leas** and **Kellogg** file a quiet title property suit against me over my easement rights. I am served a summons on Sept. 9, 2004. Interestingly, this lawsuit filing shows up in **Landis'** Code Enforcement file on me.
19. **Sept. 8, 2004,** City Planner **Jodie Sharp** sends a letter demanding that I get a permit from **BNSF** in order to keep my home occupation permit.
20. **Sept. 9, 2004, Jacks** calls me a "diagnosed functional sociopath" in a memo he sends to **Landis** and **Townsend** for their approval, prior to sending it to the City Manager, Mayor and City Council. Landis writes back, "Well done."
21. **Sept. 27, 2004, Owen** alarms **Landis** with an email informing him that **BNSF** would like to close the crossing at 144th Court, thus sending traffic to the crossing at 147th, and right through the **Campbells'** estate on the Old Camas Highway. Landis quickly sends messages to City Attorney **Charles Isely** informing him that I am being sued by my neighbors over easements which were established illegally.
22. **Sept. 27, 2004, Landis** orchestrates a conference call with **Shana Druffner,** a **BNSF** executive and attorney; **Steve Mills,** BNSF Safety Manager; **Gene Biddle** from **BNSF**; Assistant Vancouver City Attorney **Jim McNamara; Mike Wynne,** my business attorney; **Dan Lorenz,** the attorney handling my lawsuit; Landis; and me. On the call, Landis blurts out that he has been trying to shut down my home-based business at the request of **BNSF**. This, in spite of the fact that the parties to this call had agreed to recognize my train crossing deed and my home business license, I was hounded by Landis and **BNSF** for another year and a half.

APPENDIX

23. **Oct. 8, 2004, Landis** writes in his Code Enforcement log, "concerning the easement issues raised by Ms. Marshack, we have told her . . . that this is a civil issue and we will let the courts resolve this. . ."
24. **Oct. 13, 2004, Owen** emails **Landis,** questioning his continued involvement in a private civil matter. Further, she refers Landis to **Louie Benedict,** Clark County Roads and Rights of Way clerk, because, Owen says, he has more information on the "old county road."
25. **Oct. 14, 2004, Landis** emails **Benedict** and learns no evidence can be found that indicates the Old Camas Highway was ever vacated at this location.
26. **Oct 14, 2004, Landis** replies to **Owen's** query about his involvement in a private matter: "It is the City's position at this time that an underlying easement may exist, but it has never been maintained, or improved or accepted by Clark County as a public road thus when we annexed it we accepted it as a private road."
27. **Jan. 7, 2004, BNSF** sends me a contract to sign that would make me liable for maintenance and accidents at the old train crossing. They insist that I buy insurance to the tune of $50,000 a year. I don't and receive these demand letters monthly for a year.
28. **Jan. 11, 2005, Sharp** sends me another letter demanding that I cooperate with **BNSF,** or she will withhold my home occupation permit.
29. **Jan. 13, 2005, McNamara** sends a letter to **Druffner** stating that they plan to re-issue my home occupation permit without requiring cooperation with **BNSF.**
30. **Jan. 18, 2004, Druffner** continues to demand that I take responsibility for the train crossing. She says, "Routine maintenance [of the crossing] will need to be borne by you and the other users."
31. **Jan. 25, 2005, Landis** sends **Druffner** an email stating that there is a 20-foot-wide easement for a county road on my property. He also says, ". . . she [Marshack] refuses to survey to determine if it is on the south side or north side of the railroad tracks."
32. **Feb. 2, 2005,** Assistant City Attorney **Charles Isely** sends a letter to Wynne stating that the Old Camas Highway is private. Further, he states that I am required to get a crossing permit to use the train crossing.

33. **Feb. 9, 2005, Isely** sends a letter to my attorney **Zach Stoumbos** (He was working for my title company on my behalf.), that says, according to **Richard Landis**, the Old Camas Highway "is not a public road" and has "never been a public road."
34. **Feb. 15, 2005**, in a sworn declaration, **Benedict** states he cannot find records that the Old Camas Highway was ever vacated in our area.
35. **Feb. 17, 2005**, Vancouver Fire Captain **Mike Berg** evaluates safety at the 144th Court train crossing and the Old Camas Highway. In an email to **Landis** and others he says:

> "I might suggest we advise the property owners on this road we cannot meet time response guidelines into this area for fire or medical responses and also let their fire insurance companies know that we as a Department cannot operate with our normal fire ground operations and expect larger fire damage due to extreme fire access problems. . ."

I was never informed of this evaluation by the fire department—even though I'd been the one who'd requested it.

36. **Feb. 28, 2005, Stoumbos** sends a letter to **Isely**, questioning his competency. Stoumbos states, "How does staff [meaning **Landis**] reconcile the fact that the very road which was opened in the 1850s was partially vacated in the 1930s? What evidence does staff have that the County Commissioners vacated a non-existent public road." Stoumbos attaches dozens of documents verifying the road.
37. **March 1, 2005**, letter from **Isely** to **Wynne** (copied to **Landis**) announces that the City will stay Code Enforcement actions against me for my home occupation permit if I agree that the Old Camas Highway and the train crossing are private.
38. **March 14, 2005**, yet another in a string of monthly demands from **BNSF** that I sign a contract to assume responsibility for the train crossing and that I buy insurance.
39. **March 16, 2005**, letter from **Isely** to **Stoumbos** says that the City doesn't want to get involved in the private property dispute but must take a stand on the old road and the crossing nevertheless.
40. **March 17, 2005**, letter from **Isely** to **Wynne** and copied to **Landis** indicates that my new home occupation permit will be authorized only if I get a permit from

APPENDIX

BNSF. Further, the home occupation permit forbids me, my clients and guests from parking along the Old Camas Highway.

41. **March 17, 2005, Isely** sends an email to **Druffner** (copied to **Landis**) stating that I do not have the right to use the train crossing without a permit. Isely suggests **BNSF** should sue me.
42. **May 3, 2005,** letter from **BNSF** states that I am using the train crossing illegally. Throughout the summer, I continue to get demands from BNSF.
43. **June 30, 2005, Nin Beseda** (surveyor hired by my title insurance company to verify the boundaries of my property, the river easement, and the Old Camas Highway) verifies in an email to **Isely** that Old Camas Highway is still a public right of way where it passes through the properties of **Campbell, Mary Jacob, Marshack,** and the **Leas.**
44. **Aug. 24, 2005, Beseda** gives a sworn declaration to the court indicating that he found no records that the old county road had ever been vacated in our area. He supplies numerous documents to support his findings. In fact, he furnishes a document showing that all territorial roads were originally 60 feet in width. This particular road has significantly dwindled away: It is currently 10 to 11 feet in wide.
45. **Aug. 29, 2005,** letter from **Steve Turner**, the attorney representing my neighbors **Leas** and **Kellogg**, goes to **Isely**. Turner says, "Enclosed please find the latest rantings from Ms. Marshack that the driveway is a 'public road.'"
46. **Aug. 31, 2005, Isely** responds to **Turner's** letter and refers to **Beseda's** survey. "He [Beseda] can't come out and say that the asphalt between your clients' property and Marshack's is the alleged county road, right?"
47. **Jan. 4, 2006, Gathe** and **Leiker** send a letter to **Scott Campbell,** explaining the law for vacating a territorial road.
48. **Jan. 25, 2006,** email string with **Landis**, and City employees **Isely, McNamara, Zeider, Thayer Rorabaugh,** and others, scolds **Benedict** for talking with *The Columbian*'s history editor, **Dean Baker**. Much to Campbell's disliking (I'm pretty sure), Baker writes a story about the history of the old road.
49. **Jan. 25, 2006, Owen** emails **Landis,** because I have made another complaint regarding harassment by Landis. In response to Owen, Landis emails several other City employees with the information that **Scott Campbell** is talking to **Gathe**

about the Old Camas Highway. Landis indicates that the City Attorneys will handle my complaint. Satisfied, Owen does nothing to help me.

50. **Jan. 26, 2006, Beseda** files a secondary declaration after conducting even more survey work. He confirms the location of the Old Camas Highway as well as the fact that it has never been vacated.
51. **Feb. 26, 2006,** email string with **Campbell's** attorney, **Gathe,** and **Isely** fires **Landis** up to proceed with vacating the Old Camas Highway.
52. **July 4, 2006,** I am falsely arrested. I go to trial in February 2007 and am fully acquitted. During the pre-trial period, **Melanie Mooney** admits assaulting me. Her husband **Don Morris** admits taking videos of me and my family and turning them over to **Landis**. The videos were never released during our two public records request. As a result of the discovery of these stalking videos and Landis' obstructing justice, the charges against me for stalking are dismissed.
53. **July 19, 2006,** members of the Steamboat Landing Home Owners Association Board (SBL Board) report in their meeting minutes that **Landis** authorized a fence through the middle of the river easement, over the river bank and down into the river. Landis confirms that they did not need a permit for the fence because the police authorized it (the police never authorized the fence).

    At this same HOA meeting President **Toni Montgomery** admits she had authorized placing the wanted poster at the front gate. The SBL Board also discusses my complaint to the Washington Department of Ecology about their fence being built without a permit and constructed into the Columbia River. The minutes indicate that Landis said he would take care of the problem for them. The fence remains until **Judge John Nichols** orders it removed in 2008.
54. **Aug. 2006,** the property dispute goes to trial. It lasts a week. **Nichols** took six months to deliver his verdict in my favor. My neighbors appealed. I sued them for ongoing harassment and contempt of court.
55. **Feb. 2007,** two events are going on. I am suing my neighbors for violating the court orders upholding my easement rights, and I am preparing for my criminal trial (the one where I was falsely charged with harassment, assault, stalking, trespass and lying to the police). I'd first learned of the 50 videos taken by **Morris** at the contempt hearing. He admits secretly taking the videos and delivering them to

APPENDIX

Landis. During a court break, my attorney goes to **Isely's** office to confront him about the whereabouts of the tapes since they had not been produced during the public records request. Isely locates the tapes in the office of city planner **Chad Eiken.** Isely brings the tapes to the courtroom personally, with the excuse that he had never seen them, so that's why he hadn't turned them over. Instead of dropping all criminal charges against me, the City dismissed the charge that I had stalked Morris by taking videos! Then, they proceeded on the other false charges against me: (harassment, assault, stalking, trespass, and lying to the police). A jury found me not guilty on all of these counts.

56. **Over the next two and a half years,** several events are transpiring. Nationally, the country is feeling the shock of the stock market crash, which creates a host of events that impact my neighbors. **Campbell** faces bankruptcy and has to sell his home and his new office building. My legal woes continue as I am wrapped up in ongoing neighborhood harassment. Eventually, I win all cases against my neighbors for harassment, contempt, and assault. I will be fighting for safety at the old train crossing until 2014.

57. **Feb. 18, 2009, Landis** responds to a request from Campbell about my involvement with **BNSF** and the private train crossing. Landis tells **Campbell** how to contact **Druffner.** He also lies when he says that I had no concerns with safety at the train crossing.

58. **Feb. 24, 2009, Landis** sends **Campbell** the Aug.31, 2004 letter he had sent to **BNSF** Safety Manager **Steve Miles,** regarding my supposed lack of a train crossing permit. By the way, I am never copied on any of Landis' correspondence about me (so that I can correct it), but he readily sends it out to others.

59. **Feb. 25, 2009, Landis** emails **BNSF**, requesting protection for **Campbell** during a routine maintenance closure of the 144th Ct crossing. He complains that I will trespass on the Campbell's property to use the Old Camas Highway to the crossing at 147th. In fact, there is no other way to exit my property without taking the Old Camas Highway when the 144th crossing is closed.

60. **March 3, 2009, BNSF** responds to **Landis** by advising him that the 144th Ct crossing is slated for permanent closure; instead, traffic will be routed through the **Campbell** property to 147th. This is in anticipation of the **THNQZ.**

WHEN EMPATHY FAILS

61. **Aug. 2009,** meeting at the Water Resources Center celebrates completion of the **THNQZ** permitting process. At this meeting, the **FRA** representative learns about the existence of my dangerous private crossing at 144th Court. As a result, the **THNQZ** is put on hold until the safety issues can be resolved.
62. **Oct. 8, 2009,** Assistant City Attorney **Brent Boger** sends a letter to the **FRA** complaining about me and my home business stalling the THNQZ. He wrote several more letters along these lines complaining that I didn't have that much traffic to my home business, or that the Old Camas Highway was not really an issue anymore, etc.
63. **Throughout the remainder of 2009,** there is a flurry of activity by City officials, including, **Gathe, Rorabaugh,** and Vancouver Mayor **Tim Leavitt,** in an effort to help **Campbell** with the sale of his home and his business property. Campbell scribbles a hurried note during one of these meetings that reads: "Call **Richard Landis.**"
64. **2010,** in preparation to sell the **Campbell** home to **David and Martha Lindsay,** Chicago Title issues a report on Campbell's property. It says there is an "unrecorded" road across the Campbell lot. The report also indicates that Campbell has an old **BNSF** permit to use the crossing at 147th Court but none for the crossing at 144th Ct. In fact, I am the only homeowner with a deeded right to cross at 144th Court.
65. **Jan. 8, 2010,** letter from **Ronald Reis,** another **FRA** representative, explains that the **THNQZ** permit is halted until there is a diagnostic review of the private crossing problem.
66. **March 11, 2010,** my neighbor and **THNQZ** proponent **Roger Parsons** emails many distinguished citizens of Vancouver, including City officials, Superior Court Judge **James Rulli,** auto tycoon **Dick Hannah,** and others, complaining that it is my fault the **THNQZ** has been halted. He suggests the way to deal with me is to revoke my home occupation permit.
67. **June 15, 2010,** the City announces the purchase of **Campbell's** office building, thus bailing him out of bankruptcy.
68. **Dec. 12, 2012,** the FRA finally grants the City a **THNQZ** permit for my neighborhood. Several negotiations were required to finalize the deal. The City

APPENDIX

declares the Old Camas Highway vacated, but not through any legal means. They rationalize the old road's change in status was the "intent"[2] of the homeowners who sold rights of way to the train company back in the early 1900s. Hence, the City is granted a waiver to bypass any major upgrades to the historic train crossing—as long as they install LED-lit stop signs and remove rock that impedes line of sight for the train engineers.

69. **Oct.18, 2013,** "The Oregonian" newspaper's online site, OregonLive.com, reports construction of the **THNQZ** is complete. **Parsons,** the man who wanted to yank my home occupation permit and referred to me as a "snag" in one of his emails, is quoted as saying: "After many years of research, persistence, and working together both as a neighborhood and with our local and federal officials, we have a solution. It does take a village."

---

[2] The City's position was that over a hundred years ago, the intention was to vacate the road. The City, however, had never followed through with the appropriate legal filings. Yet, based on that original intent, the City considered the "vacation" done.

Fig. A. 10
    Emails passed between Richard Landis and Shana Druffner of Burlington Northern and Santa Fe Railroad Company discussing the "vacation" status of Old Camas Highway in connection with approval of a Train Horn Noise Quiet Zone.

From: Druffner, Shana [mailto:Shana.Druffner@BNSF.com]
Sent: Tuesday, January 25, 2005 11:07 AM
To: Landis, Richard
Cc: 'Gene Biddle'
Subject: FW: Application/Agreement covering the use of an existing Private crossing in Vancouver, WA (tracking #: 04-27550)

Richard:

This is the latest from Kathy Marshack. She is still claiming the road is a public road and will not agree to signing a crossing agreement.

As you can see, she claims the road has not been vacated. Please advise as to the City's position on this point.

I would really like to get this resolved and feel that the Railroad has been very accommodating towards Mrs. Marshack and her use of the crossing.

Thanks,

Shana Druffner

-----Original Message-----
From: Kathy J. Marshack, Ph.D. [mailto:kmarshack@kmarshack.com]
Sent: Tuesday, January 18, 2005 9:21 AM
To: 'Druffner, Shana'
Cc: 'Dan Lorenz'; P. S. Michael J. Wynne; 'Jennifer Redd-Sanderford'
Subject: RE: Application/Agreement covering the use of an existing Private crossing in Vancouver, WA (tracking #: 04-27550)

Shana,

The City cannot decide this is a private road. It was never legally vacated. They have no proof whatsoever that the road was vacated. In fact, I have proof that it was not vacated and that it was left for public use to the river. It is time to have the attorneys meet again to settle this problem. I have informed my attorneys to contact you.

2

Marshack - Box 1238 - 001525

APPENDIX

Furthermore, the City's claim that emergency vehicles cannot make it over the road is not true. I called the Fire Marshal and he told me there was plenty of room to get across and they have in the past. So indeed the crossing could be upgraded to public and continued as a through way for our homes and for the public to the river.

It is not my responsibility to pay for the repairs to a public road.

Thank you,

Kathy

-----Original Message-----
From: Druffner, Shana [mailto:Shana.Druffner@BNSF.com]
Sent: Tuesday, January 18, 2005 6:42 AM
To: 'Kathy J. Marshack, Ph.D.'
Cc: 'gene_biddle@staubach.com'; Roy, Robert A; Cowles, Mike; Mills, Steven A
Subject: RE: Application/Agreement covering the use of an existing Private crossing in Vancouver, WA (tracking #: 04-27550)

Kathy:

The City has declined in writing to make this a public road. As such, the roadway will continue to be private. The crossing will not need to be widened per the City's latest letter. However, routine maintenance (to the extent any is necessary) will be need to be borne by you and the other users.

If you or your attorneys would like to discuss further, I can be available early next week. Otherwise, I believe Gene has forwarded the agreement to you.

Thanks,

Shana

-----Original Message-----
From: Kathy J. Marshack, Ph.D. [mailto:kmarshack@kmarshack.com]
Sent: Monday, January 17, 2005 6:40 PM
To: 'Gene Biddle'
Cc: 'Druffner, Shana'; P. S. Michael J. Wynne; Dan Lorenz; 'Jennifer Redd-Sanderford'
Subject: RE: Application/Agreement covering the use of an existing Private crossing in Vancouver, WA (tracking #: 04-27550)

Hi Gene,

I guess I still do not understand why I alone am responsible for the wear and tear to the crossing when 13 home owners use this crossing. Furthermore, my deed indicates that the railroad is responsible to build

3

Marshack - Box 1238 - 001526

and maintain the crossing in perpetuity. Finally, the agreement on the conference call we had in September is that the City of Vancouver and BNSF would share jointly in the expense of upgrading the crossing to a public crossing. This was agreed to by the City Attorney, and Shana Druffner. So it just makes no sense to me that this clause is still in the agreement. Please ask Shana to contact my attorneys. I have emailed her and my attorneys are trying to reach her as well.

Thank you,

Kathy Marshack

-----Original Message-----
From: Gene Biddle [mailto:Gene.Biddle@Staubach.com]
Sent: Monday, January 17, 2005 1:02 PM
To: Kathy J. Marshack, Ph.D.
Cc: Druffner, Shana; P. S. Michael J. Wynne; Jennifer Redd; Dan Lorenz; Zachary Stoumbos
Subject: RE: Application/Agreement covering the use of an existing Private crossing in Vancouver, WA (tracking #: 04-27550)

Hello Kathy - You as a user are responsible for the costs of maintaining the crossing as well as the approaches since you as a user as well as your invitee's create the wear and tear to the crossing surface by driving over it (train rides on the track not the crossing surface).

What has been revised under paragraph 3 section (b) "Licensee acknowledges that the City of Vancouver has determined that the Crossing is a private crossing. Further, the City has advised Licensee that the roadway and Crossing serving Licensee's residence may not be sufficient to accommodate the passage of some emergency vehicles. Licensee further acknowledges and agrees that Licensee's use of the Crossing is at her own risk and subject to terms of this Agreement, including without limitation Section 21." The Exhibit "C" stipulations have been removed and no longer apply.

Please let me know if you have any questions.

Thanks,

Gene

-----Original Message-----
From: Kathy J. Marshack, Ph.D. [mailto:kmarshack@kmarshack.com]
Sent: Monday, January 17, 2005 2:39 PM
To: Gene Biddle
Cc: 'Druffner, Shana'; P. S. Michael J. Wynne; Jennifer Redd; Dan Lorenz; Zachary Stoumbos

4

Marshack - Box 1238 - 001527

APPENDIX

Fig. A. 11

Emails passed between Richard Landis and Shana Druffner of Burlington Northern and Santa Fe This is a sampling of the more than 60 pages of correspondence about the author's property that passed between Transportation Services' Pat Owen and Richard Landis of Code Enforcement, then to others, beginning in September 2004. Many pages have sections that were redacted before being released in conjunction with a public records request(s) by the author's attorneys. These 20 pages confirm the author's easement rights and include her Deed of Trust, Property Description (with clarification of the easements), Chicago Title report, and Clark County GIS map for both of her lots. The remaining pages of correspondence (not shown here) document similar information for the author's neighboring property owners, Mary Kellogg and Joseph and Julianne Leas, as well as several additional river access road easement holders. Landis chose to ignore all of these legal land use details, instead fostering—and spreading—the disinformation that Marshack had no easement rights.

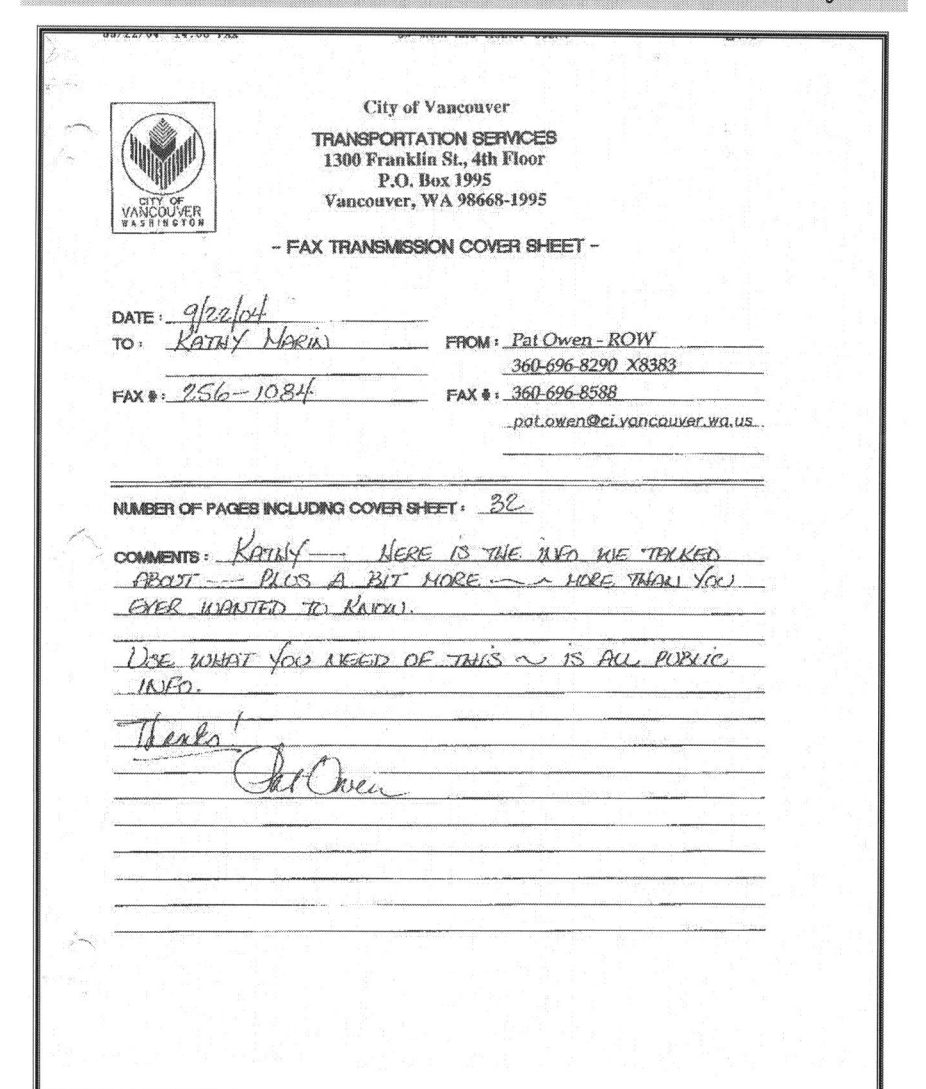

City of Vancouver
TRANSPORTATION SERVICES
1300 Franklin St., 4th Floor
P.O. Box 1995
Vancouver, WA 98668-1995

— FAX TRANSMISSION COVER SHEET —

DATE: 9/22/04
TO: Kathy Marin
FAX #: 256-1084

FROM: Pat Owen - ROW
360-696-8290 X8383
FAX #: 360-696-8588
pat.owen@ci.vancouver.wa.us

NUMBER OF PAGES INCLUDING COVER SHEET: 32

COMMENTS: Kathy— Here is the info we talked about — plus a bit more. — More than you ever wanted to know.

Use what you need of this ~ is all public info.

Thanks!
Pat Owen

Owen, Pat

From: Owen, Pat
Sent: Wednesday, September 01, 2004 2:10 PM
To: Landis, Richard
Cc: Chumbley, Traci
Subject: "144th Court" south of Evergreen Hwy

Tracking:

Recipient	Delivery
Landis, Richard	Delivered: 9/1/2004 2:10 PM
Chumbley, Traci	Delivered: 9/1/2004 2:10 PM

See exhibit of site below.

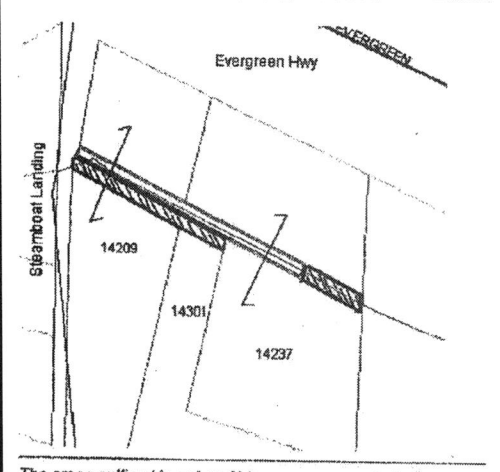

The areas outlined in red and blue are easements for ingress and egress, (private roads).

The deed for 14237 SE Evergreen Hwy, owner Kathy Marshak, contains a paragraph stating:
"TOGETHER WITH an easement for ingress and egress over and across a strip of land 30 feet in width, as said roadway now exists, leading from subject property to the "Steamboat Landing" as well as leading over and across that tract of land described as the "Old Camas Highway".

Hoping this answers the question of status of this property. Let me know if there are additional questions.
Thanks, Pat

Patricia (Pat) Owen
Right of Way Services/Records
City of Vancouver
Transportation Services
1300 Franklin - PO Box 1995

9/22/2004

APPENDIX

Vancouver, WA 98668-1995
360-696-8290 ext 8363
fax 360-696-8508
pat.owen@ci.vancouver.wa.us

MapsOnline

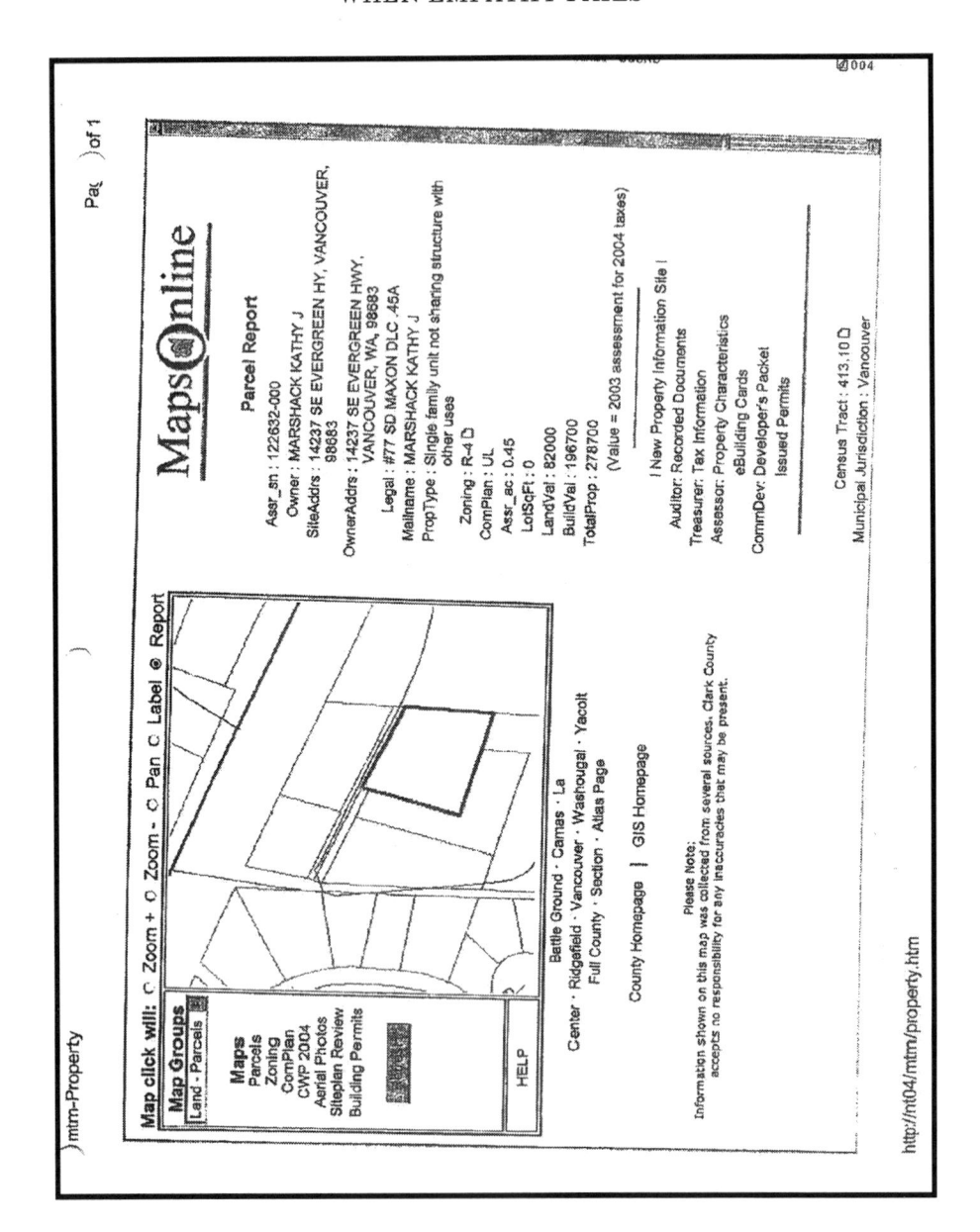

Parcel Report

- Assr_sn : 122632-000
- Owner : MARSHACK KATHY J
- SiteAddrs : 14237 SE EVERGREEN HY, VANCOUVER, 98683
- OwnerAddrs : 14237 SE EVERGREEN HWY, VANCOUVER, WA, 98683
- MailName : MARSHACK KATHY J
- Legal : #77 SD MAXON DLC .45A
- PropType : Single family unit not sharing structure with other uses
- Zoning : R-4
- ComPlan : UL
- Assr_ac : 0.45
- LotSqFt : 0
- LandVal : 82000
- BuildVal : 196700
- TotalProp : 278700

(Value = 2003 assessment for 2004 taxes)

- New Property Information Site
- Auditor: Recorded Documents
- Treasurer: Tax Information
- Assessor: Property Characteristics
- eBuilding Cards
- CommDev: Developer's Packet
- Issued Permits

Census Tract: 413.10
Municipal Jurisdiction: Vancouver

Center · Ridgefield · Vancouver · Washougal · Yacolt
Battle Ground · Camas · La
Full County · Section · Atlas Page

County Homepage | GIS Homepage

Please Note:
Information shown on this map was collected from several sources. Clark County accepts no responsibility for any inaccuracies that may be present.

Map click will: Zoom + / Zoom − / Pan / Label / Report

Map Groups Land · Parcels

Maps
Parcels
Zoning
ComPlan
CWP 2004
Aerial Photos
Siteplan Review
Building Permits

HELP

APPENDIX

Document ᴼᴬ Page 1 of 1

3106437
Page: 1 of 5
05/17/1999 10:15A
Clark County, WA
CHICAGO TITLE INSURANCE CO DT   19.00

Return Address:
Citicorp Mortgage, Inc.
P.O. Box 790021 MS-321
St. Louis, MO 63179-0021
ATTN: Document Collections

DEED OF TRUST

Reference # (if applicable): 8095062380
Grantor/Borrower:
 HOWARD H MARSHACK
 KATHY J MARSHACK
Grantee/Assignee/Beneficiary:
 CITICORP MORTGAGE, INC. , Beneficiary
 CHICAGO TITLE , Trustee
Legal Description (abbreviated): S2 T1N R2E
Assessor's Tax Parcel ID#: 122632-000 v 172633 000

K1104726P

(25 00) 2-1-2

(Space Above This Line For Recording Data)

THIS DEED OF TRUST ("Security Instrument") is made on MAY 11, 1999.
The grantor is HOWARD H MARSHACK AND KATHY J MARSHACK, Husband and Wife
("Borrower"). The Trustee is
CHICAGO TITLE
("Trustee"). The beneficiary is
CITICORP MORTGAGE, INC. , which is organized and existing
under the laws of THE STATE OF DELAWARE , and whose address is
15851 CLAYTON ROAD, ST. LOUIS, MISSOURI 63011 ("Lender").
Borrower owes Lender the principal sum of Two Hundred Forty Thousand and 00/100
Dollars (U.S. $ 240,000.00). This debt is evidenced by Borrower's note dated the same date as this Security Instrument
("Note"), which provides for monthly payments, with the full debt, if not paid earlier, due and payable on JUNE 1, 2029.
This Security Instrument secures to Lender: (a) the repayment of the debt evidenced by the Note, with interest, and all
renewals, extensions and modifications of the Note; (b) the payment of all other sums, with interest, advanced under
paragraph 7 to protect the security of this Security Instrument; and (c) the performance of Borrower's covenants and agreements under this Security Instrument and the Note. For this purpose, Borrower irrevocably grants and conveys to the Trustee,
in trust, with the power of sale, the following described property located in CLARK County, Washington:

which has the address of 14237 SE EVERGREEN HWY , VANCOUVER

http://mt04/auditor/index.cfm?fuseaction=displaydetail&recno=3106437&excise=

Document

Page 1 of 1

3106437
Page: 2 of 5
05/17/1998 10:51A
CHICAGO TITLE INSURANCE CO OT 12.00 Clark County, WA

Loan No. 9090082990

If the Funds held by Lender exceed the amounts permitted to be held by applicable law, Lender shall account to Borrower for the excess Funds in accordance with the requirements of applicable law. If the amount of the Funds held by Lender at any time is not sufficient to pay the Escrow Items when due, Lender may so notify Borrower in writing, and, in such case Borrower shall pay to Lender the amount necessary to make up the deficiency. Borrower shall make up the deficiency in no more than twelve monthly payments, at Lender's sole discretion.

Upon payment in full of all sums secured by this Security Instrument, Lender shall promptly refund to Borrower any Funds held by Lender. If, under paragraph 21, Lender shall acquire or sell the Property, Lender, prior to the acquisition or sale of the Property, shall apply any Funds held by Lender at the time of acquisition or sale as a credit against the sums secured by this Security Instrument.

3. **Application of Payments.** Unless applicable law provides otherwise, all payments received by Lender under paragraphs 1 and 2 shall be applied: first, to any prepayment charges due under the Note; second, to amounts payable under paragraph 2; third, to interest due; fourth, to principal due; and last, to any late charges due under the Note.

4. **Charges; Liens.** Borrower shall pay all taxes, assessments, charges, fines and impositions attributable to the Property which may attain priority over this Security Instrument, and leasehold payments or ground rents, if any. Borrower shall pay these obligations in the manner provided in paragraph 2, or if not paid in that manner, Borrower shall pay them on time directly to the person owed payment. Borrower shall promptly furnish to Lender all notices of amounts to be paid under this paragraph. If Borrower makes these payments directly, Borrower shall promptly furnish to Lender receipts evidencing the payments.

Borrower shall promptly discharge any lien which has priority over this Security Instrument unless Borrower: (a) agrees in writing to the payment of the obligation secured by the lien in a manner acceptable to Lender; (b) contests in good faith the lien by, or defends against enforcement of the lien in, legal proceedings which in the Lender's opinion operate to prevent the enforcement of the lien; or (c) secures from the holder of the lien an agreement satisfactory to Lender subordinating the lien to this Security Instrument. If Lender determines that any part of the Property is subject to a lien which may attain priority over this Security Instrument, Lender may give Borrower a notice identifying the lien. Borrower shall satisfy the lien or take one or more of the actions set forth above within 10 days of the giving of notice.

5. **Hazard or Property Insurance.** Borrower shall keep the improvements now existing or hereafter erected on the Property insured against loss by fire, hazards included within the term "extended coverage" and any other hazards, including floods or flooding, for which Lender requires insurance. This insurance shall be maintained in the amounts and for the periods that Lender requires. The insurance carrier providing the insurance shall be chosen by Borrower subject to Lender's approval which shall not be unreasonably withheld. If Borrower fails to maintain coverage described above, Lender may, at Lender's option, obtain coverage to protect Lender's rights in the Property in accordance with paragraph 7.

All insurance policies and renewals shall be acceptable to Lender and shall include a standard mortgage clause. Lender shall have the right to hold the policies and renewals. If Lender requires, Borrower shall promptly give to Lender all receipts of paid premiums and renewal notices. In the event of loss, Borrower shall give prompt notice to the insurance carrier and Lender. Lender may make proof of loss if not made promptly by Borrower.

Unless Lender and Borrower otherwise agree in writing, insurance proceeds shall be applied to restoration or repair of the Property damaged, if the restoration or repair is economically feasible and Lender's security is not lessened. If the restoration or repair is not economically feasible or Lender's security would be lessened, the insurance proceeds shall be applied to the sums secured by this Security Instrument, whether or not then due, with any excess paid to Borrower. If Borrower abandons the Property, or does not answer within 30 days a notice from Lender that the insurance carrier has offered to settle a claim, then Lender may collect the insurance proceeds. Lender may use the proceeds to repair or restore the Property or to pay sums secured by this Security Instrument, whether or not then due. The 30-day period will begin when the notice is given.

Unless Lender and Borrower otherwise agree in writing, any application of proceeds to principal shall not extend or postpone the due date of the monthly payments referred to in paragraphs 1 and 2 or change the amount of the payments. If under paragraph 21 the Property is acquired by Lender, Borrower's right to any insurance policies and proceeds resulting from damage to the Property prior to the acquisition shall pass to Lender to the extent of the sums secured by this Security Instrument immediately prior to the acquisition.

6. **Occupancy, Preservation, Maintenance and Protection of the Property; Borrower's Loan Application; Leaseholds.** Borrower shall occupy, establish, and use the Property as Borrower's principal residence within sixty days after the execution of this Security Instrument and shall continue to occupy the Property as Borrower's principal residence for at least one year after the date of occupancy, unless Lender otherwise agrees in writing, which consent shall not be unreasonably withheld, or unless extenuating circumstances exist which are beyond Borrower's control. Borrower shall not destroy, damage or impair the Property, allow the Property to deteriorate, or commit waste on the Property. Borrower shall be in default if any forfeiture action or proceeding, whether civil or criminal, is begun that in Lender's good faith judgment could result in forfeiture of the Property or otherwise materially impair the lien created by this Security Instrument or Lender's security interest. Borrower may cure such a default and reinstate, as provided in paragraph 18, by causing the action or proceeding to be dismissed with a ruling that, in Lender's good faith determination, precludes forfeiture of the Borrower's interest in the Property or other material impairment of the lien created by this Security Instrument or Lender's security interest. Borrower shall also be in default if Borrower, during the loan application process, gave materially false or inaccurate information or statements to Lender (or failed to provide Lender with any material information) in connection with the loan evidenced by the Note, including, but not limited to, representations concerning Borrower's occupancy of the Property as a principal residence. If this Security Instrument is on a leasehold, Borrower shall comply with all the provisions of the lease. If Borrower acquires fee title to the Property, the leasehold and the fee title shall not merge unless Lender agrees to the merger in writing.

http://nt04/auditor/index.cfm?fuseaction=displaydetail&recno=3106437&excise=

APPENDIX

APPENDIX

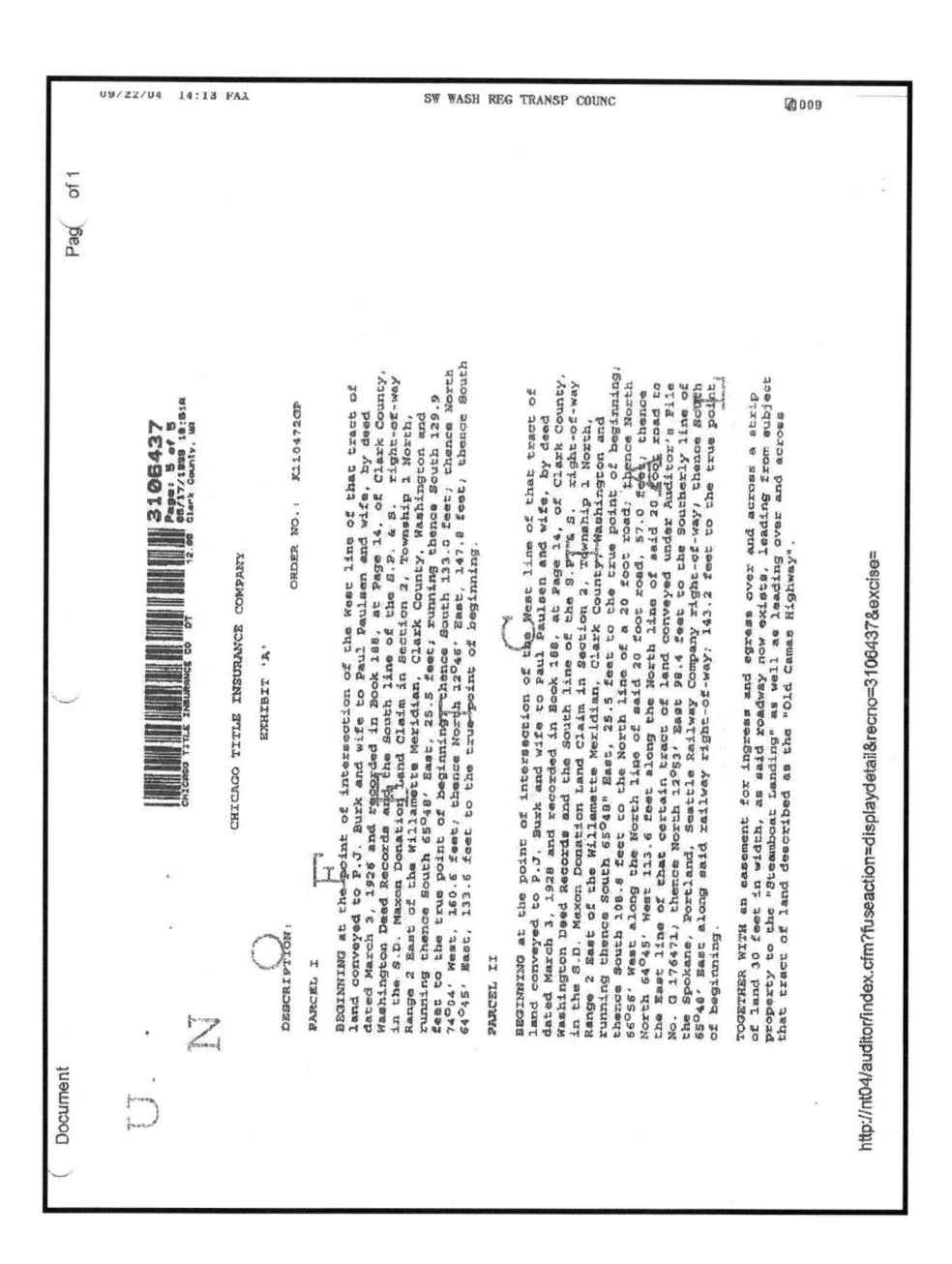

CHICAGO TITLE INSURANCE COMPANY

EXHIBIT 'A'

ORDER NO.: K104720P

DESCRIPTION:

PARCEL I

BEGINNING at the point of intersection of the West line of that tract of land conveyed to P.J. Burk and wife to Paul Paulsen and wife, by deed dated March 3, 1926 and recorded in Book 188, at Page 14, of Clark County, Washington Deed Records and the South line of the S.P. & S. right-of-way in the S.D. Maxon Donation Land Claim in Section 2, Township 1 North, Range 2 East of the Willamette Meridian, Clark County, Washington and running thence South 65°48' East, 25.5 feet; running thence South 129.9 feet to the true point of beginning; thence South 133.0 feet; thence North 74°04' West, 160.6 feet; thence North 12°46' East, 147.8 feet; thence South 64°45' East, 133.6 feet to the true point of beginning.

PARCEL II

BEGINNING at the point of intersection of the West line of that tract of land conveyed to P.J. Burk and wife to Paul Paulsen and wife, by deed dated March 3, 1928 and recorded in Book 188, at Page 14, of Clark County, Washington Deed Records and the South line of the S.P. & S. right-of-way in the S.D. Maxon Donation Land Claim in Section 2, Township 1 North, Range 2 East of the Willamette Meridian, Clark County, Washington and running thence South 65°48' East, 25.5 feet to the true point of beginning; thence South 108.8 feet to the North line of a 20 foot road; thence North 56°56' West along the North line of said 20 foot road, 57.0 feet; thence North 64°45' West 113.6 feet along the North line of said 20 foot road to the East line of that certain tract of land conveyed under Auditor's File No. G 176471, thence North 12°53' East 98.4 feet to the Southerly line of the Spokane, Portland, Seattle Railway Company right-of-way; thence South 65°48' East along said railway right-of-way, 143.2 feet to the true point of beginning.

TOGETHER WITH an easement for ingress and egress over and across a strip of land 30 feet in width, as said roadway now exists, leading from subject property to the "Steamboat Landing" as well as leading over and across that tract of land described as the "Old Camas Highway".

493

WHEN EMPATHY FAILS

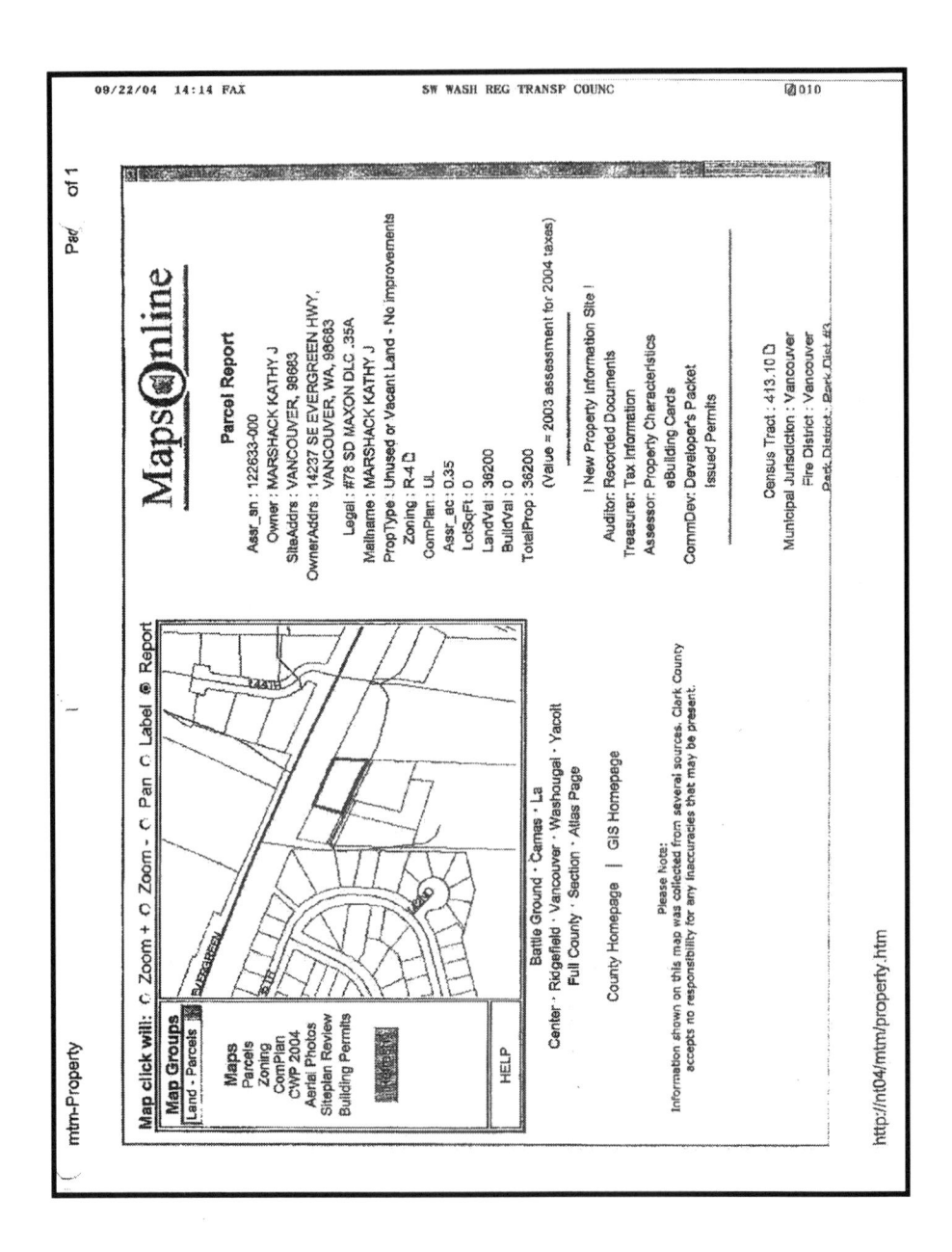

Parcel Report

Assr_sn : 122633-000
Owner : MARSHACK KATHY J
SiteAddrs : 14237 SE EVERGREEN HWY, VANCOUVER, WA, 98683
OwnerAddrs : 14237 SE EVERGREEN HWY, VANCOUVER, WA, 98683
Legal : #78 SD MAXON DLC .35A
Mailname : MARSHACK KATHY J
PropType : Unused or Vacant Land - No improvements
Zoning : R-4
ComPlan : UL
Assr_ac : 0.35
LotSqFt : 0
LandVal : 36200
BuildVal : 0
TotalProp : 36200
(Value = 2003 assessment for 2004 taxes)

| New Property Information Site |
Auditor: Recorded Documents
Treasurer: Tax Information
Assessor: Property Characteristics
eBuilding Cards
CommDev: Developer's Packet
Issued Permits

Census Tract : 413.10
Municipal Jurisdiction : Vancouver
Fire District : Vancouver

APPENDIX

09/22/04 14:14 FAX   SW WASH REG TRANSP COUNC   ☒011
Document   Page 1 of 1

2A

N

Return Address:
Citicorp Mortgage, Inc.
P. O. Box 790021 MS-321
St. Louis, MO 63179-0021
ATTN: Document Collections

310

DEED OF TRUST

Reference # (if applicable):   Additional on page __
9090082990
Grantor/Borrower: Additional on page __
HOWARD H MARSHACK
KATHY J MARSHACK
Grantee/Assignee/Beneficiary: Additional on page __
CITICORP MORTGAGE, INC.   , Beneficiary
CHICAGO TITLE   , Trustee
Legal Description (abbreviated):   Additional on page __
. OLD EVERGREEN HWY   S2 T1N R2E
Assessor's Tax Parcel ID#:   (25)(87) 2-1-2-
122632-000 × 122633-000   (Space Above This Line For Recording Data)
K1104726P

THIS DEED OF TRUST ("Security Instrument") is made on MAY 11, 1999
The grantor is HOWARD H MARSHACK AND KATHY J MARSHACK   Husband and Wife
                                                              ("Borrower"). The Truste
CHICAGO TITLE   ("Trustee"). The benefici
CITICORP MORTGAGE, INC.   which is organized and ex
under the laws of THE STATE OF DELAWARE   , and whose addre
15851 CLAYTON ROAD, ST. LOUIS, MISSOURI 63011   ("Lend
Borrower owes Lender the principal sum of Two Hundred Forty Thousand and 00/100
Dollars (U.S. $ 240,000.00). This debt is evidenced by Borrower's note dated the same date as this Security Instru
("Note"), which provides for monthly payments, with the full debt, if not paid earlier, due and payable on JUNE 1, 2029
This Security Instrument secures to Lender: (a) the repayment of the debt evidenced by the Note, with interest, an
renewals, extensions and modifications of the Note; (b) the payment of all other sums, with interest, advanced u
paragraph 7 to protect the security of this Security Instrument; and (c) the performance of Borrower's covenants and ag
ments under this Security Instrument and the Note. For this purpose, Borrower irrevocably grants and conveys to the Trus
in trust, with the power of sale, the following described property located in CLARK   County, Washing

which has the address of 14237 SE EVERGREEN HWY   VANCOUVER
                                    [Street]   (City)
Washington   98663-   , ("Property Address");
              [Zip Code]

TOGETHER WITH all the improvements now or hereafter erected on the property, and all easements, appurtenan
and fixtures now or hereafter a part of the property. All replacements and additions shall also be covered by this Sec
Instrument. All of the foregoing is referred to in this Security Instrument as the "Property."
BORROWER COVENANTS that Borrower is lawfully seised of the estate hereby conveyed and has the right to grant
convey the Property and that the Property is unencumbered, except for encumbrances of record. Borrower warrants and
defend generally the title to the Property against all claims and demands, subject to any encumbrances of record.
UNIFORM COVENANTS. Borrower and Lender covenant and agree as follows:
1. Payment of Principal and Interest; Prepayment and Late Charges. Borrower shall promptly pay when
the principal of and interest on the debt evidenced by the Note and any prepayment and late charges due under the Note.
2. Funds for Taxes and Insurance. Subject to applicable law or to a written waiver by Lender, Borrower shall
to Lender on the day monthly payments are due under the Note, until the Note is paid in full, a sum ("Funds") for: (a) ye
taxes and assessments which may attain priority over this Security Instrument as a lien on the Property; (b) yearly leasel
payments or ground rents on the Property, if any; (c) yearly hazard or property insurance premiums; (d) yearly flood insura
premiums, if any; (e) yearly mortgage insurance premiums, if any; and (f) any sums payable by Borrower to Lender, in
cordance with the provisions of paragraph 8, in lieu of the payment of mortgage insurance premiums. These items are ca
"Escrow Items." Lender may, at any time, collect and hold Funds in an amount not to exceed the maximum amount a le
for a federally related mortgage loan may require for Borrower's escrow account under the federal Real Estate Settlen
Procedures Act of 1974 as amended from time to time, 12 U.S.C. SS 2601 et seq. ("RESPA"), unless another law that app
to the Funds sets a lesser amount. If so, Lender may, at any time, collect and hold Funds in an amount not to exceed
lesser amount. Lender may estimate the amount of Funds due on the basis of current data and reasonable estimates of
penditures of future Escrow Items or otherwise in accordance with applicable law.
The Funds shall be held in an institution whose deposits are insured by a federal agency, instrumentality, or a

http://nt04/auditor/index.cfm?fuseaction=displaydetail&recno=3106437&excise=

09/22/04 14:15 FAX SW WASH REG TRANSP COUNC 012

Document Page 1 of 1

3106437
Page: 2 of 5
05/17/1998 10:
CHICAGO TITLE INSURANCE CO DT 12.00 Clark County, WA

Loan No. 9090082890

If the Funds held by Lender exceed the amounts permitted to be held by applicable law, Lender shall accou
Borrower for the excess Funds in accordance with the requirements of applicable law. If the amount of the Funds he
Lender at any time is not sufficient to pay the Escrow Items when due, Lender may so notify Borrower in writing, and, in
case Borrower shall pay to Lender the amount necessary to make up the deficiency. Borrower shall make up the deficien
no more than twelve monthly payments, at Lender's sole discretion.

Upon payment in full of all sums secured by this Security Instrument, Lender shall promptly refund to Borrowe
Funds held by Lender. If, under paragraph 21, Lender shall acquire or sell the Property, Lender, prior to the acquisition or
of the Property, shall apply any Funds held by Lender at the time of acquisition or sale as a credit against the sums secure
this Security Instrument.

3. Application of Payments. Unless applicable law provides otherwise, all payments received by Lender u
paragraphs 1 and 2 shall be applied: first, to any prepayment charges due under the Note; second, to amounts payable u
paragraph 2; third, to interest due; fourth, to principal due; and last, to any late charges due under the Note.

4. Charges; Liens. Borrower shall pay all taxes, assessments, charges, fines and impositions attributable t
Property which may attain priority over this Security Instrument, and leasehold payments or ground rents, if any. Bor
shall pay these obligations in the manner provided in paragraph 2, or if not paid in that manner, Borrower shall pay ther
time directly to the person owed payment. Borrower shall promptly furnish to Lender all notices of amounts to be paid u
this paragraph. If Borrower makes these payments directly, Borrower shall promptly furnish to Lender receipts evidencing
payments. Borrower shall promptly discharge any lien which has priority over this Security Instrument unless Borrower: (a) ag
in writing to the payment of the obligation secured by the lien in a manner acceptable to Lender; (b) contests in good fait
lien by, or defends against enforcement of the lien in, legal proceedings which in the Lender's opinion operate to preven
enforcement of the lien; or (c) secures from the holder of the lien an agreement satisfactory to Lender subordinating the li
this Security Instrument. If Lender determines that any part of the Property is subject to a lien which may attain priority
this Security Instrument, Lender may give Borrower a notice identifying the lien. Borrower shall satisfy the lien or take o
more of the actions set forth above within 10 days of the giving of notice.

5. Hazard or Property Insurance. Borrower shall keep the improvements now existing or hereafter erected or
Property insured against loss by fire, hazards included within the term "extended coverage" and any other hazards, inclu
floods or flooding, for which Lender requires insurance. This insurance shall be maintained in the amounts and for the per
that Lender requires. The insurance carrier providing the insurance shall be chosen by Borrower subject to Lender's app
which shall not be unreasonably withheld. If Borrower fails to maintain coverage described above, Lender may, at Len
option, obtain coverage to protect Lender's rights in the Property in accordance with paragraph 7.

All insurance policies and renewals shall be acceptable to Lender and shall include a standard mortgage cla
Lender shall have the right to hold the policies and renewals. If Lender requires, Borrower shall promptly give to Lend
receipts of paid premiums and renewal notices. In the event of loss, Borrower shall give prompt notice to the insurance ca
and Lender. Lender may make proof of loss if not made promptly by Borrower.

Unless Lender and Borrower otherwise agree in writing, insurance proceeds shall be applied to restoration or rep
the Property damaged, if "the restoration or repair is economically feasible and Lender's security is not lessened. If the
toration or repair is not economically feasible or Lender's security would be lessened, the insurance proceeds shall be ap
to the sums secured by this Security Instrument, whether or not then due, with any excess paid to Borrower. If Borr
abandons the Property, or does not answer within 30 days a notice from Lender that the insurance carrier has offered to s
a claim, then Lender may collect the insurance proceeds. Lender may use the proceeds to repair or restore the Property
pay sums secured by this Security Instrument, whether or not then due. The 30-day period will begin when the notic
given.

Unless Lender and Borrower otherwise agree in writing, any application of proceeds to principal shall not exten
postpone the due date of the monthly payments referred to in paragraphs 1 and 2 or change the amount of the payment
under paragraph 21 the Property is acquired by Lender, Borrower's right to any insurance policies and proceeds resulting f
damage to the Property prior to the acquisition shall pass to Lender to the extent of the sums secured by this Sec
Instrument immediately prior to the acquisition.

**6. Occupancy, Preservation, Maintenance and Protection of the Property; Borrower's Loan Applicat
Leaseholds.** Borrower shall occupy, establish, and use the Property as Borrower's principal residence within sixty days
the execution of this Security Instrument and shall continue to occupy the Property as Borrower's principal residence fo
least one year after the date of occupancy, unless Lender otherwise agrees in writing, which consent shall not be unreasor
ly withheld, or unless extenuating circumstances exist which are beyond Borrower's control. Borrower shall not dest
damage or impair the Property, allow the Property to deteriorate, or commit waste on the Property. Borrower shall b
default if any forfeiture action or proceeding, whether civil or criminal, is begun that in Lender's good faith judgment co
result in forfeiture of the Property or otherwise materially impair the lien created by this Security Instrument or Lender's secu
interest. Borrower may cure such a default and reinstate, as provided in paragraph 18, by causing the action or proceedin
be dismissed with a ruling that, in Lender's good faith determination, precludes forfeiture of the Borrower's interest in
Property or other material impairment of the lien created by this Security Instrument or Lender's security interest. Borro
shall also be in default if Borrower, during the loan application process, gave materially false or inaccurate informatio
statements to Lender (or failed to provide Lender with any material information) in connection with the loan evidenced by
Note, including, but not limited to, representations concerning Borrower's occupancy of the Property as a principal reside
If this Security Instrument is on a leasehold, Borrower shall comply with all the provisions of the lease. If Borrower acquires
title to the Property, the leasehold and the fee title shall not merge unless Lender agrees to the merger in writing.

7. Protection of Lender's Rights in the Property. If Borrower fails to perform the covenants and agreements c
tained in this Security Instrument, or there is a legal proceeding that may significantly affect Lender's rights in the Prop
(such as a proceeding in bankruptcy, probate, for condemnation or forfeiture or to enforce laws or regulations), then Len
may do and pay for whatever is necessary to protect the value of the Property and Lender's rights in the Property. Lend
actions may include paying any sums secured by a lien which has priority over this Security Instrument, appearing in co
paying reasonable attorneys' fees and entering on the Property to make repairs. Although Lender may take action under
paragraph 7, Lender does not have to do so.

Any amounts disbursed by Lender under this paragraph 7 shall become additional debt of Borrower secured by
Security Instrument. Unless Borrower and Lender agree to other terms of payment, these amounts shall bear interest from
date of disbursement at the Note rate and shall be payable, with interest, upon notice from Lender to Borrower reques
payment.

8. Mortgage Insurance. If Lender required mortgage insurance as a condition of making the loan secured by
Security Instrument, Borrower shall pay the premiums required to maintain the mortgage insurance in effect. If, for any reas
the mortgage insurance coverage required by Lender lapses or ceases to be in effect, Borrower shall pay the premi
required to obtain coverage substantially equivalent to the mortgage insurance previously in effect, at a cost substant
equivalent to the cost to Borrower of the mortgage insurance previously in effect, from an alternate mortgage insurer appro
by Lender. If substantially equivalent mortgage insurance coverage is not available, Borrower shall pay to Lender each mo
a sum equal to one-twelfth of the yearly mortgage insurance premium being paid by Borrower when the insurance cover
lapsed or ceased to be in effect. Lender will accept, use and retain these payments as a loss reserve in lieu of mortg
insurance. Loss reserve payments may no longer be required, at the option of Lender, if mortgage insurance coverage (in
amount and for the period that Lender requires) provided by an insurer approved by Lender again becomes available an
obtained. Borrower shall pay the premiums required to maintain mortgage insurance in effect, or to provide a loss rese
until the requirement for mortgage insurance ends in accordance with any written agreement between Borrower and Lende
applicable law.

9. Inspection. Lender or its agent may make reasonable entries upon and inspections of the Property. Lender s
give Borrower notice at the time of or prior to an inspection specifying reasonable cause for the inspection.

10. Condemnation. The proceeds of any award or claim for damages, direct or consequential, in connection v

http://nt04/auditor/index.cfm?fuseaction=displaydetail&recno=3106437&excise=

APPENDIX

```
09/22/04  14:18 FAX              SW WASH REG TRANSP COUNC                    ☑014
Document                                                                Page 1 of 1
```

Loan No. 9090082990

Trustee shall deliver to the purchaser Trustee's deed conveying the Property without any covena_ expressed or implied. The recitals in the Trustee's deed shall be prima facie evidence of the truth of the s_ therein. Trustee shall apply the proceeds of the sale in the following order: (a) to all expenses of the sal_ not limited to, reasonable Trustee's and attorney's fees; (b) to all sums secured by this Security Instrum_ excess to the person or persons legally entitled to it.

22. **Reconveyance.** Upon payment of all sums secured by this Security Instrument, Lender shall requ_ reconvey the Property and shall surrender this Security Instrument and all notes evidencing debt secured _ Instrument to Trustee. Trustee shall reconvey the Property without warranty and without charge to the per_ legally entitled to it. Such person or persons shall pay any recordation costs.

23. **Substitute Trustee.** In accordance with applicable law, Lender may from time to time appoint a successo_ Trustee appointed hereunder who has ceased to act. Without conveyance of the Property, the successo_ succeed to all the title, power, and duties conferred upon Trustee herein and by applicable law.

24. **Use of Property.** The Property is not used principally for agricultural or farming purposes.

25. **Riders to this Security Instrument.** If one or more riders are executed by Borrower and recorded tog_ Security Instrument, the covenants and agreements of each such rider shall be incorporated into and sh_ supplement the covenants and agreements of this Security Instrument as if the rider(s) were a part o_ Instrument.
[Check applicable box(es)]

☐ Adjustable Rate Rider   ☐ Condominium Rider   ☐ 1-4 Family Rider
☐ Graduated Payment Rider   ☐ Planned Unit Development Rider ☐ Biweekly Payment
☐ Balloon Rider   ☐ Rate Improvement Rider   ☐ Second Home Ride
☐ Other(s) [specify]

BY SIGNING BELOW, Borrower accepts and agrees to the terms and covenants contained i_ Instrument and in any rider(s) executed by Borrower and recorded with it.

Witness:

HOWARD H MARSHACK

KATHY J MARSHACK

[Space Below This Line For Acknowledgment]

STATE OF WASHINGTON
County of Clark } SS:

I hereby certify that I know or have satisfactory evidence that
HOWARD H MARSHACK AND KATHY J MARSHACK
signed this instrument and acknowledged it to be the free and voluntary act for the uses and purposes mentione_ Instrument.
Dated:

My Appointment expires

Notary Public in and for the State of Washington, re_ Vancouver
REQUEST FOR RECONVEYANCE

TO TRUSTEE:

http://nt04/auditor/index.cfm?fuseaction=displaydetail&recno=3106437&excise=

APPENDIX

CHICAGO TITLE INSURANCE COMPANY

EXHIBIT 'A'

DESCRIPTION: ORDER NO.: K11047

PARCEL I

BEGINNING at the point of intersection of the West line of that tra[ct of] land conveyed to P.J. Burk and wife to Paul Paulsen and wife, by de[ed] dated March 3, 1926 and recorded in Book 188, at Page 14, of Clark [County] Washington Deed Records and the South line of the S.P. & S. right-[of-way] in the S.D. Maxon Donation Land Claim in Section 2, Township 1 Nort[h,] Range 2 East of the Willamette Meridian, Clark County, Washington a[nd] running thence South 65°48' East, 25.5 feet; running thence South 1[?] feet to the true point of beginning; thence South 133.0 feet; thenc[e] 74°04' West, 160.6 feet; thence North 12°46' East, 147.8 feet; then[ce] 64°45' East, 133.6 feet to the true point of beginning.

PARCEL II

BEGINNING at the point of intersection of the West line of that tra[ct of] land conveyed to P.J. Burk and wife to Paul Paulsen and wife, by dee[d] dated March 3, 1926 and recorded in Book 188, at Page 14, of Clark [County] Washington Deed Records and the South line of the S.P. & S. right-[of-way] in the S.D. Maxon Donation Land Claim in Section 2, Township 1 Nort[h,] Range 2 East of the Willamette Meridian, Clark County, Washington a[nd] running thence South 65°48' East, 25.5 feet to the true point of beg[inning;] thence South 108.8 feet to the North line of a 20 foot road; thence [North] 66°56' West along the North line of said 20 foot road, 57.0 feet; th[ence] North 64°45' West 113.6 feet along the North line of said 20 foot ro[ad to] the East line of that certain tract of land conveyed under Auditor'[s File] No. G 176471; thence North 12°53' East 98.4 feet to the Southerly li[ne of] the Spokane, Portland, Seattle Railway Company right-of-way; thence [South] 65°48' East along said railway right-of-way; 143.2 feet to the true [point] of beginning.

TOGETHER WITH an easement for ingress and egress over and across a s[trip] of land 30 feet in width, as said roadway now exists, leading from s[aid] property to the "Steamboat Landing" as well as leading over and acro[ss] that tract of land described as the "Old Camas Highway".

http://nt04/auditor/index.cfm?fuseaction=displaydetail&recno=3106437&excise=

WHEN EMPATHY FAILS

Page 1 of 2

Landis, Richard

From: Owen, Pat
Sent: Monday, September 27, 2004 4:50 PM
To: Landis, Richard; Zeider, Judy; McNamara, Jim
Cc: Chumbley, Traci; Whitcomb, Bill; Rorabaugh, Thayer
Subject: RE: "144th Court" south of Evergreen Hwy
Importance: High

Bill Whitcomb has been a part of the meetings regarding the "Railroad Quiet Zones", and had the following response when asked about the future status of the "private" railroad crossing at the foot of 144th Court, south of Evergreen Hwy.

Pat, I believe that neither the city nor the railroad would support the establishment of another public crossing at this location. In recent talks with the railroad on other matters, they would like the city to consolidate this crossing if possible with the crossing to the east. It would be helpful to know what the status of the easements are etc to know if there is something that could be reasonably be proposed in the future to consolidate this crossing with the one to the east.

In the meantime, I will e-mail Mike Cowles at BNSF to see what records they have for this private crossing.

Bill Whitcomb
bill.whitcomb@ci.vancouver.wa.us

From: Landis, Richard
Sent: Monday, September 27, 2004 3:47 PM
To: Owen, Pat; Zeider, Judy; McNamara, Jim
Cc: Chumbley, Traci
Subject: RE: "144th Court" south of Evergreen Hwy

[handwritten note: Note concern about closing down train crossing.]

From: Owen, Pat
Sent: Monday, September 27, 2004 12:53 PM
To: Zeider, Judy; McNamara, Jim
Cc: Chumbley, Traci; Landis, Richard
Subject: FW: "144th Court" south of Evergreen Hwy
Importance: High

9/28/2004

Marshack - Code - CDE 2004-00204 - 000117
Marshack - Code Enforcement - 000122

APPENDIX

Right of Way Services/Records
Transportation Services
696-8290 x8383
fax 696-8588

From: Landis, Richard
Sent: Thursday, October 14, 2004 10:16 AM
To: Owen, Pat
Subject: RE: "144th Court" south of Evergreen Hwy

Burlington Northern, Steven Mills called at the request of the Railroads attorney for the call. The call is now about what they claim is that they, based on what Lou provided Ms Marshack, are saying the driveway is a public road. That is not what Lou said and he is going to respond to a set of questions I have forwarded to him. Jim McNamara is involved and will be a part of the conference call. It is the City's position at this time that an underlying easement may exist, but it has never been maintained, or improved or accepted by Clark County as a public road thus when we annexed it we accepted it as a private road.

From: Owen, Pat
Sent: Wednesday, October 13, 2004 5:07 PM
To: Landis, Richard
Cc: Whitcomb, Bill
Subject: FW: "144th Court" south of Evergreen Hwy
Importance: High

Richard,

(Bill Whitcomb won't be in the office next Monday the 18th for this 8 am "conference call" that you mentioned today.)

Who did you say made the request for this conference call?

In my last contact with Judy Zeider, she recommended ▒▒▒▒▒▒▒▒▒▒▒▒▒▒▒▒▒▒▒▒▒▒▒▒▒▒▒▒▒▒▒▒▒▒▒▒▒▒ Since this is a private civil dispute - should the City even be involved? What has Jim McNamara said concerning this?

I spoke very quickly with Bill W as he was on his way into another meeting, and it sounds like he has given us about all of the feedback he has on the subject of the RR crossing matter. You might want to call or e-mail Bill if you have additional questions regarding this, and have his explanation ready for whatever transpires on Monday.

Personally, I don't see that we, or I, can add anything to the discussion, as Louie Benedict at the County has the resources we don't have at the City and has been able to find the records that exist concerning the "old County road" in that area that seems to be in dispute now.

I will search and provide whatever info I can, but at this point it may be better to call or e-mail Bill.

Pat Owen
Right of Way Services/Records
Transportation Services
696-8290 x8383
fax 696-8588

From: Owen, Pat
Sent: Monday, September 27, 2004 4:50 PM
To: Landis, Richard; Zeider, Judy; McNamara, Jim
Cc: Chumbley, Traci; Whitcomb, Bill; Rorabaugh, Thayer
Subject: RE: "144th Court" south of Evergreen Hwy
Importance: High

Message: FW: Evergreen/144th/OldCamas

FW: Evergreen/144th/OldCamas
From Owen, Pat Date Tuesday, October 26, 2004 11:11 AM
To   ; Benedict, Louie
Cc
Subject FW: Evergreen/144th/OldCamas

From: Landis, Richard
Sent: Wednesday, October 20, 2004 8:33 AM
To: Owen, Pat
Subject: RE:

The civil suit is going to court next month, the city is not a part to it. Jim McNamara did tell Burlington Northern on Monday that we do not accept Ms. Marshack's contention that the driveway in front of her house is a city road. He did tell them there may be an underlying easement for future development to bring the road up to city standards, but until that would take place at owners expense, the road/driveway is a private road. We also forwarded a copy of the private road agreement signed by the four property owners on the south side of the tracks, which was recorded, to Burlington Northern.

From: Owen, Pat
Sent: Tuesday, October 19, 2004 3:59 PM
To: Landis, Richard
Cc: Whitcomb, Bill
Subject: RE:

Wow! Thanks for the update on this, Richard! Another case of much trouble and mis-understanding that could

Marshack - Emails - 000801

APPENDIX

have possibly been headed off by the parties handing the docs and info to someone qualified to interpret it all - like to Mike Wynne. (What a snowball effect of circumstances!)

What was the outcome of the dispute or question regarding the RR crossing, to the east at approx. 144th? Or is this part of the civil suit scheduled for next month?

Thanks!

From: Landis, Richard
Sent: Tuesday, October 19, 2004 2:42 PM
To: Owen, Pat
Subject:

Pat here were our findings concerning Ms. Marshack's complaint against the Leas and Kelloggs.

The complaint involved a number of issues of which the city investigated and coordinated with Clark Public Utilities easement expert as well as going to the site measuring the height of the fence and determine if the gate referenced in the complaint was actually installed. Per Collen McGray, easement manager for Clark Public Utilities, they abandoned that portion of the easement that led from pole 33723 to Marshack's house in that the power to her house goes from pole 33723 underground first west and south to transformer 2101 then south to Mrs. Kellogg property transformer 7869 then north to the meter located on the west side of Marshack's house. Clark PUD has no objection to the gate being place where it is to be ultimately placed. Concerning the easement issues raised by Ms Marshack we have told her and her attorney Michael Wynne that this is a civil issue and we will let the courts resolve this, court date scheduled some time in November 2004. The Leas and Mrs. Kellogg are represented by LeAnne Bremmer of Miller and Nash. At Ms. Marshack's code enforcement hearing this was also reiterated by us and her attorney, this is a civil issue. Concerning the parking of cars on the utility easement, once again the easement was abandoned years ago by PUD. Concerning the fence erected on Mrs. Kellogg's property, once again the public utility easement was abandoned and Clark PUD as a result has no concerns. A review of the plaintiffs and their properties indicates none of them have ever obtained a fence permit from the city, thus would not be aware that fences 30" or less require no permits at all. Officer Tammi Neblock measured the fence in question which is a split rail

Marshack - Emails - 000802

fence and in no location could she find it over 27" in height. If Ms Marshack had contacted her attorney, Michael Wynne, he could have explained this to her as he is a land use attorney. At this time there are no violations on either the Leas's or Mrs. Kellogg's property as outlined in the unsigned September 26, 2004 complaint.

APPENDIX

Fig. A. 12
2008 Dan Lorenz letter to Judge John Nichols requesting help in getting records from Vancouver's City Attorneys and Police.

Daniel C. Lorenz

Attorney at Law
521 SW Clay
Portland, OR 97201
Phone: (503) 222-1161
Fax: (503) 226-1321

*Admitted in Oregon,
Washington, and California

Todd Worthley, Of Counsel

B. Lynn Miner, Legal Assistant
Bette J. Watkins, Legal Assistant

August 14, 2008

The Honorable Judge John Nichols
Clark County Courthouse
1200 Franklin Street
Vancouver, WA 98666-5000

Re: Kellogg, et. al. v. Harrington, et al.
Clark County Case Nos. 04-2-04611-8 and Y6-9834

Dear Judge Nichols:

I wanted to bring to your attention with the problems I have been experiencing in attempting to get records from the City of Vancouver relative to ongoing conflicts involving the parties to this litigation. Enclosed please find a series of letters responding to public records requests, including the request for information regarding an assault by Melanie Mooney of Dr. Marshack on June 16, 2008.

As has been suggested in some of our discussions in court, because the City of Vancouver has reviewed the existing Orders of the Court and recognizes that Your Honor has intentionally taken it upon yourself to try and address inappropriate behaviors occurring in this neighborhood, the Police are not following their normal protocols, and are not responding even to the recent assault. Moreover, they are treating the matters as ongoing investigations not requiring that they supply police reports and other public records, since the matter in theory is under consideration. We have been advised that these reports, for example, are regularly forwarded to Your Honor, but that we are not allowed to see them.

By this letter, I would request that you release to the parties copies of any reports you have received from any public agency regarding the parties to this litigation, and further communicate to the City of Vancouver that it is not your intention to obstruct our ability to obtain these records in the normal course.

001379

Honorable Judge Nichols
August 14, 2008
Page 2

Thank you for your attention to this matter.

Sincerely,

Daniel C. Lorenz
Attorney at Law

DCL/bw
Copy to: Kathy Marshack
Albert Schlotfeldt
Lawrence Holzman

\\Amanda2007\public\Clients\Marshack05PropLit\CONTEMPT\LNichols081408fin.wpd

001380

APPENDIX

City of Vancouver, Washington

P.O. Box 1995 • Vancouver, WA 98668-1995
www.ci.vancouver.wa.us

July 17, 2008

Daniel Lorenz
521 SW Clay
Portland, OR 97201

RE: *Public Record Request for VPD #08-11520*

Dear Mr. Lorenz:

This is to acknowledge receipt by our office of your July 14, 2008, public record request for VPD #08-11520 in regards to Marshack v. Mooney.

The report you request pertains to an open and active investigation in which enforcement proceedings are contemplated, and is therefore exempt from disclosure at this time.

RCW 42.56.240(1) exempts from disclosure "specific intelligence information and specific investigative records compiled by investigative, law enforcement, and penology agencies, and state agencies vested with the responsibility to discipline members of any profession, the nondisclosure of which is essential to effective law enforcement or for the protection of any person's right to privacy." Police files of open and active investigations in which enforcement proceedings are contemplated are categorically exempt from disclosure. Newman v. King County, 133 Wn.2d 565, 947 P.2d 712 (1997).

At this point, I do not know when the investigation will be complete and an enforcement decision will be made. At such time as the investigation is completed, we will be glad to revisit the matter, should you choose to submit another public record request.

Sincerely,

[signature]

Judith Zeider
Chief Assistant City Attorney

001382

Office of City Attorney
Telephone: 360-696-8251 · Facsimile: 360-696-8250

Garry E. Lucas
Sheriff

July 25th, 2008

Daniel C. Lorenz
Attorney at Law
521 SW Clay
Portland, Oregon 97201

Re: Public Disclosure Request received: 7-17-08
Reference: V08-11520 Kathy Marshack v Melanie Mooney

Dear Mr. Lorenz;

The referenced public disclosure request was forwarded to me for review and response.

The item you requested contains **"non conviction data,"** as the term is defined in the Washington State Criminal Records Privacy Act, Chapter 10.97 of the Revised Code of Washington. Non conviction data may generally not be released based on RCW 10.97.050.

If you have any questions feel free to contact me at Clark County Sheriff's Office, Public Disclosure Line at (360) 397-2211 x2101.

Sincerely,

Carolyn Demmie-Supervisor
Clark County Sheriff's Office Public Disclosure

Cc: PDR file

P.S. I'm returning your check #9778 for $5.00 CD

001381

707 W. 13th St., P.O. Box 410, Vancouver, WA 98666
360 397-2211

APPENDIX

Garry E. Lucas
Sheriff
Records Unit

August 28, 2007

Daniel C. Lorenz
521 SW Clay
Portland, Oregon 97201

Re: Public Disclosure Request received: 8/04/07

Reference: copy of V07-14889-Kathy Martin, aka, Marrin, aka Marshack

Dear Mr. Lorenz;

We are in receipt of your Public Disclosure Request. Your request will be processed and reviewed with an anticipated response within thirty (30) working days of the date of this notification.

If you have any questions, please feel free to contact our Public Disclosure desk at (360) 397-2211 x2101.

Sincerely,

Carolyn Demme-Supervisor
Clark Co. Sheriff's Records

707 W. 13th St. P.O. Box 410 Vancouver, WA 98666

Daniel C. Lorenz

Attorney at Law
521 SW Clay
Portland, OR 97201
Phone: (503) 222-1161
Fax: (503) 226-1321

Admitted in Oregon,
Washington, and California

October 3, 2007

B Lynn Miner, Legal Assistant
Amanda Gaylord, Legal Assistant

Officer Tim Thomson
Badge #1240
East Precinct
520 SE 155th Ave
Vancouver WA 98684

Via Hand Delivery

Re: Marshack and Morris
Report No: V07-14889

Dear Officer Thomas:

My staff has been attempting to obtain a copy of the police report for the July 22, 2007 incident. This request was made over 45 days ago. I also need copies of all photographs and officer notes. As such, we have a hearing scheduled for October 12, 2007 at 1:30 for which I am enclosing a subpoena for your appearance. We may be able to avoid your appearance if that report and related materials are made available in my office prior to October 9, 2007. Please give me a call to discuss this matter.

Thank you.

Very Truly Yours,

Daniel Lorenz
Attorney at Law

DCL/blm
cc: client
Z:\Clients\Marshack05ProphiT\LOfficerThomson100307.wpd

001386

APPENDIX

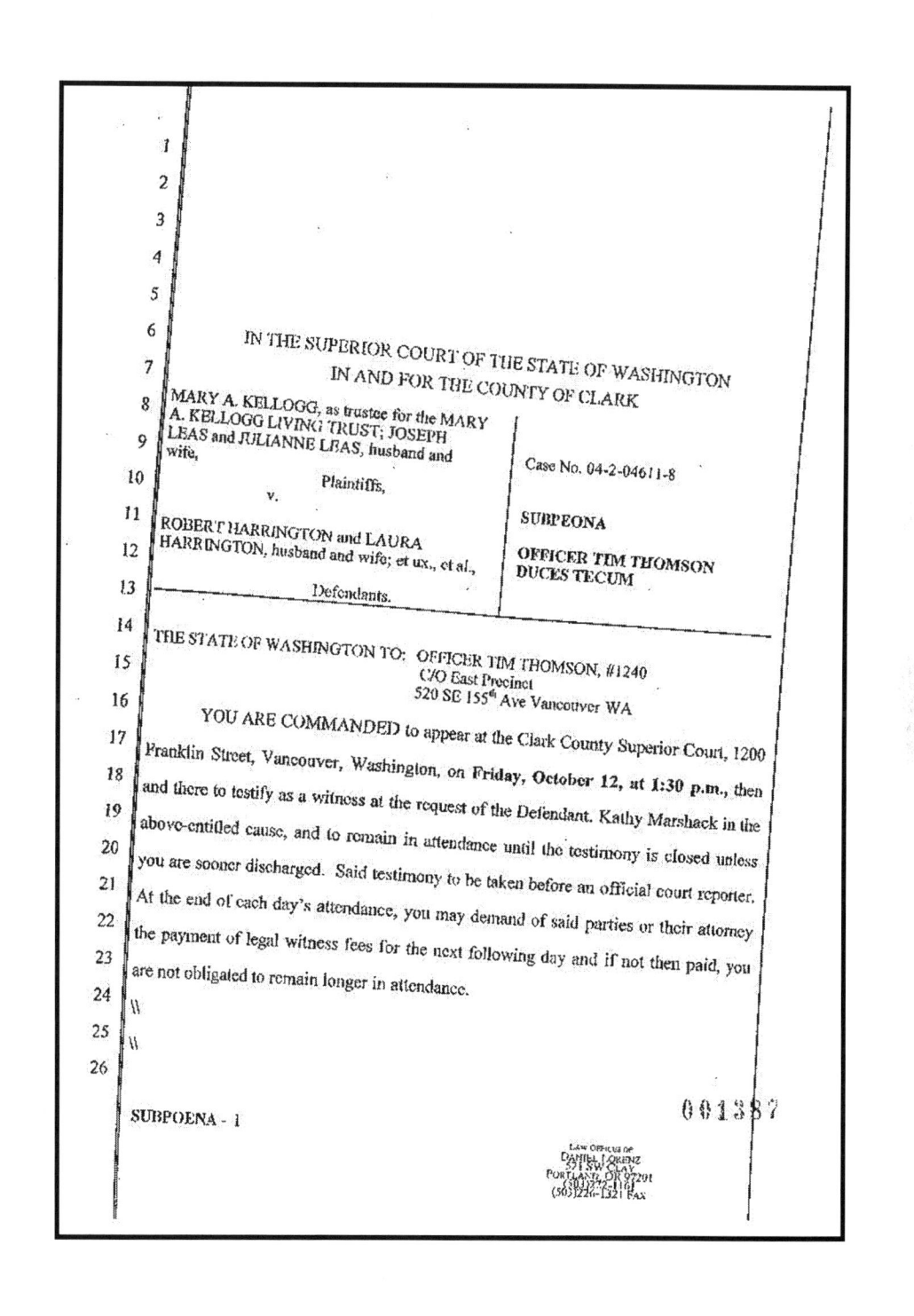

IN THE SUPERIOR COURT OF THE STATE OF WASHINGTON
IN AND FOR THE COUNTY OF CLARK

MARY A. KELLOGG, as trustee for the MARY A. KELLOGG LIVING TRUST; JOSEPH LEAS and JULIANNE LEAS, husband and wife,

Plaintiffs,

v.

ROBERT HARRINGTON and LAURA HARRINGTON, husband and wife; et ux., et al.,

Defendants.

Case No. 04-2-04611-8

SUBPOENA

OFFICER TIM THOMSON
DUCES TECUM

THE STATE OF WASHINGTON TO: OFFICER TIM THOMSON, #1240
C/O East Precinct
520 SE 155th Ave Vancouver WA

YOU ARE COMMANDED to appear at the Clark County Superior Court, 1200 Franklin Street, Vancouver, Washington, on Friday, October 12, at 1:30 p.m., then and there to testify as a witness at the request of the Defendant. Kathy Marshack in the above-entitled cause, and to remain in attendance until the testimony is closed unless you are sooner discharged. Said testimony to be taken before an official court reporter. At the end of each day's attendance, you may demand of said parties or their attorney the payment of legal witness fees for the next following day and if not then paid, you are not obligated to remain longer in attendance.

\\
\\

SUBPOENA - 1

001387

LAW OFFICES OF
DANIEL LORENZ
571 SW CLAY
PORTLAND, OR 97201
(503) 226-1161
(503) 226-1321 FAX

You are commanded to bring with you the following: Any and all officer notes, photographs and police report pertaining to an incident on July 22, 2007.

DATED this 3 day of October, 2007.

Daniel Lorenz

Daniel Lorenz, WSBA #14688
Of Attorneys for Defendant Marshack

SUBPOENA - 2

APPENDIX

Fig. A. 13

Letter attorney Dan Lorenz sent to Washington State BAR regarding Vancouver City Prosecutor Josephine Townsend's unsatisfactory treatment of the author in and out of court. These included documents in which Townsend made derogatory remarks about the author's parenting.

Daniel C. Lorenz

Attorney at Law
521 SW Clay
Portland, OR 97201
Phone: (503) 222-1161
Fax: (503) 226-1321

Admitted in Oregon,
Washington, and California

July 28, 2005

B Lynn Minor, Legal Assistant
Amanda Gaylord, Legal Assistant

Cheryl Fuji
Washington State Bar
Disciplinary Section
2101 Fourth Avenue, Suite 400
Seattle, WA 98121-2330

Re: <u>Josephine Townsend</u>

Dear Ms. Fuji:

I pulled my file from storage and have reviewed that file. I believe the following documents may be of assistance to you in view of the situation.

1. Joint Motion for Stay of Proceedings signed by both Ms. Townsend, Dr. Marshack, and Bob Yoseph, who then represented Dr. Marshack. Note on page 5 of the motion calls for 26 weeks, and not 26 sessions, of domestic violence treatment pursuant to negotiations. In recognition of prior treatment the order was made retroactive to January 1, 2004, also an unusual provision, but clearly reflecting that the parties anticipated that Dr. Marshack would be able to complete counseling with respect to the diversion by the end of June 2004.

2. Judge Swanger's Order of March 2, 2004, approving that Stay of Proceedings.

3. My file reflects faxes with Josephine Townsend beginning August 9, although I believe I had prior phone conversations with her on a number of occasions discussing the issues relating to treatment with Dr. Colistro. Dr. Colistro's formal report was August 10, and I enclose a copy of my cover letter.

4. Notice of Appearance dated August 20, 2004. I became officially involved in this case because of the difficulties Dr. Marshack had dealing with Ms. Townsend. Contrary to the prosecutors normal practice, Dr. Marshack was instructed to see Josephine Townsend personally for her monthly visits, rather than the normal diversion counselor associated with the City Attorney's office.

Page -2
Townsend/Marshack

5. Pursuant to my discussions with Ms. Townsend, and after she became adamant that 26 sessions, and not simply 6 weeks of counseling were required of Dr. Marshack, I contacted Commissioner Swanger directly to clarify his understanding of the terms of the existing diversion order. A copy of my August 20, 2005 to Judge Swanger (copied to Ms. Townsend) is enclosed.

6. In response to that letter, I received a call from Robin at the District Court office, requesting that I cite the matter on for a Thursday morning at 9:00. Pursuant to the request, I did so on August 31. A copy of that letter dated August 31 and then cited the matter before Commissioner Swanger are also enclosed.

7. On September 1, I received a phone message from Ms. Townsend, and I enclose a copy of that phone message I received. Ms. Townsend insisted that I strike the scheduled hearing and recite the matter. This note also for the first time indicated that she would be moving to revoke Dr. Marshack's diversion. I continued to believe that Ms. Townsend's reaction was a direct response to my challenges to her "interpretation" of the counseling requirements. You will note that Ms. Townsend claimed that Dr. Marshack had a "new conviction" which she failed to disclose in her monthly report. Again, the matter to which that comment refers is a civil code violation for the home occupation permit. After returning Ms. Townsend's call, I sent her a letter of September 3, a copy of which I enclose. I also attempted at the same time to confirm with Dr. Colistro that Dr. Marshack had completed her sessions as he has had originally contemplated. His confirmation of that is indicated by his signature at the bottom of my letter of September 3 to him, also enclosed.

On September 3, I also received, without prior notice, a Motion and Order to Revoke Stay of Prosecution citing the matter before Judge Schreiber on September 29 at 3:00 p.m. I enclose a copy of those pleadings. Despite my telephone contact with Ms. Townsend in response to her September 1 message, she never conferred with me regarding the scheduling or bringing the matter before a different judge.

8. My next communication with Mr. Townsend was her letter of September 6, 2004. Interestingly, the letter was done by Ms. Townsend on her own time over the Labor Day weekend. I confirmed in a later conversation with her that she personally typed the letter in the absence of any staff over the holiday weekend. Enclosed with the letter is a set of downloads that she apparently obtained off the Internet. You will note as well that she raises for the first time the qualifications of Dr. Colistro, whose qualifications are significantly greater than the basic domestic violence program. Dr. Colistro is a prominent psychologist in therapy and forensic evaluations throughout the Pacific NW. His qualifications were expressly known to Ms. Townsend when she expressly agreed to his

APPENDIX

Page -3
Townsend/Marshack

report and proposal which was incorporated into the diversion agreement.

9. Ultimately, I did strike the September 9 hearing based on Ms. Townsend's demand, not because I felt she was entitled to have the matter reset, but rather because I did not want to further antagonize the situation. I did provide Dr. Colistro a copy of Ms. Townsend's transmittal and described my contacts with Ms. Townsend. A copy of my letter of September 10 is enclosed. Despite the fact that Dr. Marshack had completed her diversion treatment, Ms. Townsend continued to assert otherwise. A copy of her letter of September 16 is also enclosed.

10. In order to placate Ms. Townsend it became necessary for Dr. Marshack not only to incur significant additional costs for me, which I believe to have been unwarranted, but for her to retain counsel to deal with the issues with the City and become more proactive, including the filing of a land use petition in Clark County Cause No: 04 2 04801 3. A copy of that petition is also enclosed for your file.

11. As I prepared to address issues on September 29, my client faced very strenuous attempts by Ms. Townsend to revoke her diversion based on what I consider to be highly improper grounds. I enclose a copy of a letter dated September 19, offering a "last chance offer." In looking into the scheduling of the matter before Judge Schreiber, I discovered that the hearing had been scheduled on his regular docket, despite the fact that it was abundantly clear that the matter could not be resolved on that docket as that docket is not intended to allow an evidentiary hearing. Mr. Townsend was very much aware that I expected to fight any attempt to terminate diversion and expected to call witnesses. In addition, she cited the matter before a judge different than the one having entered the diversion order and would have required that a second judge interpret the first judge's order. I was also concerned that Judge Schreiber would ultimately recuse himself after I had assembled my multiple witnesses. Because the case involved Dr. Marshack, who was well known in the legal community, having testified in numerous custody actions, as well as her husband, an attorney who is actively engaged in the practice of law in Vancouver, a number of the Judges had previously recused themselves and did not want to hear the matter. Judge Schreiber was sent a letter of September 20, advising of the issues. A copy of that letter is enclosed.

12. September 21, Ms. Townsend challenged my analysis and actually filed an amended Motion and Order to Revoke Stay and Prosecution. I enclose both her letter and the pleading.

Page -4
Townsend/Marshack

13. On September 22, I had a further conversation with Ms. Townsend wherein she claimed that Dr. Marshack was not tracking, hates authority figures and considered treatment a waste of time. Ms. Townsend was aware of the divorce between Dr. Marshack and her former spouse, and raised in that conversation issues related to custody and stated that the childrens' emotional problems were the result of Dr. Marshack. She claimed that Mr. Yoseph had expressly assured her that Dr. Colistro was in fact authorized to do DV counseling under the Washington Administrative Code, although Mr. Yoseph denied having ever given such an assurance or representation. As the hearing approached, Ms. Townsend and I had further conversation. Finally, it was clear that my client would not fold and was prepared to take the risk of proceeding to hearing, and that I intended to call Mr. Wynne, Mr. Yoseph, Dr. Colistro, and my client. Ms. Townsend finally relented.
An agreement was reached as set forth in my letter of September 28. A copy of which is attached.

14. As part of my evaluation of revocations issues, I had a number of discussions with Bob Yoseph, Dr. Marshack's prior attorney. He had contact himself with the Clark County Diversion Unit. He confirmed that Clark County does not revoke diversions for speeding tickets, too much junk in the yard, or other civil violations of the county code. The county does not interpret the phrase "obey all laws" in the diversion contract to incorporate civil violations, and referred specifically to Washington v. Merino, 674 P2d, 171. In addition, since there was still an appeal pending regarding the civil violation, it was not final and would not have been considered by the county diversion program to be a violation.

Finally, following additional sessions with Dr. Colistro, which should not have been required, the diversion was dismissed by the City Attorney's office at the request of Jill Petty. A copy of the dismissal order is enclosed.

I hope that this is helpful. Should you need any thing further, please do not hesitate to contact me.

Best Regards,

DANIEL C. LORENZ
Attorney at Law

Daniel Lorenz

DCL/blm
Z:\Clients\Marshack04\Ltr FujiWABAR72705.wpd

APPENDIX

Fig. A. 14
Nov. 20, 2006 Subpoena for Vancouver's Records Clerk Raylene McJilton (incorrectly spelled in Subpeona as Raylin McGiliten) to appear in person in Clark County Court with any and all documents making allegations against the author or her property. McJilton did not comply.

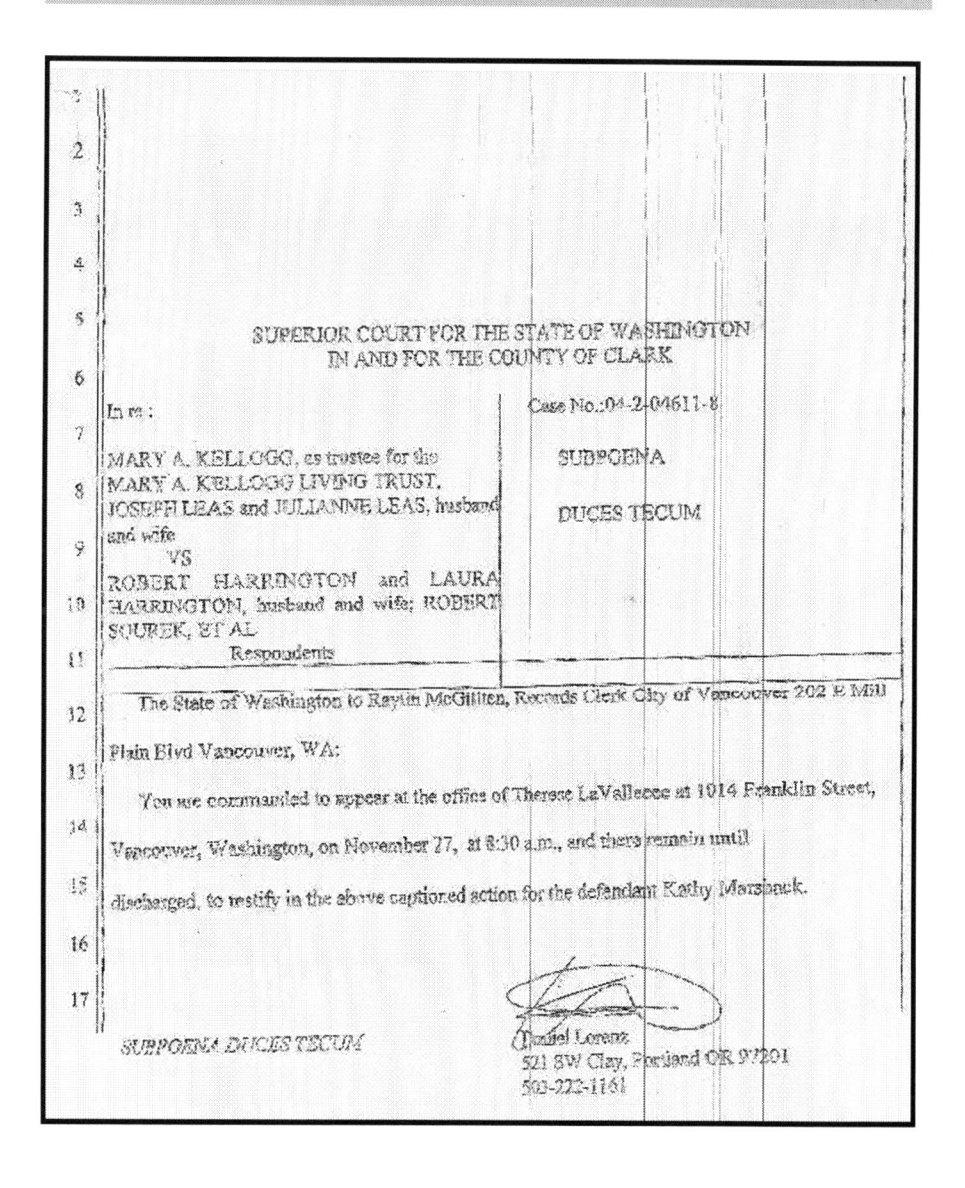

SUPERIOR COURT FOR THE STATE OF WASHINGTON
IN AND FOR THE COUNTY OF CLARK

In re:

MARY A. KELLOGG, as trustee for the
MARY A. KELLOGG LIVING TRUST.
JOSEPH LEAS and JULIANNE LEAS, husband
and wife
VS
ROBERT HARRINGTON and LAURA
HARRINGTON, husband and wife; ROBERT
SOUREK, ET AL
Respondents

Case No.: 04-2-04611-8

SUBPOENA

DUCES TECUM

The State of Washington to Raylin McGiliten, Records Clerk City of Vancouver 202 E Mill Plain Blvd Vancouver, WA:

You are commanded to appear at the office of Therese LaVallece at 1014 Franklin Street, Vancouver, Washington, on November 27, at 8:30 a.m., and there remain until discharged, to testify in the above captioned action for the defendant Kathy Marsback.

SUBPOENA DUCES TECUM

Daniel Lorenz
521 SW Clay, Portland OR 97201
503-222-1161

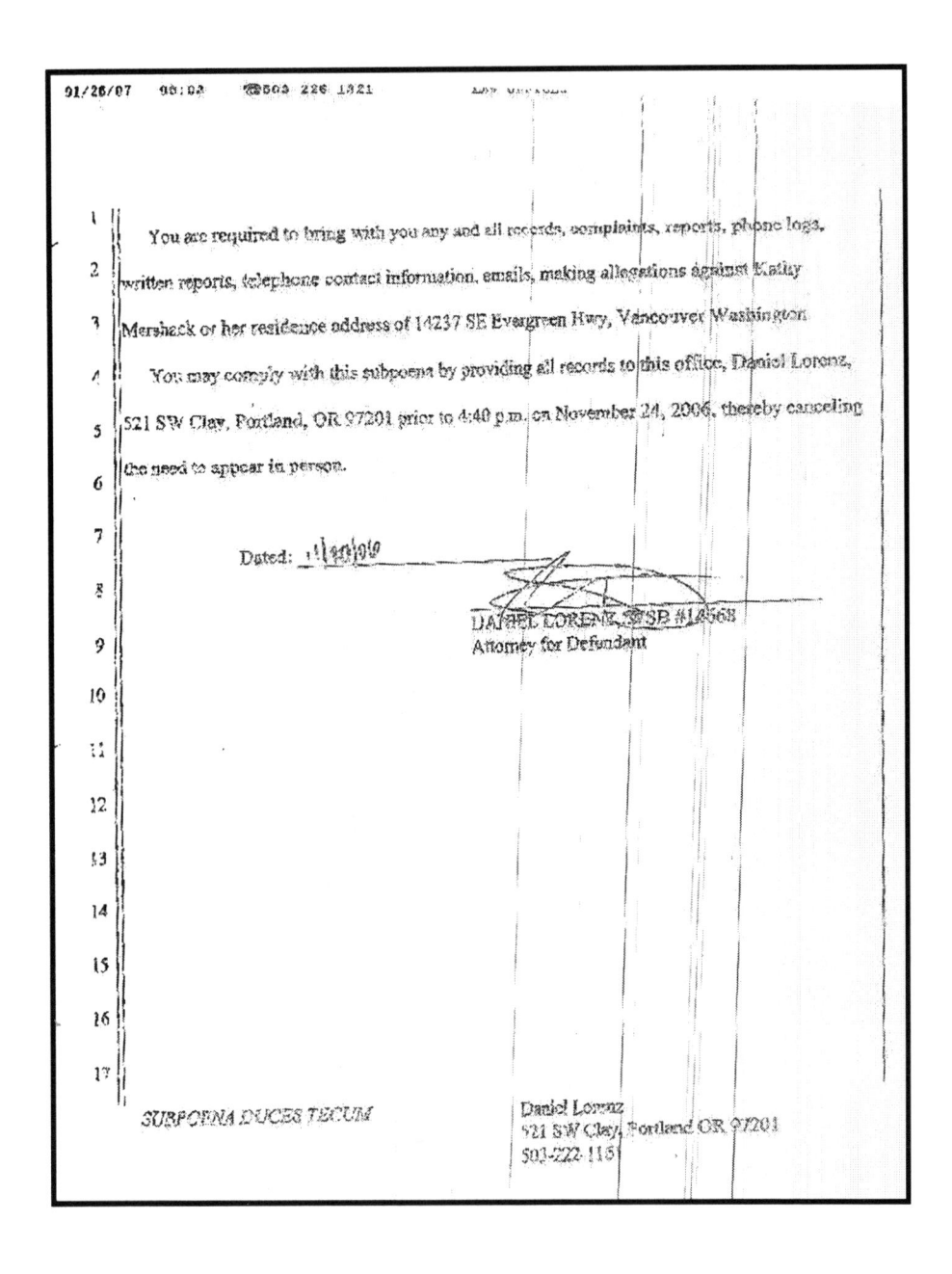

> 1 You are required to bring with you any and all records, complaints, reports, phone logs,
> 2 written reports, telephone contact information, emails, making allegations against Kathy
> 3 Mershack or her residence address of 14237 SE Evergreen Hwy, Vancouver Washington
> 4 You may comply with this subpoena by providing all records to this office, Daniel Lorenz,
> 5 521 SW Clay, Portland, OR 97201 prior to 4:40 p.m. on November 24, 2006, thereby canceling
> 6 the need to appear in person.
>
> Dated: _____
>
> DANIEL LORENZ, OSB #14568
> Attorney for Defendant
>
> SUBPOENA DUCES TECUM
>
> Daniel Lorenz
> 521 SW Clay, Portland OR 97201
> 503-222-1151

APPENDIX

Fig. A. 15

This list provides insight into the numbers—in terms of time and money—lost and cost to the author during the decade she fought fiercely and steadily to win her legal rights back and save her family.

BY THE NUMBERS

This by-the-numbers list provides a clear view of the magnitude of the perfect-storm years when private citizens and public officials with various degrees of Empathy Dysfunction came at the author from all sides. It offers a different perspective on what the author endured in order to survive, recover and, in the process, create the Empathy Dysfunction Scale, remarkable in its simplicity.

- **2 years** (2002 to 2004) of nasty court proceedings while divorcing my husband of **23 years,** who happened to be a divorce attorney himself.
- Being forced to give **half of my retirement funds** to my ex-husband to settle our divorce.
- **1 year** in a Diversion program as an alternative to jail time.
- **12 weeks** of court-ordered anger management treatment.
- **3** false arrests.
- **4 days** spent in County jail after two of the three false arrests.
- **12 years** of abuse at the hands of a mob.
- **12 years** when my daughters and I felt imprisoned in our home because we feared the intimidating and physically threatening neighbors.
- **16** attorneys hired to defend my civil rights.
- **8** judges in my court cases.
- **20-plus** legal proceedings (divorce, lawsuits, harassment orders, contempt orders, arrests, City code violations and licensing board complaints).
- **50-plus** videos made of my family and me by a stalker.

- **Half a million dollars and more** in legal fees.
- **25 percent** of what I paid to lawyers to handle my cases was what I received in settlements.
- **12- to 14-hour days**—i.e. **60- to 70-hour** weeks worked for a decade to pay attorneys.
- **9 years** of being unable to sell my house (2005-2014) because of litigation around my property rights.
- **2** refinances of my home to help pay lawyers.
- Borrowing on credit cards to stay afloat.
- **650,** my credit score after it slipped dramatically from a very high level.
- **1 year** of being cyberstalked.
- **12** precious prime-working years when every cent I made supported my family—but mostly paid lawyers, leaving me resentful about being unable to contribute to my retirement account.
- **12** years (beginning in 2005) of estrangement from my oldest daughter, Bianca.
- **4** years (beginning in 2014) of estrangement from my youngest daughter, Phoebe, and my grandson, Jameson.
- **$600,000,** the price tag on my home, which was **nearly $400,000** under market value (It had appraised at nearly a **million dollars** in 2005).
- **14** years (since 2003) of living with Post Traumatic Disorder (PTSD).

APPENDIX

Fig. A. 16
Letter from an Uber driver relaying to the author how tools she took away from reading "When Empathy Fails" helped her avoid entanglement with an Emotionally Dysfunctional passenger.

Letter to Kathy Marshack from an Uber driver regarding the Empathy Dysfunction Scale she learned about while reading "When Empathy Fails"

Kathy,

I just had a "Rider from Hell" experience while out Ubering around, and I have to thank you for letting me in on your journey in developing the EmD book. She was just like that woman you described in the "No Disney Cruise" chapter. When I arrived, with my cute little PT Cruiser that meets all the requirements as an UberX car, and even has a hatchback, she showed up with a bike, two saddlebags, a pizza box and a dachshund. She tried to get her bike in the hatchback, and of course it didn't fit, she mentioned that it was a very small space, and I pointed out that this would be even more of a problem in a sedan. She wanted me to lift the back end of the bike because, obviously, she's a small woman and having a hard time. She made me maneuver the bike around, maneuver the seats around, her pizza fell all over the front seat, her dog was wet (hot day, understandable) and the little guy ended up sitting next to her on the front seat, which is all that was left for the two of them once I got her bike in. Then she railed on about all the crime and injustice and tried to get me on board with her, naming names that I don't know nor care about. Which is part of why I didn't engage.

She heard me mention that I'm familiar with how large items fit in the car because I put my harp in there, told me she plays the flute, told me we should exchange phone numbers, so I told her I was leaving the harp in Portland while I went to Denver, but she was already on a roll, sure that she'd found her angle. She switched the channel on my radio, kept searching, looking for 89.9, had a hard time finding it, and I didn't help her. 89.9 had been on one of my presets, apparently wasn't at this point in time. I wondered if she was high on cocaine or heroin or something, but I think she was just intentionally pushing my boundaries. She ate one of the Almond Rocas I happened to have in one of my drink holders, then told her dog he couldn't have chocolate, tried to get him to eat some "duck" she had, but he wasn't interested, nor had he been regarding the chocolate though she seemed to want me to think he was, and she claimed to be worried that the easily available chocolate could harm him. She cranked up the music so I couldn't hear her talk, and continued to talk to me about how she could triple tongue on the flute, and she could sing, and was looking to find a song she could sing to. It was mildly distressing to me that I couldn't understand what she was saying because the music was so loud. On the other hand, it was easier to ignore her, and I figured if she really wanted to be heard she could turn the music down.

At this point I just wanted her out of my car, ASAP. She even pulled my mileage reporting notebook out of the slot between the seat and the console and asked me something. I turned the music down and said "What?" and she asked if I had a pen. I said no (as a fellow writer, you realize there's no way this is true.) She looked a bit surprised and asked if I wanted her number, and I said no. She asked to turn the music up again, so I did, after she said she hoped I enjoyed Denver. She seemed sincere, "seemed" being the operative word. I let her listen to the overly loud music and go on talking, I went on ignoring, and when we arrived at the destination she let her dog run into the street so I grabbed the leash and brought him back for his own sake, not hers, as I'm sure she'd have loved the sympathy that she derived if he'd been run over. I unloaded every single thing, including the pizza box she'd let the contents out of twice now, with no help from her. I had to go immediately to my next rider, and he asked "front seat or back" so I looked at the front seat and realized it was, on top of everything else, all wet, which is utterly unacceptable for doing business in. I suggested he'd find the back seat more comfortable because the previous rider had spilled water all over the front seat, so he got in back. I took a break after this so my car seat could at least dry out, which took me off the clock for the last half hour of the evening rush hour shift.

WHEN EMPATHY FAILS

As someone with an ASD, I struggle with my understanding of other people, sensitive to the fact that I often misinterpret their behaviors, even more so than the average person, and the average person might have been snowed, especially with her rapid-fire monologue that didn't provide a chance to think. If I hadn't read that section of your book, as well as many of the others, I'd have been second guessing myself about whether she knew exactly what she was doing, and was intentionally making me extremely uncomfortable. I felt like I could see, though, from what you described, how she was calibrating me, finding my sensitive places, and applying pressure. I found it easy to disengage from her because I realized she was being predatory and didn't deserve compassion, as she not only earned none, she actively chose to be unworthy of it. While it's possible she's just an idiot, which is also fine but she still doesn't warrant sympathy from me, I am pretty sure she's savvy enough to have recognized that I am easy-going and not entirely socially astute, which would normally have made me an easy mark. I imagine that's why she started pulling out the stops, pushing me further past my comfort zone, saying things that made her seem like a sympathetic character triumphing over a tragedy (she gave me a story about being mugged, and her bike wheels wouldn't come off because She's had them made permanent to avoid theft…), and now she was in a position to share some wealth. Fortunately I was able to sidestep her, with relative grace, by merely not responding to her asinine suggestions that I engage more thoroughly with her. I dropped her at The Nines; she had said things on the way that suggested we were now friends and I should join her at the hotel, which might have been appealing to someone dazzled by the thought of enjoying such a luxurious escape simply by being associated with someone who had a room booked there.

She certainly put effort into coming across as a gifted musician another harper might have wanted to connect with, if they allowed themselves to ignore a few signs that she was more talk than skill. In the end, I was just glad it was easy to drop her and leave her there. Now I have a "Rider from Hell" story.

And this is why I know your book is going to empower people to raise defenses against such predatory behaviors. I can't wait to see it in print, and get copies into the hands of my friends and family. I was going over some of the things you said in there, and thinking, "This could be the same thing!" Even if it's not, that helped clear my head so that I could see what was happening around me and to me, and make sure I DIDN'T get drawn in. I could see where she could be intentionally working me over, and that was enough to keep her at arm's length without feeling any sympathy or guilt for not helping her any more than I already did, which was above the call of duty already.

Namaste,

Laura

Author's Biography

Kathy J. Marshack, Ph.D. is a licensed psychologist with more than 40 years of experience as a marriage and family therapist and business coach. Dr. Marshack received her bachelor's degree in psychology from Portland State University, her master's degree from the University of Hawaii, and her doctorate in psychology from the Fielding Institute. She is a member of the *American Psychological Association*.

Dr. Marshack is a prolific writer who pulls inspiration from her extensive research, insight from counseling thousands of clients, and her own life experiences. Her first book, *Entrepreneurial Couples: Making It Work at Work and at Home,* published in 1998 and rereleased in 2017, explores the unique lifestyle of couples that run a business together. She was also a contributor to the nationally acclaimed book, *Sixty Things to Do When You Turn Sixty,* 2006.

After discovering how many people were struggling with a family member with Autism Spectrum Disorder, without any support or guidance, she wrote two books: *Going over the Edge: Life with a Partner or Spouse with Asperger Syndrome* in 2009, and in

2013, *Out of Mind – Out of Sight: Parenting with a Partner with Asperger Syndrome (ASD)*. Her latest book, *When Empathy Fails*, is her most powerful and intimate book to date.

Dr. Marshack has been extensively profiled in the media, including *Kiplinger's, The New York Times, Inc. Magazine, USA Today, Business Week,* and has appeared on *CNN, The Lifetime Channel, BBC,* and *National Public Radio*. She also works as an investigative journalist for the *US~Observer*.

Learn more about Dr. Marshack's articles, online consultation and therapy, as well as her International Meetup for Partners & Family of Adults with ASD, by visiting www.kmarshack.com.

Printed in Great Britain
by Amazon